To Anne

Christmas 2006.

With much love

from

Gordon & Mary

D0636535

IN THE BLOOD

by the same author

poetry
The Pleasure Steamers
Independence
Secret Narratives
Dangerous Play
Natural Causes
Love in a Life
The Price of Everything
Salt Water
Public Property
The Penguin Book of Contemporary British Poetry
(edited with Blake Morrison)
Here to Eternity (edited)
First World War Poems (edited)

prose
The Lamberts
Philip Larkin: A Writer's Life
Keats
Wainewright the Poisoner
The Invention of Dr Cake

In the Blood

A Memoir of My Childhood

ANDREW MOTION

faber and faber

First published in 2006
by Faber and Faber Limited
3 Queen Square London WC1N 3AU

Typeset by Faber and Faber Ltd
Printed in England by Mackays of Chatham, plc

All rights reserved
© Andrew Motion, 2006

The right of Andrew Motion to be identified as author of
this work has been asserted in accordance with Section 77 of
the Copyright, Designs and Patents Act 1988

A CIP record for this book
is available from the British Library

ISBN 978–0571–22803–4
ISBN 0–571–22803–8

2 4 6 8 10 9 7 5 3 1

For my brother
and
in memory of our mother and father

I have owed to them,
In hours of weariness, sensations sweet,
Felt in the blood, and felt along the heart.

'Lines Composed a Few Miles above Tintern Abbey',
William Wordsworth

Contents

Essex Plough

Mum doesn't knock, she just whisks open my bedroom door, crosses straight to the curtains, tears them apart, and flaps one hand in front of her face. 'What a fug!' She sounds angry but I know she isn't – she says this every morning, and anyway the fug isn't me, it's Wiggy, asleep by my feet. Mum's got her by the scruff of the neck now, and is dragging her onto the landing: 'Downstairs and into the garden, you idle dog. The back door's open – go on, hurry up, there you are, good girl.' I'm still half asleep, collecting my thoughts. Today it's Julia and the party. Then home again tomorrow. That's all fine.

When I open my eyes properly, mum's leaning against the doorframe with her arms folded. 'You'd better hurry up too,' she says. 'Your bus goes in an hour.' I rub my face and carry on remembering. Mum's hunting today – she's half-dressed for it already. Long socks and breeches. Baggy shirt. Stock. Yellow wool waistcoat. She peels back one of her cuffs and glances at her watch, then fiddles the strap until it sits flat on her wrist. I roll over and wait for her to disappear.

Last summer, when I was still sixteen and about to stay with a girl in London – a different girl, not Julia – mum sat on the edge of my bed and gave me a talk. Did I know what I was doing? It was embarrassing, being serious about things we usually thought were a joke. But today there's not a word about Julia – nothing before mum leaves the bedroom, nothing at breakfast, and nothing when we settle into the car. As we reach the lane I glance back at the house – at its white walls through the hedge-trees, the green roof of the stables, and the rose-arch leading into the garden. 'OK?' mum asks, meaning: do I like what I see? I nod, but say nothing.

Mum slows down when we reach the main street, so we can

wave if we recognise anyone. But we're not really paying attention. Hunting mornings are always chaotic – the horses to groom, the tack to clean, blah blah – and mum feels off-net. I'm not so bright myself. I've never taken a bus cross-country before. Worse, I don't know what to expect when I reach the other end. I've only met Julia once, at a party a few days ago, before Christmas, and the lights were so dim she was more or less invisible. Will I even recognise her? Her last name is Shelley, that's a good omen. Poetic. Mum says Julia's father is 'something to do with coal'.

We swing downhill under the bare trees, past Mrs Bunton's cottage by the ford, then up and out of the valley. Have I got money for the ticket? Will I remember to give Mrs Shelley the chocolates as a thank-you? Mum knows all this sounds fussy, so she talks in a pretend-whine. I answer in the same voice: *yaaaas; yaaaas*. We both know we're really talking about something else – about Julia – but neither of us wants to admit it. At the crest of the hill, where the lane meets the main road, we see what kind of day it is for the first time, and feel it too. There's snow in the wind. Mum makes a face, crouching forward as she waits for the traffic. But there's nothing to worry about. We can see the bus already, buffeting towards us along the roller-coaster of dips and rises. It means when we reach The Swan and turn into the yard, there's still time for her to switch off the engine so we can say our last things. What things, though? We've said all there is to say for the time being – so instead of talking, I stare. At mum's gold hair looped behind her ears; the mole on her cheek; her bony fingers gripping the steering wheel. Then the bus lumbers to a stop and suddenly I'm in a muddle. Do I kiss mum goodbye? I've got to be quick, the driver's glaring over his shoulder. Yes, of course I kiss her. I always kiss her goodbye, just a peck, but enough to catch her lemony soap-smell. Next second the bus doors have wheezed shut behind me, and I'm lurching upstairs towards the back window. I want to see mum once more, and I know she'll wait. There she is now, leaning towards the windscreen, waving with her long hand. I twinkle my fingers, feeling idiotic – I'm only going to be away for a night. Neither of us moves until the bus slides over the brow of the next hill.

I switch to the front, and lay my suitcase on the seat beside me as we pick up speed. Looking down, everything is full of surprises even though I still know where I am. I can spy into the bedrooms of houses I've driven past a hundred times, but never thought were more than front doors. Look: a woman twirling in front of a mirror with her hands on her hips, making her skirt into a bell. It's probably a Christmas present, and she's trying it on because she's going to a New Year party at the end of the week. Then we reach the first town, Braintree, with its ropes of dingy lights swaying above the main street. This is the Barclays where I've opened my first account. That's the place we buy shoes for school. Some of the people on the pavements might even recognise me, if I met them face to face. Up here I'm a ghost, watching them go about their business.

The town ends and we're in open country again, with snow sprinkled across the fields, and painful-looking cabbage-stalks poking through the hard ground. Mum said the bus would be good experience, then dug me in the ribs, daring me to ask for a lift all the way in the car. She'll be leaving home herself about now. There'll be the usual kerfuffle with the sandwiches, then a worse panic as she and my brother Kit hook the horse-box to the car, and get the animals inside. It's a tight fit, and Serenade always comes to a dead halt on the ramp, snorting and rolling her eyes while mum hauls on the halter-rope. Kit will stand behind clapping his hands, murmuring 'Go oooon', and mum will warn him to keep out of kicking range. He's only fourteen. In five minutes they'll be off, Kit's tweed jacket and mum's black hunting coat lying on the back seat beside the hard hats.

At Bishops Stortford the bus gives a final enormous sigh and I clamber downstairs, my suitcase banging against my knee. I haven't worked out what I'm going to say next: whenever I think about Julia, all I can see is her black hair and her mouth. It doesn't matter. She's as jittery as I am, waiting beside her mother on the draughty concrete, with her hands stuffed into her overcoat pockets. I glance at her face too quickly, and get a blur. White skin. Eyeshadow. Hair falling forward. That big squashy mouth – is she sticking out her bottom lip or is it always like that? And what about her clothes? Everything's hidden under her coat. Her *school* coat, obviously – I can tell by that anchor on the buttons. Doesn't she have a proper one? When she says 'Hello' her voice sounds gluey, as though she needs to clear her throat. I can't decide whether to give her a hug, and end up patting her arm.

'Come on, you two. Can't stand about here all day freezing to death.' Julia's mother is black-haired too, though heavier, and her skin is darker. She bundles us into the car and keeps chatting until we reach the house. It's a surprise – but that's good. Home is airy, full of light. Julia's house is shadowy, with laurel bushes dripping round the front door. Even their Christmas tree looks dark, with tiny silver lights almost smothered by branches. When her mother shows me to my bedroom, it's like squeezing into a burrow. I hand over the chocolates, then glance into the garden. Blowsy snowflakes are falling. Mum and Kit will be cold if the weather's the same with them. The hunt will be called off soon, and they'll head home.

Everyone wants to sound relaxed at lunch, but the conversation keeps getting stuck. When we finish at last, Julia looks straight at me for the first time and says we're going for a walk. 'The snow won't melt us.' I tell her that's fine, and she lends me a coat from the hooks by the back door, a tatty sheepskin which stinks of dog. It makes things easier, especially now she's dumped her school coat, putting on a filthy Afghan yak that smells almost as bad as the one I'm wearing. When I tell her, she says she knows, then collides with me accidentally-on-purpose as we stomp off through the back door, heading for the fields beyond the garden. She even looks beautiful with a big hairy scarf tied round her throat and half her face.

We walk side by side for a bit, then drop into single file on a headland round the plough. The hedges have all been ripped out, and the sky feels enormous – much taller than at home, and not so many birds. I stop in a gateway saying we should go back, it's freezing, and that's when Julia takes a step closer. The cold has made dark blotches on her cheek, like pennies in milk, but her skin is warm when we kiss each other. It's so simple. She's wearing the same scent as her mother – she must have borrowed it – and when we hug, the heat squeezes up inside our coats and fans across our faces.

After a while we step apart with our hands hooked together. We've done the difficult bit. 'Well,' I say, though my mouth isn't working properly, 'I still think we should go back'. Julia grabs my elbow, dragging me, and ten minutes later we're in the garden, breaking apart in case her mother's watching. But there's no sign of her – not even in the kitchen, which means we can lean against the Aga and keep talking: what we did for Christmas, what we're doing at New Year. 'Can I see you?' she asks. 'No,' I say, 'I've got a family thing.' I'm pleased she looks disappointed, and think if things are this easy, I'd rather give tonight's party a miss. Julia shakes her head. Plans are plans, and anyway she wants me to meet her friends. So at six o'clock I go upstairs to bath and change. As the door shuts behind me, I notice one of her long black hairs in my jersey, and decide to leave it there.

There's a single knock as I'm swinging my suitcase onto the bed. Julia. She must have changed her mind about the party. But it's not Julia. It's her mother, clasping her hands and peering into my face, then away through the window. I've forgotten to close the curtains, and she's watching the snowflakes sail down through the glow of my light. 'How's the room?' she asks, which is weird. She knows it's fine. Then she starts talking in a quieter voice. 'Listen, Andrew. I was downstairs in the sitting room just now, watching the news, and the telephone rang. It was a friend of your family's: Mrs Hill. Do you know Mrs Hill?' I nod, and so does Julia's mother, pursing her lips before launching forward again. 'It was Mrs Hill saying there'd been an accident while your mum was hunting. She doesn't know what happened exactly, she said your mum fell off and banged her head. She was crossing a field, I think. Anyway. There was an accident, and your mum has been taken to hospital. Mrs Hill says to tell you the people there are very good, they're doing everything they can.'

I'm still at the bedside, holding open the lid of my suitcase with both hands. Now I close it. I don't want her to see my stupid clothes. The pale blue trousers mum gave me for Christmas, which dad thinks are too tight. When I turn round, she's still clasping and unclasping her hands. I feel sorry for her, having to tell me this. But at the same time I want her to leave so I don't have to ask any questions. There are so many, I can't tell where to start. How badly is mum hurt? Which hospital? Is Kit OK? Where's dad? In the end I say 'Can I go home?' – too softly for Julia's mother to hear. Then I sit on the bed, thinking that will be better, but the eiderdown feels slippery and I might fall off. Brownish feathers on a pink background. Fishtails. When I look up again Julia's mother is standing directly in front of me. Is she going to put her hand on my shoulder? I don't want her to touch me. I want to know what she knows, then for her to leave.

'Can I go home?' I ask again, and this time Julia's mother shakes her head. 'You can't.' 'Why not?' 'There's nobody there tonight.' 'What do you mean?' 'Your brother's with friends, and your father's at the hospital – he'll be staying tonight, they'll make up a bed for him. In the morning you can get the bus back. By then your granny will be home. Mrs Hill said your granny would take charge.' 'Granny!' I want to say; 'Granny can't even look after the dog!' But Julia's mother is still talking, and I have to listen. She's telling me it's best to carry on as planned. Mrs Hill said so, and there was a message from dad as well. He thinks there's nothing to be gained by leaving now. 'I want to see her.' Julia's mother straightens her shoulders. She knew I'd say this. 'Your father doesn't think that would be a good idea,' she says, taking a pace back, then changing her mind and stepping towards me again. She probably expects me to cry now, but I won't. 'You mean I'd be in the way?' I ask. 'Is that what dad thinks?' Julia's mother presses her hands together. 'No,' she says. 'It's more that your mum wouldn't recognise you.'

I'm about to ask her why not, then realise I don't want to know, not yet. So all I say is, 'Right, then; I'll get changed', using the same flat voice that isn't my own. My throat is trying to swallow something gigantic, and I have to be alone to do that. I need time. I push myself upright, reaching towards the door, and as Julia's mother brushes past me she looks like a sad child, with her head bowed. It makes me feel we've changed places. 'I'll be downstairs if you need me,' she says in the corridor. 'We'll leave in an hour. Give me a shout if you need anything.' I shut the door with a smart click. There she is now. Gone. As she creaks along the corridor to Julia's room, I try not to imagine Julia's face, or her empty party dress lying on the bed.

Part of my brain has escaped and is hovering in space. It watches me open my suitcase, take out my clothes, then pad next door to run the bath. When I climb in, the water's too cold – but I don't mind. Everything should be wrong now, even the little things. And everything should be a question. Small questions and big questions jumbled together. What happened exactly? Have they taken mum out of her hunting clothes? How did they do that? Did the nurses undress her normally, or did they use a knife and cut them off? Is she awake? How much does her head hurt? Is dad beside her? Julia's mother was probably right. I am better off here. If I don't go to the party I'll only think of more questions. As I pull on my trousers and button up my shirt, I remember how I packed them this morning, wondering what Julia would think, and suddenly I see myself leaning out of a carriage window at Euston. Where has that come from? I'm ten years old again, waving to mum as the train shovels me off to school. But it's not her I see on the platform, it's myself, shrinking in the steam.

Julia's mother drives us to the party, which she says is twenty minutes away, and Julia sits beside me in the back holding my hand. It's allowed, because of what's happened, but I still feel I have to make a joke, and say we're like passengers in a taxi. Then I stop talking. It's better to hear the silence rush past as if I were dreaming, and when we reach a village green at last and park under a buzzing lamp, my eyes are half-closed. I come to with a jolt, and ask Julia's mother not to tell anyone what's happened. But after we've walked up the path and opened the front door, I can tell by the way people are frowning that she's rung them already. I put my head down and keep going. I need to get through the next door and be where the lights are dim and there's music. I want to be invisible, and then I want it to be morning, and then I want to be on the bus going home.

At eleven the music slows down and the lights fade almost to nothing. Julia is sitting on my knee, and we're chatting to some of her friends, who are sprawling on a sofa in an alcove. The weight of her in my lap: I like that. Her scent is soaking into my skin, and her hair brushes across my face whenever she leans forward. I don't have to say much, she's doing all the talking, so they probably haven't noticed I'm faking. These are my hands lighting a cigarette, my eyes watching people float round me like bodies underwater. But everything inside me is missing. I suppose I'll have to explain this to Julia, though when we're collected at midnight she already understands. She's been faking too. And now we're at the house again, beginning to climb the stairs towards the bedrooms, there's no need to pretend any more. 'Perhaps I'll see you in the new year?' she says, touching me on the cheek with one hand. I'm too tired to say anything except goodnight, and close my door. There's time to hear the floorboards groan as Julia tiptoes down the corridor. Then her dress rustling, and the click of her light going out. When I turn out my own lamp, I see an open field with frozen ribs of plough. Snow settles in the hoof-print moons where Serenade stumbles, then gathers herself, then gallops into the darkness.

Everything's a hurry next morning – we all make sure of that. Julia and her mother are clattering breakfast things when I park my suitcase in the hall, but none of us wants more than a cup of coffee. Then we're off, me in the passenger seat, with Julia directly behind so we can't see one another. She rubs the window, making little squeaks with her finger ends, and I stare out too, wondering what she's seeing. While everyone's been asleep, the snow has stopped; the grazing looks like old cords under the melting white, and the car tyres make a long whoosh through the slush. 'Would you like something to read on the journey?' says Julia's mother. 'No, thank you.' 'Not even a newspaper?' We're in Bishops Stortford again, with the bus shuddering at its stand. 'You must let me pay,' she says, but there's no need for that; mum lent me £5 yesterday, and here it is tucked in the back pocket of my jeans. I glance at my watch. She gave me the money almost exactly twenty-four hours ago, and now this other woman is leaning forward to kiss me goodbye. I climb out of the car and collect my suitcase from the boot. Julia's wearing her school coat again, with her hands stuffed back into her pockets.

I wonder whether I'm going to cry when I say goodbye – but that mustn't happen, even though it might help Julia and her mother. So I don't say goodbye. I just wave my hand stiffly in front of my face, then nip on the bus, pay my fare, and clump back upstairs to the front seat. The driver creaks into gear and I look down expecting to give another wave – but Julia and her mother have already gone. It's such a relief I actually smile, watching my face stretch in the window. Then it's shop-fronts again. Fields. Hedges. Outskirts. Next thing, the bus is leaving Braintree and I know where I am – beginning the roller-coaster of little bumps to The Swan. There are still so many questions to answer, but never mind. The thing to do is find Kit. It won't be long, because Mrs Hill is already here in her Land Rover, jumping out when she sees me, leaving her door to sway in the wind. She looks like a man dressed up, with her bobbly tweed skirt and her green Husky and her headscarf with bridles and horseshoes on it. It's a pity it has to be her; we don't like each other. But she tries to be kind, asking 'Did you get any sleep?' as we accelerate down the lane into the village, past Mrs Bunton's cottage.

Mrs Hill doesn't have much news; she wasn't with mum yesterday. She only knows what dad told her last night, when he rang and asked her to meet the bus. I interrupt: 'She fell off and hit her head?' Mrs Hill's hands are beefy on the steering-wheel, and she has a bulge of skin round her wedding ring. 'That's what I gather,' she says in her marching voice. 'In the middle of a field, apparently, which seems odd. Anyway, she banged her poor head and was still unconscious when they got her to the hospital. Your father said something about a blood clot and needing to have an operation, but I can't bear to think about it. It's too awful.' I rub my eyes, and let her go on. 'Honestly, your father. I don't know how he's coping but he's wonderful. And you must try not to worry. Your granny and Ruby will look after you.' 'They will,' I tell her, trying to give nothing away. Mrs Hill fidgets with the knot of her headscarf and smiles. 'Yes, I know,' she says. 'Gilly told me. Your mother, I mean; she told me what granny's like.'

I still don't want Mrs Hill to see I know what she means. It's none of her business. In any case, we'll be fine. Granny is looked after by Ruby, who was mum's nanny years ago, and Kit and I love Ruby. Look: there they are now, waiting with Kit on the doorstep as Mrs Hill turns off the lane towards the house. Kit steps forward as I squeeze out of the car, then stops still. He's looking at me as though he's never seen me before, and I'm staring back at him, feeling the same. He's my only brother. My younger bro. Except he's always been like a little man, with his straight fair hair and his wiry body. Today his face is slapped red, and he's shrunk inside his jersey – the sleeves have wriggled down over the backs of his hands. I want to hug him but we never do that and can't start now, not with these people watching. We stand close together without speaking. His eyes are wide and wet.

In a minute we'll go inside and talk, but first there's granny and Ruby to think about, and Mrs Hill as she backs away in her Land Rover. 'Remember what I said,' she shouts from the open window, anxious to be off. 'Give me a call when you need anything'. Before she disappears Ruby kisses me – I've forgotten how soft her cheek feels, like a moth – and over her shoulder I see granny dragging her terrier Janey on a lead. When she lifts her face for a kiss as well, the dog makes a sudden charge after Mrs Hill's car. 'This is mum's mum,' I think, grabbing hold of granny and feeling her thin shoulders slither like plates under her pullover. 'Mum is her daughter'. Granny gazes at me for a moment, then says, 'Andrew!' – astonished, as if she's only just realised I'm me. A second later, she whisks away again. It's Janey, surging down the drive and making coughy barks as her collar half-strangles her. 'That bloody dog,' says Kit, sounding exactly like dad. 'Do you know, we've had to lock Wiggy and Jenny in the stables?' Then he seizes my arm to steer me into the house. On the way through the hall, I see a berry has dropped off the mistletoe: waxy white, on the dark green carpet. Kit sees it too, and flicks it under the bench with the toe of his shoe.

We go straight to my room, close the door carefully, and sit side by side on the edge of the bed. Kit takes a deep breath to steady himself. Then he starts. He tells me they got to the meet without any problems, and when the hunt moved off everything had been fine too. It was snowy, but only a bit, and the ground hadn't been too bad, not hard enough to slow things down. Around lunchtime they'd drawn a wood in the middle of nowhere, just plough in every direction. People had been on point duty, checking to see if the fox broke cover, and Kit and mum were together but away from the rest of the field. When the hounds were going through the wood, there'd been the usual pheasants and rabbits.

Soon the hounds started to make a fuss. They'd found, and someone Kit couldn't see had hollered – the fox had made a dash for it on the far side of the wood. Mum said rather than trail all the way round, they should cut straight through – it would be quicker. So they popped over this little ditch and into the trees. It wasn't too bad, not as tangled as it looked from outside. There were a few fallen branches, and it was dark of course, and twigs whacking, but they managed pretty well. It was fun: they could hear the hounds in the plough ahead of them, hard on the heels of the fox.

They reached the other side of the wood and a ditch again, the same as before. There was a low branch, holly or something, so jumping out was more tricky than getting in – but nothing really, a scramble and a leap, then another scramble up the other side. Kit went first and it was all over before he knew anything. He was in the open, loosening his reins and galloping off across the plough. But he heard a stumble behind him and mum saying something, maybe 'Ouch' as she scraped against the holly. He hadn't thought it was serious. When he looked back, though, and saw Serenade hauling out of the ditch, mum was across her shoulder. The left shoulder. And mum's feet were out of the stirrups. It was unlike her, she was such a good rider. Perhaps Serenade had shied at something. Kit didn't know.

Before he looked away again, helping his own pony across the field – it was real Essex plough, terrible stuff – he noticed her hard hat was shoved forward at a funny angle. She'd banged it on Serenade's shoulder, and because mum never wore a strap under her chin it was about to come off. It had happened before, but she always said, 'I hate wearing a strap. It's infra dig'. Kit hadn't seen anything after that. He kept facing forward. But he could hear Serenade behind him, clambering through the plough. He called back once, 'Are you OK?', and there'd been some ooofing, nothing much. He thought mum had got back into her saddle. Serenade was bigger than his pony, Cavalier; she'd easily catch up. Besides, it was exciting. He could see other horses ahead of him now. They were making for an open gateway into the next field which was grass, and would be easier going.

Before he got there, he had to cross this track running through the plough – he didn't see it until he was close. A cement track for tractors, laid down like a gigantic dribble. Hideous. He knew he shouldn't gallop across it – that would hurt the pony's hooves – but he couldn't slow down. When it came to it, Cavalier didn't mind. He clattered a bit, then Kit was through the gate, picking up speed and overtaking some of the others. He thought he should get a move on, because the hounds were still some way ahead, even though he could hear them clearly enough. It sounded as though they could actually see the fox, they were making such a hullaballoo.

He reckoned Serenade would appear alongside any minute, but it didn't happen until he reached the end of the grazing. Then she galloped past going hell for leather, her ears back and stirrups flailing. The saddle was empty. He didn't think much of it at first. That business with the holly and the ditch: mum must have fallen off after all, but she wouldn't be hurt. It was only plough, and the frost wasn't too bad. So what should he do next? Try and catch Serenade, obviously, then take her back. No, someone else was doing that. A man in a pink coat, snatching at the reins. Kit glanced over his shoulder. Through the gateway behind him, half a dozen people had got off their horses and were standing in a circle, leaning inwards. He thought they looked like crows. Kit wheeled round, and as he reached the gateway one of the people on the ground, a woman, jumped back onto her horse.

'Who was it?' I ask, interrupting. 'I don't know,' Kit says. 'She pulled up in front of me and barred the way.' 'What do you mean barred the way? Couldn't you do anything?' 'Not really, no,' he says. 'Mum was lying on the track, not on the plough. She must have hung on all the way across the field, then fallen off when she got to the cement, and hit her head on that.' We stop talking and stare at the curtains, the new red curtains I chose before Christmas. 'That was bad luck,' I say. 'Bloody bad luck,' says Kit, still sounding like dad. 'A few seconds earlier, or a few seconds later, she'd have hit the plough and been all right.' He turns sideways and raises his eyebrows. I'm the elder brother. I'm the one who reads books. Don't I have something helpful to say?

I shake my head. 'So you didn't see her at all?' Kit looks straight ahead again. We can hear Ruby downstairs setting out the plates for lunch, and the tick-tick-tick of Janey's feet on the kitchen lino. He tells me he couldn't see mum's face, but she was unconscious, he knew that. She wasn't moving, and some of the people had taken off their coats and piled them on top of her for warmth. How long did it all take, I want to know. How long was she lying there? I need to have everything as clear as a photograph: the plough with the wood in the background; the low horizon and the cold sky; mum ringed by a circle of crow-people; her bare head on the cement. But I say nothing. I let Kit finish.

He says somebody rang for an ambulance but doesn't know how they got to a phone. They must have galloped off and found one in a farmhouse. Anyway, after a while this ambulance arrived, he'd heard it coming from miles away, with the siren going. It crept along the cement track and stopped, then the men took out a stretcher and rolled mum onto it. He'd seen that bit. 'And after they'd got her in the back,' he says, 'they reversed all the way up the cement because there was nowhere to turn round.' Kit stops again and we sit staring at the curtains. Mum thought such a strong colour might make the room too small, but it doesn't; it's cosy. Eventually Kit tells me someone put his pony and Serenade into the horsebox and drove them home. He went to stay with a friend for the night, as I knew. He's sorry he didn't call me, nobody had my number. I tell him it doesn't matter, we're here now, and as I say this I see Julia stepping forward in the gateway to kiss me, pulling the big ticklish scarf down from her mouth. That must have been when the accident was happening.

The plates clash again, and food smells drift up to us. It feels wrong, being hungry. But there's one more thing I have to ask: has Kit talked to dad? Not last night; dad was busy at the hospital. He'd rung this morning, though. 'And?' I ask. 'He talked to Ruby mainly,' Kit tells me. 'Granny couldn't take much in. Then I chatted to him for a bit.' 'And?' I ask again. Kit squares his shoulders. 'I don't really know,' he says stiffly. 'They did this operation to remove the blood clot, and that seemed to go well. But dad says they won't really know until she wakes up.' 'She hasn't woken up yet?' 'No, she hasn't woken up yet.' 'Do they know when she will?' 'They can't say.'

There's a scuffle at the door and Ruby appears, large and soft in her cardigan. Kit and I shift apart as though we've been caught doing something wrong. 'Are you two coming for lunch?' she asks. The kindness in her voice sparks something I haven't expected. 'Roo,' I say angrily, accidentally jabbing Kit with my elbow. 'Why will nobody tell us what's happening? We're not babies. It's mum we're talking about here. Mum. We have a right to know.' Even before I finish, I wish I hadn't started. How can Ruby help? She fiddles with her hearing aid, and for a second I think she hasn't heard me. She's been deaf ever since we can remember; mum says it's because granny talks so much nonsense – Ruby would go mad if she heard it all. But she has heard me. 'Yes, I talked to your father early this morning,' she says in her cobwebby voice, speaking slowly so I can tell it's something she's rehearsed. 'This is what he said. Someone rang him yesterday afternoon when he was at his office in London, and told him there'd been an accident. He drove straight to Chelmsford, to the hospital. He got there a couple of hours after mum arrived in the ambulance, and by that time the doctors had looked at her, and decided what had to be done. But they needed dad before they could start.' 'What do you mean?' I say, speaking loudly so Ruby can hear. 'Well,' she goes on, taking a tissue from her pocket and tweaking one of the corners. 'He told me he'd talked to a doctor straight away and apparently they had a choice. There was a blood clot on mum's brain, and if they didn't operate soon it would be too late. If they did operate it might not work.' 'What do you mean it might not work?' Kit asks. Ruby lifts her head. 'She might become a vegetable,' she says.

She pronounces the word carefully, as though I might not know what it means. But I do understand, and I smile. It sounds ludicrous. Then I see dad under the garish lights of the waiting room, talking to a man in a white coat with a stethoscope dangling round his neck. There wasn't a choice, not really. Dad had to say operate. That's what I would have done.

'They operated,' Ruby says, her mouth quivering and her right hand touching her forehead like a salute. She's speaking fast now; it reminds me of Julia's mother, the way she rattled on as though her voice was trying to escape something charging up behind it. 'They operated, but a piece of her brain came away with the blood clot. That sounds bad, I know, but dad says the doctors don't know how serious in fact, because they know very little about the brain, even in this day and age, that's one of the strange things. They don't understand what this bit of the brain does, or did rather, this missing piece. It might not be that important.'

'When can we see her?' Kit asks softly, but Ruby hears this too and presses back against the radiator. Her arm drops from her face and tightens across her stomach. 'Not yet,' she says, slowing down again. 'Dad will ring later, after lunch he said, and explain. He doesn't think seeing her is a good idea.' 'Why not?' Kit and I say together. 'Because she's still unconscious, for one thing. She wouldn't know who you were. She's not herself. She doesn't look like herself. Dad doesn't want you to see that. He wants you to remember her as she was.' A crack runs through Ruby's voice, breaking it into pieces, and we know we mustn't ask any more questions. Ruby has known mum all her life, ever since she was a baby. She goes on anyway, even though tears have started plopping out of her eyes. 'She's very bruised, you know,' she says. 'And they've cut off all her hair.' Her hair. I hold the words in a soft loop, and see myself standing behind mum at the dressing table in her bedroom. She turns to pass me her shiny blue-backed brush.

Then Ruby unclasps her arms and holds them towards us, so Kit and I get to our feet, and the three of us stand in a huddle. It's awkward, nobody knows how tight to hold anybody else, and I keep expecting Ruby to say everything will soon be back to normal, but she doesn't. She goes on crying, making odd quivery whimpers, and then Kit's crying too, and then I am. The light from outside, flicking off the bare branches of the chestnut tree, swings over us in pale yellow waves. The mattress on my bed gives a muffled creak as it recovers from our weight. 'Anyway,' Ruby says eventually, sighing and letting her arms fall. 'You can talk to dad yourselves later. He won't be coming home for a day or two, but he'll ring. And the best thing we can all do is keep going.' I say 'Yes', realising that Ruby is repeating something dad must have told her himself. We must be brave. We mustn't add to his worries.

Granny calls from the kitchen: she sounds frightened, as though we might have disappeared. The three of us give each other quick little pats on the back, then wipe our eyes and start to head downstairs. At the door, I tell Kit I'll follow in a minute, and turn back into the room. A lumpy thought is stuck in my head and I can't find space for it: I need a minute alone. I'm thinking that for most people childhood ends slowly, so nobody can see where one part of life finishes and the next bit starts. But my childhood has ended suddenly. In a day. No matter what happens to mum, nothing will be the same from now on. Then I'm thinking something else – no, not thinking. Wishing. I want to lock into my head everything that's happened in my life up to now, and make sure it never changes. If I can keep it safe, I'll be able to look back and feel safe myself. I don't want to explain it. I don't want to talk about it in the grown-up language I haven't learned yet. Maybe I don't even want to understand it. I just want everything as it was, when I saw the world for the first time.

Kit calls from the hall below: 'Are you coming, bro?' He's right, we must stick together, and I bang the door behind me to show I'm on my way. When I reach the kitchen, granny's wandering to and fro in front of the Aga, where a pan of potatoes has boiled dry. 'We'll eat in the dining room,' she says, not knowing we only do that on high days and holidays. Kit glances at me, rolls his eyes, and we take our plates from the cupboard by the sink. When I walk next door, I see granny has tied Janey's lead to a leg of the dining table. As we eat our meal, Janey makes mad lunges towards the sideboard. Every time she does this, the table shifts an inch or two, taking our food away from us.

CHAPTER TWO

Was He Dead?

Mum and dad liked telling stories about our relations, and Kit and I liked hearing them. But that was pretty much that. We almost never went to stay with other people in the family, and didn't expect them to be friends. I wondered whether there'd been arguments in the past, or one lot thought they were too good for the other. In the end I decided we preferred our own company.

There weren't many of them. Mum had one brother and his name was George. When he was twenty-something he'd taken his family to Rhodesia, where mum said things had been tricky. Although he'd married a rich woman, he'd lost a lot of money running a tobacco farm. Then he went into advertising and appeared on telly modelling shirts that were several sizes too big, with balled-up stockings stuffed inside his collar. This made him sound wonderful, even if he had once whacked mum on the back of her legs with cabbage stalks. But when he came to visit, and turned out to be a crumpled-looking man with a chimp face, we never got beyond being polite.

Dad had a younger brother and a sister, Liz, who didn't have any children and lived in a thatched cottage outside Diss in Suffolk that kept bursting into flames. Kit and I thought she was frightening – she had a moustache, and was surrounded by out-of-control spaniels. Mum said the moustache explained why she'd married Eric, who was a pansy. I didn't know what she meant, but apparently it had something to do with the fancy socks he wore, which we thought were so amazing we often used his name for socks in general. 'You're not wearing matching Erics,' for instance, or 'Change your Erics, they stink.' Eventually Liz dumped him and took up with a man who came to fix the roof after one of her blazes. Dad was annoyed about this, but not surprised. He'd never liked Eric much. We knew that, because one Christmas Eric had given him a bottle of Brut aftershave as a present. Dad didn't approve of aftershave, and pretended to think it was a liqueur. He poured it carefully into a little glass, then swallowed a mouthful and said it was delicious.

Uncle Rob owned a small farm in Warwickshire, and was an outside version of dad. Dad behaved like a countryman but looked towny: when he caught the train to London every weekday morning, his black hair was polished with Bay Rum. Rob was curly, and had purple nails because he kept hammering his hands when he was meant to be knocking in fence posts. There was something daredevil about him, too. After he'd broken up with his first wife, she married a man whose own wife then moved in with Uncle Rob. Apparently all four of them had been childhood friends, so it was understandable in a way.

Rob and his first wife had two children, cousin Peter and cousin Sarah, but mum didn't seem too keen for us to like them. She never actually criticised them, she just let us know they were difficult. 'Difficult how?' I wanted to know. 'Rebellious,' she said, which made me like them more. But nothing came of it. When we went to stay with Uncle Rob for a weekend one summer, Kit and I spent most of the time heaving bales of straw from the stubble onto a trailer, then swaying into the barn on top of the stacked-up wagon, brushing our heads on the rafters. On a winter visit, Uncle Rob showed us how to cut-and-lay a hedge. Staring at the woven branches was like gazing at an enormous puzzle. Our uncle had made this. He was a magician, and it was him we wanted to talk to, not his children.

Older relations were even further off than cousins, which meant their stories were better still. Mum's maiden name was Bakewell, and when she told me her great-great-great something-or-other Robert had been 'the inventor of the fat sheep', it made me feel important. We had a painting of him in the hall, looking just the job: a jolly farmer with roly-poly ringlets. There was another sort-of famous name on her side, too. Her grandfather had been a high-court judge. 'A hanging judge,' mum said solemnly, lifting both arms and pretending to put a black cap on her head as if about to deliver a death sentence. Whenever we went to London we drove along Cumberland Terrace, overlooking Regent's Park, while she pointed out his rooms. As time went by, almost any row of grand white houses turned out to be Cumberland Terrace, but Kit and I didn't mind. We knew mum loved exaggerating, and wanted us to think her family was as interesting as dad's. All the same, it was strange to think that such a powerful brain, my great-grandpa, had produced someone as dotty as granny.

Granny's childhood had been strict and boring, according to mum. 'She had governesses, and never went to school; it must have been awful.' Eventually granny spun out sideways and married a doctor, a GP, and settled in Beaconsfield. She was still living there now – an old lady who drove straight over roundabouts because she couldn't remember whether to turn right or left. When we laughed at this, mum said, 'It's pathetic really; granny was quite something in her younger days.' 'What do you mean?' we wanted to know. 'Look at this,' mum said. It was a photograph of granny biking down the main street of Beaconsfield in her Girl Guides uniform, her long front teeth stuck out like a rabbit. Apparently she'd run the local Guides for years, which mum said 'was really like being a general in an army'.

Mum still missed her father, the doctor. He'd died years before, when she was a teenager, but she kept his picture on the dressing table in her bedroom. A big-shouldered man with clipped moustaches and old-fashioned Christian names – 'Empire names,' dad said: George Victor. He'd been a reader of books and friendly with G. K. Chesterton, who mum said was a wonderful writer and one of his patients. Mum reckoned her father had been killed by the war – not because he'd worked in the front line, but because there'd been so much to do in Beaconsfield. There was an army hospital along the road, where they put soldiers who'd been injured in the fighting. Once George Victor spent a day treating half a dozen wounded German prisoners at the camp, waved goodnight to them in their tent, then came back next morning to find they'd all been bayoneted by some Gurkhas. 'Very tough people, the Gurkhas,' mum said.

Granny would have come to live with us, if it hadn't been for Ruby. But Ruby was always there – had always been there, ever since mum was born. People said she hadn't changed in thirty years and I could believe it: Ruby's red-haired moon-face seemed incredibly old and yet no age at all. Her family came from Cookham, nearby in the Thames valley, and although I'd never been there, I felt I knew it. Ruby had told me that when she was a little girl, there'd been a painter in her village called Stanley Spencer, who was famous. She showed me some postcard-pictures of back gardens with chubby-looking people hugging, or empty-ing dustbins. And one of a graveyard, with a dead family popping out of the ground.

Ruby's face creased into smiles when she talked about Cookham. If granny was around, she was frowning and nervous, twiddling her hearing aid, wanting to slip away because she felt one of her migraines coming on and needed to lie down. Kit and I loved her, and liked the way she and mum talked as if they were best friends, even if it did mean hearing them say rude things about granny sometimes. Ruby always leaned forward to listen, watching mum's lips move and nodding. Everything she did was slow and soft – her trips to the Women's Institute; her holidays with her brother near Cookham; her jam-making and cake-bak-ing. It didn't matter that she couldn't hear much. Standing beside her in the kitchen, I watched her sprinkle flour on the formica, then push her faded red hair from her forehead with the back of her hand. She was more like a granny than granny herself.

We stayed at Beaconsfield every three months or so until I was seven and went away to school, and after that we visited every hol-iday. We dreaded it, even though we looked forward to seeing Ruby and the tramp who sat on the signpost to London, saying he was a poached egg on toast. The journey was long, the days were dull, and granny's dogs were mad. Quivering Lassie bit us if we tried to stroke her. The pug Lucy slobbered on our hands. The terriers before Janey, and then Janey, gnawed the legs of chairs and left them covered in bitemarks. But there were two highlights. A trip to Beaconscot; and a walk round Hall Barn. Mum said Beaconscot was creepy, but that's what I liked about it. The adverts said it was a 'model village'. Really it was a shrivelled-up town; everything was doll-sized. There were tiny houses, even smaller bungalows, mini-roads, half-inch postmen delivering letters, and a station and track like the best train set I could imagine. Ruby said when Prince Charles visited, the people who owned Beaconscot let him organise a crash, and I told her I was jealous. 'Oh no,' said mum, butting in. 'You don't want to feel envious of Prince Charles about anything. He's got a ghastly job, poor little boy. And his ears! What were his parents thinking, not getting them pinned back somehow? Talk about taxi doors.'

On the other hand, mum thought Hall Barn was blissful, and we agreed about that too; it was Queen Anne she said, and the home of granny's friend, Lady Burnham. After they got married, my parents had a party in a big room at the back like a greenhouse, and we always began our afternoon walk by peering through the windows. I could imagine mum and dad stepping across the cold floor to say hello to their friends, and thought if I ever got married, I'd like to have a party there too. After that we set off towards the woods facing the house – a huge green labyrinth with shaggy walks cut between the rhododendrons, and miles of beech trees, and yews dangling their poisonous scarlet berries. There was a maze in the middle of the beeches. Sometimes the corridors here would be clipped, which was disappointing: we could look ahead and see our way to the centre. Usually it was overgrown and mysterious, which meant we had to push through cobwebs, prowling in circles but getting somewhere, cheering when we reached the end, which was a small stone Cupid. He was frozen on one leg with his bow lifted up, and his eyes were fixed on a gap in the leaves, as though he was following the flight of the arrow he'd just fired.

It was here that mum told us our favourite Beaconsfield stories. In the first she was eight, and wanted to join the village gang. The leader said yes, but first she had to jump off one of the temples in the wood. She did, and a laurel bush came to her rescue, which proved she was lucky as well as brave. In the second she was fourteen, and reaching the end of a Sunday afternoon stroll with

George Victor. She was his only daughter and liked having him to herself, chattering uphill from the deep valley where the stream cut through. It was winter, the light was fading, and they were hurrying to reach the side-gate where they'd left the car. Her father was puffing – he was a pipe-smoker, always short of breath – and the path was slippery where it climbed under the evergreens. Suddenly he bent forward, leaning on her heavily, then slipped to the ground. She told us this in the exact spot where it happened, by the last yew tree on the path to the wonky gate. Was he still breathing? 'Of course he was still breathing,' mum said, annoyed that we wouldn't keep to the pace of her story. 'But only just – he was very ill. He'd had a heart attack.' We gazed at her pale face, breathing the resin-smell of the trees. A young girl, whose father was struggling for his life. What did she do? She ran for help, of course. She burst through the gate, up the path alongside the wood, then into Hall Barn, where she found people to come back with her. What did they find? Was he any worse? She wanted to say yes, to make a better story, but she loved her father too much, and said actually he was OK, still conscious. Kit and I stared at the path for evidence. There was only the shining mud, and the burst yew berries showing their yellow seeds.

The third story belonged deeper in the wood, by one of the little man-made pools. 'You remember what I told you about the German plane?' mum asked, as we stared into the black water. 'No,' Kit and I said, meaning the opposite. 'Well, it was during the war as well, but in the summer, a hot day, and I was walking here with my father when we heard this engine overhead.' 'What sort of engine?' I asked, to show how interested I was. Mum shrugged and carried on. 'My father said it was a German plane, a Messerschmidt, but there was something wrong; it was making a funny noise like a motorbike. Barely above those trees by the sound of it.' Mum and George Victor had stopped still, feeling skinned by the engine-racket which might turn into a nosedive at any minute. Then the plane doodled into view, crossing their patch of sky. 'It was so low,' mum went on, 'I could see the face of the pilot looking down – a real face, like someone I might know, not a German face.' She even thought their eyes might have met for a second, but that was probably one of her exaggerations. In my head he was a German Biggles, with a moustache, and goggles pushed onto his forehead, and she was a pretty girl in a blowing dress, shielding her eyes as she squinted up at him. 'Anyway,' she said with a sigh, 'there was oily black stuff flapping from the engine, and the motor kept cutting out then catching again. I thought it must have been hit by one of our own planes, a Spitfire probably. The pilot couldn't find his way home and was looking for somewhere to land. The woods below were useless and he had to get away into open country.'

The story might have ended there, but because George Victor was the GP he heard what happened next. The pilot wheeled away from Beaconsfield, heading for the flat bit on top of the Chilterns where he could make a pancake landing. But he didn't have enough fuel to get that far, and decided to ditch the plane. Which meant climbing, trying to get high enough to make a parachute jump – except that went wrong too, and his parachute didn't work. Some boys working in the fields saw him falling, and ran over to see. 'Was he dead?' I asked, knowing the answer. 'Oh yes, he was dead,' said mum, then paused before adding the bit she knew I liked best: 'They had to scrape him off the grass.'

Dad usually gave these visits to granny a miss, and whenever he came with us he looked nervous. He was too big for the poky little house, always hunching his shoulders and squeezing his arms to his sides if he went near the Toby jugs. It was the fiddliness he hated – the marmalade pot at breakfast which was shaped like an orange, the boxes and photographs on the side-table. Whenever possible, he went into the garden to smoke cigarettes and talk to the gardener, Mr Bunce, who'd been shot during the First World War and still had the bullet in his chest. On the other hand, dad cheered up whenever granny's younger sister Daphne looked in. Her fiancé had been killed on HMS *Hood*, and since then she'd lived in a cottage up a cart-track in Sussex, where she kept to herself. She was bony and stylish, with an old-fashioned la-di-dah voice that said 'orf' not 'off', and 'crorws' not 'cross', and always seemed about to collapse into laughter. There was a picture of her fiancé in a display cabinet at the top of granny's stairs, and I liked to lean on the glass and gaze at his face. Smooth-looking and clever, with smile-lines round his mouth. If it hadn't been for the bomb that dropped straight into the funnel of the *Hood*, and blew all the sailors to smithereens, he'd be downstairs now, creeping round the Toby jugs with dad.

Although mum told dad there were 'just as many nutcases among the Motions', we never laughed about them in the same way. When I thought of the Bakewells I heard parties and chat. When I thought of the Mos I saw wallets and portraits. Especially the portraits in the dining room at home, where we had lunch on Sundays. When dad sat down at the head of the table, he had his grandpa Andrew in his high white collar and business suit on the wall in front, and his father in army uniform on the wall behind. 'They won't bite,' mum told us, but Kit and I still thought they were frightening.

Mo stories began with Andrew, my great-grandpa. The first I heard was: he'd been born the son of a baker in St Andrews, on the east coast of Scotland, and travelled to London to better himself. When Aunt Liz did some research, it turned out Andrew's parents had actually moved south in the 1870s while he was still a boy, leaving several dead Mos buried round the old cathedral, and a few more baking bread in the town. But that didn't change the point of the story. Andrew went into the wine trade after leaving school, then swapped it for brewing. He was hired by the Canon Brewery, in Clerkenwell, and around the same time he married Jessie Holmwood, whose family came from Clapton, near his own home in Hackney in the east end of London. Dad hummed and hawed when he got to this bit of the story, and mum stepped in to spare his blushes. I liked that. It showed that when mum and dad were alone together, he told her things he wouldn't breathe to anyone else. Then, when she thought we were ready, mum passed them on to us. It was how families were supposed to work.

Mum said Andrew's career took off very fast. 'He was licking stamps for the brewery when he was seventeen, and owned it by the time he was thirty.' That sounded amazing, but it turned out the explanation was simple. Andrew had come up with a big idea – the idea of buying free houses, so he could tie them to the brewery. He made a packet, and immediately set about turning himself into a country gent. First he bought Faulkbourne Hall, a big Elizabethan house in Essex, then Upton House in Warwickshire, along with everything inside: every stick of furniture, every picture, every snuffbox. He had a coat of arms designed, a badger on a mount, which Kit and I thought looked like a wild boar jumping over a five-barred gate. He had a family motto invented: *Suscipere et Finere*, 'If you start something, don't give up until you've finished.' He took up hunting and shooting and fishing.

'He really must have been stinko,' mum said. 'You know what people are like, turning up their noses at new money. But Andrew never had that problem. He fitted into the country, like he fitted into the brewery.' She said this with a swing, which made us feel proud, but she liked telling us how he'd come a cropper as well. Her favourite example was a story about two pictures he'd bought with Upton, which were supposed to be originals by Stubbs, who mum said was one of her favourite painters. They were scenes of people haymaking. 'If Andrew had ever been to an art gallery,' mum said, 'he'd have known the pictures at Upton were copies.' I'd never been to an art gallery, but I could see this was embarrassing. Was mum sure people didn't laugh at Andrew behind his back? She couldn't say. 'Every morning a train stopped for him on the line below the house,' she went on with a giggle. 'They let down a little pair of steps and he climbed up to his carriage. I suppose he thought it would all go on for ever. Grandpa certainly did.'

That made it sound as though grandpa had always been slap-bang at the middle of things, but his mother Jessie had five daughters first: everyone called them Pro-motion, Com-motion, E-motion, Loco-motion and De-motion. 'After that performance,' mum said, 'it's not surprising grandpa was spoiled rotten.' As far as I could see, the girls weren't exactly hard done by, either. From what mum said, they never expected to think for themselves. 'You mean they had governesses like granny?' 'Well, yes,' mum said. 'Like granny but not like granny. Do you understand what "professional" means?'

I didn't. 'Granny's family were professional,' mum said, and even though I still couldn't tell exactly what she was on about, I got the general idea. Grandpa was expected to take up where great-grandpa Andrew left off. Everything was meant to fall into his lap.

Grandpa went to Eton, because Andrew thought that was the done thing, then started at Brasenose College in Oxford. But after a few months the First World War broke out, and everything changed. Dad told me what happened one lunchtime, while we were standing in front of grandpa's portrait in the dining room. Instead of staying at university, grandpa joined the Warwickshire Yeomanry and was sent to Egypt. 'He took his hunter with him,' dad said. 'They all had to do that, but there was an accident. Their boat got torpedoed, and most of the horses were killed. It meant he had to ride some Australian nag when he got to the other end; you can imagine what he thought of that.' He laughed. 'He lived the life of Riley to start with – staying in a swanky hotel, that kind of thing. Then it got nasty. He was fighting the Turks, you see, who'd teamed up with a few local tribes. One of them was called the Senussi, and they were the worst: they tricked a whole troop of British cavalry into charging at them. Really charging – think about that! Everyone waving their swords in the air and bellowing and going hell for leather.' I did think about it: it was like a story in one of my comics – the *Victor*, not the *Dandy*. Especially when it turned out the Senussi had disappeared at the last minute, and most of the rushing men and horses had gone flying over the edge of a crevasse. One Sunday grandpa told me this story himself, sitting beside mum with his white hair and his pink face and his beautiful silvery suit. He blurred the times and dates so much, I thought he'd actually taken part. He definitely didn't say anything when mum chipped in at the end and told me it was 'the last cavalry charge ever made by British soldiers'.

When I asked dad what happened next, he went quiet. It was odd – normally he liked this kind of thing. But he only said grandpa came back from the war a Captain, which was what he'd been at the start. I wondered whether there'd been a problem. Maybe he wasn't a very good soldier? Dad shook his head, and told me that after the war grandpa had worked for the Canon until 1930, when it was sold to Taylor Walker. Then he took up farming. 'Were great-grandpa and Jessie disappointed?' I wanted to know. By now dad was shaking his head. 'Your great-grandfather left the brewery at the same time,' he said. 'Though by all accounts he was a difficult man.' 'What do you mean?' 'Moody,' dad said, then quickly told me the rest of the story. In 1926 Andrew sold Upton and moved back to Essex, to Stisted Hall, where the high ground was good for Jessie's asthma. 'Didn't stop him being pretty peculiar though,' mum piped up from the doorway; we hadn't noticed her listening. 'Andrew ploughed up the tennis court when he left Upton because he thought he'd been diddled in the sale.' 'Really?' dad said. 'Never knew that.' I looked at mum but she wouldn't meet my eye. It was probably another of her exaggerations.

Lunch was ready, so dad and I followed mum into the kitchen. But I still wanted to get to the end of the story, and kept rolling my questions over the table. It turned out that by the time Andrew and Jessie arrived in Stisted, grandpa had already got married. But dad didn't want to talk about this, and let mum take over. 'Your grand-father wasn't an easy man to please,' she said, trying to sound nor-mal, like someone reading the news. 'He went to live in Witham because it was handy for London, but mainly it suited him because he needed to be near the hunt kennels. Hunting wasn't something he did at the weekends, you know. It was his whole life. He lived and breathed it'. I didn't understand. Why did that make it difficult for dad to talk about him? After all, dad loved hunting too. I decid-ed it would be better to finish lunch, then ask mum when I had her to myself. When the time came, even she went quiet. 'Grandpa got divorced,' she said eventually. 'Surely you knew that – I mean, he and granny don't live together.' I looked at her like an idiot, and mum put her finger under my chin. 'You're fly-catching,' she said, clicking my mouth shut. 'But honestly: didn't you realise?' I blath-ered for a while about how we didn't see granny much, so how was I to know? Mum went on frowning until I stopped, then put her hand back to my face and patted me on the cheek. 'No, well, I sup-pose that's rather sweet,' she said, as if I wasn't in the room. 'Nowadays divorce happens all the time, but in those days it was a terrible scandal. Especially when the woman ran off, not the man, which is what happened with grandpa. That's why dad doesn't like talking about it. He was only sixteen or so. It was difficult for him at school and everything. Andrew was dead by then, but Jessie must have hated it too. Grandpa was the apple of her eye.'

We left it at that for the time being, but I went on thinking about Jessie. She ended up in a house called Bengeo, near Hatfield. I knew, because mum had taken me to see her when we were little. The first time we went with grandpa and dad: there was a photograph to prove it, three generations of Mos leaning over the fourth, and Jessie dressed in black with a white frilly blouse. Then mum took us by ourselves, and Kit and I played croquet on the lawn while Jessie watched from her summer house, her fingers resting on the silver knob of her cane. As the sun crossed the sky, we stopped our game now and again to push the summer house round on its swivel, so Jessie was always in the shade. The last time I was seven; mum told us Jessie was dying, and we had to say goodbye. Kit and I were spellbound, and didn't even mind driving for hours through the snow. When we reached Bengeo, we found a nurse waiting in a high wooden hallway that smelled of chrysanths – it was like going to church. The bedroom had wooden walls too, and the air inside was blurred by the snow-light, coming through the net curtains. I'd expected a feeling of struggle, but Jessie looked more like a fossil than a person, propped on huge pillows in the middle of her four-poster, with the top sheet folded under her tiny hands. She didn't speak, and her eyes were shut, and I thought she was asleep. Then, after we'd bowed and were starting to leave, one of her fingers lifted. 'Jessie,' mum whispered. 'I've brought the boys to see you.' Jessie's face tightened, like the skin when I put my spoon into custard, and it was all mum wanted. 'There,' she said to us. 'You see? She knows you're here.'

Jessie died a day or two later, and was buried in Stisted beside Andrew, who'd been waiting twenty-six years. Mum decided Kit and I were too young to go to the funeral, but we knew something important had changed. Grandpa was the head man now, and when he came to Sunday lunch, mum tried harder to make him laugh at her jokes. It was OK, because he made a great performance of getting on well with her, too; he was always patting her hand, and saying she was marvellous. Kit and I thought it was like having royalty to visit – and why did grandpa always walk in that strange way, with his legs stiff? Mum explained he was helping with money for school fees. He had pound notes stuffed into his trouser pockets; that's why they rustled.

Mum told us we shouldn't complain about grandpa; his visits never lasted very long. Every time he drove off, she told dad how grateful she was about the fees, then added something about him being good-looking: no wonder half the women in Essex were in love with him. At the same time, I could see he made her fidgety, so I wasn't surprised when I overheard her mumbling to dad, soon after grandpa's car had disappeared. She was doing the washing-up, and speaking more quickly than usual. 'Grandpa's not interested in the boys,' she said. 'Not really. Just like he wasn't interested in you, when you were little.' 'He was,' said dad, sounding sulky. 'No, he wasn't,' mum said. 'And neither was your mother, come to that. They just got Nanny Goody to look after you, and she brought you down from the nursery from time to time, for them to coo over you like a prize vegetable. That's no way to bring people up.' Dad didn't answer straight away. He was putting knives and forks in the kitchen sideboard and I could hear them clinking into the little trays. 'But that shouldn't surprise anyone, should it?' mum went on. 'After all, grandpa's always done exactly what he wanted to do. Hunted, and hunted, and hunted.' Dad laughed but I knew mum was right. I'd heard her talking about this before, saying grandpa's reign as Master had lasted nearly thirty years, and gobbled up most of Andrew's money. I tiptoed away, thinking I'd heard enough. It wasn't all bad about grandpa, though. People who liked him thought he was a hero. An old lady had once told me he didn't even get off his horse when he wanted to pee. He stood up in his saddle and did it over the side.

There was something I couldn't understand. Why hadn't grandpa been able to hang onto granny if he'd been so handsome and dashing? And why did he get divorced if he cared so much what people thought of him? Nobody said, and there wasn't much chance of finding out from granny herself. She lived in Westleton, on the Suffolk coast, but as I'd said to mum, we hardly ever saw her. It was usually when we bumped into her at point-to-points in the Easter holidays, and she invited us to watch a race from her car – a Sunbeam, which is why we called her granny Sunbeam. Her metal-coloured hair looked tight as a helmet, her face had been whacked red by the wind, and she kept letting fly with un-funny laughs when she twisted round to offer us a glass of cherry brandy. 'Very good against the cold; here, have a swig' she said, without looking me in the eye. It was even worse when we went to her cottage. Kit and I hung around the garden counting Red Admirals on her buddleia bush, then crouched under low beams in the dining room. Once, when I stood up to help clear the table after we'd eaten our soup, I thumped my forehead so hard I almost knocked myself out. Granny banged the table with her fist. 'I told you to duck, you clot,' she said, and pulled mum down into her seat. 'Let him get on with it, Gilly. There's only one way for them to learn.'

'Granny Sunbeam is a very unhappy woman,' mum said, and I thought about this in secret. Unhappy? More than unhappy, by the look of things. We could see it in her puffy face, and even her handwriting was strange. It slumped down to the right in her Christmas cards, as if each line was falling asleep. But the question was, did that make granny Sunbeam any weirder than the rest of the family? They were all peculiar, and even though I prayed for them every night, they were far off as well. Grandpa was the only one we saw much. The rest of them – dotty granny and sad granny, the invisible cousins, hairy Aunt Liz and Uncle Rob with his purple nails, the judge who sent people to the gallows, the doctor who died young – they circled in the sky above me like a flock of seagulls. I didn't have to bother with them if I didn't want to.

All the same, I felt they were teaching me things. That's why I liked it when dad dragged the family Bible out from his desk – the huge monster, big enough for a church, which left brown stains on our hands as we opened it. There on the first page was the family tree – the top half written in black spider-scribbles by goodness-knows-who, the bottom bit in Jessie's pale blue ink. We knelt on the carpet, and I ran my finger down the branches. It only took a few seconds to get from Scotland and the oldest baker Mo at the top, to my own name and Kit's squeezed in at the bottom four hundred years later. 'There's hardly any room for you,' dad said, in a voice which was meant to be happy but sounded sad. I felt a weight on my shoulder as if he'd touched me, but of course he hadn't. We almost never touched. Kit and I giggled. Dad went on staring, his breath like a miniature sea rushing in and out.

CHAPTER THREE

Eggs

Three years after the war, when she was twenty-one, mum left granny's house in Beaconsfield and moved to a flat in Cheyne Row, near the Thames embankment in London. She was renting it with her friend Jenny, who got there first. Mum turned up a couple of days later, clutching two suitcases and a bundled-up sheet stuffed with odds-and-ends. As she leaned forward to ring the bell with her nose, the door yanked open and a young man barged out. Mum lost her grip on the sheet, which burst open and spewed onto the pavement, but the young man marched off towards the Underground without even looking round. 'Who was that?' mum asked, when Jenny appeared in the hall. 'Richard Motion,' she was told. 'He lives in the downstairs flat, but I don't know him. The landlady says he's in love with her daughter, and she doesn't approve. Apparently he boils his eggs in the kettle. It'll give him warts.'

That's the story mum told me, anyway. When I asked dad, he smiled and said mum was fibbing again – but he didn't mind. In fact her flat was down the road in Chelsea, and they'd met nearby at a drinks party given by a friend called Robert Eden. I went back to mum, and told her what dad had said. 'Oh really?' she mumbled. 'Well, yes, perhaps. We certainly did see each other at Robert's.' 'And did you know at once?' I wondered. 'What do you mean, did we know at once?' I chose my words carefully: 'Did you like each other?' 'We did like each other,' mum said in a slower voice, to show me she was telling the truth now. 'We liked each other very much and went to a lot of other parties together, that sort of thing. And to see granny Bakewell, of course – and grandpa. But we liked it best in London, even though there was still rationing and everything was pretty dreary. Your father's a wonderful dancer, you know.' Now it was my turn to go slow. Dad, dancing? No, I didn't know, but I pressed on with the story because we were nearly at the end. 'When did you decide to get married?' I asked. 'Oh, after six months or so,' mum said, in the same dreamy voice. 'Wanting to marry someone is something you feel in your guts. You'll see – you'll find out yourself one day.' 'Yes,' I said, speaking faster again and suddenly wanting to change the subject.

Mum liked to pretend she was scatty, but really she knew how to make things happen. Her brother George had been sent away to school when she was six, and because her parents were busy – George Victor doctoring, and granny bossing the Girl Guides – she learned how to fend for herself. At thirteen she was parcelled off to boarding school – in Malvern, Worcestershire, which she hated. 'The boater was hideous,' she told me, flinging out one arm like a dancer. 'On the last day of my last term I opened the window as my train crossed a bridge coming back to Beaconsfield, and skimmed the blasted thing into the river. I can still see it floating away.'

She always said she was middling at school, but that didn't stop everyone liking her. Whenever she took me to meet old friends, they drew me to one side and said she'd been their favourite. I believed them. She was prettier than other mums, with her thin face and beautiful gold hair, and she was a different sort of mix-ture, too – giggly and cosy, but also delicate, which was the word dad kept using. It made people want to laugh and look after her at the same time, and didn't sound middling to me. When I asked her about school again, she showed me her exercise books, which she kept in her desk. Science and maths were 'a complete blob', but English was better. She opened the pages at a poem she'd written about a monkey who went for a ride on a whale, and then – in older writing, but with the same hole in the loop of every 'l' – at an essay about 'The Hound of Heaven'. 'I've always liked that poem,' she said. 'It's gloomy, but then he had a very unhappy life you know.' 'Who did?' 'Francis Thompson, who wrote it. Very unhap-py.' I shrugged and didn't know what to say. Poems were for grown-ups. On the other hand, this one might be about a dog. 'Girls didn't go to university after school,' mum went on, inter-rupting my train of thought. 'It was all I could do to persuade granny I should even have a job.' She meant that she'd worked for a while as a typist in the Beaconsfield film studios, where she said she'd got to know the funniest man in the world. He certainly had a funny name, Peter Ustinov, but it didn't sound as though she'd known him very well. 'I say *knew*,' she sighed. 'I should probably say *met*.' After that, she went off to stay for a year with family friends in South Africa.

Mum said the trip was good experience, and among her crinkly photographs were several of a fellow called Wally. Dad sometimes pointed at them and said the name in a soft wail, as if he was calling across miles of water: 'Waaaaly.' How could mum possibly have been interested in *him*, with his thick black specs? Look: here he was buried up to his knees in the sand outside Cape Town – didn't he mind looking a fool? 'I wasn't interested,' mum said quietly. 'Not really.' But she kept the alarm clock he'd given her – 'Wally's clock' – on the shelf above the Aga in the kitchen, beside the Radio Malt. When I stared into its salmon-coloured face I thought of shimmery distances and the sawn-off top of Table Mountain, and wondered what it would be like to have Wally as a father. Hotter, by the look of things.

George Victor died soon after mum got home from South Africa, and the house on the main street of Beaconsfield was sold. Mum didn't like to talk about this: she just said that when granny moved down the hill with Ruby into the smaller house I knew, it was time for a change of scene. Time for Chelsea, in fact. 'So dad never knew your dad?' I asked, finding this hard to imagine. 'No, they never met,' she said, and then added, 'I was always very sorry about that.' I could see why she minded, but I felt sure dad had looked after her from the start. I didn't like to say this, though; dad hated people who wore their hearts on their sleeves, which mum said was to do with Nanny Goody and being a prize vegetable. 'Did I ever tell you what my father always told me?' dad said, whenever I spoke out of turn at meals. 'Little boys should be seen and not heard.' I wasn't sure whether he wanted me to pipe down, or show me that he felt hard done by.

When dad was eight he was sent to a prep school – Wellington

House – and then to Stowe when he was twelve. But if I asked him for school stories he looked at his hands and said, 'I don't have any.' I knew this couldn't be true. What was his house called again? Ah yes, Bruce. Was he taught by T. H. White, who'd written *The Once and Future King*, which mum said I would read one day because it had a marvellous bit in it about a boy who turned into a fish? Another shake of the head. I couldn't work out whether this meant he'd forgotten, or been so miserable he didn't want to remember. Mum had told me the teachers were foul to him because he bit his nails: they sewed his hands into his trouser pockets. That was much worse than what happened when I bit mine: I only got Bitter Aloes smeared on my fingers, or had to wear red nail varnish. But nails couldn't have been the whole story with dad. He'd obviously been popular with the other boys, and he was clever – good at French and German, mum said. He liked cricket, too, and played in a school team. That's all I could gather, but it fitted with the photographs. Dad had never been a child, not properly. Grandpa had always been champing for him to grow up and go to university, then get a good job, then have a family.

But dad never made it to university. During his last year at school, 1939, he realised another world war was bound to break out soon, and decided he should join the army. He wanted to join the Essex Yeomanry, but they couldn't take untrained officers any more. Dad would have to wait until he got his call-up papers, then do the training and ask them again; they'd do their best to keep a place for him. So dad bought an old banger which had an orange box for a passenger seat, and went to work for Barclays Bank for a year. Then the army papers came, he trained, and after a few months he joined the Yeomanry just as he'd hoped.

'I saw English weather then,' dad told me one evening, when he was more relaxed than usual. 'Pissing rain on Salisbury Plain, pissing rain on Catterick, pissing rain on Wales. Pissing rain everywhere for three years. Learning about gunnery.' In the spring of 1944 he moved down to Southampton, and in June went over to Normandy in the first wave of the D-Day landings. He never said much about this either, but when I started learning about the Second World War at school, I quizzed him about it. He still kept pretty quiet, and I decided he didn't want to get upset. All the same, the story came out in bits and pieces. Dad was in charge of a flat-bottomed boat filled with soldiers and armed personnel carriers. They set off across the Channel when the invasion started, but turned back because the weather was bad, then went again the next day. A few yards out from the beach at Aromanche their boat ran into a spike, so when the first vehicle drove down the ramp it sank, and everyone inside baled out. Dad made it, though. He revved up the beach while his vehicle filled with water, took cover while one of his sergeants demolished a pill-box, and finally met up with his batman who handed him some dry clothes. When he stood up to change, his commanding officer bellowed: 'Motion! Do you want your bloody head shot off?' 'It wasn't that,' dad told me. 'It was just that if I was going to be killed, I wanted to be wearing dry trousers.'

'The idea,' dad went on, 'was to keep going until we reached Berlin, which is what we did. Early on, we were stopped by some tanks firing from a wood, and several of our lot were killed. Later it got worse, when we were trying to take a bridge, and got dive-bombed by Stukas. My driver and I took cover in a ditch, otherwise we'd have had it.' 'Was this the driver who died when you got a direct hit?' mum asked. Dad looked at her and frowned. 'That never happened,' he told her. 'My driver was never killed; you must be thinking of someone else.'

It was winter when dad told me this, and we were sitting round the fire in the drawing room, sleepy after supper. Dad was leaning back in his chair, dotting his cigarette into the ashtray on the arm. Maybe it was Christmas, and I'd just opened a new toy for my army collection: that would explain why we were talking about the war. Then, after he'd finished his cigarette, dad went to mum's desk by the window, opened the bottom drawer where they kept the photographs and precious objects, and pulled out one of his earliest albums. I'd looked at it before, but not carefully like this. 'These are Berlin,' he said, showing me dark little streets filled with rubble, skull-heads peering round doorways, and the railway station with the roof ripped off. He stared at them, pursing his lips. 'We ended up at Bremen, actually; that's where I was demobbed. But I drove to Berlin and this is what I saw. I went to the Nuremberg Trials, too – I'd done German at school, so I could understand what was going on.' It was the longest I'd heard him talk about the war, and I didn't want to say anything in case he stopped. Then he passed me an envelope. Inside there was a French phrasebook in a see-through plastic bag – the bag he was given before leaving England in 1944 – with his pencil squiggles and stars in the margin. 'I am your friend,' he said, taking the book from my hands and reading aloud in a pretend-stuffy voice; 'I have come to liberate you.' Then I reached inside the envelope again. Roneo-ed sheets this time, like the ones we had for tests at school, only the purple ink was more faded. It was a seating plan of the Trials, with the names of the Germans in little boxes, to show where they were meant to sit. Dad looked over my shoulder, his jaw chewing silently. 'I was wondering what to do with it,' he said. 'I was thinking I should probably chuck it out.'

I looked up amazed, but he was perfectly serious. 'No, don't, dad,' I said, hoping I wasn't breaking the spell. 'Just put it back and keep it.' To my surprise, he did as I asked, then sat down again and went on talking. He told me that when the Yeomanry got into Germany they were held up by more tanks in another wood, and when the firing stopped a head stuck through a hedge next to him. This head said that he was a friend of Uncle Rob, who was wounded and in the field behind him. 'Extraordinary, isn't it?' said dad. 'The coincidence, I mean. I hopped out of my tank and went through the hedge and there was Uncle Rob. A shell had burst in a tree above him, and the shrapnel had caught him in the back. It was nothing serious, but he had to go home for a bit.' He hesitated again, with his eyes half-shut. 'You know,' he said eventually, 'It wasn't him being wounded that seemed so strange. It was the thought of us being side by side. It was as though all the counties of England were on the move, creeping across France like an animal.'

Dad came home in early 1946 and went to work for the Taylor Walker brewery in the London offices. He stayed for the next forty-odd years, sticking to it through all kinds of upheavals and buyouts. He always said people were pleased to see a third generation of the family go into brewing, but he didn't expect any favours. 'I wanted to succeed on my own merits,' he said, when I was old enough to be thinking about what job I might have myself one day. 'Though I sometimes wonder what would have happened if there hadn't been a war. I'd probably have done something with languages. Maybe even the Foreign Office! Who knows? Can you see me and mum in Paris?'

I liked the idea that dad and mum would have been together, no matter what. But it didn't surprise me. There wasn't much sign that he'd had a proper girlfriend before they met. Sometimes I saw him glancing at mum when someone called Peggy was mentioned. Occasionally mum gave one of her inefficient wolf-whistles if dad said he'd be getting back from work later than usual. But it was all a joke. They were devoted to one another – Kit and I knew that, even though they almost never touched when we were around, or kissed one another. Mum said we were 'about as cuddly as lamp posts, all you boys', but she said it smiling.

It was the same smile in the photograph of her and dad walking through the churchyard after their wedding in Beaconsfield, eighteen months before I was born. Mum was hanging on dad's left arm and he was steering her – not much, because he didn't want to give anything away while people were watching. 'We make a lovely couple, don't we?' mum said in her soppy voice, pointing at the picture on her dressing table. I bent over her shoulder to look more closely. They did. The people lining the path were interesting too. The old ladies from the town who had known mum since she was a child. The little girl with sandals and white socks. The woman who'd flung up one arm to stop her daughter slipping from her shoulders – it looked as though she was making a hosannah. She was standing behind my parents, this woman, and as they gazed towards the camera into the future, they couldn't see what she looked like. But I saw her, even though I was only a gleam in their eyes.

CHAPTER FOUR

Little Brewers

Mum and dad never planned to live in London. London was for work and parties, not marriage and babies. But they couldn't move too far into the country, because dad still needed to get to his office in Clerkenwell. So they settled on Kimpton, a village in Hertfordshire squeezed into a patch of green between Luton, Stevenage, Welwyn and St Albans. It was nothing much – a main street, a pub, a shop, and a small converted mill, which they bought in 1950. I arrived two years later, driven home in dad's Riley after mum had given birth to me in the Westminster Hospital. 'Why there?' I asked her later. 'Because we thought it would be handy for you to have London as place of birth in your passport,' she told me. 'In case you go globetrotting. Though really it should say "In the lift". That's where your head appeared, on the way to the delivery room.'

For a while the Mill was perfect: black weatherboard, with a pond in the back garden which drained into a pipe that ran under the sitting room. When mum bounced me on her knees in front of the fire, she could hear the invisible current burbling under her feet. She liked the sound so much, she told dad they should put in a glass floor, so she could watch the water as well as listen to it. He said it was bad enough as it was; all that tinkling and slithering made him want to pee. He didn't mean it, though. He liked the house, and when the pond froze during my first winter he photographed it with his Box Brownie. Mum wore her white skates, and wheeled me across the ice in my pram while he clicked the camera and laughed, blurring the picture a little.

A few years later, after we had moved, we were driving through Hertfordshire and took a detour to look at the Mill. Mum and dad were excited: they wanted to know how much I recognised. I wasn't interested – I'd found a small Union Jack stuck in the rabbity lawn beside the pond. What was it doing there? Why was it so tiny? Dad told me to leave it alone, speaking crossly as though I'd picked up something disgusting. When I twisted round, he and mum were facing away from me, staring at the black house without speaking. I prodded the flag back into its hole. This had been my world for two years, but it hadn't left a trace.

Kit was with us that day – my bro who made my parents sell the Mill. Mum thought if she had a new baby on the way she wouldn't be able to keep an eye out for me, in case I fell into the stream. Besides, dad was getting on in the brewery, making more money, and they wanted a bigger house. They'd found one thirty-odd miles north-east, still just in Hertfordshire, and it was called Little Brewers. Nobody knew where the name came from: the house wasn't that little, and had nothing to do with brewing until we arrived. We moved before Kit was born in April 1955, when I was two and a half.

Little Brewers had been built at the edge of Hatfield Heath, which was a straggle of houses round a common where travellers grazed their ponies. There was a line of shops, including Bucks Stores for sweets and toys; a butcher with sawdust on the floor; a pond which lapped the side of the road in winter and shrank to a sticky puddle during the summer; a church surrounded by poplars; and a pebble-dashed council estate. None of us liked the village much, which made me realise mum and dad hadn't quite found what they were looking for. 'It's not proper country,' they kept telling each other, but they made the best of it. Mum said we were lucky to have so many rooms, even if some were a bit dingy, and the kitchen was a cellar, and the long upstairs corridor made the house feel like two buildings not one, and the traffic outside was 'awful, and bound to get worse'. When our terrier Jack was run over and killed by a car, she told dad it would be 'the children next', but dad thought that was overdoing it. If a better house came up, then he'd think about moving again. Meanwhile we should count our blessings.

Whenever I overheard these talks, I hoped nothing would come of them. I couldn't imagine anywhere more interesting than Little

Brewers. The house was dark and twisty, like a rabbit warren, and I loved the field where we kept the horses – the two horses my parents had always wanted, and the two ponies which joined them when Kit and I were old enough. This field lay at the end of the lane alongside the house, and was dotted with may trees, the oldest-looking things I'd ever seen. Even the smallest twigs had arthritis. I sheltered from a downpour there once with dad, watching the rain rip through the red-and-cream blossom. 'Only a clearing shower,' he said, as the petals plastered our faces. It didn't matter that people could spy on us from the new housing estate through the trees. The idea that the field might not last much longer, might be sold and disappear, made me like it even more. We were seeing the end of something but at least we'd seen it.

On the other hand, there was the mill over the road, opposite the front door – surely nothing could ever change that? Not a mill like Kimpton, with its guts torn out, but a huge yellow barn with front steps like a mounting block, dust-clouds billowing from the front door, and a miller. Sometimes I saw him from my bedroom window, resting on the top step with his arms folded, gazing at nothing in particular and breathing the clear air. He wore a meal-coloured overall, a peaked cap, and a white apron with a big wooden hammer in the pouch. The whole of him – including his enormous hairless arms and his wide face – was pale with flour. By day, the traffic drowned out the sound of his grinding-stones, but at night, lying in my bedroom, I could hear their endless dry rumble. Fee fi fo fum. If he could smell the blood of an English man, he would sniff out an English boy too. But when I peeked through my curtains he was nowhere to be seen. There was only the bolted front door and the narrow window above, with its glass fuzzed by cobwebs.

When I went with mum to buy feed for the horses, the miller turned from a ghost into a man. He let me run after his cats as they dawdled across the floorboards with their tails in the air. He slipped his hands under my arms and hoisted me so I could peer into the rafters and see the mice paths in the flour dust. He let me hold one side of the sack as he opened it under the grain-shoot, and the bran whooshed out like heavy soapflakes. When the sack was full, he pulled a tangle of binder twine from the apron pocket where he kept his hammer, and tied it with a sliding knot. Because he liked mum, and could see she was 'just a skinny thing', he carried the sack home himself, heaving it across his wide back and grunting as he dumped it down in our hayshed. 'That should keep you going for a bit.' The horses snickered in their stables.

Compared to the mill, what dad called our outbuildings were just huts and shacks. They were wonderful all the same. We reached them from the side lane, where double doors in the clapboard wall opened onto the place we used to park the car. Both cars in fact – though dad's was usually at the railway station in Bishops Stortford, which meant the way through to the yard was clear. A strip of cement spotted with rainbow puddles of petrol; open beams above, where the swallows built their mud huts; and the scullery drain where Kit and I once found a grass snake snoozing on the cushion of its own coils.

The yard was a small square which sloped inwards towards the centre, and was covered with gravel that glued into the horses' hooves if they had mud in them. To the left: the coal cellar under the kitchen window, with a sparkly asphalt lid that whispered when I scuffled across to surprise mum through the glass. On the right: three stables and a woodshed. One of these stables was divided by a wooden panel with a see-through iron barrier along the top. It was like the book mum gave me to read when I went away to school: *Zong the Hill Pony*, which ended with a stable fire. I couldn't look at our second stall without thinking how easy it would be to get trapped there, face pressed to the gaps in the barrier as the flames rose.

In the far right-hand corner of the yard was a faded green door with a latch that never worked properly. It led through to the veg garden, but the greenhouse came first, and that was split into two as well. The first part was for flowers. In winter it was always dark, because of mum's peppery-smelling chrysanths, and in spring it was full of bedding trays where she pricked out her 'things for the garden'. I couldn't connect these spindly shoots with anything that grew outside – certainly not the big papery heads Kit and I thwacked as we rode past on our bikes, waving our bamboo swords like grandpa in his cavalry charge.

The further part of the greenhouse was for veg, where the gardener Mr Manning spent most of his time. He wore a tramp's suit with the waistcoat wrinkling across his stomach, and used a belt like a cow's tongue to hold up his trousers. Mum said she 'couldn't possibly manage without him' because he did all the heavy work including digging the flower beds. All the same, she thought he was 'very rude'. He even glared when dad spoke to him, and swore at me and Kit if we rode too near his precious cold-frames. Sometimes, if it was cold or rainy, he came into the kitchen for his tea at eleven, clasping both hands round his special mug with the haymakers on it. The mud flaked off his fingers as it dried and fell onto the tabletop. Usually he sat in the shed by the greenhouse, swigging from his thermos and unwrapping sandwiches from a parcel of greaseproof paper. 'Really he's impossible, he'll have to go,' dad said occasionally. But Mr Manning never did go, not even when we came back early from an outing, and found him lumbering up the pavement away from Little Brewers towards his own house 'with enough cucumbers and whatnot under his coat to feed an army,' mum said.

Did Mr Manning stay for the money, or did he like us more than we thought? There was no way of knowing and, as things turned out, we needed him as much as he needed us. Mooching round one day at the far end of the greenhouse, puffing bug poison over the tomatoes, he heard something splosh into the tank which stood between his veg and mum's flowers. It was Kit, who was now face-down in the water, not moving. Mr Manning fished him out, squeezed him, and handed him to mum as if he were giving her a basket of potatoes. 'But of course he'd really saved Kit's life,' she told dad when he got back from work that evening. 'Actually saved his life. We can't complain if he takes home a few marrows after this, can we?'

Beyond the greenhouse, at the join of two hawthorn hedges which marked the end of the garden, was the manure heap. The smell here was so strong it made the air ripple, but Kit and I were never bothered by this, just as we never minded the grey fur on the dung-dollops, or the sloppy gravy which oozed round the base. Some days there was a little puff of steam hanging over the top like Vesuvius, and mum said if we poked a stick inside, the heat would eat it. What would happen if we fell in ourselves? Would we disappear too? We pedalled at top speed along the path from the stable yard, taking it head on, but always lost our nerve at the last minute and wavered off along the furthest edge of the garden, talking about something else. The vegetables, for instance. Rhubarb in rusty dustbins with their bottoms knocked out; raspberries in a netting-cage where blackbirds got trapped but were so busy gobbling they hardly noticed; the asparagus bed like someone's grave; Brussels sprouts I had only to look at to feel the frost numbing my fingers; scruffy cabbages like upside-down dolls' dresses. Mr Manning was king here. If Kit and I snatched a bean pod or a sweet pea as we whizzed past, we had to hide it until we were out of reach in the poplar spinney.

This spinney was the furthest we could get from the house and still be at home. In winter the tree trunks were like the walls of a church, leaning together at the top as if they were pointing at the squirrel's dray which swayed at the highest point of all. In summer the whole place was splattered with yellow light, which made us dump our bikes and lie down, so we could stare through the leaves. Gazing so hard, after a while I started to lose my grip on the earth and hurtle off into space. But the leaf-mould was damp under my shoulders, and the ivy trails tickled. So we were off again, heaving our bikes up the weird earth mound that stood on the edge of the spinney. Was it a part of the war, a shelter of some kind? There was no way in, and nothing to show where a door might have been. Or was it something to do with the water supply? We let our bikes slither away behind us, and stamped on the top. There was no echo, only the solid thump of our gumboots. It was a mystery. We called it Teaser's Hill, after dad's Labrador: she liked to bury bones here, then come and look for them without remembering where they were. The sides were pitted with her scrabblings.

Kit and I trundled out of the spinney then hopped onto our bikes again as we reached the real garden. First came the scruffy bit: two blocks of tall grass spotted with poppies, and a mown strip down the middle where we played cricket. The clover here was especially sweet, and if I tweaked out one of the flowers and sucked the stem, a shoot of honey squished on my tongue. There were lost things, too – tennis balls and hankies and penknives and coins which were waiting for us, if only we could be bothered to search. We sped up the central path, the bulgy yew hedge on our left and the orchard to our right. We called it the orchard, anyway; really it was a few old trees hiding the neighbours' tennis court. Their trunks were so gnarled, and their grey branches so spotty with fungus, I couldn't believe they'd be carrying apples again next autumn. Then we'd have to pick them carefully, as if we were unscrewing light bulbs, laying them on the shelves in the hayshed and making sure they didn't touch.

Next came the Tree of Heaven, which I thought was a private name invented by mum. Most of the year it was a miserable-looking mess of droopy branches covered with bristles. Then spring came and the branches shivered like a bird shaking off raindrops. The muddle was suddenly a shape and the leaves began to show. Pale yellow at first, but hardening as the summer warmed up, and turning a deeper green. Finally, when none of us wanted it to be autumn, the leaves exploded into red and crimson and yellow. It was like the song about the ugly duckling that mum sang to me when she said goodnight. The tree was beautiful, the most beautiful thing I'd seen, but it took time. We had to be patient.

We still had the tunnel to explore, the one inside the laurel hedge that grew alongside the main road. Kit and I climbed off our bikes and wheeled them through the side door. This wasn't a proper door, just a battered gap. And it wasn't really a tunnel either, only a path under the leaves. We fell into single file, me leading and Kit crouching behind with the front wheel of his bike squealing chirpily. It didn't sound right, but never mind. We had plans to camp here one of these nights, to see if it actually was a fox that lived in this big hole under the blackbird nest, where the mud was smelly and trodden down hard.

At the mouth, which was big enough for us to stand side by side again, we faced the house for the first time. We weren't ready for indoors yet – there was the rest of the garden first, the flowery bit. In fact there was mum now, shoulder-deep in her border, wearing her straw hat. We were under orders not to ride our bikes too close, in case we squashed something, but flowers didn't interest us much anyway. The crab-apple tree at the far end – that was more. like it. It had a handy low branch, which meant we could climb into its fork, checking on the pale green fruits and wondering why they never turned red.

The cherry tree at the nearer end of the flower bed was even better. Not for blossom, which we saw everywhere in the village, but for the white marble bowl half-buried in the grass underneath. One day we dug it out, discovered it was too heavy to lift, and sat down to stare. What was it for, exactly? Why did it have those strange dents in the lip? How come it was so wide at the top and narrow at the bottom, when that meant it kept falling over? We rolled it to and fro, trying to make it go in a straight line. We dropped in some cherry stones and ground them to a pulp, then left the bowl outside all night to see how much rain it collected. In time everything turned sooty, and bits chipped off the rim so we could see the inside sparkling with tiny crystals. But the bowl stayed a mystery. I told Kit it was like something the Aztecs had left behind in the jungle and he asked what Aztecs were. I didn't know. I'd heard they lived in forests years ago but didn't any more.

We left the bowl lolling in the shade and headed back to the roses in front of the drawing-room windows – two rows, spiky and dull for half the year, but in summer more like brushstrokes than flowers. This was dad's place, if ever he was home. He stood here on autumn Sundays with the collar of his mac turned up, pointing out the best spot to snip them – there, above that crease on the stem where a shoot would come in spring. His hands shook as the curved jaws of the clippers sliced shut, then flinched as the dead head fell away. Now we biked along the flagstone path which divided the two rows, taking care not to wobble against the spikes. When we reached the earth-bump at the end, we turned sharp left onto the patio.

'Don't call it a patio,' mum said. 'Patio is suburban.' So we didn't. It was the suntrap, a triangle of crazy-paving, sheltered on one side by the wall of the stable yard and on the other by the hayshed. This shed was important. Every autumn a local farmer filled it with a wagon-load of straw bales, which we used for bedding in the stables during the rest of the year. When the shed was full, it was difficult getting bales down from the top. If we weren't careful the twine broke as they hit the ground, and the straw went everywhere. But by summer, when stocks were low, we'd given up thinking we might need them and decided to play on them instead. 'You'll have to watch it, ragging in there,' mum said. 'If that lot falls on you, you'll be strawberry jam.' Sometimes the bales swayed beneath us, as if they were about to bulge like a castle wall hit by a cannonball. It was OK, though. The worst that happened was my penknife slipping out of my pocket – my silver penknife, the first I'd ever had – down one of the whiskery cracks. I pressed my face to the dark, thinking I'd see the blade winking like a stone at the bottom of a pool. When it was autumn again, and only a few broken bales were left on the floor of the shed, it was still nowhere to be seen.

The shed always caught the light, bouncing it across the suntrap whatever the weather. This was partly why we liked sitting there; it felt summery, even when the days started to draw in, and we could smell the sour nip of the dahlias mum grew along the back wall. They looked plastic, but dad told us they were 'special'. 'Blister my kidneys, the dahlias are dead,' he said, whenever he looked down from his bedroom window at this time of year. 'He's quoting Jorrocks, you know,' mum added from the dressing table, brushing her hair. I didn't know; Jorrocks was the name on a big grey book in the drawing room. 'It means when the dahlias die, it's time to start cub hunting,' she said.

Kit and I were done with the garden for now. We dumped our bikes and wellies by the woodpile, and barged in through the back door of the house. Little Brewers wasn't much to look at from the outside. It was too tall, too thin, and the bricks were grimy because they were nearly a hundred years old. But inside it felt snug. The hall ran back to front, with corridors off to our playroom and the drawing room on one side, and steps down to the kitchen and a dining room on the other. The floors were bare boards, splintery, and the carpet wrinkled as we skidded to a halt. 'Careful, boys, you'll break something,' mum called from the kitchen, so we stood still for a moment, smoothing our hair before we jumped down to her.

She was cooking lunch; Wally's clock on the shelf said half-past twelve – nearly time. But it could have been evening: the light here was dim and warm, though mum turned off the Aga during the summer and switched to the Baby Belling where she was standing now. We always ate the same food in turn – kedgeree, fish pie, macaroni cheese, bangers, shepherd's pie, chops, that sort of thing. 'What is it today?' we wanted to know, but she wasn't interested. 'I'm not ready yet; go and find something to do and I'll give you a shout.' She was scraping potato peelings into a bucket. I knew if we dithered she'd change her mind and ask us to help, but I stopped in the doorway all the same, and glanced back at her. She looked tired, with her shoulders slouching as she bent into the sink again. Was there something the matter, something I didn't know about? Once I'd found her in the drawing room with dad, and heard him telling her she must rest like the doctor said. 'I'm fine, darling,' she told him. 'A bit weary, that's all.' When I saw her gardening, pressing one hand against her chest or leaning on the rake, I thought she might be fibbing. Then there was the day a whole dish of kedgeree had slithered out of her oven gloves and smashed on the kitchen floor, fish bits, rice and china everywhere. She didn't know I'd seen her kneeling in the mess, crying.

Today she didn't seem too bad, so off we went. Back into the hall past the grandfather clock, which only dad was allowed to touch, then the downstairs loo where Uncle Rob had got stuck in the window frame wearing a Father Christmas costume, and into the drawing room. At this time of day, with the cushions plumped up on the green sofa, and the fire laid with fresh kindling, it wasn't the place for us. There was a whiff of cold ash from the grate – a grown-up smell for this evening, when we'd have music and 'civilised conversation'. Mum said I was ready for that, now I was six years old. I'd kneel in front of the record player, choosing *My Fair Lady* or *Gigi* from the LPs stacked in the bottom part of the cabinet. When I'd decided, I'd open the front flap and stick my head and shoulders inside so I could see properly to lower the record over the shiny rod, down onto the mat, then pick up the needle-arm by the little wing sticking out from its head. 'Careful you don't scratch,' dad would say, but the harder I tried to keep my hand steady, the more it wobbled, meaning the first notes were always *blurp* before they settled down. 'I'm looking for a piano, a piano, not any old piano . . .' I pulled back my head like a tortoise. The fire was blazing. Mum was in her armchair doing her tatting with the standard lamp pulled close to her elbow. Dad was on the window seat, patting the cover of my *Observer's Book of Birds*, which I'd left for him to find. The curtains behind him were drawn across the rose beds and the view down to the Tree of Heaven.

If dad was in a good mood, he'd give me one of his tests – the only kind I liked, because I knew the answers. Turning the pages of the book, and sliding his free hand quickly over the names of the birds, he'd hold up the pictures for me. Blackbird too easy, robin too easy, thrush too easy, and then on towards the ducks with their quiffs and mad orange eyes, the godwit scratching its ear with one stick-leg, the whimbrel I'd never seen in real life. When I got the names right, he moved on to 'haunts' and 'calls', but now it was more like a game than a quiz. We pursed our lips and blew 'wee, wee' for the curlew, or experimented with the 'delicious, liquid "tooi"' of the ringed plover. Dad smelled of trains and cigarettes if we did this during the week. At the weekends, it was cigarettes and cold air from outdoors. He liked these pictures so much I couldn't understand why he didn't live differently, where he could be outside all the time. 'I have to work and make money,' he said, if ever I asked him. 'But you don't have to worry about any of that yet.'

Kit and I left the drawing room and turned next door into the playroom, where mum meant us to wait for lunch, playing with the train set. It had started with just one engine; now the track had its own green table, like a ping-pong table only lower, which meant there was space for me to add new bits from the Hornby catalogue. But I didn't add much, except when people gave me presents at Christmas and birthdays. There was one station, no passengers, and a grey plastic bridge that had dog chew-marks up one side. When the train pulled out, it went straight into open country – the flat green littered with scrumpled-up balls of wire mesh, which were meant to be hills. I didn't enjoy playing here as much as everyone said I did, but I kept the thought to myself. Trains were my hobby, and boys needed a hobby. Dad said so.

There was still nothing from the kitchen except the burble of radio music, so Kit and I started upstairs. The banister rail shivered by the sticky patch on the turn, which mum said was generations of sweaty palms. It was a good place to sit – we could hear our parents talking when they thought we were out of earshot. One day I'd caught dad telling mum he thought I was funny, meaning he laughed at my jokes. It was the first time I'd heard him sound as though he liked me. But it wasn't the moment to sit down now, or to look into the upstairs rooms either. Lunch would be ready soon. It didn't matter because everything was already laid out in my head like a doll's house. The heavy wooden seat in the loo by mum and dad's bedroom, which crashed down when I was peeing unless I held onto it. The bedroom itself, with the headboard Kit ruined with his penknife: he carved the sides off one of the square bars, trying to make it look prettier. And the dressing table.

The dressing table stood in the far right-hand corner of the bedroom, with a window over the suntrap on one side, and a window facing down the garden on the other. 'I need the light,' mum said, 'so I can see when I'm doing my face.' It had a green-rimmed glass top that fitted exactly, drawers either side of the knee-hole which were covered by pale blue curtains, and three mirrors at the back – the middle one head on, the other two sideways so she could see different parts of her face. Mum had tucked photographs beneath the glass top: dad holding a salmon with his fingers hooked into the gills; Kit in his highchair; me on my bike under the cherry tree.

And there were more photographs in frames among the blue-backed brushes and make-up boxes. Her father George Victor. Dad in his dark suit with a carnation in his buttonhole. Their wedding picture with the little girl about to fall off the woman's shoulders.

Mum said no one was allowed to go near the dressing table – only her. This was where she sat down first thing in the morning, brushing her hair and dabbing her face with the ticklish powder puff, and where she 'finished off' after breakfast – checking the powder, stroking on her lipstick, then gumming her lips together on a Kleenex so they left a kiss-shape she chucked into the wastepaper basket. In the afternoon, she checked it all again, and again in the evening before dad came home from work, and one more time last thing in her nightie, before smearing off the powder with a special cloth, rubbing in cream. Sometimes, in the mornings and early evenings, she let me help. I stood behind her stool, watching her pull faces as she tilted her head first one way and then the other, gazing at her herself from all angles. After a while, she handed over the brush, and asked me to do her hair. I had to be careful. If I let the bristles hit the mole at the crown of her head she didn't like it, and neither did I; it made my stomach lurch. And it was tricky, too. If I watched my hands in the mirror they got confused and didn't know which way to go. 'It's like steering a ship,' mum said, but that wasn't much help. Everything was doubled in the main mirror in front of us, multiplied over and over in the smaller ones on either side. Her face and mine. The powder box and the scrumpled tissues. The lipstick with its wet-looking red tip. The scent bottles with their gold labels and French words and glittering tops. They made me think the dressing table went on for ever, with its photographs trapped and smiling under the glass skin.

The bedroom was for early or late, not lunchtime. So what about the laundry cupboard next door: anything interesting there? Maybe the cat, Flick, on the specially folded rug that was really a nest of her own fur. Not today. On to our own bedroom, then – Kit's bed in the corner, mine jutting into the room from the left-hand wall, between the door and the wash-basin. Nothing there either. After I pulled the door shut, Kit followed me past the bath-room and into the back part of the house, which ran out towards the stables. We didn't usually come here unless granny and Ruby were staying. The corridor was always cold and so were the rooms – 'unlived in,' mum said, though I often thought someone visited when none of us were looking. See? A vase of dried flowers had dropped a petal onto the carpet, and a wasp was dying slowly against the window. How had it got in? Kit and I were above the kitchen now, and as we clattered off the carpet onto the brown lino of the back stairs, we heard the wireless making its pips for one o'clock. That meant getting a move on – gripping the rail, in case we lost our footing. At the foot of the stairs we passed the scullery, where Mrs Lambert cranked the mangle on washing days, then the lumber room where dad didn't like us to go, because he thought we'd make it untidy. We were on tiptoe now, creeping up to the kitchen door – then bursting it open to give mum a surprise. But she'd heard us coming. She was standing at the head of the table with one hand on her hip and the other holding a battered spoon. Like a fat cook in a picture, except she was so thin the light from the stable yard shone straight through her.

CHAPTER FIVE

Close Fielding

It was lunchtime again, and I told mum I didn't see why Kit always got his food first. She said I was being silly, he was only little, but I went on moaning. Then she did something amazing. She told me she'd got a disease when Kit was born, and had to go into hospital for a year; that was probably why I felt clingy. A whole year! How could so much time have disappeared without me remembering? But she nodded and said it again. A year. 'We made sure you were looked after properly, of course. Ruby was here. You liked being with her.' I asked her what the disease was called. 'Brucellosis,' she said. 'Normally it's something only cows get. One of my kidneys had to be chopped out.' I looked at my plate, and wasn't hungry any more.

I tried to forget what mum had said; there was nothing I could do to get the time back. Besides, I had Kit to worry about. He annoyed me because he kept changing. One minute he was a yowling blob in a highchair, the next he was pedalling round the garden, turning out to be better than me at a lot of things. He was skinny as a sparrow and his face had slap-marks when he got cold, but he was brave. When the ponies arrived and we started riding, he aimed at ditches that looked like the Grand Canyon and bounced across them as though his body was a balloon tied to the saddle. And if friends came round from the village, we'd play as though he was really as tall as me. In fact when Adam hurled himself out of the ash tree by the rockery, and broke Kit's arm, Kit made so little fuss it took a day for mum to think of driving him to a doctor. Dad was always telling us we mustn't be wet; Kit cried more than I did but everyone knew he was really dry as a bone.

So I loved him. He was funny, fidgety and small – and mum was right, he had 'a heart like a lion'. All the same, I didn't want him to forget I'd been around longer than he had. That meant I was the one who decided which games we played, and it was me who had the smooth end of the bath, while he jammed up against the taps. If anyone told me to let up, I said I was helping, like an elder brother should. I was the 'ice-breaker', wasn't I? Well, then. But Kit went on doing things that put him in the lead. Like drinking sherry from the picnic basket in the back of the Hillman at the gymkhana, and doing a clear round. Or losing his temper with an au pair we both hated, Jane, and shooting her fat, hairy leg with the airgun. It turned out Jane had shut him in the laundry cupboard and tried to clean out his mouth with soap. When mum heard about this, she sacked Jane and told Kit she didn't blame him.

Dad took the shooting more seriously: he told us we were bloody fools, and locked the airgun in the cupboard along with his 12-bore. This was typical. Dad always thought there was a right way and a wrong way to do things. That's why he had so many routines, most of them to do with saving. Going round the house turning out lights. Not filling the bath right to the top. Telling us to finish our food and chew our mouthfuls thirty-three times (or was it thirty-two? I could never remember). Rescuing half-burned bits of coal from the fire in the drawing room, and using them when he made it again. It meant we had to mind our p's and q's when he was at home – not that we ever had much chance to talk. On weekdays he left for work before Kit and I got up, and came back after we'd gone to bed. He was away most weekends too. On winter Saturdays he went hunting, and most Sundays, all year round, he was with the Yeomanry. 'Playing soldiers,' mum called it.

Because they were rare, the times we did see him felt special. Evenings were best of all. When I was in bed falling asleep, I heard his car door whacking shut in the drive-through, his shoes tramping through the hall, his overcoat and bowler hat and umbrella clicking onto their pegs by the back door, then his shoes again, scuffing upstairs towards me. He lit a new cigarette in my doorway, which made his face glow red in the dark. But smoke wasn't the only thing I could smell. There was something sooty as well – trains, or London, or maybe just tiredness. He held the cigarette away when he kissed me, and his bristles scratched like Desperate Dan in my *Dandy*. Did mum like that? It felt peculiar, but I could see he was handsome, with his open face and black-black hair. He was a soldier, firing questions, even when he wasn't wearing his uniform. 'What sort of day have you had?' He only meant to be friendly, but I had to prove I hadn't been wasting my time. 'Well, I helped to muck out the horses this morning, then we had lunch, then mum had her rest and I lay on my bed for a bit, then Kit and I played in the garden.' 'Didn't you exercise the horses?' He sounded annoyed; I'd forgotten the most important thing. 'Oh yes, of course, sorry dad, we rode this morning.' 'Was it fun?' 'Great.' He tousled my hair, then stood up and paused in the doorway to say 'God bless', drawing a half-circle with his cigarette end. Before I fell asleep, I heard him laughing with mum in the kitchen. This was what she called unwinding.

On army days dad was coiled tighter than usual. Before leaving for the HQ in Chelmsford he took his Sam Browne and boots into the kitchen, laid some newspapers on the table, and polished them patiently, huffing on them, peering with narrow eyes, as if he couldn't focus properly, then setting to again. Eventually he lowered them down to the floor and asked whether I could see my face in the toecaps. I could, squashed like in a spoon, only dark. While this went on, mum sat by the window sliding a brass contraption under the buttons of his uniform to stop the Brasso staining the cloth, shining them with quick little strokes as though she was hitting the buttons, not polishing them. She didn't want him to go, but things had always been like this. After he'd changed, and come downstairs again with his uniform buttoned up, his boots on, his cap in his hand, his swagger stick under his arm, she kissed him on the cheek then licked her fingers and rubbed off the O of her lipstick.

None of us ever went with him to Chelmsford, but we did drive to Salisbury Plain once, to watch the regiment do their exercises. Mum, Kit and I stood under a hedge overlooking a grassy valley while some of dad's officer friends talked to her, using their sticks to point out a cardboard tank in the distance, which they said would blow up any minute. Their faces looked like skulls in the shadow of their caps, but they thought mum was pretty: I could tell from the way they crowded round her, treading on the end of each other's sentences. She never looked back at them, but shielded her eyes and stared towards the tank. There was a muscle twitching in her cheek. It meant she was bored. She wanted this over, and dad home again. Where had he got to? There, someone told her, seizing her wrist and using her own hand to point. I winced, but stared in the same direction. In the far distance was a cross between a tank and a personnel carrier; I knew the name because dad had given me a toy version for my army collection. It bucked across the chalky green, with the stubby gun jutting dead ahead, and a ridiculous long aerial swaying up and down at the back. There was a flag at the tip, and this was snatched off when dad zoomed under the low branches of a tree. Would he get into trouble? One of the men beside me went 'Whoops' in a big fruity voice, but he shut up when dad's gun suddenly started coughing out clouds of smoke like a cigar. Seconds later we heard the crack of the shots – they sounded tiny under the enormous sky – and then the other tank, the pretend one, staggered and burst into flames. My father had done this. He hadn't let us down. The men behind me started cheering and we cheered too, but much more loudly than them, really meaning it. Then dad disappeared round the back of the hill. A few weeks before, when I'd been getting dressed in my parents' bedroom, I'd put on my underpants back to front. It had made me think I'd never be much good in the war, and I switched them round quickly before anyone noticed.

'The army is dad's world,' mum told me, when we were back in the kitchen. This made her sound sad, but she liked the regimental dinners. Kit and I hated them because they meant an evening alone, with a stranger looking after us. We sprawled on our parents' bed, messing up the counterpane, while dad hooked his dress uniform out of the cupboard: tight jacket, narrow black trousers with a red stripe down the side, spurs, a white shirt with a stiff collar. Wasn't that all a bit pansy, like Eric's socks? It wasn't the right moment to ask. Mum was busy at her dressing table, twisting her head to get all the angles, squirting herself with Blue Grass, taking the mothballs out of her sparkly evening bag. 'Will you bring us back something?' Kit said, though we'd asked a dozen times already, and knew she'd remember. Sure enough, next morning there was a marzipan sweet on our bedside tables, and a creased card with the autograph of the bandsman, Tommy Kinsman. I didn't collect autographs, but I did have several copies of this one, and each was exactly the same: zigzag letters like a snazzy tie, and always in pencil with the last bit of the second 'n' in 'Kinsman' nipping back under the word to underline it.

On hunting mornings dad was different again. These were the days he enjoyed most, getting up early and padding downstairs in his slippers to find the breakfast things mum had set out the night before: the egg cup in its saucer, the tea leaves in the teapot. I was too young to go too, but I could hear him clearing his throat in the kitchen below me, then the scrape when he took his hard hat and riding crop from the bench in the hall. After that, I rolled over and thought how different he'd be when he got home. 'A changed man,' mum always said. He smiled at her across the kitchen table with the mark of his hat brim still creasing his hair, and freckles of dried mud on his face and hands. He talked more easily than usual, reeling off the names of woods he'd jumped into, farmers he'd met and farmer's wives who'd given him mugs of tea. After he finished, mum told me I'd see all this for myself in a few years. 'Can't wait,' I said, and because it didn't sound very convincing, she added, 'If you want to.' 'Of course he'll want to,' dad butted in. 'It's in the blood.'

Maybe he was right: I was only six but I already knew how to ride. In two or three years, depending on how I was managing, I probably would be hunting. Cubbing, at least. What if I didn't like it? That would be wet, and dad would be angry, or think I didn't like what he liked. All the same, there was something funny about the whole business. Why did dad want to kill an animal he liked so much? If ever a fox came into the garden, slinking through the hedge beyond Teaser's Hill, he rushed to the drawing-room windows and gazed in wonder. When I asked mum about this, she said it was a mystery, but a lot of country people felt the same way, it was one of those things. We'd talk about it again later, when I was old enough to go out for the first time.

Meanwhile I went on riding, and liked it. My pony was called Snippet – a dark brown bomber from Exmoor with a shaggy mane falling into his eyes and a bum like a Thelwell cartoon. He had a habit of suddenly lying down for no reason, then rolling over and trying to flatten me. Kit and I thought this was hilarious, and I rode with my stirrups on the tips of my toes in case I had to bail out. He also farted a great deal, very loudly, especially when I was trotting beside one of mum's friends. Their boring questions dropped down like pebbles, and Snippet never failed. Even though it sounded like a motorbike, nobody said anything. Did they think it was normal? I knew if I caught mum's eye, I'd get the giggles. The best thing was to slip the reins between my fingers and let Snippet make a dive for the grass, so I'd fall behind and the questions would dry up.

After Snippet there was Tommy. He was gingery-marmalade – cat-coloured. Tommy-Tomcat, Bosscat, with a barrel stomach and a gypsy blaze down his nose. I was frightened of him: the wet gleam in his eyes showed that he knew the whole world was his enemy, and he was waiting for exactly the right moment to kick it to Timbuktu. But I loved him as well. He was perky and had an 'I-don't-care' way of hammering down hard lanes. Dad said trotting like this was a bad idea, but he liked it in Tommy and that was a relief. Even though it was mum who first taught us to ride, Kit and I knew she'd pass us over to dad in the end. On the way there'd be gymkhanas and the pony club, which dad thought were child's play. Hunting was the only real thing. The closer I got to my first meet, the less chance there would be of saying no. If I refused, I'd be a sort of traitor.

I'd never be that, no matter how scared I was of hunting. There was something in dad I didn't want to upset. I couldn't say what, exactly – I just knew it was there because of his tiredness when he said goodnight, and the way his jaw set when he went off to work or in uniform. He was always bracing himself, and that made me want to look out for him, even though he was dad and meant to be looking out for me. Why was the fourth finger of his right hand so flat at the tip? Because he'd sat in a deckchair when he was little, clamping his hands round the wooden frame. When the chair collapsed it caught him, squishing his nail. And why did he always tell me not to sit with my chin in my hands? Because when he was my age he'd perched on the end of his bed, and his feet had slipped off the rail, and he'd bitten so far through his tongue a doctor had to sew it on again. And why did he wear Bay Rum in his hair? For the shine and the sweet smell of course. But when I sat in the back of the car on holiday in Ireland once, and stared at his head after we'd been swimming, I saw that without the oil his hair was curly. Curly like mine – or at least like someone who wasn't serious all the time. It reminded me of the morning Kit and I went into our parents' bedroom and dad was standing at the window, saying he'd shot a bear which had come into the garden during the night. Look, there it was, lying in the suntrap. Kit and I stood on tiptoe. Sure enough – an enormous shaggy dead body. A monster. Though it did look a bit familiar. Dad kept us guessing until breakfast, then told us it was the hearthrug: he'd thrown it out last night because it was flea-ridden. It didn't matter that we'd been idiots. We liked seeing him laugh.

Mum was always happiest when dad unwound, but she liked him being good at things too. He was a director of the brewery now, and tipped to be Colonel of the regiment, as well as Master of the hounds. Although this meant he was even more of a top dog at home, we knew he counted on her. That's why she could tease him when he got pompous, and tell him he worried too much. Sometimes people were just dotty, she said. Including grandpa. Because dad believed her, they never had rows or sneaked on each other – though mum did sometimes promise to soften dad up, if Kit and I wanted something he thought was expensive or rubbish. 'You know what he'll say, though, don't you?' she warned us. We did. He'd tell us the story about great-grandpa Andrew, who was offered a bowl of peaches one day and said, 'The biggest are not always the best.' Dad repeated this so often it might have been the family motto.

Usually we asked for things early in the day, when we bundled along to my parents' bedroom after dad had left for work. It was our favourite time with mum – deciding what we were going to do, hearing Jack de Manio muttering from the wireless on her bedside table, watching the flies potter round the lampshade in the middle of the ceiling. Just being there together in the same heat: that was all we wanted. On weekends, we were meant to let them lie in, but by eight o'clock we'd lost patience and tiptoed along the corridor with our clothes under our arms, so we could get dressed at the foot of their bed if dad didn't want us to climb in. Usually he slipped out when we poked our heads round the door, leaving a warm hollow beside mum like a rabbit's nest. When he started to shave in the corner basin, I pressed down the sheet to watch his brush twirl a Father Christmas beard across his face. 'Is that real badger hair, dad, from a real badger?' His red lips twisted among the white cream. 'Yes,' he said, but the word came out oddly, stretched like a piece of chewing gum. 'Do they have to kill the badger to get the hair, or do they pull it out?' Dad bent closer to the mirror without answering, and mum told me to pipe down, couldn't I see he was concentrating? I could – but it was so rare to see dad like this, just him and his body, which was like my own only bigger. I held the sheet tight over my chest, and watched his razor scraping in careful strokes until he was patched together again. Then he patted his face with a towel and disappeared next door to his dressing room, still without saying a word.

The only time dad was sure to stay in bed after we'd arrived was at Christmas, when we squeezed between him and mum and set about our stockings – his long grey Stowe rugby socks, lumpy and smelling of tangerines. After we'd got down to the toes there was a lull, and we lay still under mounds of shredded wrapping paper. Dad said we looked bloated, but we hadn't eaten anything yet. We were saving up. Anyway, it was their turn now, and we wanted to watch. They rolled sideways and delved under the bed for presents they'd bought each other, then passed them over our heads. Dad went first, and after that it was mum's turn. But there was a problem. She couldn't reach under the bed properly, and as she tugged out her present, she knocked it against something hard. The bed frame. There was the horrible fizzing sound of breaking glass, and we stopped talking. Mum sat upright, straightening her dressing gown round her shoulders. 'I think I'd better open it,' she said in a small voice, and as she began pulling off the wrapping dad said 'Never mind, darling, never mind', but she wasn't listening. She was crying, turning the present round in one hand. It was a decanter, cut glass, beautiful, and shaped like a tear. A sliver was missing from the top, where it should have been smooth for pouring. 'Never mind, never mind' dad was still saying, almost smothering me and Kit as he reached across to look. Mum held it towards him without letting go. 'I've ruined it,' she said eventually. 'No, you haven't. Of course you haven't,' dad told her. He'd forgotten about me and Kit – they both had – and we slithered down the bed. Something embarrassing was happening, and we didn't want to see. As we closed the door behind us, and went back to our room, I heard the crackle of the paper we'd left lying between them.

I didn't mind feeling left out, if I thought there was a good reason. And the bust decanter was definitely a good reason – not like that other time, when we'd watched dad play against the Gentlemen of Essex. Up to then, I'd always thought he was expert at cricket. He knew what to do when Kit and I hammered our stumps into the strip between the rough grass at the end of the garden: '*Never* use the blade of the bat, boys, always the handle downwards like *this*.' He was a member of the MCC. He had promised to take us to Lord's when we were older, to watch Wes Hall and Fiery Fred. But suddenly here he was miles from home, in a village we'd never seen before, staring across this enormous bright pitch and rubbing his chin. 'He's really a batsman you know, not a bowler,' mum had said in the car, twisting round to us in the back seat. I remembered this as I watched dad take his place in the outfield. At least nobody would expect anything from him yet; he could stay there among the daisies until it was his turn to go to the crease.

As the match got under way, Kit and I walked round the boundary, sometimes stopping to poke the line of whitewash with the toes of our shoes. It wasn't the game that interested us, only dad – standing close to us now and fielding at deep cover, his whites looking sadly yellow. He gave a low wave, then turned away and began his stroll inwards as the bowler trundled up to the wicket. There was the crack of the bat hitting the ball, and its echo skidding into the trees. By the time dad turned round, we'd moved on. Why was he using that old tie to hold up his trousers, like so many of the others? Was it a kind of uniform?

When we reached mum again, she was sitting in a row of deckchairs with the other wives. They rippled as we got close – it was the sun bouncing off the cars behind them. Mum was at the far end, leaning forward to pour tea from the thermos into our ivory-coloured plastic mugs. Everything about her had the same dazzle – her hair falling over her face, her white and yellow dress, the skin of her bare arms. She looked beautiful. And a man was stretched at her feet, propping himself upright on his elbows. I didn't recognise him, but he was obviously a friend, even though he was on the opposite team – one of the Gentlemen of Essex. He was wearing pads and a dark blue cap which pressed his head into a square. Because his bat was lying on the grass beside him, I could tell he was about to go in. 'Oh, hello you two,' said mum, sploshing a dribble of tea. Her cheeks were flushed. 'You don't know . . .' She flapped a hand towards the man, who closed one eye to look at us. 'Hello,' we said like a couple of parrots, then added 'sir' because dad liked us to do that. Although the man bunched up his legs to make room, I could tell mum was annoyed. She had a little frown between her eyes, which meant she was thinking, 'Why don't you two buzz off and play somewhere; you've got your bat and ball in the car?' But Kit and I didn't want to play. We wanted to be a part of whatever was happening here, and watch the match with the grown-ups.

I swivelled round to ask for a cup of tea, and noticed a button on mum's dress was undone, the third button from her throat. The cotton had sagged open and showed the edge of her bra. Had the lolling man seen this? He must have done – mum had been leaning forward. Should I tell her? Surely she'd want to know, and do it up again? I had to think of an excuse, and get her to myself. That would be awkward, because the man would think I had some childish problem, and laugh at me when I came back. I opened my mouth then shut it quickly again as the air shivered behind me. It was one of the batsmen – he'd just given the ball a colossal whack. By the time I looked round, several fielders were already dashing across the grass yelling 'Catch it!' – though the ball itself had disappeared. No, there it was, falling very slowly back to earth, into the space between dad and the man next to him. They were both rushing towards it with their arms straight, and their heads twisted towards the sky. Everyone could see what was going to happen next – everyone except dad and the other man.

They met head to head and stood still as snowmen, frowning into each other's eyes while the ball thumped down beside them, rolled a few feet, then lay still. 'Oh look, look!' said mum, as dad and the other man melted apart. She skipped across the padded legs of the stranger and reached dad almost as soon as he crumpled to the ground. Kit and I got there soon after. Was he really hurt? Would he have to stop playing? Could we go home?

We did have to go home, but only after dad got better and finished the game. By that time his accident had turned round. It wasn't funny or painful any more, it was brave: the captain said dad had 'flung himself into the breach'. Better still, his team had walloped the others and he didn't have to bat, which meant he could sit with us, and the stranger went away. By the time we climbed into the car, the sun was low, slicing through the hedges and turning the surface of the lane into fudge. We were happy and quiet, and dad said his head didn't even hurt any more. 'Oh mum,' I said, suddenly remembering, 'you've got a button undone on your dress.' I was thinking about the sunset, expecting her simply to bend forward and do herself up. But she snapped at me: 'When did that happen?' 'Earlier,' I said, wishing I'd had time to work out a lie. 'When you were talking to that man.' There was a pause, and the watery purr of the wheels on the gravel, then a rumpus. Why hadn't I told her then? How could I have been so thoughtless? Couldn't I see how embarrassing it was? I sank back as the heat boiled into my face, and dad chipped in, giving the last word as usual: 'Yes, honestly, Andrew. You could have said.' I looked down at my hands and kept quiet for a moment, then glanced at Kit. He shrugged, which was strange. Usually he enjoyed it when I was in trouble.

It wasn't like mum and dad to join ranks; usually dad laid the law down, and mum tried to fit in – which just went to show how sensitive she was. That was one of the words her friends used about her, when we overheard them talking: 'Gilly is such a sensitive person.' If they meant she felt more strongly about things than most people, they were right. But that wasn't the only way she was different. Most mums wore chunky skirts and rollneck jerseys with fake pearl necklaces bouncing up and down on their bosoms. She had bright dresses and dolly boots like the ones in magazines. She talked differently too, as though she wanted to know what people thought, even when she didn't agree with them. And she read books sometimes, which nobody else did. When these books were finished, they went into the whirligig in the drawing room. Elizabeth Bowen. C. P. Snow. The life story of Francis Chichester. I wanted to know why the names of some writers were bigger than their titles, and mum said it was because they were famous and people wanted to read everything they'd written. What, everything? Yes. Even everything by Iris Murdoch, who apparently couldn't stop? Yes, especially her.

'Eventually you'll read stories yourself,' mum told me one evening, when I was hanging around the dressing table on my way to bed. I picked up the book at her elbow, but she snatched it back. 'What's the matter?' I asked. 'Oh, nothing,' she said quickly. 'It's rather grown up for you at the moment, that's all.' I wasn't sure what she meant, but I told myself I'd have a look later, when she was asleep. I wouldn't, though. I wasn't interested in books. What I liked was sharing a secret with her. 'And if you enjoy that sort of thing,' she went on, 'books, I mean, then we can go to the theatre. Even the ballet, perhaps. I haven't been to the ballet for years. *Nutcracker* would be good to start with.' She was talking faster now, brushing her hair with fierce little tugs. 'Why don't you go with dad?' I said, and she slowed down suddenly, smiling at herself in the mirror. 'Poor dad,' she said. 'He doesn't have time to read.' 'I mean the ballet,' I said. Mum put down her brush, still smiling. 'Ballet isn't really dad's cup of tea.'

There was no need to ask what she meant. I'd heard dad snorting at the telly one Saturday evening when he'd seen some dancers hopping across a bare stage. I thought about it some more after I'd gone to my room, said my prayers, and climbed into bed to wait for mum to come and say goodnight. She and dad were different, but that made them sound separate, and they weren't. Mum was gentler in dad's world, that was all. I'd watched her on holiday in Norfolk last summer, grabbing the binoculars to follow a buzzard. Her mouth had fallen open and she'd actually gurgled as the sun lit up its wings. And I saw her with her dog every day – with Beauty, the collie we got after Jack was killed on the road outside the house. Beauty was always nervous, twisting her lips into a half-smile, and if ever she saw the postman she tried to nip him on the ankles. But with mum she was easy, even when she had puppies.

Kit and I had known another litter was on the way, but we'd lost patience waiting. Then mum whisked us along to the woodshed, and there they were. We knelt down in the smell of chopped logs and milk. Three of them, but they could have been moles: shiny black fur, eyes bulging behind their lids, paddling feet with see-through nails. When I stretched out my hand to touch, Beauty growled at me. When mum did the same, Beauty just gave a sneezing shake. Then mum lifted one of the puppies, the largest, and gave it to me. It wasn't like a mole, it was like a Slinky, pouring through my hands. Mum tickled it with a finger, rubbing the fur the wrong way so I could see the skin underneath, with its deep blue ink-blobs. I'd heard someone say 'lost in admiration', and now I understood what it meant. Mum had forgotten me and Kit. She was staring and staring at the puppy, flicking her little finger against the long yellow tuft between his back legs. Then she nestled him back into the straw beside Beauty. I couldn't imagine dad doing this, not with his trembling hands – the puppy was too delicate. Neither could I hear him talking under his breath all the time like mum: 'Good girl, good girl, good girl.'

Mum kissed me goodnight and went downstairs, leaving the door ajar. Her gentleness wasn't the only thing. She let go of her feelings, and dad didn't. That was how he'd been brought up, and he wanted us to be the same. But why was he jumpy so much of the time? And come to that, why was mum ill so often, with her brucellosis, and her bad back, and her colds, and her skinniness? Maybe things weren't safe after all. Maybe mum and dad felt like me, when I lay in the dark every night with my hands clasped behind my head. I could hear the mill grinding its wobbly teeth on the far side of the road, and the leaves of the Virginia creeper rustling along the wall outside my window. But mainly I could hear the cars, and see their headlights crossing my ceiling: more and more of them as time went by. The hedge running along the side of the garden was too thin. When I got out of bed and opened the curtains to look towards the Tree of Heaven, smashed bits of light were spreading across the lawn like a disaster.

CHAPTER SIX

A over T

The two cars were like the two dogs. Dad's had a pedigree, it was new and reliable, and we used it whenever we went anywhere smart. The Daimler. British Racing Green. Mum's car was a Hillman Estate, registration 473 AJN, which she said stood for 'Old John's Knickers'. Dad said that was nonsense, 'old' had an 'o' and 'knickers' had a 'k' – two out of three wrong was stretching a point. 'I mean "auld" as in "auld lang syne"', mum said. 'Well that still leaves *ker*-nickers,' dad told her. 'What about them? *Ker*-nickers?' Kit and I looked at each other and shrugged. This was their joke, not ours. Anyway, we preferred the Hillman, even if it did have bolt-upright seats and a heater that roared without blowing any fug off the windows. 'So what *is* it about mum's car?' dad wanted to know. 'If it's got all those things wrong?' 'It holds the road better,' I told him, nodding my head like an expert. 'The Daimler makes us feel sick.'

When I started at primary school, we used the Hillman to get there and back. The Barn was eight miles away, in a village we normally never visited: Much Hadham. Mum said the buildings were only bungalows, and not many people went there, but the teachers were friendly. That was good enough for me. I knew she wouldn't have made me go unless she had to, and I was sure she'd fetch me away again if I didn't like it. 'Besides', she said, 'there'll still be weekends and holidays. Enormous long times, when we can do everything you want. Maybe even go to a film in Harlow. Would you like to see Elvis Presley?' I told her it was OK, school was fine. Especially if I didn't have to talk to the headmistress, Mrs Lucas. She was a small square body in a small square tweed suit, with half-moon glasses and wire hair. Hardly a woman at all, I thought, the first time I saw her. More like a badger, and probably as bad-tempered.

But she never taught me, and apart from meeting parents, and leading prayers at the start of the day, she kept herself to herself. On the other hand, I could see her shadow at the edge of everything. At midday, for instance, when the whole school tramped down the village street in a crocodile for lunch in the Copper Kettle, Mrs Lucas took the lead, calves shaking as she clipped along the pavement in her sensible shoes. After we said grace, her eyes followed every forkful into our mouths and her Adam's apple bobbed as we swallowed. When we were back at school and she disappeared into her office again, we could still see her through the wrinkled glass of her door. Then she wasn't a badger any more. She was a spider.

Mr Lucas was a blotchy-skinned man with soft moustaches who taught art. He blew into my classroom once a week on a cloud of pipe tobacco, rummaged in a cupboard by the teacher's dais, handed out jamjars, told us to fill them from the tap in the washroom ('*carefully*, children, and one between two, *please*'), helped us put up our easels, and arranged a bunch of flowers on his desk. 'This is your subject for today, boys and girls,' he said, pressing his thumb gently on the tobacco in his pipe, then dropping it back into his pocket. 'You haven't got a view here, so I've brought one for you.' I liked it best when the flowers were irises: the skinny stems, the purple and blue like the head of a baby bird, the yellow smear inside. But my fingers were never steady enough, or the powder paints glued into hard lumps on the paper, or the water dribbled in coloured stripes when I wanted a clear space, or the shape I was making was nothing like the shape I could see. The lesson was my favourite part of the week, though it made me want to tear my hair out.

Then Louise Oliphant, who had the desk next to mine and was a pretty girl with a red smudge on the back of her neck, which she said showed where the stork had carried her as a baby, told me Mr Lucas didn't know what he was talking about. He wasn't an art teacher at all, he was married to Mrs Lucas. What did I think of that? I remembered the day Louise had peed at her desk – a terrible flood that smelled of veg soup. Why should I trust her? All the same, if what she said was true, it was puzzling. How could Mr Lucas do his job, if he didn't know what he was talking about? There was only one way to find out. At the end of my first term, I asked him whether he'd do a painting of the flowers at the same time as us. 'Of course,' he said, giving the crushed smile that made me think of Mrs Lucas stamping her feet. When he'd finished we all knew it was brilliant – even Louise. It made me think not all painters were like the man who had his workshop outside the school, where our path met the main road, and who mum said was famous. His name was Henry Moore, and he glared at us sometimes if we made a racket when lessons ended.

None of us thought lessons with Mr Lucas were work. Work was something we did with Miss Vickery, who smelled of mothballs and took us for everything except art. Writing, first. She gave us an exercise book each, which already had our names written on the front. The outside was green and furry like suede, and the pages inside were cream with faint blue lines. 'I'm going to put one or two sentences here on the blackboard,' she said, 'and I want you to copy them into your books as carefully as you can.' It sounded easy, but turned out to be impossible. Miss Vickery's letters were round as stones on a beach, and mine were saggy, or shrinking, however tightly I gripped my pencil. In fact, the harder I tried, the messier they got. Why didn't my hand do what my brain told it? And what was that scribble doing further down my page? I hadn't been anywhere near there.

Next came sums, which were worse than writing. For this Miss Vickery wiped her stumpy letters off the board, and put up numbers instead. Even if I hadn't seen her writing, I'd have known they belonged to her. They were so clear. Miss Vickery obviously didn't have anything nervous inside her body, otherwise her hand would have shaken like mine. Her 2, for instance: it sailed along the line like a swan. Mine always hit a rock underwater and tipped forward. Mum called that 'going a over t' but wouldn't tell me what the 'a' or the 't' stood for. I pressed on – we all did – and copied the numbers into our books. After that, we stared at them with our backs straight and our hands in our laps, chanting out loud. 1, 2, 3,

4, 5 , 6, 7 . . . The sounds didn't mean anything to start with. Then I understood them for a moment (one chicken plus one chicken makes two chickens). Then they didn't mean anything again. They were just a noise – and made me feel sleepy, like saying prayers.

There were only two more lessons before the bell. Geography first. Miss Vickery turned to a rolled-up map, which hung on the wall behind her dais. When she untied the purple ribbon, it rattled down and hung straight, blocking some of the paintings Mr Lucas had pinned there. The map was very old and made of canvas, which meant that every time it unrolled, pieces flaked off, and made me feel the world was over and done with. 'Can you see?' Miss Vickery wanted to know. 'Yes, miss,' we told her, all together in our singsong voice. 'Very good. Now then.' Miss Vickery opened her desk drawer and pulled out a stick like a billiards cue, tapping it against her palm. 'Where are we? Does anyone know?' My hand shot up. The green of England was the same colour as the garden at home, and if I pressed my face close enough to the canvas, I'd probably see the worn-down grass where we played cricket, or the worm-bobbles in mum's flower bed. 'Have you been paying attention, Andrew?' Miss Vickery asked. 'Yes, Miss Vickery,' I said, feeling my skin prickle. 'Good. Then answer the question. Where is England?' I pointed – and she believed me. 'And what does it look like?' she went on, turning to the whole class. 'A witch riding a pig,' we chanted. 'Good. Now draw it'. For the time being, my shaking hand wasn't a problem. As I looked up at the map and down again, the trembling line of the coast turned into a wriggle of seashores. Later, I'd put in the blue lines of rivers, the hills like brown seagulls, the black dots of towns, the small X of the Barn, and the pinprick of Little Brewers. Names would have to wait. I didn't know how to spell most of them, and even if I did the letters would have staggered off across the hump of East Anglia into the North Sea, spoiling everything.

After geography, reading. Miss Vickery stood on her chair so we could see her fat legs, rolled up the map and tied it with the purple ribbon, then climbed down and faced the blackboard again. Her hair wobbled as she wrote up more of her tidy letters, and told us to practise our vowels. 'Come on, all together. *Aaaa* like *baaaaath*.' The sounds came out of my mouth sounding right, even though I didn't think about how to make them. In Mr Lucas's art classes, there was nothing I could do to make my hand copy exactly the flowers in front of my eyes. Reading was different. I could learn the words off the blackboard and make them private. Actually I'd made some of them private already, from the stories mum read me at bedtime. *Peter Rabbit* and *Mr Tod*, which she said was 'exactly how foxes behave in real life'. These two were my favourites, but there were others as well: *My Father's Dragon*, which had a mouse that got his letters in a muddle and said 'bum cack' when he meant 'come back'. And a story about a rat who liked groceries called *Tim Minds the Shop*. Granny had given me that one, and it was too long. I usually asked mum to stop before she got to the end, and make something up herself. She enjoyed telling stories – she kept stopping and laughing to herself in the darkness, then rushing on again. She'd ramble about what the dogs did when they were dreaming, or what the horses said when we weren't listening. I listened with my eyes closed, thinking I was afloat in the Dead Sea, where Miss Vickery said there was so much salt, people drifted on their backs for hours and never drowned. But it couldn't happen every night. Mum would run out of ideas. Besides, I wanted my own stories as well as hers, even if reading them was complicated.

When Miss Vickery held up her dictionary, it looked as though language went on for ever. How would I remember all those words, and if I did, how would I use them? 'Words have rules,' said Miss Vickery, which meant more learning. Not just grammar, but which words were good and which bad. This was the bit of school that mum and dad most often asked me about. 'How does Miss Vickery talk?' they wanted to know. 'What do you mean, how does she talk? She's got a funny sort of voice. It sounds soapy.' 'No, not her voice,' mum said. 'What sort of words does she use?' 'How do you mean?' 'Does she say "toilet", for instance?' I couldn't remember, but I knew some of the other people in my class did, when they put up their hands and asked to be excused. 'You must never say "toilet",' mum went on; she was being so serious it made my clothes feel tight.

'Why not?' 'Because it's non-U,' she said. 'What's non-U?' Mum frowned, then said, 'It's the way people like us don't talk.' 'How do people like us talk, then?' 'We say "loo",' she said firmly. 'Why?' 'I can't tell you why. We just do. We always have done.' That didn't help. 'Tell me some other words I should use,' I said, trying to turn it into a game. 'Well,' she said, 'here are a few for starters. "Looking glass", not "mirror", "Christmas" not "Xmas", "sorry" not "pardon", "sofa" not "settee", "drawing room" not "lounge", "pudding" not "sweet", "perfume" not "scent", which is for hounds. When you're older I'll show you a poem by a friend of granny's friend, Joan Kunser. Do you remember Joan? No, well, never mind. His name's John Betjeman, and the poem's about fish knives'. She gave a little laugh. 'What's so funny about fish knives?' I asked, remembering we had some of our own in a drawer in the dining room. 'Oh, Joan's friend thinks they're ghastly,' she said. 'Beyond the pale.'

It would have been easier to see what mum meant if 'non-U' words were actually bad, like swear words. But the rules didn't work like that. Miss Vickery said swear words were bad, and my parents used them a lot. The dogs were the bloody dogs, the weather was the ruddy weather, and if anyone ever tripped, or banged themselves, or pinched a finger, they always said 'bugger'. Dad said 'God', too, and 'Christ' if it was really serious, and he sometimes made rude jokes as well – things like bubbles in the water being fish-farts, that sort of thing. Why was all this OK at home but not OK at school? And if 'toilet' was so awful at home, why did nobody mind at school? I didn't understand – though I could see how to deal with it. Have one language for home, and one for the Barn. And never use slang anywhere, except with people my own age. One lunchtime I walked back from the Copper Kettle to school with Alex, the dark-haired boy who sat behind Louise. He explained that slang could be very handy, even if grown-ups kept telling us it was lazy. 'What do you mean, "handy"?' I asked. 'You might have had a car accident,' Alex said, flicking his black hair out of his eyes. 'You might be staggering up the road covered in blood with a terrible cut in your head and a broken arm. And you're looking for help.' He paused, wetting his lips. 'And?' I said. 'And,' he went on, 'you find someone. You find someone, but you haven't got the energy to say a word as long as "accident". You're about to faint, you see, from loss of blood.' 'And?' I said again. 'You say "prang",' he said with a foxy grin. 'You get it? A quick little word you can say before you faint. That's why we have slang.'

Just when I thought I knew which language to use in what place, I lost my way again. In another crocodile back from the Copper Kettle, Alex told me the worst word in the world was 'fuck'. He couldn't explain what it meant; he only knew it was terrible. 'Fuck,' I repeated softly, keeping in step. 'It's so short. How can it be the worst? It's tiny.' 'I don't know,' Alex said. 'It just *is* the worst.' I decided there was only one way to test this. When I was at home that afternoon, hanging round mum as she stirred some white sauce in a pan on the Baby Belling, I asked her. 'Is it true that "fuck" is the worst word in the world, mum?' She dropped her wooden spoon, and the sauce splattered on her hand so I thought she must have burned herself. Then her face was inches from my own, smelling lemony as usual. 'You must *never* say that word,' she breathed. 'It will make people very unhappy.' I wanted to say I was sorry, I hadn't known, but I was too shocked. Instead I said, 'You and dad use swear words, and they don't make people unhappy.' 'No,' mum said, standing straight and hoiking her spoon out of the pan. 'But we never use *that* word. It's quite different. Now off you go and tidy the playroom before we eat. And give Kit a shout too. I don't know where he's got to.'

There were so many other words I was allowed to use, a few missing 'fucks' and 'mirrors' were no problem. Besides, Miss Vickery said I was good at writing, and that made me cheerful. 'It's nice being told "well done", isn't it?' mum said, and I nodded. But not everyone felt the same, which was why they were lazy sometimes, or cheeky. Stephen, for instance, who was always standing in the corner because he never did his lessons. Or Harold, who bullied Louise and had to leave. 'You're a goody-goody,' Harold hissed in my ear before he went. I was astonished and told him I liked reading, before I could stop myself. But Harold wasn't interested. He bludged up the path to the main road, kicking flints while we watched from the front door. Then Miss Vickery shooed us back to our desks and told us to keep quiet. That was difficult. Harold was horrible, but had he been telling the truth? I looked round the classroom, the frowning faces, the poster of mushrooms that were safe to eat, and Miss Vickery on her dais with her arms folded. No, Harold hadn't been telling the truth. He was a liar and a bully, and that's why he'd left.

Then Mrs Lucas was standing in the door of our classroom, bristling. She was back to being a badger again. It must be Harold: they must have had an argument. I looked away and saw Miss Vickery stretch her whiskery lips wider than usual. 'What do you say, boys and girls?' she asked. 'Good afternoon, Mrs Lucas,' we chanted. There was no reply. Just Mrs Lucas lifting her right hand and pointing at me, even though the bell was about to go, and the day would soon be over.

Mrs Lucas bent her finger and beckoned. Perhaps she was looking at someone behind me? I swivelled round, but there was only Alex, flicking his fringe from his eyes. That meant it was me she wanted. I stood up, and all the muscles in my legs turned to rubber bands, which made following her difficult. I couldn't see anything properly, either, when we got to her office. Blurry heaps of paper. An ashtray full of paperclips. A painting of some purple flowers – that must be by Mr Lucas. 'Now,' Mrs Lucas began, as I sat down facing her. 'Do you want to tell me about this business?' My mind went red. 'What business?' 'What business, *Mrs Lucas*.' 'I'm sorry, Mrs Lucas, I don't know what you mean, Mrs Lucas.' 'We have no room in this school for dishonest boys.' 'Dishonest, Mrs Lucas?' I was trying to keep my voice under control but it kept escaping and turning into a squeak. 'No games, Andrew.' Mrs Lucas clenched her fists on her knees; the hem of her petticoat was showing. What games did she mean? 'I'm not playing, Mrs Lucas.' 'You know perfectly well what I mean. I'm going to give you a moment to think.' Mrs Lucas thumped her legs with both fists and glared into my face. Supposing I told her she could give me all the minutes she liked, and it wouldn't make any difference? I could hear mum's voice cutting across, telling me not to be rude. The only thing to do was tell the truth, and the truth was I hadn't a clue what she was on about. She must have confused me with someone else. Or was it a test I could pass by saying the right thing?

'I have no idea, Mrs Lucas,' I said, as seriously as I could. 'Honestly. Ask the others.' 'That's exactly what I have done,' she said, lowering her head until the whole of her grey eyes appeared above the top of her half-specs. I didn't understand that either. How could she have asked the others when they'd been in the classroom with me? Then I had a brainwave. She didn't mean she'd asked the others. She meant she'd asked Harold. He'd obviously told a lie about me, and Mrs Lucas had believed him. 'Which others?' I asked. 'That's not your concern.' 'Do you mean Harold, Mrs Lucas?' I went on. She took a deep breath and leaned back in her chair, gripping the arms. 'I want you to be honest, Andrew. I don't want you telling tales about others.'

I shook my head. Harold told tales, not me. Mrs Lucas had put everything the wrong way round. 'So?' she went on. 'Are you going to tell me now, or are you going to be stubborn and stupid?' She pronounced it 'stupit', and a fleck of white spit bobbled into the middle of her bottom lip. I shook my head again. Everything in my brain was used up. 'I'm sorry,' I said at last. 'I really am, Mrs Lucas. I don't know what you're talking about.' I wanted to go on, and tell her I wasn't a dishonest person, that Harold didn't like me. But then Mrs Lucas would think it was me who invented things. I stared down at the flower patterns in the toes of my sandals, and my grey socks wrinkling under the strap. Why could I never get them to stay smooth? Mrs Lucas took another deep breath. 'Very well,' she said, in a big flat voice. 'You are a stubborn child, Andrew, and I'm very disappointed. You can go now.' She dragged her chair closer to her desk, and began shuffling papers. 'I said you can go now.' It was the same hissing voice she'd used when I'd first come into the office. I hadn't changed her mind about anything.

'Thank you, Mrs Lucas.' I had no idea how my voice worked, but the words appeared anyway, and hung in the air like dust. Then I saw the door open when I touched the handle, my satchel come off its peg in the corridor, and balloon-faces bobbing on the path as I started running. There was mum ahead, in the shadows under the trees by the main road. She was gassing and didn't see me until I charged into her. 'What's the matter, what's the matter?' she said, wrapping her arms round my head so I could disappear into the dark. The buttons of her pullover pressed into my cheek. 'Please,' she said. 'How can I help you if you don't tell me?' I shook my head again, peering round her arm into the back of the Hillman. Kit and the dogs were in the back, and the shopping in mum's wicker basket, and the rug with its hairs like hundreds of tiny cracks.

'I don't want any bloody talk,' I said. 'What?' mum asked. She'd never heard me swear before, and I couldn't tell whether she was angry. I was a bit surprised myself. I hadn't meant to say 'bloody', it just popped out. 'Nothing,' I said. Mum bent over me again. 'Would you like me to go and see Mrs Lucas?' 'No!' I told her, almost shouting. Surely she understood? I broke away and climbed into the passenger seat, ignoring Kit's questions. 'What's the matter, mum?' he asked, as she settled behind the steering wheel and crashed the car into gear. 'Why's Andrew crying? Is he in trouble?' 'No, of course he's not in trouble,' she said quietly. 'He's upset, that's all.' I let my satchel slip onto the floor mat as we swung away from the kerb, pulled up my knees and leaned my head on them, eyes shut. I'd talk to mum soon – but not now. I wanted to turn over what had happened. Either that, or push it out of my mind altogether, like a nightmare, or the thought of mum's missing year. When I glanced up, we'd reached the end of the main street, where the big lime trees in Henry Moore's garden dropped their sticky juice on the road and made it shine. Whatever had happened was already falling behind us. It didn't matter so much about Mrs Lucas. School wasn't my real life. This was. The road opening between the hedges, then the lane off the main road beside the house, and then the stable yard where the horses had left their shoeprints on the gravel.

That evening after prayers, mum sat on the side of my bed and asked me to tell her my troubles, even though she knew perfectly well. Then we imagined a bottle with thick glass and writing on it, like the ones dad's brewery used for Celebration Beers, and I stuffed my thoughts inside. As soon as I'd done that, mum made a hissing noise which was the top going back on, went to the window, and threw her arm as if she was hurling the bottle away – not towards the road and the mill opposite, but into a swirling river which carried everything out to sea while I fell asleep. Except it didn't quite work. In the morning, I still had a wrinkle in my mind. And later, the next day, there was Mrs Lucas herself, with her tight mouth and her metal eyes. She passed over my face in the crocodile as though I didn't exist.

I'd have to do something else – something that showed I wasn't the person she thought. Trying harder in lessons might do the trick. Then again, more people might believe I really was a goody-goody. Anyway, Mrs Lucas didn't know what happened in lessons, she was hidden away in her office. I'd have to find something more surprising. This turned out to be a piece of paper, pinned on the school notice board, which asked pupils to put down their names for a singing competition. It would be held in the village hall, and everyone would sing the same song: 'Ducks Go a-Dabbling, Up Tails All'. Mr Lucas would play the piano. 'I didn't know you felt musical,' mum said, when I told her I'd put my name on the list. 'Oh yes,' I answered, as if it was well known. 'Are you sure?' she went on. 'The song does sound a bit soppy.' 'Quite sure,' I told her, and left it at that. I didn't want her to think I might have made a mistake, but I could see she was right about the words. They were awful. Nobody said 'a-dabbling' when they were talking in real life.

Mum didn't ask any more questions about the competition. She agreed with dad, who said 'it needs guts to do something like this', and told me she'd 'back me all the way'. She took me to special lessons; she practised with me at home – just the words, because we didn't have a piano; she drove me to a rehearsal in the village hall, then again on the big day. The hall was big as an aircraft hanger, with thousands of metal chairs in rows, and huge planks of light crashing through the side windows. The stage was enormous too, a splintery desert with a piano in the middle which looked as though it had dropped from the sun. While the seats filled up, mum and I sat side by side in the front row, next to the five other singers and their parents. 'Only six of you?' mum whispered. 'That's not very many!' 'No,' I said blankly. I couldn't decide whether it made me braver than ever, or more stupid. I peeped round the corner of mum's shoulder. None of them was as nervous as me, and I could tell from their clothes that they were all better singers. The girls had short jerseys and stiff dresses, which made them look like egg cups. The one other boy had glasses and a bow tie.

'Watch the clock on the back wall. Imagine there's a fairy sitting on the clock and keep your eyes on her. Then you won't worry about the audience.' That's what Mr Lucas had said at the rehearsal, wiping his soft moustache so it didn't creep inside his mouth. I wished he'd chosen something other than a fairy. The girls might like that, and maybe the boy with specs. But not me. When my turn came to climb the chipped stairs, I tried to imagine something else there. What could it be? A goblin. Like the one in that illustration to *Babes in the Wood* by – what was his name, the one mum liked? Arthur Rackham? No, not a goblin. A goblin wouldn't help. I let my mind spin as my feet clunked across the stage. A girl. A miniature girl with fair hair, like my sister if I had a sister. She was wearing a pale pink ballet dress and sitting with her legs crossed, her chin in her hand. She wanted to know what on earth I was doing, but it was too late to explain. Mr Lucas was already splashing into the song, picking up the notes and waggling them like shiny duck-tails, while I clasped my hands behind my back and took a deep breath. I knew the tune. I'd practised it dozens of times. But suddenly there were no words in my head. I looked down at mum, expecting her to be gazing at her hands and fiddling with her wedding ring, or fixing me with her 'Go on, you'll be fine' look. She wasn't doing either of these things. She was leaning back in her chair, perfectly relaxed, smiling as though we were sitting round the kitchen table. It didn't matter. That's what she was telling me. It was just a song. I smiled back at her, and started to sing.

I was no good, but it wasn't terrible. I remembered the words. I came fourth. By the time this sank in, mum and I were driving home again and the stage, the hall, the faces, the clock, the song were all slithering out of my head. Not out of dad's, though. When he got home from work that evening, he said, 'People will look at you differently now. It'll make you more confident.' I was impressed by this, and remembered it a fortnight later, when another sheet of paper appeared on the school notice-board. 'Any child wanting to buy the *Encyclopaedia Britannica* should write their name below, and a salesman will visit their home to make arrangements.' Dad was right. I did feel more confident. But after I'd put down my name on this new list, I still wondered whether I'd made a mistake. The *Encyclopaedia Britannica* was serious – the biggest *and* the best encyclopaedia in the world. Any fool knew that. So why did I want it? Long words were still a problem. Maybe my parents would like it? That was a good idea, but not completely good. Mum had her padded parcels from the Book Club. Apart from that, books didn't fit at home.

I left the paper flapping in the breeze, and told myself I didn't need to worry. A teacher would see my name on the list and realise I hadn't meant to put it there. I'd never hear any more about it. The next thing I knew was a booming bang-bang-bang on the front door at Little Brewers – the one friends never used. It was late in the evening, after seven, and dad had just got in. I stood behind him in the hall, ready for bed in my pyjamas and dressing gown, squinting round his waist. A bald head was shining under the outside light. A tired-looking man wearing a blue mac, and tipped over to one side because he was carrying a heavy suitcase. 'Dad . . .' I started, taking a step backwards into the hall. It was too late. The man was already wiping the rain off his forehead with a hanky, explaining that I'd asked him to call.

Mum stepped up from the kitchen, wiping her hands on a drying-up cloth. She touched me on the shoulder, and walked me into the playroom. Dad and the bald man followed. Shouldn't they ask him to sit down? They were normally so polite. But they kept him standing. 'Have you really asked this man to come and see us, old boy?' dad asked me quietly, as if we were alone. I wished I could say of course not, what on earth would I do with the *Encyclopaedia*

Britannica? But a part of me did still want it, so I nodded my head – and as if that was a secret sign, the man suddenly knelt down on the floor. I knew the bare boards were hard, but he said nothing. He just opened his case and held up one of the big books inside, which he called a volume. Dad took it in both hands as if it was hot, and flicked over a few pages. 'How much will this set me back?' he wanted to know, clearing his throat. 'One hundred and twenty-five pounds' the bald man said quickly, then added before dad could interrupt, 'Quite amazing value, considering the amount of information and the number of volumes.' Nobody answered him. A hundred and twenty-five pounds! It was a fortune. No wonder the book was suddenly heavier in dad's hands. I glimpsed columns of tiny print, and a coloured picture of a man standing on a rock wearing a headdress. Underneath it said 'Red Indian Chief in the costume of . . .' But it was no good. I couldn't understand the rest. Clumps of pages flipped through dad's fingers, closing on one another with a delicious *chomp*.

'Do they pay you a wage for this?' mum suddenly asked the man. 'Or do you get paid for every copy you sell?' She hadn't meant to be rude, but the question made the man wince. It wasn't rain on his forehead anymore. He was sweaty. 'I get a percentage of every sale,' he said, not meeting her eye, and I repeated his answer to myself until I understood. Now it was my turn to clear my throat. The man probably had a wife and children at home, waiting to ask how many copies he'd sold today. I'd want to know, if I were his son. I hated myself for getting his hopes up, and making him kneel in front of us. Look at him! Twisting his head round, as though dad was about to kick him. Spidery red veins wriggled in the corners of his eyes.

'I'm sorry,' dad said after a minute, handing back the volume and wiping his palms on the sides of his trousers. 'It's too much for us.' 'Of course, it is a great deal of money,' the man said eagerly, as if dad had said the thing he most wanted to hear. 'It is a wonderful investment, though, and if you prefer, you can stagger the payments.' For a moment I thought the man might keel over, to show dad what he meant by stagger. 'No,' dad said again. 'I don't think so, thank you. Now, let me give you a hand with that.' He stretched forward to help, but the man was having none of it. He packed his case neatly, without looking at us.

'I'll do the dogs, Richard, if you'll show out Mr . . .' Mum didn't finish her sentence, and as she brushed past me towards the kitchen she whispered, 'We'll talk about this in a moment.' I couldn't tell whether she was upset or not; her voice was too low. Then I was in the hall again, watching dad and the man face one another on the front step in the rain. 'Let me leave you my card,' said the man, switching his smile back on. 'In case you change your mind.' Dad thanked him, then shut the door carefully, as if he was fitting a lid on a jar. He put his hand on my shoulder and steered me towards the kitchen. 'In future,' he said, 'let us know before you do something like that, will you?' He wasn't angry, but there was something hurt in his voice. 'Of course, dad,' I said. 'Sorry.' 'No harm done,' he said. 'You're not disappointed, are you?' 'Not at all.' 'Good. That's that, then.' He opened the kitchen door, and as we sank down into the warmth mum said, 'Has he gone?' She might have been talking about a tramp she'd seen hanging round the end of the garden. 'Yes, he's gone,' dad said wearily, picking his whisky glass off the table and swirling it. 'I said to Andrew, no harm done.'

Mum and I talked about the *Encyclopaedia* at bedtime, but not much. 'You really do understand, don't you?' she said. 'It's an awful lot of money.' 'It is,' I told her, and because I knew it would help, I added, 'Dad's right.' She smiled faintly and reached for the light switch. 'Anything else?' she asked in the darkness. 'Only the man,' I said. 'Oh, the man,' she answered, in her velvet late-night voice. 'Try not to think about him. He has other fish to fry.' I nodded, hearing his footsteps again, as they sizzled through the puddles to the front gate. He was still tilted over to one side by the weight of the volumes. I didn't believe her.

CHAPTER SEVEN

In the Wood

Mum and I were sitting at the kitchen table after tea, watching Wally Clock wipe his face on the shelf above the Aga. We were day-dreaming, waiting for the news at six. 'Dad and I think it's time for you to leave the Barn and go to a different sort of school,' mum said suddenly. I thought for a moment I might have made it up. 'Pardon?' I said. 'Not "pardon",' she told me. '"Sorry".' 'Oh. Sorry,' I said. '*Sorry.*' She leaned forward and held my two hands down on the tabletop. 'Starting next term, when the summer hols are over and you're nearly eight.' I looked into her eyes; she had a flick of white goo in the corners, which meant she was tired. 'What do you mean, a different school?' 'It's called Maidwell Hall,' she said. 'It's in Northamptonshire.' 'How far away is that?' I asked, worried she might say Miss Vickery should have taught me. 'About a hundred miles,' she went on, in the same quiet voice. 'A hundred miles!' It was even further than granny. 'It sounds a long way, I know, but it isn't really. We'll be able to whizz there in the car.' She was gripping my hands more tightly now, and I knew she was lying. Nobody whizzed a hundred miles; it was impossible. 'I told dad I'd talk to you,' she said. 'It's a prep school. You know what a prep school is, don't you?' I was trying to concentrate, but Serenade was clattering her stable door across the yard. She must be hungry. Wouldn't it be better if we fed her now and talked about this later? 'I'm not sure,' I said vaguely, but mum pressed on. 'Prep school is like the Barn. Except you stay there all the time during term.' 'What, sleep there and everything?' 'Yes,' she said. 'You mean, I wouldn't see you?' 'Of course not,' mum said, then twisted her mouth as though she'd swallowed something sour. 'I mean of course, *yes.* Dad and I will visit sometimes – as often as we're allowed. The good news about Maidwell is, it's run by a friend of grandpa's.'

I heard myself say 'Fine' – quite flat, as if mum had told me it was raining. I didn't mean 'fine'. I meant something was pinging my ears and I couldn't think straight. But mum had obviously made a mistake, and we'd sort it out this evening, when we were saying goodnight. After that, she could talk to dad and make him change his mind too. 'Honestly, mum,' I said, 'I think we'd better go and feed those horses.' She gave my hand a squeeze, and pushed back from the table.

That night I waited until I'd said my prayers, then deepened my voice as much as possible. 'I've been thinking about what you said,' I told her, 'and I've decided I don't want to go to a prep school. I'd rather go to a day school, like Tim. You know, Tim across the Heath.' Mum stared at me in the darkness, then slowly laid her head beside me on the pillow. I wrapped my arm round her shoulders. I hadn't done this before, and her thin bones made me nervous. After a while, she sat up again and patted me on the cheek. She wasn't going to agree with me, I could tell. She wanted to, but she couldn't. 'I know, darling,' she said softly. 'But it's what happens. Everyone has to go away at your age. All the boys, anyway.' I'd thought she might say that, and had my answer ready. 'It's not true,' I told her. 'What about Tim? You're just saying what dad says, aren't you?' I never talked to her angrily like this. 'I am saying what dad says,' she answered. 'But it's what I say too.' She paused, then picked up speed. 'He's very nice, grandpa's friend who runs the school. You'll like him. His name's Beak.' I saw an eagle's head stabbing down at me. 'Beak?' I said. Mum half-laughed. 'Well, Beak's not his real name. His real name's Oliver Wyatt, but you'll call him Beak. It means "teacher". It's Latin or something. Dad and I thought it would be a good idea if he came to lunch one weekend before you go, so you can meet him.' I stared at her grey face in the darkness but didn't answer. What was the point, when nothing would make any difference? Then I rolled over onto my side, facing the basin, so mum wouldn't be able to kiss me goodnight. That would show her how much I minded. The washer on one of the taps was almost gone. It sounded like someone sucking a sweet.

She left the door ajar, and as she creaked downstairs I flipped over to call her back. It was too late; I could hear her in the kitchen already, mumbling to dad. A saucepan lid dropped, and gave an echoey rattle across the floorboards. Was that because she was upset? I fell asleep with my thoughts foaming into each other like streams rushing from opposite directions. It would all be better in the morning. That's what mum always said, even when we didn't put things in the bottle and throw them out of the window.

The moment I woke up, I knew I'd go to Maidwell when the summer ended; there was no choice. And I knew something else, too. Before I went, I needed to see what it felt like being a hundred miles away from home. I waited until after lunch, when we all had our rest. Then I lay on my bed for five minutes and read the book dad had brought back from work as a surprise the other day, which told me about Tommy Steele and Lonnie Donegan and Cliff Richard, and what colour their eyes were and what their girlfriends were called. It was more interesting than I thought, and I almost changed my plan. But when I saw Kit had dozed off, I got up, straightened my counterpane, and tiptoed downstairs to the pantry. There was a plastic bag in the wicker basket under the bottom shelf, and I dropped an apple into it, along with a hunk of bread and some cheese from the fridge. How long would I be gone? I had no idea. Then I clinked the latch on the back door as quietly as possible, crept round the edge of the yard so my shoes didn't scrunch the gravel, and slipped into the lane.

It was a hot afternoon, and by the time I reached the Heath I was dizzy. Most of our rides began here, and I knew where I was. There was the butcher waving to me now – Mr Reynolds, under his blue-and-white striped awning. I hoisted my bag and looked away to the pond beside his shop. Mum said last spring that all the mallards and coots had built their nests in the middle because they knew the pond would dry up as summer went by. She was right. Their stick-messes were still afloat, even though the water had shrivelled into a puddle. 'Creatures understand things we don't,' mum said. 'They're cleverer than us. They can see into the future.'

I'd have to become more like a creature if I was going to survive. When I needed something to drink, for instance. But if I stopped at the pond here and lapped at the edge like a dog, Mr Reynolds would see me and know something was up. If I waited, I'd find somewhere more private. I turned my back and came to the edge of the Heath, where the traffic whanged to and fro along the road to the Barn. Sunlight bounced off the bumpers and fell round me like pieces of tin. This was the great divide, and I had to be careful. I waited for a gap, then ran across and clambered over a five-barred gate. I'd made it. I was somewhere I'd never been before, and on my own.

It was a gigantic stubble field, one of those English prairies dad complained about because he liked hedges and the birds. 'Those bloody farmers who rip out everything in sight,' he said, 'they're only interested in money. It's a disgrace.' I shielded my eyes and stared towards the horizon. That dark green in the distance was better than a hedge. It was a whole wood. A wood might have a pond, and a pond would be a drink. The drink I now wanted more than anything – though an apple would help. I pulled it from my bag and began chewing as I set off again, but the mouthfuls soon turned to mush, and when I didn't swallow quickly, I felt thirstier than ever. The stubble was hard going, too. On my way over the road, I'd noticed the tyre-tracks of a combine harvester on the tarmac, like Indian war paint. They must have cut the corn here in the last few days – no wonder it was so spiky.

I could soak my feet in the pond, as soon as I'd had my drink. That would be good. The trouble was, the sun was so hot I couldn't even be sure I was keeping in a straight line, or how far I'd got. The trees ahead were still miles off, but if I turned round I could hardly see the gate where I came in. It was like sleepwalking, which I'd never done, though Kit had once. Only the ground felt real. Stubble poking through the patterns in my sandals. Clover. Gravy-coloured clay underneath it all. My feet whispered as they swung forward step by step, and the next thing I knew, a tune was stuck in my head. 'I'm looking for a piano, a piano, not any old piano, a piano that can sing . . .' It was maddening, but it gave me an idea. If I followed the tune all the way through, it took a couple of minutes. A couple of minutes carried me a hundred yards. Twice through was two hundred yards. I'd reach the wood eventually. Then I'd be safe again and in the shade.

When I got to the ditch round the trees, the song immediately disappeared. I stood still, the plastic bag swinging in my hand, and listened. Such a huge silence. Heavier than anything I'd heard before, and seeping into me like rain. It wasn't really silence, though. Now I was breathing more quietly, I could tell the whole wood was watching. Holding its breath and wondering what I was going to do next. If I listened really hard, I could even hear the hiss of leaves slithering over one another, and the click of yellow eyes. I stared back at them, still not moving. Nothing here was used to people. The trees never heard about them, and neither did the birds or the foxes. All they saw was a tractor sometimes, or the combine. It made me want to kneel down and ask permission before I went any further.

That was ridiculous. I wiped my face with my free hand and ran at the ditch. The brambles on the other side were just a thin wall – I knew they would be – and when I got into the shade, the floor was clear and easy. A spongy bed of dead leaves, with a few nettle clumps, and crumbling branches I could step over. I stood still again. It was like being in church. Grey tree-pillars soaring into the darkness on either side. Was this the centre of the wood? All along, I'd thought there were bound to be edges and a middle, and the middle would be the most important bit, where I'd find the pond. But it turned out woods didn't have one centre. They had lots of centres. My giddiness came back, and mum's voice telling me to be careful. It was like that rhyme she sang in the evening sometimes:

> My mother told me
> I never should
> Play with the gypsies
> In the wood.
> If I did, she would say
> Naughty boy to disobey.

It should be 'girl', really, not 'boy' – mum always explained that she only said 'boy' because I was a boy. The meaning was the same, though. Woods had magic powers and confused people. This one would spin my head until I hadn't got a clue where I was. It would close round me and shelter me and make me sleepy with its leaf-noises. It would drop twigs on me until I was nothing but a bump in the ground. If anyone ever came looking for me, they'd think I was an old bit of tree, and walk straight on.

I sat down on a log and prodded it with my finger; the bark came away in soggy rolls. Eventually I was down to the hard middle and a red spider crawled out, bright as a pinprick. The thought of its feet on the damp wood made me thirsty again – but it was strange, I didn't have the energy to look for the pond any more. Or get the cheese out of my bag. Or move at all, come to that. It was a giant effort even looking towards the patch of brambles where I'd broken into the wood. That would be my way back, if I ever went home again.

The word 'shame' slithered into my head. It was one Mrs Lucas used when she was angry: 'You should be ashamed of yourself.' Why had I remembered that? It must be because my journey was a flop. I'd been away a couple of hours and I was already thinking of home. Pathetic. I hadn't even found the pond for my drink. If only I could do that, everything would be changed. Mum would probably be angry with me, but at least I'd be able to tell her something she didn't know.

When I did stand up again, it was like climbing out of bed. But look, after all that muddling, the ground sloped away to the left, so it was easy to know which direction was best. A pigeon fluttered my face with its wing-tip – disgusting, as if I'd been smeared with charcoal – but I shrugged it off. I was back in control of things. Totally in control, so it wasn't surprising the trees ahead of me suddenly shimmied like dancers on telly – and there was the pond after all. Just a hollow, but brimming with water. I fiddled up a stick to poke it, and made a hole in the green skin. A hole where the blackness shone like ebony, but so clear I could see all the way down to the bed of curled-up leaves. I stretched out my hand, scooping a thimble of wet. Then I drank it, tilting back my head and swallowing as slowly as possible. There was the dry coppery taste of pennies, especially when I rolled it round my mouth, tightening my lips and squeezing it between my teeth.

On the way home, I spent so much time practising what to tell mum I forgot to think what she might say to me. But when I turned into the yard and saw the white blob of her face at the kitchen window, I knew I'd made a mistake. A moment later, when she whipped open the back door, I realised it was more than a mistake. Mum's face had shrivelled up, and I could see the whole of her skull under her skin, and the pulse fluttering in the dip beside her forehead. Her eyes were red like someone staring into a flash.

'Where have you been, where have you been?' she kept saying, wrapping her arms round my head. I didn't know what to tell her. The truth sounded idiotic, and my brain wasn't working fast enough. It was still lopsided with the sun and the stubble and the wood and the red spider and the green weed. Mum wasn't interested in them anyway, I should have seen that. She wanted to know *why*. How could I explain, if she didn't know already? 'I went for a walk,' I said, mumbling into her dress. She pushed me away, keeping her arms rigid and holding me by the shoulders as if I might spin round and vanish again. Then she stared at me. Had I got a scratch? Did I need to blow my nose? No, it wasn't anything like that. I pressed my hands down on the inside of her elbows to break her grip, and squirrelled up close again. 'I'm sorry,' I told her. 'I didn't think.' I wanted it to sound like the truest thing I'd ever said, but my voice wouldn't do what I told it. It was too light, and I wasn't crying. As the words soaked into her dress, the horizon of the wood stretched out in my head, making a cloudy smudge above the stubble. The pond was still there: a black eye with a lid closing over it. I had a secret now. Nobody could take it away from me, because nobody else knew exactly what it was. Only me.

CHAPTER EIGHT

The Glass Door

I was in my listening-place at the turn of the stairs, watching a spider wrestle with a bluebottle in the window overlooking the yard. The spider had won, and was squirting tiny threads round the fly's wings, wrapping it up like a chrysalis. Then the telephone rang in the drawing room and mum's voice drifted up. Something about a swimming pool. The horses. My name. I switched from the fly and stared at the carpet, ears tingling. 'Well, it was terrifying, of course,' mum was saying, in a more bubbly voice than usual. 'I'd no idea where he was. And it lasted for hours. I thought he'd been kidnapped by gypsies or something. Worse.' There was a pause, and I could imagine her nodding, stretching the plaited brown telephone cord with her free hand. Then she burst into life again. 'I know – but it was all fine in the end. He just came wandering back into the yard. He'd got hungry – you know what boys are like. He said he'd completely lost track of time, and found some wood or other, I don't know. He was having an adventure, but it wasn't an adventure for me, not by a long chalk. Anyway, he's safe now, that's the main thing. The police were very good about it. Apparently it happens a lot.'

The police! She hadn't told me about the police. At the same time, I could see she was turning the whole thing into a joke, so no one would think she'd done anything wrong herself. I'd been silly, that was all, and now we could get on with the next thing, which was Beak coming to Sunday lunch. 'Remember he's grandpa's friend,' mum kept saying. That didn't help. It made me think when school started, Beak would ring up grandpa and gossip to him about everything I'd done wrong. Then grandpa would talk to dad, and dad would be angry as well as my teachers. 'Tell me more about Beak,' I said the evening before he came, when we were sitting round the fire in the drawing room. 'What do you want to know?' mum said in her reasonable voice. I couldn't think of anything; I just wanted to know what he was like. 'Is he married?' I said eventually. Mum glanced above my head and made a face at dad, but I couldn't understand what it meant. 'No,' she said quickly. 'He's not married. Anything else?' 'Where does he live?' Mum explained that Maidwell was a big old country house, built in a square, but there was a bit off to the side which was Beak's home. He had been there for thirty years. 'The school's been his whole life,' she said. 'I think that's marvellous. He treats all the boys as if they were his own.' Dad was on the other side of the fireplace, staring into his whisky. 'That's right,' he said. 'It's marvellous.' I couldn't understand why he said it in such a sad voice. I thought it was mum who didn't want me to go, not him.

Grandpa didn't get to Little Brewers until nearly one o'clock the next day. I was in the kitchen helping mum get the plates ready, and suddenly he was talking to dad in the hall, telling him he'd stopped on the way over and put some flowers on Andrew's grave. That was strange. Why did he think I'd died? Then I realised he was talking about great-grandpa, and mum put a hand between my shoulder-blades to show me I should go into the hall and say hello. Grandpa was still on the doorstep, a black silhouette with a couple of smaller shapes behind him. They were dark too, I couldn't see their faces, but one was a woman. I wasn't expecting that. Hadn't I been listening properly? I made it to the playroom door, and waited for them to notice me. There was a water-blob on my shirt where mum had wet the hairbrush to flatten the hair on top of my head. It always stuck up if I didn't do that.

Dad finished helping off coats while I kept still like a sentry in a sentry box. He obviously didn't want to introduce me here, and the others were waiting for the right moment, too – which was after I'd followed them into the drawing room. The woman tramped across the bare floorboards to the side table, opened the silver box where dad kept the cigarettes, clamped one between her bright jam lips, lit it, and turned to stare at me. I remembered now. This was Joanie, who mum said was grandpa's girlfriend, even if she was married to someone else. She was Beak's sister: short grey hair, thick shoes that could have been sawn-off hunting boots, and a face like a sparrowhawk. As she opened her mouth, a smoke-cloud sagged into the sunlight; that must be why she sounded so raspy. 'So you're the son and heir, are you?' It was a question but didn't sound like one, and I needed a moment to work out what she meant. There wasn't time. She grabbed my chin with her brown hand and bent my face towards the light. It was like the vet yanking the ponies' heads when he tried to see their teeth. Did she want me to open my mouth and show her? 'He's the spitting image of you, Richard,' she said loudly, without looking at dad. 'Though he's got Gilly's hair of course, lucky little sod.' She breathed more smoke at me – there was lipstick on her teeth – and pushed me towards grandpa. He made me smile by bowing as though I was a prince. He didn't mean it to be funny, but it was. Then he took me by the hand, and when he'd finished shaking it, he held on. I could smell roses on the hanky in his breast pocket. 'And this,' he said gently, still holding my hand and twisting me sideways, 'is Beak.'

Mum had got it wrong. Beak wasn't Latin. Beak was called Beak because of his nose. Not that it was like a bird's bill. More like a candle stub, when the wind blew and made a puddle of wax. Except it was purple, not white. Dark red, anyway, with thousands of tiny veins crawling all over it. And drooping, which really was like wax. Beak's nose had melted down so far, it was resting on his moustache. I knew I should stop looking at him like this, it was rude to stare, but he was putting me under his spell. To make it worse, grandpa was helping, passing him my hand as if it was a present, so Beak could hold it in his own for a moment while he gazed into my face. I kept on gazing back. His cheeks were the same Ribena colour as the nose. Bald head. Eyes sunk, and black. Moustache very thick and grey, like metal only velvety. He didn't look unkind, but he did look something. Was he embarrassed? Surely someone like him wouldn't feel shy about meeting a boy? He must have met thousands. When he said 'Hello, Andrew' there was a wet chuckle in his voice. 'Hello, sir,' I answered. 'Hello, *Beak*,' he said, still chuckling, then let go of me at last and took the glass of sherry dad was holding towards him.

I didn't see Beak again until the beginning of term, but I often floated his face into my head. It was difficult, because his red cheeks and droopy nose kept swirling like a kaleidoscope. His moustache crawled round his mouth, his black eyes sunk further and further into their sockets, his soft hand moused backwards and forwards across my palm. I wanted to like him, because then I wouldn't miss home so much. But I couldn't. He gave me the creeps, which made me feel odd about mum and dad too. They wouldn't send me to a school they didn't think was good for me; maybe grandpa was bullying them? He was paying the fees, after all.

'Where will you go for clothes?' Dad wondered, sitting round the unlit fire after supper. 'Billings and Edmonds?' 'Oh, I think so,' mum said at once, as though everyone knew it was the only place. I looked at her and frowned. 'Billings and Edmonds, darling,' she repeated more slowly. 'It's in London . . .' 'I got my clothes there when I went to Wellington,' dad interrupted. He lit another cigarette and dotted the ash into the blue glass ashtray before there was anything to shake off. 'What's that now, let me see, almost forty years ago? It's a wonderful place.' He paused to take another drag, then hurried on. 'They have everything. And there's a model of Gulliver, too. You'll love that.' I shook my head: who was Gulliver? I obviously couldn't ask dad – he thought I should know already. My heart felt as though it was shrinking, and I looked into the fireplace – at the crumpled newspaper, and the soot that had fallen down the chimney during the summer, and the pale strips of kindling. This fire would be lit when I wasn't here to see it. And that wasn't all. Going to Maidwell wasn't like a trip to granny, where I knew my way around. It was like walking into a room which led to lots of other rooms, which were all joined by secret corridors and underground tunnels. There was no path back, only forward.

On shopping day, mum and I caught the train from Bishops Stortford to Liverpool Street. It was how we always went to London – not that we did go much, only when we needed to buy something special, or grandpa took us to the Palladium at Christmas. London was dad's world, and when mum called it 'the smoke' she made me think he disappeared into a cloud like a magician as soon as he got off his train. At the same time, the name made me remember shiny things that had nothing to do with smoke. Taxis. Handrails. Black lions. Umbrellas. Piccadilly Circus. Metal steps on the escalators in the underground. I liked escalators so much, we'd been to Tottenham Court Road once or twice in the past, because mum said it had an especially long ride. We just sailed up and down for half an hour, enjoying ourselves. 'Be careful, get ready to jump,' mum said the first time. 'You don't want to end up like the boy who got his toes stuck.' 'What happened to him?' I asked, though I could guess the answer. 'The engineer people had to stop the whole thing, and pull him out.' 'Was he hurt?' 'He was definitely hurt,' mum said, sounding excited, like she did when she was telling me about the Messerschmidt pilot who'd crashed in the war. 'His toes were minced up like a rabbit in a combine.'

Mum said we didn't have time for the escalators now – there was too much else to do. 'You'll have to be brave,' she whispered, as we walked through the front door of Billings and Edmonds. 'If you start, I won't be able to stop myself.' I was pleased she said that, but I knew she was nowhere near crying. She was in her businesslike mood, dodging the other mums and grabbing one of the men so she could wave my list at him. Two pairs of grey flannel shorts, two tweed jackets, six pairs of underpants, six vests, six white shirts, a tie with special blue stripes, and a trunk – that one, green like the Daimler, and my initials to go on top, please: APM. 'Oh yes,' she added, pointing to a dark brown cardigan with leather buttons up the front. 'We'll have one of those, too.' She smiled as the assistant held it across my shoulders to make sure it would fit. 'It'll keep you warm,' she said. I grinned and left her at the counter. That way, I didn't have to see how much everything cost.

I found Gulliver. He was the same size as me, but a man – he had a grown-up face with lines – and he was lying in a big glass case. Not just lying: struggling; his suit was full of wrinkles. I bent towards the glass, watching him come and go as my breath made clouds. No wonder he was unhappy. Dozens of tiny people were scurrying over his body; they were like greenfly on a rose, except they were tying him down with white cotton. More like spiders than flies. And it was amazing how many there had to be, to keep him still. Even with dozens of them, it still looked as though he might get fed up any minute now and shake them off. I held my breath so I could see them clearly for a longer stretch, and when I ran out of puff a man was staring at me through the other side of the case. An old man, with a face like a walrus. He was rubbing his hands together and talking to me: how much had I missed already? 'And that's when he came into the shop,' he was saying. 'Ever such a long time ago. Now all the boys look at him and remember, like you will. You'll always think of today when you put on your clothes, and see him lying there.' I stared back at the man, not knowing what to say. Did he work here, was that why he was wearing a smart suit? Or had he wandered in? I twisted round to see where mum had got to, but she was busy paying. When I turned back again, the man was still crouching beyond the case with his hands on his knees. The light sliding over the glass made everything blur, and he didn't look like a walrus any more. He looked like Beak. Or like a mixture of Beak and Joanie. A man's face turning into a woman's. Lipstick melting into a grey moustache. Face powder and wriggly veins.

I didn't tell mum – the man was too difficult to explain. Anyway, we were feeling quiet when we got back to the train, and didn't say much on the way home. I wasn't tired, exactly. It was more that I wanted to keep thinking, even though thinking made me unhappy. It was the same all next week, right the way through to the last supper when mum said I could have anything I liked, and we chose bangers and mash. Neither of us wanted to make a fuss, but after prayers mum sat on the edge of my bed for longer than usual. I was hoping she wouldn't say anything about Maidwell – I didn't want it to be real and tomorrow. But we'd talked about everything else at supper, and now we'd run out. 'Are you dreading it?' she asked, with her back straight and her hands in her lap. I wished she hadn't said it like that. 'Dread' was a word we only used when things were deadly serious. I swallowed to keep my voice steady. 'Not dreading it, mum. I don't know what it will be like.' She touched my face, then pushed the hair out of my eyes; the ends of her fingers were wet. 'It's six weeks until half-term,' she said. 'That's forty-two days, forty-one not counting today.' I grabbed her hand and held it, so she wouldn't stop talking, but she did. In the silence, I felt my skin tightening. It was because all the things I wanted to say were saved up inside me like water behind a dam. If I said one of them, the dam would burst and I'd never be able to control them. Mum understood this, though. She let out her breath very slowly, using it to cover my face like a cloth when I had a temperature. 'Can I have my hand back now?' she said eventually. I laughed, but there was something stuck in my throat. 'No,' I said, and let go. She got to her feet at once, and when she sidestepped onto the bright land-ing it looked as though the light was solid, like a sheet, so she dis-appeared as soon as she reached it.

Next day the journey took three hours – mum had warned me about that. It was the Daimler, too, because dad said it would be easier. 'Do we have to?' I heard mum hiss in the hall, when they thought I wasn't listening. 'Have to what?' dad said. 'Can't we take the Hillman? If we go in the Daimler he'll be sick as a cat.' 'Of course not,' dad said. 'The Daimler's ideal. We'll get there in half the time.' They both sounded annoyed, and I didn't want mum to go on. I already felt sick; dad's car wouldn't make things any worse. 'Well, don't blame me,' mum said, and banged the door behind her as she went out to the yard. After a moment's hush dad called out to me in his holiday voice. 'Are you there, old boy? We're ready for the off.'

It was almost dark when we got to Northamptonshire, and by then the road was more like a lane, swooping up and down between stone walls. We'd had to stop twice for me to be sick, and I could tell mum was feeling queasy as well; she hadn't said any-thing for miles. Her left hand was gripping the door handle, and her right was clenched on the little leather arm-rest between her and dad. Then suddenly she was speaking again. 'Here. Here.' The map crinkled against the dashboard, and she went on angrily.

'Why do they put the bloody lights in such a stupid bloody place? They're almost on the floor. Do they think we've got eyes in our feet?' Dad laughed, but he knew she wasn't joking. 'Here, what?' he said. 'We're *here*,' mum told him, as a village sign floated past my window: MAIDWELL. There was time to see the little studs glittering like cat's-eyes in the letters as dad slowed down. Then he swung right and the Daimler juddered across a cattle grid. 'Wasn't expecting that. Think you're going to escape, do they?' Mum unclenched her hand and laid it on his arm, shooshing him. She didn't want me to notice, but I saw when I leaned forward and stuck my head between them. 'Very smart,' dad was saying, meaning the driveway. Mum and I said nothing, but shaded our eyes and bent closer to our side windows. Dark branches – yew, probably – then a wide lawn with a cedar tree in the middle. 'That'll be good for climbing,' dad went on, but again I said nothing. I could see the house now: rust-coloured, four stories, with windows in the roof and towers at the corners. The towers were like a castle, only too small, and they had pale green roofs. That was all I could see. That, and the lights in every window on every floor. Had they done that on purpose, to make us feel welcome? On second thoughts, it wasn't welcoming. In the windows on the bottom floor I could see dark rows of desks, and one or two boys wandering up and down like goblins.

Round the front of the house, where the drive ended, we found a patch of grass and a man standing on one leg. He wasn't wearing any clothes, just a hat with wings. But I didn't look for long – there was too much else to see. The other cars, for instance, and boys hauling trunks out of boots, and mums powdering their noses in driving mirrors, and dads standing on tiptoe by open doors, stretching their arms above their heads. 'Well, you're taller than him,' dad said, parking by the statue with the hat, and nodding towards a slug-boy oozing from the back seat of a Van den Plas. 'Don't stare, Richard,' mum said, but it was too late, the boy had seen us, and flinched away because he knew what we were thinking. 'Poor chap,' she went on. 'How awful for him. I wonder whether he'll be in your dorm . . .' A gaggle appeared from the twilight, clapping the slug-boy on the back. 'Oh, I see,' mum said, suddenly sounding like granny. 'That's good. He's got *some* friends, at least.'

I was still only half paying attention. Dad was right – it was a relief to know there was someone smaller than me. Probably quite a few people, actually. And he'd been right to bring the Daimler, too. It was nicer than most of these old bangers, though there was a Rolls the other side of the statue, with a tall blonde woman leaning against the bonnet, gazing at her nails. 'We know who gets the prettiest girl prize, don't we?' dad said, leaning round and grinning at me. 'It's mum, isn't it?' I grinned back, but before I could say anything, he widened his eyes and reached to pat me on the knee. We had to get on with it. If we sat there any longer, things would get worse. So I slithered across my seat and climbed out his side. When we'd got the trunk ready and were waiting for mum to join us, I glanced into the passenger window and saw she was crying. I jerked away, then towards her again. She looked underwater. Her hand was moving slowly up to her cheek, and her mouth was open as though bubbles were trickling from her lips. Dad put his hand on my shoulder. Was he holding me back, or showing me I should open the door and help? I stood still and watched.

'I'm afraid poor mum is rather upset,' dad said softly, as though he was letting me into a secret. His hand was on my shoulder now, patting me again. It was like the way he stroked his horse when he was riding. He said it made things peaceful. It made me peaceful, too. Sleepy, even. This wasn't my hand opening the car door. It wasn't my voice telling mum she mustn't worry, I was fine. These weren't my new black indoor-shoes slipping on the gravel because they had leather soles and we'd forgotten to scratch them to make them grip. This wasn't me helping dad cart the trunk towards the glass front door. These weren't mum's steps hurrying after.

We were in a long hall – panelled walls, yellow wood floor. And there were boys everywhere, walking in groups, or running and sliding then strolling again if they thought a grown-up was watching. They looked like little men in their tweed jackets, and one of them – dark-haired, with freckles across his nose – stepped straight up to me as if I'd asked him a question and he was going to answer it. He tapped me on the chest and said 'You'll have to hand that in.' 'What?' I said, baffled. 'That cardigan,' he said. 'It's got buttons. Only prefects can wear cardigans with buttons. You might as well take it off and give it to your parents now.' I saw a flash behind my eyes. This was the cardigan mum had bought as a treat, before I'd seen Gulliver. I looked round at her – was she going to tell the boy to mind his own business? She raised her hand, and for a second I thought she might be about to swat him like a fly. But no. Her hand went on lifting, until she was rubbing the frown between her eyes. As the boy wandered away she shrugged. There was nothing she could do, even though she was mum.

Then she changed tack, suddenly twisting her head to and fro, looking for Beak. She needn't have bothered. I'd found him already – by the stairs, with parents mobbing round him. It meant I'd only seen him in bits and pieces so far, but I knew he wasn't the same man who'd come to lunch. He was bigger and harder, as though all his wax had stiffened, and his black eyes fidgeted away from people as they talked to him, flickering over the boys in the hall. He was probably checking to see if anyone was unhappy. The dark red tip of his tongue kept appearing like a lizard's, licking the edge of his moustache. It made him look as though he was eating flies.

He noticed us and pushed a way through, shaking mum and dad by the hand. That was good. It was what they'd told me: he was grandpa's friend. I folded my arms across my chest so he wouldn't see the knobbly buttons on my cardigan. Then it was bad again. Beak was talking quickly to mum, darting his wet eyes sideways every few words. He was saying it would be best if they went away at once, because there was lots for me to do this evening, I needed to settle in, and anyway they must be exhausted after such a long drive, and wouldn't they want to get some dinner somewhere on the way home, and not do the whole three hours in one stretch? It made me breathless, listening, and it was stupid, too. He must know I could hear him. Why was he talking as if I didn't exist?

It made a mess of my plans. All the way in the car, I'd broken the journey into miles, and half miles, and quarter miles, and hundreds of yards, and inches. That way, I still had ages with mum and dad, if we took the trunk upstairs to my dormitory together, and unpacked it together, then came downstairs together and said goodbye. I could make every second feel like an hour. But Beak had decided we were at the end. As the thought sank in, my neck suddenly felt floppy and I stared at the floor. There was an orange Spangles wrapper stuck between the boards; how had the cleaners missed that? It must have been there all summer.

I looked up again and concentrated on dad. Surely he'd say we had to unpack together? He was still dad, after all. I looked up at his hand, and saw his fingers closing round his thumb, like they always did when he felt nervous. 'All right then, Oliver,' he was saying, in a voice that might have come from the ceiling, it felt so far above me. 'If that's what you think. But Gilly did want to see where he was going to sleep.' 'Do that at half-term,' Beak said. 'He'll be more used to things by then. It's all for the best, believe me.' I turned to mum, wondering whether she'd sound so far away too. She didn't sound anything. She just cleared her throat and stared at some boys trudging round the far end of the hall. She was going to cry again – I could see the swimminess in her eyes, and that meant I knew what to do. I had to help her. Immediately. I unfolded my arms and went to hug dad, gripping him tight round the waist. He swayed a little, and his hands landed heavily on my shoulders, getting ready to push me away if I made a fuss. I breathed in the cigarette smell from his tweed and let him go. Then I turned to mum, quickly, so dad could see I wasn't going to kiss him. He wouldn't want me to do that here. Mum would, though, on the cheek. I stood on tiptoe, and as our faces bumped, her hair slid across my eyes, shutting out the light in the hall. She was saying something I couldn't hear. What was it? She'd already stepped back, and now the light was glaring again.

Then mum tapped me on the tip of my nose with her finger and it was brilliant, like a magician sending me to sleep. After that, she caught hold of dad's sleeve and they moved away. It's done, I thought. I'm on the other side of saying goodbye. But as the glass door closed behind them, mum peeped over her shoulder. She was really crying hard now, so when she tried to blow me a kiss her lips crumpled, and wouldn't make the right shape. Dad's arm was stretched across her shoulder, and there were wrinkles in his elbow like Gulliver. Was he pushing her forward? He didn't need to do that. She never stopped walking, not even when she turned round to look at me for the last time, as their footsteps started to crunch over the gravel.

CHAPTER NINE

Running and Sliding

Beak swung at a white-haired boy glowing through the hall: 'Will you *please* give a *hand* getting this *trunk* upstairs *immediately*?' Now mum and dad were gone, he already had a different voice, which was dozy and bossy at the same time. On the other hand, perhaps there was something wrong with the boy, and he could only understand if people slowed down when they spoke to him. Really, his hair was very white, and he didn't have any eyelashes either. He looked like one of Beauty's puppies, even though he was probably about ten, three years older than me. It made me feel I had to make a special effort, so when he finished saying 'Yes, Beak, of course, Beak', and grabbed one end of my trunk, I gave him a big smile. He ignored it. Eventually, as we were scuffing upstairs, I tried talking. 'Are you my nanny?' I knew about nannies: mum had said every new boy got one to show them the ropes. The boy sneered at me; there wasn't anything wrong with him after all. 'God no,' he said. 'I don't do nannying. That'll be some stig or other.' We were on the upstairs corridor now – blue lino with a metal clamp along both edges, and shiny white doors stretching the whole length of the house. 'You're in Blue,' he went on. 'That's where newbugs usually go. In here.' He knocked a door handle with his elbow and we lurched sideways, the wooden band of my trunk grazing the paint. I looked around for a moment. Blue walls, of course, but darker than I expected, so they looked freezing. Eight beds. Folding chairs. Bare floorboards. One chest of drawers – no, another behind the door. Long windows with leaves scrabbling against the glass. There must be Virginia creeper on the front of the house, like at home. I hadn't noticed when we were outside.

Seeing the beds made me feel tired. 'Dead beat,' mum would have said. I couldn't ask the boy what time we had lights out; he'd think I was stupid. So I stood still in the middle of the room as he turned on his heel and left. Dad's voice came into my head. 'Don't worry,' he was saying. 'You'll work things out for yourself. It's all common sense, really.' And suddenly I saw what he meant. As the boy ran off down the corridor, I heard him slithering into a long skid when he reached the head of the stairs. Running and sliding. I'd seen it in the hall, earlier, and it explained why all the nail-heads in the floor were worn-down and shiny. It was a Maidwell habit. Like having your name on the end of your bed. There was mine now, halfway along the wall to my right and under a picture, a copy, which showed some people sitting on a riverbank in the sun. Then I looked down at the piece of crinkly paper, glued above the pillow. 'Motion I,' it said. Why 'I'? Did I have a second bed somewhere else? Another boy's face popped up in the far corner of the room, before I had a chance to think straight again. This one had red clown-blobs on his cheeks; that must be because he was kneeling to unpack his trunk, and all the blood had rushed to his head. 'Are you a newbug?' I asked, hoping I'd got the right word. 'God no,' he said grumpily, sounding just like the first boy. 'You must be, though, or you wouldn't ask.' 'I was wondering why it said "Motion I" on my bed,' I told him, trying to sound as polite as possible. 'You've got a bro, haven't you?' the clown-boy answered. 'Yes, Kit,' I said, but that wasn't right either. 'I didn't ask you his *name*, for God's sake,' he groaned. 'I just asked whether you'd *got* a bro, that's all. Don't be nervy.' Nervy? What did that mean? 'I'm sorry,' I said. 'I didn't mean to be nervy.' The boy nodded. 'It's all right,' he said, suddenly kinder. 'It works like this. If you've got a younger bro, then you're Motion I and he'll be Motion II, even though he's not here yet. If you had two brothers, the third would be Motion III, but that doesn't happen very often.' I thanked him, and started to walk my trunk to my bedside, waggling the ends from side to side. I half-thought that now we were friends he might come and help, but I couldn't hear him making a move. I turned to look, then shied away. The boy wasn't unpacking any more. He was crying; his shoulders were shaking, and he was dabbing his cheeks with the back of his hand. This was much worse than seeing him angry.

'What's your name?' I asked, laying my trunk down flat as though I hadn't noticed a thing. 'Sims,' he said, with a watery quiver in his voice. 'Just Sims?' I said, keeping my own voice steady. 'No I or II?' He didn't answer.

It got easier when I realised my name wasn't only on my bed but all over the place, like clues in a treasure hunt. On the cupboard where I put my clothes – though the drawer wouldn't shut afterwards because of my cardigan, which I'd hidden at the bottom. Then in the bathroom along the corridor, by the peg where I hung my towel and we brushed our teeth: 'Motion I', in the same wriggly biro. But I'd been wrong, thinking this was a treasure trail. It was more like something in the Bible, where God knew exactly what was going to happen ahead of time. Here was my name again, on the mug for my toothpaste, inside a special plastic label. I washed the mug carefully under the tap, scraping off the white goo round the rim, and filled it. The water tasted of pennies. At home it tasted of chalk.

I turned to the wall and put on my pyjamas, then lay in bed watching the other boys when I thought they weren't looking at me. There were only seven of them but they felt like seventy. A skinny one with a narrow face: the ridge of his nose showed white through the skin. An older boy who was the prefect in charge: he had a double-barrelled name so the paper stuck to his bed was twice as long as anyone else's. Then Sims. He wasn't crying any more, but he was holding his teddy bear. And a tiny newbug – much smaller than me – with a Scottish accent: his bed said he was Mackay. He was shaky; I'd seen his knee tapping the inside of his trouser leg when we were changing into our pyjamas. What were we all doing, I wanted to ask. But no one else was talking, and I couldn't be the one to start. Maybe there was a rule. Or perhaps everyone was tired, like me. So tired I wasn't even homesick at the moment. I just wanted this bit of the day over, then I could fall asleep. Tomorrow everything would be better. I wouldn't have to work out how to take off my clothes without everyone seeing. Or what time Beak would come round, now we were ready. The sheets were tucked in so tight I felt like a sausage in a sandwich, but at least my feet were warm. Mum had worried about that – about me getting flu because the school was going to be cold. But what about her? Was she home yet? I could see the dogs in their basket by the Aga, lifting their ears whenever a car went by in the lane. Mum would be telling dad they had to hurry, Wiggy would be popping.

Then I couldn't think about her any more; that little bit was enough. Instead, I slid my hand under my pillow and searched. When I'd unpacked my truck, I'd put my Bible there, the new one mum had given me for going away. There it was – so soft, the heat from my head must have already melted through the pillow. I squeezed it, and the leather felt like a hand. I'd do that every night, I decided. It would be a routine, like running and sliding, and maybe God would travel up my arm and get into my brain, to help me with my work. That was a good idea, but it would be easier if I was lying on my front. When I was over on my back like this, I'd be bound to get pins and needles.

I had to stop, because Beak was in the doorway, wearing the same green whiskery suit as before, but with slippers now. Red leather ones, like dad's except older, with the heels trodden flat so he shuffled when he came to stand by each of our beds in turn. I tried not to look at his nose or his moustache, and concentrate on what he was saying. Was I happy? Yes, Beak. Had I got all my things sorted out? Yes, Beak. Was I looking forward to the term? Yes, Beak. I wouldn't talk after he'd gone, would I? No, Beak. I waited a moment, wondering whether he was about to mention grandpa and hoping he wouldn't. Otherwise I'd have to explain to everyone. But it was OK. He nodded then slithered on to the next boy. After that, the lights were out and I could hear him next door in Camel, asking the same questions.

That didn't matter. What mattered was darkness, prickly and heavy like a blanket. I wanted to pull it down over me, but that was another impossible thing – there were too many other people, even if I couldn't see them. At home, Kit was usually asleep by the time I went to bed; I couldn't even hear him breathing, he lay so still. I knew he was there because I could smell him: a milk-about-to-boil-over smell – he'd had it ever since I could remember. There was nothing like that now. Tonight there were boys sniffing, boys scratching, boys scuffling like mice, boys burrowing. Why had Beak bothered to tell us not to talk? We wanted to think and remember – that was all. I closed my eyes and waited for mum and dad to rise towards me like divers from the bottom of the sea. Were they home yet? Nearly: Dad's face was glowing in the lights from the dashboard, but at least mum had stopped crying. In fact she was chatting – about me, and what she was going to do tomorrow. The last few miles whispered past her window, then the car came alongside Little Brewers and swung left into the lane. They were safe. Now I could fall asleep, not minding if the noises went on around me. What was it mum had said? 'Get yourself orientated.' I hadn't heard that word before, but it was easy to see what it meant. I'd do that in the morning.

Next day, when I started looking round properly, getting orientated turned out to be difficult. Everything was equal – either equally important or equally pointless, I wasn't sure. The house, first. It was only a hundred years old but looked more, with its towers and its creeper and its green roof. The classrooms were squeezed up one end, and divided by screens which could be folded shut or opened, depending on the number of boys in a form. The desks were all the same; they were what dad called 'a job lot', with the writing bit joined to the seat by two metal S's. There was a drawer under the lid, where we kept our books, and a white china inkwell in the right hand corner, which only masters were allowed to fill in case we made a spillage. Either people had broken the rules a lot, or the masters were clumsy, because there was ink everywhere. Dots and dashes on the floorboards, doodles on the panelled walls, and tattoos where the names of boys had been gouged into the desktops and coloured. There was always ink on our hands, as well – a deep blue birthmark inside my index finger that only came off when I rubbed it with pumice. And ink on my tongue, with a dry metal taste like the water. It got there because I sucked my nib to make it work properly – everyone did that. It was the nib I collected from a store cupboard Beak opened after lunch, where I could also get sello and blotch. Then, if I had any weekly allowance left, I could get tuck; Sherbet Fountains tasted best, but wine gums lasted longer and they could be traded.

That was one half of the ground floor: the work part. The other half, across the big hall, was for everything else we did in the day-time. First came the library, but nobody went there much because there weren't many books that looked interesting. Only old stories with tiny print and mossy covers, which were usually lying on their sides because the shelves were half-empty. And opposite the library, the dining room. We had sixty-two boys in the school, which I knew because this was where I counted them – juniors at little tables round the edges, and seniors at two big trestles which ran up the middle. Every day, three times a day, we knew exactly where we were in the pecking order – which was another of dad's phrases. But that didn't mean all meals felt the same. At breakfast we hardly spoke, because we were waiting for Mr Thwaites to drown us out. He was the deputy head, and at eight o'clock he yanked round in his chair, switched on the heavy black wireless that stood on the shelf behind him, and turned up the news full blast. The same names kept whistling towards me – Sir Alec Dou-glas-Home, Mr Macmillan, Mr Wilson, Mr Brown, Mrs Castle – but I didn't know who they were so I didn't listen. I just hid in their voices. At lunch and supper we had no wireless and everyone felt more chatty, which meant eating was more fun. Sometimes the racket got so bad, a master had to bang on the table with his spoon, then shout out a boy's name and put him on silence for five min-utes. I didn't mind when that happened to me. It gave me time to think what I was going to say next.

The masters told us Annie the cook was an angel, but she didn't look like one, so far as I could see. Boys weren't allowed into her kitchen, which was across the corridor, and when she stood in the doorway she seemed more like a smoke-puff than anything else – always dissolving into the steam curling from the huge shiny caul-dron behind her. Anyway, she could have been a whole army of angels: her food was still disgusting. It was carried to our tables on grubby wooden trays by a man with slicked-back hair and a short white coat, Mr Honey. Some boys thought he wore make-up like a woman, but I could never be sure. The lines round his eyes were very dark, though that might have been his lashes. Anyway, we liked his name and we liked him too, because he helped us when the food we hadn't eaten at one meal was brought back for us to finish at the next. He must have known it was foul, which was why he never said anything when he saw us hiding especially repellent things in our pockets, so we could chuck them away later in the grounds. Butter beans. Gluey mash. Meat-slabs with gristle like squashed binder twine. He even emptied food from the drawers in the dining tables, if we managed to dump it there without being seen. And once he scraped some smelly butter off the ceiling, which a boy had flicked up with his knife. The smear-mark stayed for years, shaped like a bird's wing. Mr Honey must have used a feather duster to whisk it off.

Beyond the dining room the corridor got darker: this was where the masters had their Common Room, behind a heavy chipped door with a roll of tobacco smoke lying along the bottom edge. It looked like the entrance to the cave where Merlin disappeared, but wasn't as safe as that. The door might swirl open at any moment, and someone would ask us what we were doing – so the thing was, to pass as quietly as possible, as if we were really keen to reach the changing rooms. This bit of the house was modern, and must have been built when Beak started the school: it had bricks which crumbled when I poked them, metal window frames, radiators miles apart, and a skiddy red tile floor.

Before the changing rooms: the loos, which were called the Rears. First there was a long line of stand-ups where we peed, and which hissed like granny's pug, then came a much longer row of green wooden cabins. 'What do you mean, "cabins"?' mum asked, when I told her about them later. 'Do you mean like bathing huts?' I didn't know what a bathing hut was, but I could guess and said 'Yes', which made her smile. Then she stopped smiling, and started shaking her head, when I told her the walls of the cabins didn't reach the floor or the ceiling, and the doors didn't have locks. 'What do you do, then?' she asked. 'What happens if someone else barges in?' 'They can't,' I said. 'You sit on the loo and lean forward, with one hand against the door.' 'What, all the time you're in there?' 'Yes, all the time,' I said, and changed the subject. I didn't want to tell her any more about the Rears. Not about the smell, which was a mixture of sick and drains. And not about how we had to line up outside the cabins after breakfast, then got waved inside by a prefect when a place was empty. Sometimes boys forgot to leave their doors open after they'd finished, which meant a loo might not have someone inside even though it looked full. To stop this happening, the prefect walked up and down the cabins all the time, sticking his foot under each door in turn and shouting 'In?' Whoever was there had to answer by saying their name. If we didn't say anything, or mumbled, then the prefect kicked the door open and everyone could see us with our trousers round our ankles. It was horrible, but nothing compared to what might happen next. When we couldn't go to the loo for two days in a row, we had to own up, then see the Matron, Miss Gibbon, who gave us a Senokot. If this didn't work, she took us into her surgery and told us we had to have an enema. I'd never heard this word before, but Sims said you had to take down your trousers and pants, then lie on Matron's table so she could stick a rubber tube up your bum and pour soapy water into it. It sounded so disgusting I didn't believe him. But I never dreamed of lying to Miss Gibbon. Nobody did. That meant she gave me an enema once or twice every term – along with most other people.

After the Rears the corridor got brighter again as it ran towards the changing rooms. These stank too, but not so bad. Socks and wet wool, with dubbin or cricket-bat oil mixed in, depending on the time of year. Next door was the shower room, which kept dissolving in blasts of drizzly wet that smelled like fresh air, but turned out to be sticky when it drifted over our faces and hands. The layout meant we had to spend a lot of time paddling about in the nude: undressing by our pegs, then taking our towels to another row of hooks near the water, then nipping across the duckboards to wait in line for our turn, then slipping into the showers at last and washing ourselves, then hopping back to the towels, then drying, then finding our clothes again. Most people faced the wall as much as possible, and didn't look anyone in the eye, but nobody actually said they were embarrassed. I couldn't tell what I felt. I wanted it all over and done with, but I remembered dad saying country people didn't mind this sort of thing. It was like seeing cows climbing on top of each other in fields. Natural. Some boys obviously didn't think so – the ones who bent double and kept their hands shoved between their legs. I thought they were silly, but I felt sorry for them too. Especially when the master in charge told them to walk slowly, and keep their hands by their sides, which usually made them burst into tears. Then again, the showers were a good place for crying. No one could tell the difference between tears and water, and you could always say you'd got soap in your eyes if anyone asked why they looked puffy.

I'd never had a shower before Maidwell, only baths. Baths were upstairs, though, and we weren't allowed to go there until we'd finished our prep and it was bedtime. We used the back way unless we were prefects, which was narrow and dark, and meant we missed seeing the pictures Beak had put on the main stairs, where parents could notice them. These were like the ones we had in our dorms – copies of famous paintings. I couldn't believe Beak had actually paid for them, but I realised they were part of a plan. If anyone complained that he was mean and didn't want us to have anything nice, he could always say: what about the pictures? Don't they prove how much I care? It made me want to ignore them, but I couldn't help myself. They were too interesting, and not like anything we had at home. The slobby-looking man in a flower-pot hat and bumbags, for instance, who was on the wall above my bed in Blue. Although he was sitting beside a river, there were factories in the distance. Maybe he worked there, and was on holiday? It felt like Sunday when I looked at him. Sunday was the best day in the week because there were no lessons, only church; that's why the man looked so relaxed.

Even better was the big picture on the main stairs, which I could see if I hung over the top banister. It was Palm Sunday, and Jesus was arriving in Jerusalem on his donkey. When Beak found me staring at it one day, I thought he was going to tick me off. But he leaned forward and put his elbows on the handrail, so he was down at my level. Then he told me the painter had put portraits of his friends in the crowd – this one gazing seriously at the ground was the poet William Wordsworth, and this red-faced one, side on, was John Keats who had died young and was marvellous. 'Marvellous how?' I wondered. 'Because he wrote such beautiful poetry,' Beak said, 'And had such an unhappy life.' I nodded, and turned to another, smaller picture that hung close by. I liked this one as well, even though it was black and white. It showed some frightening men sitting behind a table, and there was a boy standing on a footstool in the middle of the room. The boy looked rather like me: his hair was longer but the same yellow. Beak said the men were asking the boy to sneak on his dad, who was the king, Charles I. If I looked closer I'd see the title across the bottom: *And When Did You Last See Your Father?* I thanked Beak, and took the question away with me, then remembered it after lights-out, when I thought about my own dad coming back from work. I saw him parking the car in the drive-through under the swallows' nests, as mum called out to him from the kitchen, 'Is that you, darling?' She always said that, even though she knew the answer perfectly well.

Beak reckoned upstairs was for calming down. That's why he had pictures here, and why he didn't allow running and sliding on the lino. We knew better. Upstairs was really the place for feeling sad. The colours of the dorms, for instance – Blue and Camel and Mauve and Green: they reminded us of whatever colours we had in our rooms at home. Colours which were nicer, and which we'd chosen ourselves. All the same, I didn't hear boys crying in their beds so often, once the first few weeks of term were over. But there was still a struggling sound, and I knew what it was, even though it was difficult to explain. It was the sound of boys thinking about time, which is what I always did myself, as soon as the lights went out. Counting the days until the end of the week, or half-term, or the end of term. Hurrying up the clock. Wishing it was the last day. Rolling my head to and fro across the pillows, kicking the sheets so even the hospital corners came undone. When I closed my eyes at last, a few more minutes had gone west.

Time went faster outside, so I decided to make the grounds into a circle, like at home. Mum had always said the Maidwell gardens were Beak's pride and joy, which meant I kept seeing his face in tree trunks, and the creepy orchids he liked so much. The grounds were big, though, that was the thing. I could get lost in them. It meant slipping out through the side door in the changing rooms and across the yard where Shep the boiler-man threw out his clinkers to make a hard surface. There was a tall yew hedge straight ahead, hiding the rose garden, but I didn't want that. It was too near the house. I was heading for the back drive, which curved past the village church and ended in the wood everyone called the Wilderness. Yew trees, mainly, with branches like enormous hat-feathers, and poisonous red berries that were always trying to plop into my mouth. And there were paths. Rabbit paths. Secret paths. Boy paths. Main paths. Some joined the little clearings people had made over the years. Some just wandered off into mounds of dead leaves and stick-piles. But it didn't make any difference. The light was always the same dim green, so it was like walking on the seabed, surrounded by sunken wrecks and the skeletons of sailors who had fallen overboard. The branches were nearly black, with blood-streaks on them, and sore little weeping-spots. I pushed inwards, where the sky faded almost to nothing. This is where boys had dug their huts – dozens of them, going back ages. Maybe I'd have my own one day. I'd organise a gang with other boys and we'd dig a hole in the ground as big as a room. It would be difficult because of the roots, which were everywhere, like white veins. Then we'd put planks on top, and pile the earth back. And we'd leave an entrance hole, but narrow, so masters couldn't see us. They wouldn't even know if I started smoking pine needles rolled up in pieces of Bronco loo-paper, like some of the older boys. The footsteps would just bounce on the planks overhead, then disappear because I was invisible.

Where the Wilderness was widest, the yew trees made space for a bamboo clump, which had a space in the middle where I could put back my head and watch the sky as if I was staring up through a funnel. This was a hideaway too, but it wasn't as safe as the huts, and Lety said there was a bad atmosphere. We all knew why. It was where Beak cut the canes he used to beat us with – green whippy ones if he wanted to give an extra sting; thick paler ones for a whack like the kind you might give to a carpet. I felt slightly mad whenever I stood inside the clumps, as though I was daring the canes to hurt me. Besides, they were always tapping and rustling, which made it difficult to tell if anyone was coming. Or was someone watching from nearby in the carpentry shed? This shed must have been a barn in the old days; now it was where we disappeared once a week to learn how to saw wood in a straight line, and how to hammer nails without bending them. The idea was, one day we'd make something useful to take home to our parents, but none of us were any good. I made a tray once, then spoiled it by covering the bottom with what was meant to be a picture of mum's horse, Serenade. Mum said she was pleased, but she put it under the Teasmade on her side of the bed, so the machine covered it and no one could see I'd made it for her.

Beyond the shed wasn't the Wilderness any more, just a line of trees dividing the grounds from the main road. We weren't allowed to go onto this road – it was one of the strictest rules – and so far as I knew only one boy had ever done more than gaze over the wall. He came back with a story about strange paint-marks he'd found on the pavement by the back gate. They'd been put there by the police, he said, to show where they'd found a dead body. A hitchhiker, probably a woman. She'd been murdered by a stranger who'd given her a lift, then flung her out of the car while it was still moving. We wanted to know why he was so sure about the paint, and the boy said he'd seen a programme on telly in the holidays. Oh? we said. Yes, he went on. When the police took a body away after a murder, they drew its shape on the carpet to help them with their inquiries. It was like that, only it was the pavement this time, obviously, and not indoors, and the paint was blue and yellow, not white. Rather like the paint used by the Gas Board, but not the Gas Board.

This part of the grounds didn't have a name; it was the furthest point from the house, and no one came here much. There was a

Wellingtonia, which had a gingery trunk that looked hard but turned out to be soft when I punched it. It made me wonder: if the bark was so spongy, wouldn't the studs on my football boots stick into it? And did that mean I might be able to run up it like Spiderman, sticking out at a right-angle? It was better to think about that than try it – I might fall off and squash one of Beak's orchids. This was mainly where he grew them, though they took some finding. Purple petals struggling through tangles of wet grass. White ones, freckled like birds' eggs. Leaves as big and flabby as a dog's tongue, only green. And such thin stalks, even looking at them made me want to break one. But I never did that, and I liked it when I was a bit older and Beak talked about them when he came round my dorm in the evening. Mum was right, they were his 'pride and joy', but that wasn't the whole story. When Beak said their names, his voice got deeper, as though he was talking about people who were dead or lived a long way away. 'Creeping Ladies Tresses'. 'Twyblade'. 'Marsh Helleborine'. 'Frog Orchid'. 'They're his children,' Waggoner said once after lights-out one night – straight out bang like that in the darkness. No one answered, but it explained why I thought about Beak so clearly when I looked at the flowers. They were a part of him. Actually bits of his body. Spindly and peculiar, as though he'd grown them inside his hairy tweed suit.

The path ended by the front gate, where dad had made his joke about escaping. We could see the road home from here, and there were usually one or two boys hanging around with their hands in their pockets, treading on the bars of the cattle grid as though testing to see how hot they were. I thought that was a mistake, and always left them to it, turning back towards the house and the games pitches. We played here every afternoon: rugger in winter, football in spring, cricket and athletics in summer. It was hard to tell how much anyone minded about games. The goalposts and the lumpy grass, then the white lines and the cracks round the cricket crease: they were no joke. Nor were the masters, bellowing when we made a mistake, or cheering when we did well. But whatever anyone said, Maidwell usually lost. I thought it might have something to do with the school colours being yellow. Yellow was the

colour of cowardice, like custard. Cowardy cowardy custard. That's
what Bilton Grange and the other schools chanted from the touchline when we played against them. Why on earth had Beak chosen
yellow? Did he *want* us to lose?

When it snowed or there were floods, we were let off games and
played Subs and Cruisers instead. Cruisers were meant to protect
boys as they trotted round the grounds in convoys, and Subs were
submarines, which meant lurking in a bush, then rushing out as
the convoy went past. More like a wolf than a submarine I thought,
but it came to the same thing. If a Sub tapped someone on the
shoulder they had to go back to the beginning of their run and
start again. It was like what happened with food, and fine for people who could run quickly. But if you were fat and slow like Bishop II, who looked like a seal, you were always going back to the
beginning, and soon got exhausted. You might not even have
reached the lake by the time the whistle went, and the lake was the
best bit.

It lay beyond the games fields – an acre or so, which had been
dug out when the house was built. The banks must have been clear
curves once, or even straight lines; now they were blurred by roots
dangling into the water. They looked puffy, and so did the willow
branches rotting into the shallows, and the iris-jungles, and the
black mudbanks, and the birds' nests crumbling on crocodile-
branches. The birds were moorhens, mainly – though there were
coots and swans and two grebes as well. I'd recognised the grebes
from my *Observer's Book*, and I could hear them at night, fighting
with their metal voices while I was falling asleep. I thought: boys
here must always have heard that, and it made me like the place a
bit more. Sometimes I even pretended Maidwell was home. Here I
was, striding downhill from the games fields, past the statue on
one leg, under the low branch of the smaller cedar tree. What was
it mum used to say? 'Monarch of all he surveys.'

Then I came to the stepping stones. They must have been neat
brick-piles once, with paving slabs on top. Now they were rotten
teeth, and some wobbled so badly I had to make myself light in case
they gave way completely. I couldn't do without them, though – not

if I wanted to reach the middle of the lake, where the stepping stones ended and someone years ago had propped an elm plank, wrinkled like elephant skin. It was my favourite place in the garden, because when I sat here, lowering my feet slowly until the water came right up to the top of my boots, I was completely hidden.

The rules said only prefects were allowed on the stepping stones, but no one minded as long as I didn't fall in. When I was close to leaving Maidwell, I worked out that in five years I must have spent almost a month sitting alone on the plank in the middle of the lake. It wasn't only that I liked being secret. The whole point about the stepping stones was they were somewhere else, not nowhere. What sort of place, I couldn't say, exactly. I just felt closer to the things around me. I could stare into the summer sky and count the dragonflies – dozens of them, brilliant kingfisher blue, like gashes in the air. Or I could gaze into the water and watch its skin suddenly tighten when one of the golden orfe swam up close. Sometimes I could even feel their soft mouths nudging my boots, and see their skin breaking the surface: not gold, really, more like goldfish-orange. Or I could look along the lake into the distance, and find the birds going about their business as if they hadn't noticed me. The moorhens with their mad head-jerks. The mallard suddenly losing control and burying each other in splashes. The swans making no effort, but swimming faster than anything else, with their wings half-lifted like meringues.

It wasn't quite as secret when I walked round the lake, but it was near enough. If I went anticlockwise there was rough grass and no path until I reached the boathouse. This was a ruin, surrounded by more yew trees, and when I pushed through, I came slap up against a hole in the back wall. I looked inside. The punt was still there, sunk into a giant mud-bubble and filled with water the colour of mercury. It was like the King Arthur story in my Ladybird book – the same one that told me about Merlin's cave. When Arthur was dying, his people laid him in a boat and pushed him onto the river outside his palace. They never saw him again, but the current kept him safe through the mists and rapids until he reached here, Avalon, when the boathouse was still new. Then Arthur got off his bed and walked across the lake like Jesus, into a blazing light. The boathouse doors swung shut behind him, and the punt was forgotten – the cushions crumbling, the birds stealing gold threads for their nests, the duckboards turning into pulp, and the whole boat settling into the mud until eventually it was like this. A thin charcoal outline, which might have been a reflection.

I never stayed long at the boathouse. These yew trees were like the others in the Wilderness – they wanted to squeeze their poison into my mouth, or drop it down my neck. So I parted their heavy branches and came to the next thing: the lake corner furthest from the house, where the swans came ashore and made their messes. That was a funny coincidence, because the next bit of the path was tidier than anywhere else, with neat flints packed into cement. The workmen must have done it when they built the swimming-pool, which was here on the right, behind a box hedge. We used the pool every afternoon in summer, but nobody liked it much. The water was too cold, there were too many people, and the whole place smelled like the Rears. In winter we weren't allowed to go near, in case we fell in and nobody noticed. This was an easy rule to keep: whenever I looked over the box hedge, there'd always be a vest someone had forgotten, mouldering in the long grass by the diving board, or dead leaves disintegrating in the water, shaped like a question mark. It made the place too sad to bother with – except for one time. It was the middle of winter and there'd been a frost overnight, so when I woke up the whole garden was white. White grass, white cedar tree, white on the bowed-down yew branches. The lake was still spellbound when I set off to walk round it in break, and every leaf in the box hedge by the pool had a rim of fur. I peered over. The water had been frozen, as the wind whipped it into little crests. Was it rushing or standing still? Both – and so far, I was the only person who knew. I nudged open the gate and sat cross-legged on the paving stones. I couldn't remember anything as beautiful as this, and the harder I looked, the better it was. There were even leaves frozen in some of the waves – little black ones, like fossils in a rock, along with grass stems and pointless white bubbles. And a pair of swimming trunks, red woollen ones, twisted into a bloodstain.

'What are you doing here, Motion I?' It was Mr Thwaites, the second master, with his big spitty voice. He'd crept through the gate and was now so close behind me, I thought he might be going to kick me; he was always angry and lashing out, unless he thought his wife might notice. His favourite thing was to ask us what we were doing, and if we started our answer by saying 'Sir, I was trying . . . ,' he interrupted us by shouting, 'You *are* trying, boy. *Very* trying.' The only good thing was, he thought this was funny, and if we pretended we thought it was funny too he didn't punish us.

I knew it was rude to stay sitting down, and I knew I shouldn't be here. But I was too frightened to move. The word 'petrified' slid onto my tongue, which I'd just learned meant 'turned to stone'. I shook my head and said, 'I'm looking, sir.' 'Looking at what?' Mr Thwaites wanted to know, but he asked more gently than I expected, even though the answer was obvious. 'The ice, sir.' Mr Thwaites said nothing, and I could hear the breath whirring through the hairs in his nose. Didn't his wife mind that, and tell him? Then he gave an odd grunt, and squatted down beside me. 'Very strange,' he went on, still quietly, and poked at one of the waves with the metal end of his walking stick. The ice didn't echo, quite, but pinged, and the ping raced outwards, hardening in all directions until it hit the edges of the pool and died. 'Yes, very strange,' he said again. 'You're not going to walk on it, are you?' 'No. I wouldn't do that, sir.' 'I'm sure you wouldn't do that,' he said. 'You might fall through and drown.' His voice sounded tired, as though he was half-asleep, or remembering something he didn't want me to know about. 'All the same,' he went on eventually, 'you'd better be going, don't you think?' 'Yes, sir,' I said again. As we stood up, our shoes left frosty scrapes on the paving stones, and I could see how close we'd been to each other. Not any more, though. Now Mr Thwaites was holding open the gate, so I could step back onto the path and finish my walk. He was showing me we were back to normal again. As I slipped past, I thought he might cuff me round the head, or even slash at me with his stick. But he kept still, and waited until I'd disappeared. We never mentioned the ice, when we saw each other again.

A few yards further and I was under the beech tree, beside the far end of the stepping stones. My circle was nearly done now – I could already see the mound ahead, where we were allowed to have little allotments by the church wall. I wanted to do that, and maybe give Annie some spuds she could cook for me, but it wasn't going to happen yet. I had to be older. Anyway, there was the rock garden to see first – a miniature valley, with close-together boulders so we could leap from one to the other without touching the ground, blind then not blind then blind again as the sun crashed through the leaves overhead. We might fall off and hurt ourselves, the boulders were shaky, but at least teachers didn't come here. The slope was too steep, so if they wanted us they had to stand at the top and blow whistles until we appeared. It was like coming up from underground – not as deep as the huts, with earth in our hair and root-scratches, but with the same fox-feeling of rising into the light.

. The next place was the last, and almost back to the rose garden. The trees here were spaced out, and the path climbed away from the lake until it met the drive. The only way to reach the water was to steady yourself under the big chestnut, then hurtle down the slope and hope you stopped before you got to the edge and the boggy bit started. Not many people managed that, which meant the shore was badly chewed-up. But the mess was worth it. There was a small island a few yards out, and a clump of silver birch where some of the coots nested. I could watch without disturbing them: they knew I couldn't reach. And the shore was good for playing, too; we were allowed to bring our toys here, and make tracks for them. That's why it was called Dinky Farm, though Dinky toys were too small and wouldn't work properly because they got clogged up with mud. My army toys were much better – the ones dad gave me for Christmas and birthdays. I could build roadways with them, using the back of trucks to cart the earth, then make camps and plan battles. Or that was the idea, anyway. I liked it better when I was staring down the slope, imagining it all. My tanks with mud in their tracks, powering over wriggly roots. My rocket launcher in a hollow with spiders and yew-berries.

The whistle went, and as I looked back at the lake I could see it had already forgotten me. A moorhen was jerking out from the reeds by the stepping stones. One of the grebes had just dived for food, leaving ripples like a target. The dripping shadows by the boathouse had all joined up. It wasn't the end of the world: that's what mum would have said. But it was the end of something. I picked my way between the beds of the rose garden and came to the changing-room door, where a handful of boys were knocking mud off their boots. One was showing Lety the skeleton of a bird's skull, and Lety wanted to buy it. So did I. I'd have to talk to him later, then write to mum and ask her for the money. As we shuffled into line and passed through the door, Mr Thwaites gave me a shove between the shoulder-blades, hurrying me forward.

CHAPTER TEN

The Swish

When Beak came round Blue on my first evening, he said Miss Hardwick had been teaching junior boys ever since he started the school, and I liked the sound of that. I liked it when I saw her the next morning, too. She was about Ruby's age, and soft-looking. Grey hair with wisps escaping over her ears. Big doughy face. Black specs with gold stars by the hinges. Red cardigan with bulging pockets where she kept spare pencil-stubs and Kleenex. Green tweed skirt, like Beak's suit but not so hairy. Sensible shoes. I wasn't the only one who thought she must be friendly. After we'd been given our desks, and were sticking up our hands to ask questions, lots of boys called her mum by mistake. And if anyone burst into tears because they didn't understand, or because they got an attack of homesickness, she put her arm round their shoulders and didn't mind if they blubbed into her cardigan.

All the same, I couldn't decide whether Miss Hardwick was pretending. If she was really like Ruby, surely she wouldn't want to hang around in the Common Room and breathe the tobacco fug? I thought I'd better do a bit of pretending myself, until I could make up my mind – so I told the other boys I liked her, and kept my questions to myself. 'You're very quiet, Motion I,' she said at the end of lessons, or as we tramped between the wide bit of her classroom, where we had our desks and lockers, and the narrower part under the tower where we sat cross-legged on the floor for reading and spelling bees. 'I'm fine, miss, thank you,' I told her, wishing she'd stop noticing me: I was quiet because I wanted to be invisible. 'Not missing home too much?' she went on. 'No, I'm fine, thank you,' I told her again. What else did she expect me to say? She'd already told us we must try to forget our mums and dads because thinking about them only made us miserable. That was why we weren't allowed to make telephone calls home. And that's why Sunday letters had to be checked, in case we said something upsetting.

I discovered this my first weekend. I wrote my letter as carefully as possible, sitting at my desk in Miss Hardwick's classroom, and after I'd explained to mum that I was completely unhappy, I begged her to come and take me away. I was sure it would do the trick. Mum would understand because she felt the same way herself, then she'd soften up dad and he'd understand too, and the next thing I'd know would be the sound of the Hillman parking beside the statue of the man standing on one leg. Mum had never let me down before, so why should she now, when things were more serious than ever? I carried my letter to Miss Hardwick's desk because she'd asked to read it before I popped it into the envelope – mum had tucked a supply of ready-stamped ones into my new brown leather writing case. She spread it on her desk. As I stood beside her, I looked into the nest of her hair: how did she get it to lift up and over like that into a giant bun? Then I concentrated again; this was all taking too long. 'Oh, Andrew,' she sighed at last, and I knew I was in trouble because she'd used my first name. 'You see how unhappy this will make your mother, don't you?' 'No, miss,' I told her, too surprised to think. 'Well, I can tell you,' she went on sadly. 'It will make her very unhappy, and you don't want that, do you?' 'No, miss,' I said again. 'In that case . . .' Miss Hardwick didn't finish her sentence, but leaned back in her chair and tore my letter into two pieces. Then she fluttered them into the bin beside her desk. 'Now,' she said, 'try and write her a letter that will make her feel happy.'

That's when I knew Miss Hardwick was like the other teachers – though she went on pretending to be nice for weeks. Until she gave her first hair-pull, in fact. We'd heard about this from senior boys – they'd told us her nickname was Haggie Hairpull, but we thought we must be better behaved than them, which was why she hadn't lost her temper with us. Then she did, with Sims, for spilling ink on his prep. One minute she was still Miss Hardwick, smiling and stuffing her hands into the pockets of her cardigan so the wool stretched tight over her shoulders and looked about to give way. The next she was Haggie, and her face was the colour of a raspberry. She had Sims by the hair, hauling him clean out of his seat. 'I warn you, I warn you!' Sims was shouting, with his hands clasped over hers, so her ring poked through the tangle of fingers like a staring purple eyeball. I couldn't understand at first. Why wasn't he just bellowing with pain? I soon got it. Sims had hair that came out very easily – it was sandy and fine and flopped into his eyes unless he gummed it straight across his head with water. He knew if Haggie gave a hard yank, she'd scalp him like a Red Indian. Which was exactly what happened, and by now Sims was crying hard. I wanted to look out of the window but I couldn't take my eyes off Haggie. She was standing over him with a mouse-coloured tuft in her left hand. Her right hand kept taking parts of this tuft and laying them back on top of his head, patting them, as if they might suddenly sprout roots and start growing again. 'Now you've done it. Now you've really done it,' said Sims, heaving out the words, and for a moment it was exciting. He was going to complain to Beak, and then Haggie would get into trouble. But we knew this would never happen. Nobody ever complained, because nobody ever listened. Not even our mums and dads. We reckoned it was because the same sorts of thing had happened to them, when they were at school. They thought it was normal.

The worst thing about Haggie was simple. She was a woman. That meant she ought to have been like mum, or at least like Ruby. After we'd seen our first hair-pull, and knew it might happen again at any time, we had to change our minds about women. It didn't take long, because we already knew about Matron. 'Hardly a woman at all,' said Eyot. 'Probably not even human.' I didn't trust Eyot, he had sharp elbows which stuck out suddenly when he was walking along, and poked whoever happened to be passing in the ribs. But he was right about this. Matron's name was P. C. Gibbon, as though she was a monkey and had been born into the police. The rumour was: her real name was Phyllis. This was bad enough. Worse still was the look of her – skin as smooth and cold as soap, flabby face with a hairy wart where her chin should have been, and a flat accent that made her difficult to understand. She wore a uniform all the time, whether she was standing in her dispensary or squeaking up and down the corridor outside our dorms in her rubbery shoes. This uniform was a stiff cap like a seagull's wing, a dress of narrow green and white stripes, a white bib with an upside-down watch, and a canvas belt like a girth, which had a painful buckle at head-height. She was disgusting. When I watched her hands, with their fatty rolls round the finger-joints, I imagined them levering open my mouth to drop in a Senokot. Or spinning me onto my stomach so she could stick her red tube up my bum. When I heard her talking I remembered the way she shouted at night, if someone couldn't get to the loo in time and was sick on the floor. When I looked into her piggy eyes, I thought of what she'd seen the night I heard her screaming. It was late and I'd already been asleep for an hour or two. Then I was woken up by the sound of people fighting in her sitting room at the end of the corridor. At least it sounded like fighting, but it couldn't be, could it? I tiptoed out of bed and told myself that if anyone asked what I was doing, I'd say I was going to have a pee. When I got to the dispensary, there was the Gibbon sunk down against the wall and huddled up with her shoulders shaking. 'Poltergeist!' she said, looking straight through me. I hadn't got a clue what she meant, but through the open door of the sitting room behind her I saw cups and plates lying on the floor, some of them smashed into pieces. When I turned back to the Gibbon again, her head was bowed onto her arm. The best thing to do, I decided, was nip back to bed and hope she wouldn't remember in the morning. She didn't, either. At least, she never said anything.

Miss Ford, the deputy matron, was more like it: Scottish, and jolly, and likely to give us a day in bed without asking too many questions. We loved her because we loathed the Gibbon so much, and thought she talked sense. 'I'm *faintly* surprised,' she once told me, her words springing along like lambs, then suddenly pausing here and there to roll in a few r's, 'no, *more* than faintly surprised, that you boys are not ill *all the time*, given the state of the *lavatories* downstairs. Speaking *personally*, I'd look *twice* at them if I were a *dog*.' This kind of thing made me think she was on my side, but I knew she couldn't do much to help. The Gibbon saw to that, just as she squashed her other assistant, Miss Johanssen. We didn't expect much of Yo-Yo, though. She was only twenty, and Swedish, and so beautiful dad noticed her at once in the school photo, with her ton of black hair piled on top of her head. 'Does she look after you at bathtime?' he asked, making the same clickety-click noise inside his cheek that he always did when Petula Clark was singing on telly. 'She helps us wash our hair,' I told him; even though it made me go red, I couldn't quite see what he was getting at. Probably he meant 'It'. Mum sometimes talked about 'It', and I thought 'It' meant pretty – something like that. Well, Yo-Yo was pretty, but I didn't want to get up in the middle of the night and look through the keyhole of her bedroom like Eyot. That just proved what an idiot he was.

The other woman in the school, apart from Annie the cook, and Jenny the hunchback who taught the piano, was Miss Anderson, who did maths. She had tree-trunk legs and stank of ammonia. I sometimes smelled her in the corridor by the dining room, but I was never in her class – which meant that when Haggie stopped teaching me, the only women I saw during term-time were the Gibbon and her deputies. This seemed odd, when I looked into books or at the telly: outside school, women were everywhere. I didn't think about it much – partly because books and telly didn't have anything to do with me, and also because I didn't see many women in the holidays either. There was mum, of course, but she was mum. There were granny, Ruby and Daffers, but they were family so they didn't count either. Then there were mum's friends, but they never spoke to me. And further off still, like smudges on the horizon, there were a few girls. But they were all Kit's age, and I didn't talk to them. It wasn't that I thought boys were better, it was just that boys were all there were.

I decided it must be another Maidwell trick. Beak was trying to convince us the school was normal, by making it hard for us to know about anywhere else. And mum and dad went along with him, because it had been the same for them. But I had a secret weapon – all the boys did. We knew that underneath the surface, most things at school were the opposite of normal. As long as we remembered that, everything was separate from us – especially the masters. Not just the ones we saw most, like Booster Thwaites, or That Fool Wooley and Froggie Learmonth. But people like Mr Morris, who had a face like a pitbull terrier and sneered all the time – you had to look out with him, because he slapped people so hard round the ear it sometimes made them deaf. Or Mr Dease who came from Malta and had a top-heavy wife; his name rhymed with 'tease', which wasn't surprising. When Kit arrived, and Maltese Dease didn't know when to stop, Kit stabbed him in the head with a pencil, which got him into bad trouble but made him a hero. Or Mr Porch, who talked like a hissing snake and used Greek e's on the blackboard. Or Mr Randall, who everyone called Rhubarb, even to his face sometimes. He looked like a garage-man with his black specs and straight-back hair, but was the only one I liked because he taught me English, and asked me to write stories about things like 'A River in Flood'. He said that when I was doing a description, I couldn't be right or wrong, just better or worse, and that made me feel I could relax.

Rhubarb didn't teach poetry – Beak did, even though his subject was Latin. Once a week he told us to close our Shortbread Eating Primers and open our anthologies instead. This should have been good news, because Latin was difficult, but Beak made poems boring. First we read one aloud, taking the verses in turn, then we learned it by heart while Beak caught up with his marking. Was he trying to be kind when he gave us funny poems like 'The chief defect of Henry King/ Was chewing little bits of string'? Probably – though he didn't feel kind very often. The day I stuck up my hand and asked what 'conies' meant, in 'Nod' by Walter de la Mare, he said 'rabbits' so impatiently I thought he'd rather be shooting them than explaining. Why didn't Beak give poems back to Rhubarb, if he couldn't be bothered? I worked out the answer soon enough. If we hadn't learned the poem by the end of the lesson, Beak wrote down our names so he'd remember to whack us later. Rhubarb might have let us off.

Beak enjoyed beating. He beat us if we did badly at work, if we were cheeky, if we walked with our hands in our pockets, if we left the middle button of our jackets undone, if we walked on the grass by the statue standing on one leg, if we slammed doors, if we barged ahead of masters, if we swore, if we made a mess in our lockers, if we didn't hang up our towels, if we had fights, if we damaged the flowers, if we hid our food. Some of these things didn't matter much, and Beak dealt with them when he came round the dorms at night. 'Who are the sinners?' he asked, sneaking through the doorway in his red slippers while we stood beside our beds in our pyjamas. Anyone who had something to report would own up, then bend over while Beak did a little hop, flicked one of his slippers into the air, caught it, gave his wet chuckle to show how nifty he'd been, and handed out a few slow wallops. There were never more than six, but the heel of his slipper was hard as wood through the flannel of our pyjama bottoms. It was embarrassing. Sometimes boys farted with shock, and got teased afterwards. Worse still was waiting my turn, after I'd been caught running down a corridor, or nipping across the cut grass when I thought no one was looking. I kept thinking how I'd bought my pyjamas with mum at Billings and Edmonds, and wondering what she'd think if she could see me now, with my hands about to clutch my knees in front of grandpa's friend. While the beating lasted, all these thoughts disappeared in a fog. But when Beak had moved on next door and the lights were out, I plotted how I'd come back when I was older. I'd steal one of dad's 12-bores from the gun cupboard, and I'd drive the Hillman to Maidwell, and I'd shoot Beak under the Wellingtonia so he'd fall over and bleed to death on his orchids.

The slipper was 'whacking'. Cane was the Swish, and much worse. It was for serious things like talking after lights. Beak read out the names of people he wanted to see at lunchtime, but he didn't actually do the swishing until the evening. This meant we had all afternoon to imagine what it was going to be like: practising how to sit down lightly, trying to swallow Annie's supper without being sick, then finally turning into the black passage opposite the dining room, which ended at Beak's study. We knew he was already seeing the first boy because the door was shut. It was a heavy door too – thick, pale wood, with carving round the edge, like a door in a church – but not heavy enough to blot out noises. As we stood in line waiting our turn, we heard Beak's deep voice on the other side, and the lighter sound of a boy trying to explain. When the voices stopped, there was a shuffling silence, and the swishing started. It made my skin tighten everywhere and hot up, and my ears twitched like a horse – at least I thought they did, but when I asked someone if it showed, they said it didn't. Then after another silence, the door opened and the boy came out, tucking in his shirt, and not looking anyone in the eye so we knew he must be crying. 'Come!' Beak would call, still invisible, and the next boy went in.

The study was a poky little room overlooking the rose garden, and even though I went there five or six times a term I never looked round carefully. I knew it had bookshelves, a pale-coloured sofa with cushions, and a flat-topped wooden desk. I wasn't interested in seeing any more, because I knew everything was just for show. Especially the cushions, which mums would like because they had roses on them. For me, the only important things in the room were Beak himself, standing by his desk and red in the face, as though he'd been for a run, and the wastepaper basket in the corner behind him, where he kept his canes. Would he turn towards the canes, or would he let me off? He always turned. Next question, then: would he choose a whippy cane or a stiff one? It depended. The whippy ones, which hurt most, were for things like being rude to the Gibbon or talking after lights. The stiff ones were for doing badly in lessons. 'You must try harder,' Beak said, glancing at a test sheet one of the masters had passed through to him, which had my marks ringed in red biro. 'I do try,' I told him, clenching my hands. Beak stroked a hand across his face, and when the tips of his fingers rubbed against his moustache, I heard the hairs prickling. My skin prickled, too, but silently. I wanted to tell him I wasn't stupid; it was just that I couldn't think straight, if I knew I was going to be beaten when I got it wrong. But there wasn't any point. He was going to beat me anyway, and then he'd tell grandpa, and grandpa would tell dad, and dad would be cross too, and the holidays would be spoiled. 'I'm going to give you four,' Beak said, as though he was being generous. Then his left hand gripped the back of my neck and bent me forward. His fingers felt like claws, and he wanted me to think he was trying to stop me running away. Really he was steadying himself while he took aim.

There were usually about half a dozen people a night for the swish, and afterwards two or three in every dorm for whacking. 'You must be very naughty little boys,' mum said, when I told her this. I knew she didn't want to talk about it, so I hurried on to something else, feeling guilty. But I wanted her to know we were the opposite of naughty. We were good. Innocent, I told myself, when I knew what the word meant. It was simply that Beak enjoyed what he did, and he had us trapped. The surprising thing was, we didn't all gang together and hate him, not even when he lost his temper and gave really bad beatings. This happened once or twice a term, if boys tried to run away, or got caught stealing, or did something so awful we were never told about it, like Bishop II. We only knew Bishop II had been swished because we saw him in the showers – he had purple lines with blood in them, all over his bum and across the backs of his legs. It looked as though someone had pelted him with Queen Anne's pudding. 'Does it hurt?' we wanted to know. 'Not much,' was all he said, before queue-barging into the showers and starting to sing.

Beak didn't just stop us ganging up on him. He made us gang up on each other. Tomkins I was the worst. When I was still a junior, he lurked around the boathouse with his friends during Muck-About and over the weekends, pouncing on people who looked feeble or lost. That's all he wanted: to make people who already felt bad feel worse. He got me once, and dragged me off to a squashy bit of ground at the edge of the lake, where he tied me to a tree and made me pull down the top of my boiler suit, so he could whip me with canes he'd cut from the same place Beak got his. It was horrible, even though it didn't hurt much – not until Rhubarb came past, and saw what was happening, and let

Tomkins I carry on because he thought it was all a joke. Then the bamboos started to sting all right, and I felt a fool, and I thought if I ever met Tomkins I later I'd get him with dad's 12-bore at the same time as I killed Beak.

Tomkins I untied me when the whistle went for the end of Muck-About, and I heard myself thank him. It was like the way we had to thank Beak after getting the Swish. When I was thinking about it later, after lights-out, I wondered how it made me feel, to say things I didn't mean. Was it like lying, which was definitely wrong? I decided it wasn't – or not always. The best way to deal with school was to say all kinds of things I didn't mean, but people wanted to hear, until they joined up and became like a kind of skin. The other way to get by was to keep most of the little rules, so nobody would know I wanted to break a big one. Really I was only interested in breaking a big one. Not big like stealing. Big like going for a Midnight Walk, which all the naughtiest boys did.

I liked the sound of Midnight Walks because I thought I'd get the grounds to myself twice over. There'd be all the secrets I had in the daytime, and lots of new ones in the darkness. But it was dangerous. Beak knew Walks happened, and sometimes he stayed up late, keeping a look out. If he heard anyone sneaking down the stairs, he'd let them go, lock whatever door or window they'd used to escape, then wait in his study with the light on until they were tired and asked to be let back in. After that he'd beat them on the bare bum like he had Bishop II, before sending them back to bed. But I decided it was worth it – and still worth it when my alarm clock went off at three o'clock in the morning, and my mouth felt as though I'd been sucking sandpaper. I tiptoed downstairs past the picture of Jesus arriving in Jerusalem, and the boy keeping quiet about Charles I, along the corridor to the changing room, and out through a window I made sure to leave on the latch.

The air felt so cold through my pyjamas and dressing gown, my eyes splashed awake: here were the same yew trees in the Wilderness, the same white roots in the pathways, the same tingling bamboos, the same shaggy bark on the Wellingtonia. But every one of them had been turned inside out, to show they were made of silver and rolling mist. The lake was best of all: like ice, and slithery, which made it difficult to tell whether it had edges, or stretched all the way to the horizon. It was so much like a dream, I made sure I got some mud on my fingers – then in the morning I could check. Like a dream, or like one of the engravings in the library, where if I looked carefully I could see each of the tiny scratch-marks the artist had made. My brain felt like that. As though the point of every twig, every blade of grass, every rush by the lake, every dart of moonlight, was a kind of nib, scraping inside my head. The shapes they carved would stay with me, like the dampness creeping through the soles of my slippers and the frosty air sparkling into my nose and mouth. Not even Beak could take them away – not even if he had found my window, and shut it behind me.

There was only one boy who understood all this – Miller II. It took me a while to find him, because Beak didn't like us making real friends. He thought if two boys were together a lot, they must be planning something. In the end, Miller II and I decided to ignore him, and after a while people started to think we were like brothers. I'd first noticed him because he looked nicer than anyone else, with his straight yellow hair falling into his eyes, and his smooth muscly skin. But this wasn't the only thing that made him special. He didn't seem to care about the rest of us, and was always disappearing into the Wilderness looking for moles, or searching for mushrooms on the far side of the games field. Was he unhappy? His brother was. Miller I was so miserable he kept having what Miss Ford called 'real *fits* of rage – and I mean *fits*'. They were so frightening, Maltese Dease wanted to use him as a secret weapon in the rugger team, and turn him loose on other schools. It didn't work, though. Miller I never lost his temper when he was playing games, only when he was waiting for a bath, or doing his prep, or something ordinary like that.

Miller II said his parents were divorced, which explained a lot. I'd never met anyone with divorced parents – apart from dad. There was a problem, though. I thought if I asked him to stay for a weekend in the holidays, he'd be bored. Everything was normal at home. So I waited until he asked me to his house in Devon, and that turned out to be great. Mrs Miller had a huge bosom and she smoked all the time, even when she was doing the washing-up. She was snappy, too, and didn't say hello to Mr Miller, when he arrived to take us gliding. Gliding! As soon as I squeezed into the little plane on Dartmoor, and a huge rubber band had boi-oinged me off the runway and into a loop-the-loop, I thought I was going to die. When I was back on the earth and still alive, I felt something so important had happened that Miller II would be my friend for ever.

Even so, we didn't help each other much at school, or make plans about how we could make it better. We kept our heads down and waited for time to pass. Scribbling out the days in a little calendar I kept inside my Bible. Counting down towards the holidays, or the visits our parents were allowed to make twice a term. These visits were called exeats, which meant that after the last lesson on Saturday morning, mum and dad would be waiting outside in the Daimler, parked where they'd left me on Day One, by the statue whose name I knew now was Mercury. The plan was always the same. They took me to the Black Swan in Market Harborough, where they were staying, then brought me back to Maidwell for the night, then whisked me away again on Sunday after church, before driving off home in the evening. I liked this routine so much, I could hardly bear it. From the second I rushed through the front door, which we were only allowed to use on special days like this, and flung myself towards the car, I was already counting the minutes we had left together. It was great until lunch, when we were still talking about how the dogs were, and what Mrs Lambert the cleaner had said about needing a new hoover, and what had happened in the village. After that, when we got onto school, and lessons, the clock speeded up and I could see mum was worried too. She kept sneaking back the sleeve of her jersey to look at her watch. She didn't think I'd noticed, but I knew we were both wondering what it would be like when we said goodbye. 'Try and pretend,' I told myself. 'Do what Haggie says.' So I lay in front of the gas fire and read my *Dandy* and *Victor*, which mum had remembered to bring because we weren't allowed comics at school. Or tramped across the field at Naseby if it was sunny, and waited for dad to make his joke about 'The Naseby Knob', which was a monument that told us about the Civil War battle. I couldn't pretend for long enough. The minutes sped up and blurred into hours, and the sun sank into mist in the street outside the Black Swan, and it was almost a relief when we clattered back over the cattle grid on Sunday evening, and mum and dad were nearly gone again.

'What will you do for the rest of the evening?' mum always wanted to know. 'So I can imagine you.' It was just like Beak to have planned something good: he must have known parents would ask. Sunday night was the time he read aloud to us in his sitting room. If it was an exeat day everyone would be quiet, slipping off their shoes at his door and trying to make sure their new tuck didn't rustle in their pockets, then finding a space on Beak's pale blue carpet where they could lie face down. That's what I liked to do, anyway. It made it easier to think of dad's headlights burrowing through the dark outside, and mum tipped forward beside him, falling asleep with her hankie still in her hand. Easier to hide our faces, too, in case we started crying, and to dip in and out of what Beak was reading while the smell of socks got thicker, along with the old food-pong that always floated round our trousers. When I thought mum and dad were probably home, and the smell had made me woozy, I started listening to Beak properly. Weeks ago it had been *The Box of Delights*, by John Masefield. Then *The Memoirs of a Midget* by Walter de la Mare. Now it was *The Lion, the Witch and the Wardrobe* by C. S. Lewis. This was the one I liked best, because of the White Queen, who had turned a whole wood to winter with a drop of her magic potion. And because of Aslan, who was a lion but something else as well, only I couldn't quite see what.

When Beak got to the end of the story, and the table cracked, he told us Aslan was really Jesus Christ. I'd already worked it out by then, but I was glad to be sure. Beak believed in God. We all did. That's why we had grace at every meal, and said prayers in the evening, and went to Matins on Sundays in the village church, like at home. The only thing was, God didn't seem to be helping much with my work. I told myself this must be because I needed to do more than hold my Bible under my pillow as I was falling asleep. So I tried saying the Lord's Prayer seven times every night as well, because Sims had told me seven was a lucky number. But it was difficult to concentrate after the fourth or fifth time – the words kept sliding away. After that, I decided I ought to make a bigger effort in Scripture; that wouldn't be difficult, because we were doing Samuel I and Samuel II, and I liked the stories. I joined the choir, too, because it was run by Rhubarb, who was friendly to me even though I couldn't stay in tune all the time.

None of this made any difference. I obviously wasn't getting God's attention, and needed to test myself more. That's when I had another brainwave, and put my name down for Confirmation; I wasn't ten yet, but I could start the classes straight away. They happened twice a week after prep, and were run by the village priest, whose reddy-brown face was the same colour as the walls in Northamptonshire. Everyone said he was kind. All the same, I felt wobbly as I walked through the churchyard towards his front door – I was out of bounds. That was partly why the classes were special. Better still, they ended in Confession. After that, I wouldn't have any sins.

But there was a snag. I couldn't think of enough sins to make a really good Confession. I'd broken a lot of little school rules, but the only big one was Midnight Walks, and I didn't think God would mind about them as much as Beak. So what about home? At home Kit and I didn't sin. It was true that once I'd taken some change from mum's purse. But I'd put it back after a while, because I couldn't work out how to spend it without her knowing – so that didn't count. In the end, I decided the only thing to do was explain things to the vicar, and stayed behind after one of the classes so I could have a private word. He looked upset when I explained my problem, and his face went from stone-colour to plums. Then he scuffled in his desk, which was the untidiest I'd ever seen, and fished out a creamy booklet. I must take it away with me, he said, and read it somewhere quiet, because then I'd remember the past more easily. The booklet listed hundreds of sins, and as I turned the pages my heart sank. I'd never done most of them, and I didn't understand lots of others. 'Playing with yourself', for instance. What was wrong with that? I'd spent loads of afternoons walking round the lake alone, or trundling my army trucks through Dinky Farm, and not even Slapper Morris had told me off. Never mind, I put 'Played alone' on my list anyway, along with dozens of others. When the big afternoon finally arrived, and I knelt down at the altar rail and gave my confession, the vicar sat beside me in a wooden chair which creaked like a saddle as I read out my list. It was the first time I'd noticed he smelled of Brut, like Hamilton-Patterson, who was a prefect, but I didn't let that put me off.

When it was over the vicar forgave me, and said I must feel much better now I'd made a clean breast of everything. I was so relieved I'd done what he wanted, I shot off my knees and bobbed outside without remembering to thank him. I didn't have any sins! But the list in my hand was still embarrassing, even if it was old news. I decided to bury it, quickly, under the holly tree by the gate back to school. I turned back through the churchyard, ducked under the low branches of the tree, gouged out a slab of earth with my finger-ends, crumpled up the paper, and stamped the earth back on top. I'd probably committed a few new sins by now, without even realising it, but with a bit of luck God would still be looking after me. He'd make sure no one found it. On the other hand, someone might – that's what I started to think after lights out. And sure enough, when I went back a few days later to dig the list up again, and bury it somewhere even safer, it wasn't there. I darted my head to and fro, in case the thief was still near, not minding the holly leaves pricking my forehead. Then I got under control again. It didn't matter. No one would know the list was mine – they wouldn't recognise my writing. It was probably like that dead thrush I'd found. The one I'd buried in the Wilderness so all the feathers and meat would rot away, and I'd get a perfect white skeleton. When I looked after a week or so, that had disappeared too.

The vicar's classes ended, and the time came for me to be confirmed. It should have been done by the Bishop of Peterborough, but he fell down the steps of an aeroplane, which meant his friend the Bishop of Colombo had to do it instead. He was very old, the

Bishop of Colombo, and his face was so brown and wrinkled he looked like one of the dead saints that Catholics kept in glass boxes. When he put his hand on my head, and leaned down with all his weight, I could feel the bump of his ring through my skull, and my knee-bones grinding into the altar steps. I didn't see God, and I still wasn't sure he was going to help me like I wanted. But as I came out of the church with mum and dad on either side, holding the new Bible granny had sent, and a book from grandpa called *Daily Light*, I looked round at the graves and realised something had happened. A big chunk of time had fallen off my life at school. I suddenly felt older, and that meant I was nearer to leaving.

CHAPTER ELEVEN

The Gate and the Shadow

I was flipping my army lorry off the bottom step of the stairs at Little Brewers, seeing how far it could leap down the hall without crashing onto its side. Why wouldn't it do what I wanted? Even when the wheels landed flat, the soldiers bounced off their seats in the back and scratched across the floor like the beginning of a headache. 'What are you doing?' mum called from the kitchen. 'I'm only . . .' I began, but she hadn't finished her questions yet. 'Can't you stop that filthy racket? Have you washed your hands for lunch?' I spread my palms flat and turned them over; they were clean enough. Mum was obviously fed up about something, unless it was just tiredness. 'Yes,' I called back. 'Then why don't you find something useful to do?' she said. I clipped the soldiers back into my lorry and parked it neatly beside the banisters. 'Like what?' I said. 'Like tidying the playroom.' 'Done that.' 'Or your bedroom.' 'Done that too.' 'Well, think of something else.' 'Such as?' I meant to say this lightly, but it came out wrong and sounded bored, which was a mistake. Boredom wasn't allowed. It meant I didn't have inner resources. 'Oh, I don't know darling.' Mum was half-shouting now, sizzling a saucepan into the sink. 'Have a look at *The Midnight Steeplechase.*' 'The what?' 'The picture above the bench. Have a look and tell me what's strange about it.'

I was so amazed, I sat fly-catching for a moment. No one at home looked at pictures, and it was easy to know why. Every one of them was more or less the same – apart from the ancestors, of course, and the two shiny flower paintings in the drawing room, which mum said were famous in Holland. The rest either showed women riding side-saddle, wearing dark blue skirts and veils like Joanie, or men in pink coats who stuck their feet forward because they were in mid-air, flying across a ditch. Sometimes it was only the people and the horses, like cut-outs. More often there was a field in the background, and a pack of hounds catching up with a fox – but the fox never looked frightened, because a picture was only a picture, and the horses were stiff as animals on a merry-go-round. 'Well?' mum called out again. 'What can you see?' 'Give me a mo,' I said, and scrambled onto the bench to get a closer look.

I was glad I hadn't said anything at first. Otherwise mum might have known I'd never looked at the picture before, not properly, even though I'd passed it hundreds of times. I couldn't have done. It didn't have hounds anywhere, for a start, and it wasn't about hunting. It was a horse race, and it was happening at night. That man in the middle was flapping a black cloak behind him like a highwayman; he'd already galloped over the hill in the distance, whizzed across an empty field, and now he was jumping a five-barred gate. Because he was alone, I couldn't tell whether he was in the lead or lagging behind everyone else. He was in a hurry, that was obvious. His horse had walloped the top rung of the gate, and smashed it to pieces. There was only a tiny moon to show where he was going, so he was lucky he hadn't fallen off. The strange thing was: even though the man was safe, everything about him felt miserable. His face was white as a gravestone under his shadowy hat. The mucky brown fields were like the bottom of a pond, and the bare trees stuck up like fish skeletons. Is that what mum wanted me to see? I felt confused, as if what the man was feeling had escaped from the painting, and slithered into my own head. 'Mum!' I called out in a sudden panic. 'Have you found it yet?' she answered – and like a miracle I immediately saw what she wanted. The gate had been broken by the horse's hooves, but the shadow of the gate was whole. There it was, stretched on the grass. Five dark green stripes of the paintbrush, and one slashed across them, holding it all together. A perfect gate.

The fog drained away from my mind and I hopped off the bench into the kitchen, where mum was ladling out Irish stew. She was her old self too, and so was Kit, who had appeared from the yard where he'd been talking to Mr Manning. 'You found it, did you?' she said. I nodded, not wanting to break the spell. 'Do you think he did it on purpose?' she went on. 'Who, the painter?' I asked, looking straight into her face to make sure Kit knew he wasn't a part of the conversation. 'Yes. Do you think it's a deliberate mistake?' 'Probably,' I said. 'Because it makes the picture more interesting.' 'How's that?' mum said. 'You're not sure which is true,' I told her. 'The gate or the shadow.' Then I skewered a forkful of stew. 'You know,' I said airily, 'I think I might be a painter.' I was just taking a breath to explain what I meant, when I saw Kit laughing. 'What's so funny?' I wanted to know, turning to mum for support. She was laughing as well. Holding her water glass to her mouth as a disguise, but definitely laughing. 'Nothing,' she said eventually. 'It's a bit of a turnaround, that's all. Last week you wanted to be a gardener.'

After lunch I thought about the painting again, while mum was having her rest and I was mugging up on some birds, in case dad tested me when he got home. Why had I liked it so much? That was simple. The gate and its shadow were like a password. When I'd cracked it, I'd climbed into the frame and stared about me as if the trees and the field and the sky and the moon were all real. I'd felt the cold wind on my face, and heard the sparrows fidgeting in the hedges. On the other hand, why had mum wanted me to look at the painting in the first place? She liked that kind of thing more than dad, and she thought the mistake was fun. But that wasn't the answer. It fitted with other things she and dad had been telling me in the last few weeks. I needed to concentrate more at school. Beak had said so in my report, and I'd promised dad to start paying attention, before it was too late. What about this for a plan? Tonight I'd ask dad if I could start hunting next winter. Hunting was the main thing at home, after all. The horses, the talk, the friends, the pictures, the mags like *The Field* and *Horse and Hound* on the long stool in the drawing room, even some of the books in the whirligig. They were nearly all about horses, or hounds, or both. I put down my book of birds and stared through the window. A white smoke-cloud was hanging over the mill. The first time I looked it was a Red Indian, but when I turned back again it had changed into an eagle.

'What are you thinking about?' Kit asked from his bed across the room. When I realised the answer was the sky, I decided not to tell him. 'Hunting,' I said, but dreamily, so he wouldn't be interested. By now I was remembering a Sunday lunch last summer, when grandpa said I ought to have a morning's cub hunting as soon as possible. That way, I'd learn something useful and so would my pony Tommy, who might go mad otherwise when it was time for proper hunting. Mum and dad had nodded, like they usually did when grandpa suggested something, then changed their minds afterwards. I wasn't ten years old yet, mum said. It was too young. Hunting could be dangerous. But I knew dad wouldn't be able to resist when I mentioned it later today. I'd be ten by next Christmas, and mum would have the whole of next term to get things ready. She'd buy me a new tweed coat and new breeches. She'd put more oats in Tommy's feed, but not too much because of the madness grandpa had talked about. She'd find me a crop with a red tassel, and have my initials put on the silver collar round the handle. The thought of it made my heart beat faster, and the bird names flapped around on the page in front of my face. 'What are you thinking about now?' Kit said, just to be annoying. 'Being a painter,' I told him, then decided our rest was over and went downstairs to the garden.

When I got home after the autumn term, my report said I'd paid more attention than usual, even though I was still near the bottom of all my classes. This meant I was stupid, but mum said I shouldn't worry, and for once dad didn't care. He wanted to talk about Saturday, which was my first day cub hunting. 'I wish I could come with you both,' mum said, when we were sitting by the fire in the drawing room. 'But the doctor says I mustn't.' She wouldn't tell me what the matter was, and dad wouldn't talk about it either. Kit thought it probably had something to do with her brucellosis, and I wanted to think he was right. It was a name we knew from years ago, and that stopped it being frightening. Besides, she still had more fizz than most mums. When I went up to bed that night, I found she'd laid out my clothes for next day on a bed in the spare room – the Viyella shirt and tweed coat and breeches and gloves all arranged as if there'd once been a body inside them, but it had melted. *My* body, I thought, when it was Saturday at last and I put them on. My body, which had been a fake, and disappeared, and was now back again and real. I clumped into the kitchen and did a little turn round the table so mum could see how well everything fitted.

The meet was only half an hour away, in Hatfield Broad Oak, but dad and I set off in good time – him in his pink coat and shiny black boots, me like a tailor's dummy, or that's what Kit said. 'Hang on tight,' he shouted, as we jingled out of the yard, then clapped his hands to give Tommy a jump, which showed how jealous he was. 'For God's sake,' I said, glaring down at him, but he laughed and said, 'Keep pulling on those reins, bro, keep pulling on those reins.' As he disappeared round the corner, I looked down at my new yellow riding gloves. They were made of string, which was meant to help me grip, but the fingers were too long, and flopped around like curls of lemon peel. Kit knew if Tommy bolted they'd be useless. And Tommy was about to do just that, even though dad had a leading rein attached to his bridle. The muscles in his shoulders had thickened into cords as fat as the one round my dressing gown: maybe mum had given him too many oats after all? Every time a horse-box rumbled past us in the lane, he shivered as though he'd had an electric shock. There was even sweat on his neck, a white shampoo smear, and his tail was slightly lifted, ready to flutter out when he reached top speed. Still, dad looked pleased. I was keeping up, which is what mum had told me I had to do, when she'd grabbed Kit by the collar, and waved us off from the yard. 'Sit up,' dad kept telling me, but using his kind voice. 'Sit straight. Sit back.'

Mum had often driven me to Hatfield Broad Oak in the Hillman. Our family doctor had his surgery by the village sign, and further on was a shop selling expensive jerseys. Mum always said it was a pretty village, prettier than ours. There were neat red-brick houses either side of the main street, and a church at the end with a yew by the gate which should have been an oak. But as dad and I trotted on, leaving behind Bucks Stores, then swinging past the willows at the corner and starting the long straight climb uphill, I realised I'd never looked at it properly. Especially not the long field to our left. Normally it was a blur through the car window, splashed with yellow in summer and brown in winter. Today it was packed and heaving – black horses, grey horses, chestnut horses, top hats glittering, pink coats, red faces, and in the top corner, below the doctor's house, the pack of hounds wriggling like maggots in a tin. The moment Tommy saw it all he stopped dead, blowing through his nose like a stallion. It made me laugh aloud. He'd never done that before. How did he know it was a grown-up horse noise? Had he been watching films? 'Remember,' said dad, winding the leading rein round his fist. 'He can feel what you're feeling. Show him who's boss. That's the way. Now let's get through this gate here and we'll be fine.'

We squeezed into the field and waited side by side for a moment. It was drizzling; if Tommy got any big ideas, the leather reins would be slippery between the fingers of my gloves. There wasn't time to worry about that now. Dad was clicking with his tongue, leading me slowly forward and keeping close to the hedge, so we were out of the way. It didn't stop people calling out to us – or to him, at least. 'Morning, Richard.' 'You've got your boy with you then, Richard.' 'First time for him, is it, Richard?' 'See if we can't get him blooded, eh, Richard?' I kept my head down, watching the water drops collect like champagne bubbles on Tommy's mane, and wishing my hat didn't make my ears stick out so much. What if I let dad down, when I knew how important people thought he was? And what if they thought Tommy always looked like this, as though he'd been rolling in a ditch, when really it was only the weather?

By the time we reached the top of the hill, Tommy was shaking so badly I could see my legs wobbling where they pressed against the saddle-flaps. At least that meant no one could see I was nervous too. More than nervous, actually. When dad gave me a nudge with his crop and introduced me to the Master, I felt a cramp. And when I went to doff my hard hat, I fumbled the strap with my stupid wet finger-ends, hoisted the hat a couple of inches with the elastic still under my chin, then let it thump back onto my skull so hard I thought I must have cut the top of my ears. The Master couldn't be bothered. He was gazing over my head, his face as long as the Duke of Wellington's. All I had to do was get dad to take me back down the hill, then we could hide until everyone was ready to set off.

First I wanted to have a good look at the hounds. It was the dog pack – I could tell because of one of them was slouching back on his bum, slobbering over his willy. They weren't really like dogs at all. The bones in their heads and chests and legs were huge as statues. Some were completely lazy, sprawling on the grass any old how. Some were squirming on their backs where they'd found a dollop of muck, dragging their heads through it and smearing their mouths open as far as their back teeth. Some were still as doorstops. Others were scratching, going at their ribs hard, with long brown nails, as though they wanted to bust through their own skin. Some were fooling around like puppies, giving each other pretend bites. It made me grin – I couldn't help it. They were so rubbery! Idiotic, really. Even though they did smell of disgusting dead meat. Just milling and ragging, so brown and white got muddled and I couldn't tell which was which.

The Master had stopped making his long face and was lifting his hunting horn to his lips. He gave a flat blast, with three or four whoops at the end. It was just noise, not like language at all. But Tommy understood. He thought it meant: go mad. He yanked his head round to prove it, and showed me the polished conker of his eyeball. Then he twisted in the opposite direction, leaped into the air, and set off downhill so fast there wasn't a hope of dad holding onto the leading rein. 'Woah!' I shouted, then bit my lip, because it didn't sound nearly serious enough for hunting. But what would be serious enough? I could try leaning back in the saddle with my legs as straight as the man in *The Midnight Steeplechase*, standing up in my stirrups and hauling at Tommy's mouth. It didn't make the slightest difference. Tommy's jaw and tongue had turned into concrete – but no one else knew that. To them, I was just a fool who couldn't ride properly, even though the rest of my family were experts. 'Isn't that Richard Motion's boy?' a man muttered, plinking past me in the opposite direction. Other voices joined in. 'Hold hard, there.' 'Look what you're doing.' 'For Christ's sake.' A big chestnut flashed out a sideways kick like a cow. A girl with a grey hard hat, a pretty girl with hair in a pigtail, winced and fiddled with her tie. And all the time the slope of the hill got steeper, the grass boggier, the sky blurrier, so when Tommy reached the gate where dad had led us in, his legs had completely lost control. Whips of foam streaked out of his mouth onto my breeches. 'If I aim at the hedge,' I thought, 'that's bound to do it. If I can't stop him before that, the hedge will.' I was almost right. Tommy saw it rearing in front of him, tightened as if he really believed he could jump twelve foot, then went watery again and squirted off sideways into the road.

After a few hundred yards he started to run out of puff. I was picturing dad's face behind me, the shadow of his top hat pouring into his eyes, the tails of his pink coat smacking the rim of his saddle, and it made me want to look over my shoulder and yell it wasn't my fault, I couldn't help it, Tommy was a lunatic and ought to be put down. But that was a bad idea. Complaining would be wet, and wetness had probably started Tommy's charge in the first place. I hadn't told him who was boss. And I wasn't telling him now, either. I was hauling at the reins like a baby, and even though we were slowing at last, it was only because Tommy was tired. His fat stomach was ridiculous, heaving in and out between my knees. And the foam on his neck, his gingery hair with the rain-streaks, the soggy fingers of my gloves: they were all ridiculous too.

As dad drew alongside his horse made a tinkling curtsey like a charger in a King Arthur story, then he quietly leaned across and took hold of the leading rein which was still dangling from Tommy's bridle. 'Are you hurt?' he asked. I told him I wasn't, but carefully, because I was still waiting for him to shout at me. He didn't, though. He went on talking in a soft voice, telling me he'd seen what had happened, and it wasn't my fault. I stared into the hedge, where a dead cow-parsley showed crinkly-brown against the black twigs, then glanced into his face. I thought he might be smiling. He was – and frowning too. As I smiled back, I started to understand. He could remember feeling ashamed like this. Had grandpa been kind, like he was being kind? I didn't think so.

'I've spoiled your day,' I said, and was sorry it sounded so feeble. 'It's not my day,' he said, 'it's our day' – and looked at the grey horizon beyond Hatfield Broad Oak, where the hunt had disappeared. 'What would you like to do?' he asked. I glanced at the knees of my new breeches, soggy with rain. I thought of the sandwiches mum had made for lunch, stiffening inside their silver paper in my coat pocket. I heard the hunting horn give a faint blast, and imagined the horses and their riders galloping across a rolling field of grass. 'I think we should try and catch them up,' I said. Dad turned towards me again, giving a different sort of frown. 'If you're happy with that,' he said. 'But first I think you should trot on a bit, and we'll see if everything's OK. You came down that hill at quite a lick.' I quickly gathered up the reins and booted Tommy in the ribs. 'I thought so,' dad said, trotting along behind me. There was heaviness in his voice, which made me think of wet cardboard. 'He's lame. It's all that clattering on the road after you'd come through the gate. You're a bloody fool, Tommy. A bloody fool. We'll have to turn you into cat food.' He swished him weakly across the rump with the end of the leading rein, then unclipped it from the bridle and tucked it into his pocket. 'At least you won't be needing this any more,' he said, clicking his tongue. We set off home side by side – me on the grass verge to spare Tommy's foot, dad's horse on the road. The shoes made soft little popping noises when they lifted out of the puddles.

Tommy stayed lame for the rest of the holidays, which mum thought was just as well. 'We don't want to put Andrew off, do we?' she asked dad in the kitchen one evening, when I was listening at my place on the stairs. I thought he might say something impatient, which would show he'd only been pretending to be kind after Tommy's charge. But 'No,' he told her. 'No, we don't want to do that.' He sounded completely serious – though it did cross my mind that he felt relieved. He could still go hunting himself and not have to look out for me. I wasn't about to complain. I needed time to forget the whole business, or better still turn it into a joke.

And that's what happened. By next summer, whenever Kit set off for a gallop across the stubble, he said he was me, looping Musket's reins behind the pommel of his saddle and shouting 'Woah, woah, help, I'm going to crash.' I didn't mind. I was better at making Tommy do what I wanted now. Before I went back to Maidwell for the autumn, mum took us cubbing one or twice, and it turned out to be easy. Mainly we stood in the plough outside woods, banging our riding crops on our saddles to stop the foxes escaping, while the hounds rootled around in the undergrowth. Then we galloped to another wood, and did the same thing again. Tommy's shoulders trembled sometimes, as though he was being dive-bombed by invisible flies, but he stayed put, even when the hounds started making a racket. Had he changed, or was it me? Me, according to mum: I was the boss now. That made me sit straighter in my saddle, which dad always wanted, but it wasn't the best thing about cubbing. The best thing was leaving home early, and being out in the fields when the sun came up. The plough smelled different – smoky, so when I breathed it in, I was like Beauty doing one of her deep sniffs at the kitchen door, which took her brain right through the paint and out the other side. The trees too: watching sunlight catch the high-up branch of an oak and belt it with yellow, I could feel the sap tingling under the bark like my own blood when I stood on tiptoe with my arms above my head.

I never saw any fox cubs, and I didn't think about them much. 'You're not squeamish, are you?' Kit asked when we were out one morning. 'Of course not,' I told him. 'Are you?' 'God, no,' he said, and we left it at that, staring at the wall of trees in front of us, and the pheasants peeking through the brambles. I'd told Kit the truth. Most of the people round home, including mum and dad, made all sorts of excuses for hunting if anyone said it was cruel. They said animals didn't feel pain in the same way as human beings. Or they explained that foxes were vermin, and if hounds didn't kill a few every year, then farmers would shoot them, or worse still poison them, and that wouldn't be nearly so sporting. I liked it better when they just told the truth, and said they didn't see anything wrong with hounds chasing foxes and killing them.

When we got home for the winter holidays, dad said there was good news. The first proper meet was at Hatfield Broad Oak, so I'd know my way around, wouldn't I? Kit was standing in front of the fire when he heard this, and because he remembered Tommy's charge there, and wanted to do a really huge laugh, he tipped back his head – without realising he'd grown tall enough to hit the mantelpiece. He clonked himself so hard he rocked one of mum's ornaments, the china blue-tit. At least we could change the subject. And when we came back to hunting again, dad said Hatfield Broad Oak really was a good thing, no, seriously, Kit, because we could ride up the lane without having to bother about a horse-box.

Dad was keeping his horse at livery now, so a man drove it round on the big day, when mum and Kit and I were ready at last. There wasn't room for all four of us in the yard, and even in the lane we had to ride in pairs: dad and Kit in front, me and mum behind. Dad said Kit looked 'just the job' in his tweed coat and breeches and short brown boots. My coat was too small because I'd put on a spurt since last year. I tried not to notice how my sleeves shot halfway up my arms when Tommy tugged on the reins. Kit saw, though, and when we were through the village he cantered up the verge, to prove that last year I'd been making a fuss about nothing. As we reached the gate into the long field below the doctor's house, dad told him to be sensible. Then he turned to me and said 'Aren't you proud?' – which I didn't know how to answer. Yes, I was proud of him: he looked like one of the pictures at home, come to life. Mum looked smart enough to meet the Queen too, in her black coat with the pink collar. But her face under the shadow of her hat was thinner than ever – clay-coloured. And the way she swayed with Serenade: it made her look as though she was about to float off like thistledown.

'You all wait here,' dad said. 'I'm going to have a quick word with the Master.' As he set off towards the hounds in the top corner of the field, and the main crowd of horses, I stared towards the jumble of trailers – at the girls twiddling their hair into hairnets, which made it looked trapped and repellent, at the mums handing out sandwiches, at a groom in a brown overall, ducking behind a Land

Rover and taking a nip from his flask. This was where I'd blundered through on Tommy last year. This was the hawthorn hedge he didn't jump. This was the gatepost with bright green moss round the top, where I'd nearly crunched my knee. Was there anyone here who remembered? As I glanced up the slope and made out the Master with his Duke of Wellington face, mum whispered into my ear; she was still wearing her lemon scent, even though we were outside. Dad wasn't saying anything embarrassing, she told me. He was letting the Master know it was my first proper meet, and if we killed anything I should be blooded. Not me and Kit. Just me. Kit's turn would come later. While I went on looking, I waited for the Master to shake his head, or laugh. But nothing like that happened. When dad finished, they both scooped a glass from a silver tray that suddenly twinkled towards them. That was a good sign, I thought. Dad was smiling anyway. And still smiling when he ambled back down the hill towards us, lifting his hat now and again like a king making a tour.

We moved off a few minutes later, and when Tommy heard the Master blowing his horn, he shook so hard I thought he was about to bolt again. But this time he just arched his neck, picked up his feet, and that was that. Grandpa's silvery face galloped through my head, then dad's: this was the thing they liked best in the world. By the time we were past the church and through a five-barred gate into open fields, dad had moved ahead with the other men, to be near the hounds. Mum and Kit and I were halfway back. 'Not too much with the children,' Kit hissed, but we ignored him. We had to be ready to turn round at any moment – dad had said that – so the middle was the best place to be. And when we reached the wood on the far side of the first field, it turned out the Master had seen us, and now he'd come back to ask mum: would she take us to the far corner, so we could be on point duty together? 'Yes of course,' mum said, sounding out of breath. The Master's long face crinkled, showing his grey teeth, and mum swung away like a nervous little girl, doing what she was told.

It was an oak wood, and the ground by our corner had been ploughed weeks before, so the furrows had stiffened into shiny waves. It meant Tommy's feet wouldn't sink in too much if we had to whizz off, but he still didn't like standing there, and neither did Musket or Serenade. They couldn't find the right distance between the furrows to get their feet comfy, and jingled their bits, and biffed their heads up and down as if shaking off cobwebs. Mum didn't mind any of this. She had her right leg stretched forward, and was rapping her saddle-flap with her crop. 'You do the same, boys,' she told us. 'Come on. We've got to stop anything escaping.' Her face was so serious it made me smile, but when I'd wound the snake-tail of my own crop into a circle, like she'd done, and started my tapping, it turned out to be more complicated than I'd thought. I had to keep Tommy calm, and concentrate on the wood, and not notice it was getting hot inside my coat – hot enough to make me feel sleepy, so the puddles in the plough slid out of focus when I gazed at them, and their boggy brown melted into sky blue, which bounced onto the mud and turned that blue as well.

'Psst,' went Kit, and I snapped back to myself. 'I think they've found something.' The hounds were close now, hidden by the trees but right in front of us. They must have worked outwards from the middle of the wood and reached our corner at last. The huntsman was talking to them, along with two or three other voices – one of them was dad, wasn't it? Talking and calling. 'Good boys. Good boys. 'Ware rabbit. Good boys. Fetch him out.' It was a sort of song, but frightening, and we could hear branches crackling, and pheasants bursting out of their hiding places – one slung itself into the field behind us. We needed to make more noise, to keep everything inside the wood. Mum was shouting 'Get back, get back, get back' – in a funny accent for some reason, so it sounded like 'Git bike, git bike, git bike' – and really thumping her saddle now, with Serenade champing and dribbling saliva-strings onto the plough.

Then they both stopped and mum lifted her crop, pointing at the wood. A thin face in the brambles. A gingery triangle. Flap ears and a grizzled mouth with black lips. 'Did you see him?' mum whispered. I had, but I couldn't be sure. 'Yes,' I told her, overlapping with Kit, who said 'I think so' under his breath. 'Keep banging, then,' said mum. 'We don't want him getting past.' I walloped my saddle so hard, Tommy shimmied sideways. 'Steady on,' said Kit. Nothing was going to get past us now, because there was nothing left in our bit of the wood. The flame-noises had stopped, and there was only a soft whoosh, like stubble after a fire. Then someone the far side of the wood was shouting 'Goooone awaaaay!' – they sounded as though they'd banged their finger in a door. 'What do we do now?' I was about to ask, but mum bundled her reins in her fists, jerked her feet hard into the stirrups, and bounced off across the plough. Musket followed and so did Tommy, skimming the hard waves as if he was racing on water. When we came round the edge of the wood and saw the others – the black coats and the pinks coats like patterns on wallpaper – they were half a field ahead. Tommy barged through the stragglers into a thin water meadow. There was a copse at the far end, a tangle of willows and elder, and what was that in front of the trees? Barbed wire. That was why everyone ahead of us had slammed on the brakes and started chewing round in a circle.

It took less than a minute of galloping to reach them, but it felt like hours. Wind gushed through my head and emptied it. The hands of my watch scuttled from morning to afternoon. Daylight faded. The willow leaves slipped from gold to silver, lifted off their branches and shivered in the wet grass. Then I was up by the wire close to dad, with mud streaks on my face and hands. 'Ah,' dad said, as if I was the answer to a question he'd been asking himself. 'Ah. Good.' Then he turned away, staring into the tree-gloom ahead. He stayed silent when mum and Kit arrived, but mum popped her eyes, to show she knew what dad was thinking anyway. A splodge had landed beside the mole on her cheek, and for a moment I couldn't tell which was which. Dad swung his right leg over the pommel of his saddle like a cowboy, jumped down, handed her the reins, and whipped off his top hat before crouching through the wire. His black hair was plastered flat to his skull, but lifting into a little curl where the rim had squeezed it. 'Good luck, darling,' said mum, lifting one hand to her mouth.

He bowed to her. I couldn't tell whether they were joking or not.

The fox had gone to ground inside the wood, and the terrier man went in to dig him out. I could imagine it all. The hounds were flopped down on a ditch-bank, licking the black pads of their feet and nibbling out the thorns. The terrier man had finished hacking at the entrance to the earth, and now he was slipping the terrier – she was a girl – out of his inside jacket pocket as though he was smuggling something illegal, and popping her into the hole with secret whispers. And I could follow the terrier underground, scuffling and gruffing down the narrow tunnel, fixing her yellow eyes on the green eyes of the fox, then bristling straight up to him and fighting him with no room to move, and no fear either because that's what she was bred to do. In the end she latched her teeth round the fox's neck and bit through his windpipe, dragging him back towards the light. It was heavy work, and slow, and dusty mud from the roof of the tunnel kept trickling into her eyes and nose like pepper. But the O of sky was swelling behind her, and the man could see her now, and was making high-pitched whoops, slapping his tweed cap on his knee and saying, 'Gooood girl, goooood girl.' When her stubby white tail finally appeared he snatched it, scooping her under his arm, and shouted, 'Let go, let go, let go.' The fox dropped onto the ground like a useless old rag that had been used for wiping and rubbing and polishing until it was nothing.

I opened my eyes again. The brambles in front of me were shaking, and the hounds clamouring. Something important was about to happen. Tommy knew it too – his shoulders were trembling – but he never moved when the leaves opened and the Master appeared in his pink coat and shiny boots. He was doing a kind of slow dance, with one hand over his face to shield his eyes from the brambles. His other hand was hidden by nettles, so I couldn't see it properly and thought he might actually be holding the fox. He wasn't, of course. The fox had been eaten. That's what all the yowling had meant a moment ago. 'Now, Andrew,' he said, squeezing through the wire fence and standing beside me. 'Let's have you, then.' Close up like this, I could see his face wasn't chalk-coloured, which was what I remembered from last year. He had hundreds of tiny purple veins scribbled over his cheeks and nose. He was tilting his head, which meant he wanted me to bend towards him. Did he? Where was dad? He'd know the answer. There he was. Shouldering through the brambles, following where the Master had made a track. Because he was smiling, I knew I must be doing the right thing.

I took off my hat, and bowed like I'd done for the Bishop of Colombo at Confirmation. There was a pause. Should I say something? The Master's hand leaped towards me, so quick the fox's pad was only a blur between his fingers. But cold, definitely cold, with a strange breeze which chilled my skin before it actually touched. Then I felt three freezing stripes: one across my forehead, one on my left cheek, one on my right. And after that, warmth. Gluey heat, which meant I knew exactly where the blood lay on my face, even though I couldn't see it. 'I expect you'd like to keep this?' the Master said, and before the question was finished he flipped open my coat pocket, the one where I had my sandwiches, and pressed the pad inside. As soon as it was done, he turned away busily, to show he didn't want me to say anything. Dad took his place, holding his top hat by the brim, which made him look as though he'd just thrown it into the air and caught it again. He squeezed my knee and said, 'Well done.' When I turned round, Kit said 'Well done' too, then 'Urgh.' Mum kept quiet, and when I smiled at her she wiped her cheek with one finger, knocking the dried mud-spot onto her coat.

It was dark by the time we'd got home and done the horses, so everyone thought we should have our baths before tea, which would be crumpets as a treat. I went upstairs to the bathroom, locked the door to keep Kit out, then delved in my pocket and found the fox's pad. It was much smaller than I remembered. Smaller, but more beautiful and more interesting. The nails were browny-black, like hooks made of tortoiseshell. The pads underneath were a chubby clover. The bone-end and the sinews, where the Master had cut through with his penknife, were white as lightning. I hung my head, then filled the basin, took my flannel, wiped my face clean, and looked in the mirror. The bars of blood had broken as soon as I touched them, but I could still see where they'd been. The skin was definitely redder there, and tighter, as if I'd been burned.

CHAPTER TWELVE

Condensed Milk

Mum wondered: now I was in double figures, would I mind coming back from school by train, when term ended? She'd meet me in London, and we'd do the last bit together. Of course not, I wrote to her, but really I felt disappointed. On the other hand, maybe mum was tired – and the bus from Maidwell to Northampton station might be fun. I'd never been on a bus before, and when I looked down from my seat, I thought this was the highest I'd ever been. I was forgetting the upstairs of houses, or the haystack in the shed at home, and when I told Innis I, who was sitting next to me, he crinkled his eyebrows so I knew I'd said something stupid. I didn't mind. I could see over the box hedge into the rose garden, and there was the gleam of the rain gauge in the middle, by the sundial. Normally a prefect had to check that every day, and work out how much rain had fallen. By the time we came back next term, it would be bunged up with leaves, which showed Beak didn't really care about rain.

Innis I tapped me on the shoulder; Slapper Morris was the master in charge, and he was talking into a microphone by the driver. 'I want you to remember something,' he said, in his high-pitched voice, which had a scream trapped inside it. 'Until you're actually with your parents, and even after that, you're still pupils at Maidwell Hall. You must make the school feel proud of you.' Then he wiped the side of his hand across his mouth, so we could hear his moustache rustling into the mike. 'I'd like to wish you a happy holidays,' he went on. 'But I won't do that yet, because I'm going to be coming with you all the way to London.' Normally when a master said something like that, everyone groaned as a joke. But nobody groaned with Slapper; he was too frightening, and bound to keep a special eye out. All the same, I couldn't help wondering about him. He was wearing a pale tweed suit I hadn't seen before, which smelled of mothballs, and there was a neat little suitcase parked by his seat: green canvas, with leather corners. Was he going to stay in London after we'd all said goodbye, and get up to something?

'No running! Remember what I told you, boys! Remember you're still pupils!' We could hear Slapper behind us, now we were out of our carriage and sprinting along the platform at Euston. But the steam-squirts hissing out from the wheels of the engine meant he couldn't see us clearly any more. We were safe. Wallace even had his tie off, and was stuffing it into his pocket as he ran – that was because his dad was rich, and he was going to the Bahamas for the holidays, to get brown. When he shoved past, I slowed down. It should have made me feel excited, this rushing. But it gave me a little wallop of sadness instead. As soon as I saw mum, the clock would start counting towards next term – and that would be any second, because she was probably over there, in that scrum the other side of the barrier. No. She'd got round it somehow, and – woah! – here she was in front of me, wearing her new beige overcoat. It must be the one she'd written to me about, and said she liked even though beige was a non-U word, so we'd have to call the colour something else. She looked like a tent blowing away. I threw myself forward and asked God to stop the clock, actually asked him aloud, but not for mum to hear.

As she wrapped her arms round my head, I could feel a bit of my brain sliding off sideways, trying to live the last five seconds all over again, and remember how she looked when I first saw her. Her face was older, and her eyes more sunk-in. Her hair had more grey in it, too. Had she always been like this, or had I forgotten? When I pushed away and checked, everything seemed normal. 'Do we have to say goodbye to anyone?' she wanted to know. 'Just Slapper,' I told her, and she said she'd do that. I waited by a pillar and stared more carefully. I'd been wrong. She wasn't thinner than usual. She was thin like always – not that Slapper minded either way. While she talked to him, his face went from yellow to pink, and he wiped his moustache so quickly I thought all the hairs must be standing on end, full of electricity. 'What an extraordinary little man,' mum said when she found me again. 'I wonder where Beak dug *him* up?' I glanced over her shoulder, and Slapper was waving. I waved back and wished I hadn't.

The big question was: would the animals recognise me? I hadn't been home since half-term, which was six weeks ago, and if one dog year was the same as seven human years, then six weeks was something like three-quarters of a year. Mum said she'd been reminding them, but I couldn't tell whether she was joking. Anyway, it took ages for us to chuff into Bishops Stortford, then find the Hillman in the car park, then wiggle through the back way to Little Brewers. First I had to say hello to Kit, who was reading in the playroom. He wasn't pleased to see me – that was obvious – but mum had warned me about this in the train. 'He's got used to being the only pebble on the beach. He thinks now you're back, he's not going to get a look-in.' 'He will,' I said, frowning. 'Anyway, he'll be at Maidwell too in a couple of terms, so he won't have to worry.' This didn't quite say what I meant, and when I looked at Kit now, peering over the top of his book with his hair sticking up, I wished we hadn't given up kissing each other. We didn't even hug any more. I gave him a shove on the shoulder and asked what he was reading, which was a silly question. He'd only picked up the book because he'd heard the car in the yard.

Then I went to change out of my school clothes, which meant tiptoeing past the kitchen, because the dogs were shut in there, and already suspected I was back. Beauty was snuffing round the edge of the door, and Wiggy was making her funny whine, like a kettle about to boil. A minute later, I was downstairs again in my jeans and my favourite blue jersey with the turnover collar. 'You do the door,' I told Kit, heading towards the drawing room and sitting in mum's green chair, where the dogs could find me easily. He only had to touch the handle and they were charging past him, skewing the rug, scrabbling on the bare boards of the hall, and leaping at my chair before they'd decided whether they wanted to be on top of me or beside me. Both, as it turned out: slobbery tongues over my face and hands, Beauty stuffing her nose under my arm so she could sniff out school on the other side of whatever soap mum used for my jersey, Wiggy quivering and grovelling, and scratching me with her nails. 'They'll pee on you if you're not careful,' Kit said from the doorway – and he was right; I knew I was being ridiculous. But even if it was disgusting, there wasn't any person I could hug like this, and I couldn't go round the house telling tables and chairs how pleased I was to see them. In a minute, I'd see the horses; they wouldn't be much good either. Tommy allowed me to keep my arms round his neck for about ten seconds before he started jerking his head up and down. It was only the dogs who let go of everything and didn't mind. Our hugging sessions were like slipping underground. I needed to lie there for a bit, before all the clocks started ticking again.

Dad got home around seven, stopping on the threshold so I could see his black hair gleaming in the light over the door. And that red dent the bowler left on his forehead, like an extra wrinkle. We didn't kiss each other either, but after he'd hung his hat and coat on the peg, dumped his briefcase and *Standard* on the bench, and poured his whisky, he wanted me to sit down and tell him everything. We were either side of the fire mum had lit in the drawing room. I started with work, then went through games, teachers, gangs, being orderly because I knew he liked that. In a week, when my report came, he'd make me stand beside his desk, while he went through the things masters had written about me. The more I told him now, the easier that would be, especially if I could persuade him all the teachers were idiots. Then, when he saw Haggie's bubbly writing, or Mr Porch's Greek e's, he wouldn't believe everything they said. He'd still be stern, but I could deal with that because I knew underneath it all, he wanted me to be happy. That's why, when the end of our chat by the fire came in sight, he said, 'You do enjoy it, old boy, don't you? I mean, school's school, but Beak and everyone are friendly, aren't they?' 'Yes, dad,' I said, wanting him to be happy too. After that his glass suddenly needed filling again, so I went through to help mum get supper ready in the kitchen.

Next morning when Kit and I were in the tack room cleaning our bridles, I was thinking that even though I'd just been doing something I enjoyed – riding – I didn't really feel the holidays had started yet. It had been obvious at supper last night that mum and dad wanted to give me a lesson in growing up, and were suddenly talking about friends to help make it happen. 'You've got friends at school, haven't you?' Kit asked, dipping his sponge into the soapy water and squeezing until he was holding bubbles and nothing else. 'Not really,' I told him. 'Why not? Aren't you popular?' I wasn't sure I knew, so I answered a different question. 'It's not that,' I said. 'It's more that I don't like many people. Only the ones I like.' It sounded silly, but I ploughed on. 'I mean,' I said, 'there aren't many people I *do* like. You'll see, when you start. It's not the same as the Barn, you know.' Kit was rubbing his sponge over the reins, leaving streaky soap-marks on the plaited leather at the ends. 'I like lots of people,' he said stiffly, sounding like dad. 'I think you ought to try a bit harder.'

I was too surprised to be angry, and we left it at that. But mum must have been listening, because soon afterwards she asked: did I want to have anyone to stay? It couldn't be Miller II, because his dad had taken him skiing. Mum tried again: what about people from nearby – just to see? 'There aren't any,' I said. 'They're all Kit's age.' 'There's Tim Spencer,' mum came back at me smartly. I stared, making sure she wasn't pulling my leg. Tim was a joke, didn't mum remember? Wet as a swamp – she'd said that herself. And now he was in the Boy Scouts, which made him even worse. Last holidays he'd knocked on the front door wearing his drippy uniform with its hanky round the neck, and asked whether we could give him a bob-a-job. Next thing I knew, he was on his hands and knees weeding the crazy-paving by the front gate, which no one ever used unless they were strangers. I'd peeped from behind the curtains in my bedroom, and when I'd seen Tim bending over like that, I wanted to kick him. Surely mum didn't think I ought to join the Scouts too? This talk about friends was more serious than I'd thought. There was a campaign going on, and if I didn't work out how to deal with it I'd get lumbered.

I said I'd like to see the Routledge twins. Their dad and mum were farmers, and they lived beyond Tim's house, down a track lined with elm trees. Peter was the younger twin and looked like a ferret – little and bony and always planning something. He knew how to tickle fish, and the pockets of his dungarees were full of bits of string, and matchboxes with pinpricks in the lid, in case he found a caterpillar. Andrew was bigger and more galumphing. When I eventually went over to play with them before tea one afternoon, and we tried to hoik a fish out of the stream below their house, his shadow got in the way. Peter had been lying in the grass on the river bank, perfectly quiet while everything got used to him, and his hand had been in the water for so long it was going wrinkly. He looked dead still but actually he was working his fingers forward incredibly slowly, tightening them into a kind of half-fist. He must have found a fish, a perch probably, alongside the reeds ahead of us, and was about to pounce. That's when Andrew moved, and Peter called him a silly arse and we all went indoors. I'd have liked to go back and try again another day, but they didn't ask me. Perhaps Kit was right. I was unpopular.

The Franklin family lived up the road in Sheering. The two boys didn't interest me much – the older one, Simon, was so dozy he always had sleepy-dust in the corner of his eyes, and the younger one, James, had white hair and felt mad: he hid in the hedge and chucked stones at cars. There was an elder sister, Emily, and she was weird too – she walked as if she was on wheels, and talked about her 'bodily needs' in a posh voice. Come to think of it, they were all pretty strange, including the parents, who were usually red in the face and laughing. Sometimes the doctor even mopped tears from his eyes with a hanky. 'They're such good fun,' mum always said, but I wasn't sure. The first time I met them, Mrs Franklin ordered everyone into the back of her sky-blue Zephyr, folded the roof back, and drove us to Harlow as fast as she could, even though it was raining and we all got soaked.

The Franklins made me tongue-tied, and as soon as that happened I felt boring, and then mum thought I was being wet. With Rosie, who came between Emily and Simon, it was even worse. She was the craziest in the whole family, and told filthy jokes without smiling, then burst into laughter when nothing funny was happening. She was gorgeous, too. Easily as pretty as the girl on the Lux packet, with the same fair hair and blue eyes. This meant I badly wanted her to like me, even though I didn't know what might happen if she did; after all, she was the only girl I'd ever met properly. Would I kiss her, for instance? I couldn't think about that, but Kit did. 'Is she your girlfriend?' he asked, after I'd spent an afternoon with her. 'Don't be an idiot,' I told him. 'I haven't got a girlfriend.' He didn't believe me, and I didn't blame him. How could I, when the whole business of girls was so mysterious? Was it usual, for instance, for their faces to float into your head when you didn't expect it? Every time this happened with Rosie, she looked so real I thought everyone else must be able to see her too. I even liked her little golden moustache, which was the kind of thing I usually hated.

Then dad had a work dinner in London; he'd be staying in a hotel, and mum wanted to keep him company. She told us at teatime, when Kit and I were round the kitchen table. 'You wouldn't mind spending the night with the Franklins, would you?' she asked, in the hurried voice which meant we had to agree with her. Kit shrugged, and I said, 'Of course not.' I was trying to sound relaxed, but the timing went wrong and it came out too high, so Kit gurgled under his breath. 'Am I missing something?' Mum asked. 'Nothing,' I said, glaring at Kit, then left the room without finishing my tea. This was a mistake, because now mum knew I was upset. Last time I'd been to the Franklin's house, Emily had announced that I had a crush on Rosie, and for once Rosie had laughed at the right time. Immediately. Then she smiled at me sideways through her eyelashes.

We got through the afternoon, but only just. Rosie wanted to play a kissing game called Postman's Knock, which I'd heard about and dreaded. I knew she'd either fix things to make sure she kissed me a lot, or not at all. I didn't know which would be more embarrassing – but the answer was neither. The sun came out, and Mrs Franklin made sure we stayed in the garden, riding our bikes again and again down the slope outside their playroom window. Kit hurt his leg falling off, but he didn't cry as much as usual. Maybe because mum wasn't around, and he knew Mrs Franklin would tell him to get on with it? I couldn't decide because it was supper time now, and we were allowed to have it on our knees in front of the telly, which was a treat. 'Do you think Jesus really looked like that?' I wondered, pointing at a picture above the sofa. It showed a man with a soft brown beard, standing in a clearing. He had the sun behind him, and everything was shimmery with white and purple, especially his cloak, which looked huge because his arms were stretched out sideways. Lots of birds had appeared from the trees roundabout, and a few children too – they were looking at him with the sun in their eyes and their mouths open. Nobody spoke for a bit, and I started to think I'd said something clever. Eventually Rosie put on her laziest voice – the words sounded as though they were lying down and snoozing. '*Is* it Jesus?' she said. 'I've always thought it might be St Francis of Assisi.' 'Because of the birds, you mean?' She turned to me with a slight frown, chewing a slab of her yellow hair. Then she burst into laughter and slapped her leg so hard, the fork shot off her plate and fell on the carpet. It still had baked beans stuck on it. 'Yes, because of the birds,' she said in a weak voice. Emily and Simon and James stayed watching the telly; they thought this was normal. Kit was staring at me. He could tell I wanted to go home.

Rosie disappeared before bed, and I felt happier by the time I went upstairs too. I'd only have to see her at breakfast, then mum would come and collect me. But after I'd said goodnight to Kit along the corridor, and turned off the bedside light, my door opened again. There she was. In her pyjamas now, though they must have been Simon's, because the legs were rolled up as if she was about to push out a boat. I didn't say anything, and for a moment she stood still, with the landing light glowing in her hair like the picture of Jesus. Then she lifted one of her arms, which was even more like Jesus. Or maybe St Francis. She was holding a small tin, with white paper and blue writing. 'Would you like some?' she said, using a deeper voice than usual. How did she know I wasn't asleep? Perhaps she'd seen my eyes – I should have kept them shut. Still, it was too late now. She was stepping forward and closing the door behind her. 'Where are you?' she said. I forgot to answer because I could smell something sugary. Had she put on scent, or were all girls like that? Probably not – and anyway, I recognised the tin now. Condensed milk. 'Here I am,' I said, suddenly remembering to speak. 'Here,' I said again, more loudly.

Rosie hadn't needed to ask. She could see perfectly well. How else did she lift back my top sheet and blankets without fumbling, then slide into bed beside me? The heat of her leg was burning, and I wondered whether the soft hair on her lip was actually everywhere, all over her body, like one of Beauty's puppies. I was tempted to put my arm round her to stroke her, but I thought she wouldn't like that. She wasn't a pet, after all. On the other hand, what did she want? I decided the best thing would be to lie still, flat on my back, even though her hair had drifted into my face, tickling so much I couldn't help blowing it away with a 'fffffffp' noise. That made her laugh again. 'Don't you like me?' she said, propping herself on her elbow. In the half light, I could see the top of her pyjamas had sagged open. I swallowed, making a little clunk in my throat, meaning to tell her yes, I did like her. But just as I was opening my mouth, she held the tin over my head. What was she doing? Giving me a drink of the milk, that's what. When I thought she'd disappeared off to bed, she must have been downstairs in the kitchen, finding the tin and making holes either side of the lid with a can opener. Now I could see their jagged little triangles above me, and the gluey milk plugging one of them. It took for ever to bulge through, swelling and shining like the white of an eye, but slowly turning into a tear, then a snail track, then a miniature rope. When it touched my tongue at last, the taste was slippery, not like milk at all, and the sweetest thing I'd ever tasted.

I swallowed again and wanted some more. But that wasn't Rosie's plan, and she was in charge. She handed me the tin, lay back, and opened her mouth as if she was going to the dentist. I didn't like this so much, especially because she pursed her lips as soon as the milk touched them. 'Urgh,' she said, shuddering and wiping her mouth. 'I don't know how you can touch that stuff. Give it here.' Then she was sitting up, shoving me flat in the bed again, plonking the tin on my chest, and settling herself beside me. She wasn't like a puppy any more. She was a cat twitching her tail, and it was my fault. But she didn't leave. She lay quietly and so did I, with my arms folded behind my head to keep them out of the way. I didn't want to touch her anywhere by accident: that seemed important. I couldn't do anything about my leg, though, which lay against hers all the way down, getting hotter and hotter. I decided I had to keep chatting, to take my mind off it. Stuff about school, mainly. How I liked English and not Maths. It didn't help. By now, my leg was glowing like one of the horse's shoes when the blacksmith hammered it on his anvil – and Rosie felt even more bored. I could tell, because she kept giving the same answer: 'Oh really?', 'Oh really?', 'Oh really?', no matter what I said.

Eventually I tipped over into a huge yawn. I thought that might happen, and I'd been taking deep breaths secretly to stop it, because I didn't want Rosie to think I was rude. Actually she seemed pleased, hopping out of bed and back into the doorway almost before my mouth shut again. I lifted one hand in a dreamy wave, and she darted forward to rescue the tin. Then she whisked onto the landing, the door clicked tight, and silence settled round me like water in a tank. Had I made a fool of myself? I couldn't tell. But I did know I'd never talked to her for so long without her laughing in the wrong places. Perhaps she really could be my girl-friend? Perhaps I could write to her at school, and she'd write back?

Mum would approve, because she thought Mr and Mrs Franklin were good fun. But I didn't want dad to laugh at me for liking a girl. These days, I even felt awkward if he caught me listening to a song which had anything about love in it. Lonnie Donegan was OK: 'My Old Man's a Dustman'. The Beatles, though, and the Searchers and the Rolling Stones: they were always saying something about girls. That's why I'd bought Tommy Steele's 'Little White Bull'. Because it was about a cow. Or a bull, rather. On the other hand, dad liked the Franklins as much as mum did, so maybe he wouldn't mind about Rosie? There was more to think about this, but I couldn't keep my eyes open, and when I closed them I saw nothing to do with Rosie or music. There was the steep slope outside the Franklins' playroom, and light rushing into my face as I freewheeled downhill for the umpteenth time.

I started to fret as soon as I woke up. Would Rosie talk to Emily, and would Emily say something that made me look stupid? I needn't have worried. While I was mooching round the kitchen, waiting for my boiled egg, Simon told me Rosie had got up early, and gone out for a long bike ride; she'd probably be away until lunch. That turned out to be right. She didn't appear even though mum turned up late, and then went into the drawing room to talk to Mrs Franklin before taking us home. Normally mum would have said Rosie was being rude, but she seemed quiet all round – probably because she was tired after London and the boring dinner. Her face was whiter than usual, and the veins in the dip beside her eyes looked full up. They bulged, even when she wasn't talking.

There was something else going on, I knew it. When she sent Kit off to the playroom after tea that afternoon, and told me to sit and finish my sandwich, I was ready. Was it OK with the Franklins? she wanted to know. 'Yes.' 'What did you do?' 'Bike riding.' 'And after supper?' 'We talked.' 'About what?' 'About Jesus,' I said, and mum laughed. 'No really,' I said, and started to explain the picture and the arms and the birds. 'And what about later?' mum wondered. 'What do you mean, later?' 'Bedtime,' Mum said, without looking up, swirling the tea round her cup. Suddenly I understood. Mrs Franklin knew about the milk. That's why she'd wanted to see mum, and why Rosie had been away this morning. I began to blush, which I always did when I was in trouble, and hated my face. Why couldn't I have dark hair and white skin like Mackay? He never went red, even when he'd done something wrong. 'I went to bed,' I said. 'That's not what I heard,' mum replied.

The kitchen door creaked open and Kit appeared on the top step. How much did he know? Everything, by the look of it. He was grinning so hard, his top lip had dried out and got rumpled on his teeth. 'Buzz off,' mum said. 'Yes, buzz off,' I echoed, but I needn't have bothered. Kit turned round in pure shock, taking his grin with him. Mum never talked to us like that – and if she was cross, I'd better look out. At the same time, I was peeved. Rosie and I'd just drunk some milk, that's all. I hadn't even touched her by accident, and there was no way she could have seen what was inside my head. All the stuff about puppies and whatnot. I glanced up quickly, to see whether mum was pretending. Her face looked hollow, and the skin round her eyes was grey as a pigeon. 'Tell me what happened and I won't mind,' she said. Her voice sounded exhausted.

I did tell her, and she wasn't angry. But she didn't believe me. When I'd explained how Rosie had taken the milk and gone back to her own room, and I'd fallen asleep soon afterwards, she said, 'So you didn't play doctors and nurses, then?' I hadn't heard of this game, but the blood rushed into my face like never before. 'No!' I said, loudly. 'No, not at all! Is that what Mrs Franklin says?' Mum stuck out her bottom lip and stared at me, nodding her head slowly. Eventually she said, 'Mrs Franklin wasn't there, so Mrs Franklin doesn't know.' Then a much worse thought struck me. 'Is it what Rosie told her?' Mum nodded again, but harder.

I looked at my sandwich lying on my plate. There was a jagged bite-mark on one side, where I'd taken a mouthful, and it reminded me of the hole in the milk tin. Is this what happened when you felt guilty? Did everything in the world gang up against you? 'That's not right,' I explained. 'We never did what you just said.' 'Do you mean Rosie's lying?' mum came straight back. 'Why should she do that?' I looked at my plate again: the bread of my sandwich was already stiff. It was amazing how quickly that happened.

'Do you promise?' mum was saying. 'Yes, I promise.' Mum shoved back her chair from the table, rubbing her hands together, wiping off crumbs. 'OK then,' she said. 'We won't talk about it again. Now give me your sandwich if you're not going to finish.' I handed over my plate and tried to smile. 'Will you tell dad?' I asked, as she turned to put our cups in the sink. 'I don't need to, if you've told me the truth, do I?' she said. 'No, you don't,' I told her, keeping my voice as level as possible. 'Well, then,' she said, and took a deep breath so I saw her shoulder-blades stirring through her cardigan. 'Now why don't you go and play with Kit until bathtime?'

I stood by the steps which led up to the hall, and put my hand on the doorknob. 'Mum?' I said. 'Yes,' she answered, still looking into the sink. 'I won't have to see them again for a bit, will I? The Franklins, I mean. Or other people like Tim and the Routledges. I want to do our things.' Mum still didn't turn round, but she hung her head a little. The hair parted at the back of her neck, and long white bones stood out like a skeleton. I thought she said 'Not if you don't want to', but I couldn't be sure. My ears were blocked by the splatter of tap water hitting the sink. 'Thanks, mum,' I said. Her thin shoulders rolled again, as she whisked the mop round my plate. It made her look as though she'd once been a bird, and was remembering her wings.

CHAPTER THIRTEEN

Bellum, Bellum, Bellum

Mum said she couldn't drive me back to school any more. 'There's a train from London, you know, like the one you came back on that time with Mr Whatshisname. Morris. Only going the other way, of course.' We were sitting in front of the telly in the drawing room, and the evening news was about Cuba. I knew it was serious because I'd heard dad talking about it the other day, and seen a scary cartoon in mum's *Express*. It showed Fidel Castro and President Kennedy: they had a sports car each, and were about to have a head-on collision. Underneath the picture it said, 'I'm sure he's going to brake first!' 'Are you happy about that, darling?' mum asked. 'What?' I said, without taking my eyes from the screen. 'About going back by train,' she said. 'After all, you're grown up now, and you've got Kit with you, so it won't be too bad.' A line of grey ships steamed across the middle of nowhere, and their shadows looked like whales. 'Honestly, darling,' she went on, speaking more smartly now. 'You must pay attention when I'm talking to you.' 'I do pay attention, mum,' I said. 'And yes it's fine to go back by train. Fine.' I didn't mean it, but there was nothing else I could say. She'd decided, and dad would back her up. 'Are you sure?' she said. 'Of course,' I snapped. 'Now can we stop talking about it? There's still a week of the hols to go.' 'That's right,' said mum. 'A whole lovely week, but we'll have to get both your trunks ready tomorrow, so we can send them PLA.'

PLA stood for Passengers' Luggage in Advance, which mum thought was a good idea. 'If you're not packing,' she explained, 'you don't have to think about leaving.' I wanted to agree with her, but it wasn't true. Everything about the last week had something to do with leaving. Like visiting Mrs Manning, so she could give us a box of Newberry Fruits, which we hated. Picking beans in the veg gar-

den, and thinking I'd never do it again on a Wednesday, or a
Thursday, or whatever. Shopping in Bucks Stores, and waiting
while Mr Buck toddled very slowly round the long arm of his
counter, and gave us a free Flying Saucer. 'Anyone would think we
were going to Australia,' Kit said as we biked home again, but that
only made me frown. Homesickness was far worse than going to
Australia. It meant having a lead weight wrapped round my whole
body, like in a coffin. My head went dark, and my stomach
squashed down flat. In the end it got so bad, I asked God to make
time get a move on – which made me wonder whether I was going
mad, and would soon start sprouting hair on the palms of my
hands. Why else would I want to get rid of the things I liked best?
It turned out mum understood perfectly well. 'It's the waiting, isn't
it?' she said, when we'd finished our prayers at night. Then she slid
off my bed to stand in the doorway, so Kit would know she was
talking to him as well. I felt sorry for him. Because I was older, I
always did most things first – and people thought life was easier for
Kit. It wasn't always, though. And certainly not at Maidwell. He'd
been there a couple of terms now, and hated it. 'It'll be better when
you get there,' mum was saying. 'Then you can start crossing off
days again.' I thought more about that, after she'd pulled the door
almost shut and creaked off downstairs. Time was behaving very
oddly, now there were only a couple of days left: every second was
precious and awful at the same time, like the countdown for a
rocket which was bound to crash. On our last evening we had the
condemned supper, which was bangers and mash, our favourite,
but difficult to swallow. Then came the last time mum kissed us
goodnight, which had to be quick because she couldn't bear it.
After that, in a blink, it was the last morning and we were saying
goodbye to dad. He tapped his bowler onto his head and buttoned
his black overcoat, while we stood in the hall and waited for him to
squeeze our shoulders in turn. I didn't mind him not being cosy –
it made things easier, because I didn't want him to see me cry. At
the same time, it reminded me how much worse I'd feel in an hour
or two. Unless I broke my leg, of course, or came out in spots
which turned out to be infectious.

Maybe the dogs would give me a disease? I lay on the floor of the drawing room and Beauty licked inside my ears, then right over my lips. It was disgusting, she smelled of manure, but all it did was make me dizzy. When I stood up again, I told myself not to be ridiculous, and walked round the garden the wrong way, starting with the roses, to make sure I was seeing everything from a surprising angle and wouldn't forget it. 'Have some of this,' mum said, when I wandered back to the kitchen. It was a glass of milk: gold top – even that was something we wouldn't get at school. I took it up to my bedroom to drink while I changed into school clothes, but had to pour the dregs into the corner sink: it was too creamy to fit down my throat. By the time I came downstairs again, mum had already shut the dogs in the kitchen, so I called to them. When Beauty woofed at me, tears spurted from both my eyes as if I'd been kicked. 'Are you OK?' said Kit, who was waiting in the car under the drive-through. His eyes were dry, but I could tell he'd been crying too: he had red blotches on his cheeks. The parting in his hair was white as a scar.

We parked by the wooden passenger bridge in Bishops Stortford, the one dad walked over every day before he caught the train for London. London. I said the word over to myself as we steamed away from the platform, and thought it should sound longer, since it was such an important place. I let my eyes glaze, playing the game of sticking an enormous super-sharp knife through the window, and chopping down all the trees, telephone poles, lamp posts and signals as we rattled along. Mr Manning had never been to London; he thought Harlow was as big as towns should get. Did that mean my life was more interesting than his? I hardly knew London myself. It was the place we went for treats, like the trip with the Franklins to feed the pigeons in Trafalgar Square, or to Madame Tussaud's where I'd pulled the hair on the man's arm and he'd turned out to be real, or the pantomime of Jorrocks with grandpa. Otherwise it was for things mum and dad thought were too important to do at home – such as buying school clothes at Billings and Edmonds, and seeing Mr Peebles the dentist in Harley Street, and Mr de Main the barber in Dover Street. Peebles and de

Main. Those were odd names too. They might have been people in Happy Families, which we sometimes played with mum because she liked the Bung family, who were brewers the same as us . . .

'What are you thinking?' Mum wanted to know. 'Nothing,' I told her, because it was too complicated to explain. The truth was, I didn't mind what popped into my head, as long as it didn't have anything to do with what came next. Liverpool Street. Then a taxi to Brown's Hotel, which would be quiet for lunch even though we'd only have soup. Then another taxi to the little cinema at Piccadilly Circus, where they showed Bugs Bunny and The Flintstones and Road Runner on a loop, so we could come in whenever we liked, and still see everything in an hour. The films were funny, but the real point was, they made time disappear. And when they ended, we had to go straight to Euston. Was I imagining things, or could I smell the train-steam already, while I was still on the pavement looking at the statue of Eros, which was like the one at Maidwell only bigger? No, I wasn't imagining. There was definitely smoke curling round my new shoes. Their toes were glittery, which dad said put his army boots in the shade. My tweed jacket wasn't so good, though. It had leather buttons like miniature buns, and they were too big for the holes.

'I won't hang around,' mum said when we came into the station, which was a relief. After she'd said hello to Rhubarb, who was the master in charge, and never had a new jacket at the start of term, she just crouched down and quickly hugged us in turn, as if we were on fire. I'd almost run out of goodbye feelings by now, and watched the other mothers over her shoulder – the country ones with their round red faces and fleecy ankle-boots; the town ones with their fair hair and chunky gold earrings. Dad was right. Our mum was the prettiest. The others all hugged their boys as if they were packing down in a rugger scrum, and didn't know how to be sad. Our mum looked as if she might fall over, now that I'd let her go. 'You know what I'll do next, don't you?' she said, laughing with red eyes. I told her no but I meant yes: she always did the same thing. 'I'll go and buy some clothes to cheer myself up, but I won't be concentrating and I'll get something hideous.' 'Make sure you wear it when you come to take us out,' I said, hoping this sounded grown up enough. 'Then we can tell you.' I waved at her, as if I was already inside the carriage, and grabbed Kit's arm so we could turn away together, like brothers were supposed to do. I knew mum would watch until the train disappeared, but it felt better if we walked off and she stayed still, rather than the other way round.

From London to about Stevenage, boys chatted pretty easily. Bishop II had a new penknife to show off, and most of the others wanted to swank about what they'd done in the holidays. Nobody talked for the second part of the journey. I saw Lety, who was normally tough, leaning his head against the window and staring at the fields getting dark. He was crying. So was Mackay. Kit said he felt sick, and I told him to see Rhubarb, who thought it would be a good idea if he went to the loo. When I waited outside the door to make sure he was OK, I could hear he was crying too, even though the wheels underneath us were clanking like a fairground. By the time we reached Northampton, all this had changed again. We were sleepy now, and when I sat beside Kit in the bus that took us the last bit, my eyes shut. When I opened them again, we were clattering over the cattle grid, and the headlights were on the Wilderness. I nudged Kit awake. 'Here we are!' said Rhubarb, standing up by the driver, and giving the smile which showed his pointy tooth. Mercury hopped into the glossy window behind him, holding up the bow with no arrow as if it were a bunch of flowers.

Kit and I stopped in the hall, watching the boys walk slowly in circles. They looked like prisoners in a war film, trudging round their yard as they swapped cigarettes and plans for escape. 'Got that smell?' Kit asked. I had. Cabbage and drains from Annie's kitchen, dead butter beans from the dining room, socks and sweat from the floorboards. I touched Kit's arm again. At home, we usually forgot there were nearly three years between us; at school, it was a difference as big as the Alps. But we weren't ready to say goodbye yet, and when I decided to go upstairs to my dorm, which was Mauve this year, Kit followed. There was my trunk waiting by the bed, even though the chalk letters of PLA had been rubbed into a smear so nobody could read them. 'That's magic,' I said. 'How do you think they knew it was mine?' But Kit's mood had changed. 'Aren't you going to talk to me?' he asked. 'Of course,' I said, speaking quietly in case he got more upset. 'What would you like to talk about? Home?' 'Yeah home,' he said. 'Well . . .' I hesitated, trying to be sensible. 'We can't very well talk about home now, can we? I mean we've got to unpack, then the gong will go for supper, then . . .' "That's what I mean,' Kit interrupted. 'They make you switch from one thing to another, and that's that. I'm not your bro any more – not until the end of term, anyway.' 'That's not true,' I said, though I could see what he meant. 'It is,' he said, quite steady. 'But I don't blame you. I blame them. They're all bastards.' I stared at him. I'd never heard him say that word before – I didn't realise he knew it. 'They are,' I said, to show I was keeping up. 'They're complete bastards. And if they hear us call them that, they'll prove it by whacking us.' Kit gave me his straight look, right down into my eyes. 'Oh well,' he said with a shrug. 'See you in twelve weeks. Have a good term.' He turned towards the corridor, then twisted back and said over his shoulder: 'Hope your work goes better.' As I watched him disappear, I thought he should have been the elder brother, not me.

In my first couple of years at Maidwell, work hadn't mattered much. Because I'd known how to read and write before I arrived, and some of the boys in Haggie's class didn't, she'd spent most of her lessons with them. I still had to do spelling bees and learn lists of new words, but none of the tests were difficult, and there'd been plenty of time for things which were partly work and partly not. Nature notebooks, for instance, where I'd collected bird feathers and dried flowers, and written their names underneath. Cress was good too. Haggie had spread some flannel in trays on top of our lockers, and if I remembered to keep the flannel wet, the cress grew so fast I could practically see it happening, and got a star. Several stars in a week meant taking your report card to Beak, but that never happened. On the other hand, several minuses in a week meant taking your card to Beak as well, and getting swished for not paying attention. Arithmetic was the worst. I could do addition and subtraction, but must have been in the sickroom for the lesson about fractions. Haggie had tried to help, but it was like having a rock instead of a sponge inside my head: my brain wouldn't soak up anything.

At the end of my first year, I left Haggie's class and started what mum called 'the long trek'. She meant from now on I'd have different classrooms, each with a different teacher. Maltese Dease for Geography, in the room next door to Haggie; Beak for Latin, in a cubbyhole under the stairs; Booster Thwaites for Scripture in the big school; Rhubarb Randall for English in Tower. This was the place I liked best, with the honeysuckle round the window where the flycatcher nested, and the iron radiator as big as a ship's boiler. When Rhubarb asked us to explain how to lose some sentences from a page without spoiling the sense, it didn't feel like work, more like a game. Other subjects were never like that – especially Maths, which was the name we used for Arithmetic now, and was taught by Miss Scott, who had fingerprints on her arms. When she put her tidy red figures in the margin beside my own sums, which always looked like a fallen-down wall, I still couldn't get the right answer. French and Latin weren't much better, especially Latin, which Beak said was never difficult because it had such clear rules. I knew he was fibbing because mum told me. She'd hated Latin herself, when she'd been at school. 'Really?' I asked, leaning forward from the back seat of the Hillman. 'You did Latin?' I couldn't believe something so awful had lasted so long. 'Oh yes,' she said in a hollow voice which must have been her teacher's. 'Bellum, bellum, bellum. Blah, blah, blah.'

English was the only good subject, and the best part about it – even better than précis – was writing stories. I'd first tried them with Haggie, and words just floated into my mind, including some I didn't understand. 'Where do they come from?' Haggie wanted to know, but I couldn't tell her. Probably they were things I'd heard mum and dad say. In any case, it wasn't only the writing that felt good. It was showing the stories to someone else, like a present I could give away and keep at the same time. That's why I'd carried on writing in the holidays, and taken some stories into mum's bed one morning, so I could read them to her. 'They're very violent,' she said, which surprised me. Violence was one of the reasons we had to turn off the telly in the evenings. 'They're not,' I said. 'They're hardly violent at all.' 'They are, darling.' She laughed, and rolled away to turn up the *Today* programme, which meant I could see the sunlight lying along her shoulder like wax. 'Cowboys and Indians,' she went on, under her breath. 'Car accidents. They're all violent, aren't they? Especially the one about soldiers killing their prisoners. Why don't you write about something peaceful? Or better still, a poem. You like the poems you do with Beak, don't you?' 'No,' I told her in a hard voice. Mum raised her eyebrows. 'Why not? Poems are lovely and peaceful.' 'All we do is learn them,' I said. Mum sighed. 'You'll be grateful when you're older. What you learn now will stay in your head for ever.' I smiled, and said, 'Softly along the road of evening, in a twilight dim with rose, wrinkled with age and drenched with dew, old Nod the shepherd goes.' 'You see?' said mum, smiling back. 'What did I tell you?'

In my first year, Haggie always made us feel the world was coming to an end if we got a minus. This was nothing compared to what happened in the senior forms. Suddenly the masters started losing their tempers all the time, and saying we'd never pass the exam to our next school, and sending us to Beak to be whacked about once a week. It made me feel I was walking into a tunnel that was getting steadily narrower and darker, and soon the ceiling would be pressing so hard on my head, I'd never be able to think straight. God was no help, even though I still kept the Bible under my pillow. And friends? I wrote to mum about this, because I knew from the muddle with Rosie that she wanted me to find some new pals, and got an answer from dad instead. He told me I should have a hobby, because that's what he'd done at school. What about stamps? I didn't like stamps, they were boring, but I took the hint. If I got interested in something, that would make me interesting, and then people would talk to me more often.

There was Miller II, at least; we weren't such good friends as before, but he was better than most people. Could I give him a hand with the moles? He goggled at me, as if I'd asked to borrow his underpants, and said no. I wasn't surprised. The moles were a big thing at Maidwell. They kept invading the lawn by the cedar tree, which Beak wanted to be smooth for the parents, and Miller II was mole prefect because he knew how to catch them. He set traps every evening after games, then went to inspect them in the morning while the rest of us were queuing for the Rears. I bumped into him once, holding one of his victims with his hands cupped, like the Rev. Jones said we had to do when we took Communion. 'A perfect little gentleman,' said Miller II, bending to look more closely at the clean pink palms. 'What do you do with him next?' I asked. 'I'm making a waistcoat,' he said – and explained that Mr Chisholm, who took us for carpentry, had given him some salt-petre for curing the skins. He had several pegged out already, and soon he'd have enough to start making clothes. 'Clothes?' I asked. 'Yes,' said Miller II. 'A waistcoat first, then maybe some trousers.' A few weeks later he wore the waistcoat for church on Sunday. It was definitely mole – I could see the body-shapes in the fur – but it didn't have the velvety feel or the shine I expected. In fact it smelled of chemicals and was dandruffy, and turned out to have fleas, too, which made Miller II scratch so badly the Gibbon told him he had to throw the waistcoat away. He got his revenge by catching a squirrel and letting it go in the main hall. No one could prove it hadn't got in by mistake.

By this time I had my own hobby, which was making models. It had been embarrassing to start with, because mum sent them by post, and I'd been getting so many a lot of people thought I must be wet. Especially Eyot, who'd never liked me. When I'd been sleeping in Tower dorm, at the top of the house along a dark cor-ridor, he jumped on me one night, and I slammed him in the face with my elbow out of pure fright. I hadn't meant to hurt him. He thought I had, though, and when he attacked me in the bath queue next day, he made my nose bleed. I thought he might be sorry and waited for him to apologise, but all he did was look for another chance to get me. After the parcels started to arrive, he found one. He said mum must be stupid, sending so many. That made me want to hit him again, on purpose this time, to see if I could make his nose bleed too. But he was taller than me and had very long bony arms, and I thought he might come out on top. So I tried a different tack. I told him I loved making models, and if he wanted to help me he was welcome. He stopped being foul after that, and when I told mum, she said, 'Well, it's called making the peace. You've definitely learned something there.'

The models were Airfix: aeroplanes like Spitfires, Mustangs, Messerschmidts, Dorniers, Lancasters, Wellingtons, Heinkels, Mosquitos, Hurricanes, biplanes (or one, anyway); and ships like cruisers, an aircraft carrier, and a motor torpedo boat which fitted together so well I could float it in the lake. Most of them took a Sunday afternoon to build, as long as I didn't get into a mess with the pilot and his gearstick, which was fiddly as an earwig, and didn't hurry with the windows because otherwise I smudged glue on the glass, which meant no one could see inside the cockpit. The glue came in a yellow tube and smelled funny – it made my head spin. But really, making was the easy part. It was painting that took the time – and on a different day, too, or the glue wasn't hard enough. It needed as much concentration as chess, which I'd never played, but everyone said was the most complicated game in the world. Smearing green blobs and brown blobs for camouflage, but not letting them touch. Getting the wheels black but not the middle, which had to be silver. Floating off the transfers of flags and numbers in a saucer of water, then sticking them on straight with no wrinkles. And when they were finished? I zoomed them round Dinky Farm, or under the desks in my classroom, but it wasn't nearly as much fun as I made out. Nothing like the glueing and painting.

The best place for building models was the window ledge in Tower classroom. If I sat there for long enough the radiator heat made school disappear as it wobbled up through my brain and mixed with the glue-smell. I could still see the games field outside, and the rugger posts glowing like enormous white H's. There were boots scraping along the drive, too, and billiard balls clacking next door. But the real world was me. It was my fingers, fitting together the grey puzzle-shapes. Imagining how mum had bought them and posted them. Knowing she was thinking of me, at exactly the same time as I was daydreaming about her. She'd be back from shopping now it was nearly dark, and starting to get supper ready for dad. The dogs would be fussing round her feet, waiting for their food, and if she didn't stop peeling spuds soon, and do their bowls instead, she'd tread on Wiggy's foot and then there'd be a rumpus. 'Don't be a bore, girls,' I could hear her saying, as their nails scrabbled on the bare floor. 'Don't be a bore,' I said under my breath, pressing the two sides of a wing together and wiping quickly with my special cloth, so no glue showed. 'Don't be a bore. Don't be a bore.' 'What's that?' said Miller II, who had crept up behind me. 'Talking to yourself?' I put down the wing carefully, and changed the subject. Did he realise you could still see the remains of the flycatcher's nest in the creeper outside this window? He didn't. Well then, I'd show him in the morning, when it was light again.

Miller II knew a lot about birds, but not as much as me, now I'd joined the Royal Society for the Protection of Birds and the Northampton Ornithological Society. They sent roneo-ed sheets which told me what to look for, depending on the time of year. Better still were the descriptions of birds I'd never see – either because they were like nightjars, or green woodpeckers, or hoopoes, which didn't live in the grounds at Maidwell, or because they were special kinds of eagle and never even visited England, let alone Northamptonshire. I liked the way people wrote about them too – grown-ups who were obviously mad keen, but trying not to let it show. I felt the same, when I tiptoed round the lake on Sunday afternoons with the binoculars mum had given me for my last birthday. My heart beat so loudly I thought all the grebes on the lake were bound to hear, and dive for cover. When they didn't, and I kept one in focus for long enough to check the quiff on its head wasn't black at all, but green as a gun barrel, I felt I'd understood something special – something like a shout and a secret mixed together. And it meant I always ended my trips feeling disappointed, no matter how much I'd enjoyed myself. A black drop in my stomach, the same as being hungry.

I thought it might help to write everything down, so I started keeping a special bird book. Just short notes of times, and what the weather was like – the sort of stuff dad put in his Game Book after he'd been shooting, only without the shooting. I did something for the school magazine, too: half a page, which told people if they wanted to find nests they should look for droppings on the ground. Dad laughed when I showed it to him, because normally we said 'poo', not 'droppings'. But I'd never had anything published before, and wanted him to be proud of me, like mum was. It made me think I should stick to my notebook. In winter that meant hanging round the lake, creeping over the stepping stones and watching the grebe disappear underwater for ages longer than I could hold my own breath. During the spring and summer, the rest of the grounds got interesting again, even if the birds were only common ones: blackbirds, thrushes, blue-tits, wrens, robins, finches. They always saw me long before I could find them, no matter how quietly I moved. That made them better than humans, even though they were so much smaller, and silly when they belted off through the leaves, giving the game away.

I tried to tell Miller II about this. 'How do you mean, better?' he said. We'd scraped away a molehill by the cedar on the front lawn, and were cleaning the hole in the grass underneath, before slipping in the trap. 'I can see a kestrel might be better, or an eagle, or something that's especially big. But a sparrow? How's that better?' He was setting the trap carefully, keeping his fingers clear in case it went off by accident. The metal was grey and cloudy, like the new gate in the horses' field at home, which mum thought was hideous, and another reason we ought to leave Little Brewers. 'I can't explain,' I said, half-wishing I'd never started the conversation. 'They can fly and we can't.' 'But lots of animals do things we can't,' he replied. 'A cheetah, for instance. We can't run as fast as that. Nothing can.' 'No,' I said. 'But at least we can run a bit fast. Birds do something completely different.' Miller II looked at me sideways, and shuffled the earth back over the trap with the side of his boot, so no light shone into the tunnel. Then we started to tramp back towards the changing rooms.

'You know what?' he said suddenly, as if it followed from talking about cheetahs. 'Beak's right. You need to fit in more.' I stopped still, and stared into his face. He was perfectly serious. Frowning, even. 'What do you mean, Beak's right?' I said. 'What do you mean, fit in?' 'Did I say *fit*?' he said, which was confusing. I'd expected an answer, not another question. 'I meant to say join. You ought to *join* in more. Beak said so the other day, when I was talking to him. He knows we're friends.' 'And you thought it was OK to talk behind my back?' I said, using words that weren't really my own, but belonged to the masters. Miller II looked puzzled. 'Beak wasn't being horrible. He's worried about you, that's all. He's seen you making your models and things, and wants to know if you're all right.' I blinked. 'Well, you can tell him I'm fine, thank you,' I said, and started to walk off. Miller II soon caught up. 'Don't get in a woofer,' he said. I looked at him more carefully this time – at his fair hair falling straight over his forehead, and the way his body slithered around inside his boiler suit. I wanted to hug him. None of my friends had talked to me like this before, being kind and grown up at the same time. And that wasn't all. His right hand was stuck out towards me because he wanted me to shake it. 'OK,' I said in a softer voice, and put out my own hand. 'I'll think about it.' 'When?' asked Miller II, as if he'd promised Beak I'd stick to a timetable. 'Tonight,' I said.

I started as soon as Beak had finished his rounds and shuffled off to his study. What had he meant, 'join in'? I couldn't very well join in when I was working in class: the masters wanted us to pip each other to the post all the time. And the sort of thing I liked doing in muck-about, my models and bird-watching – they weren't things you did with other people. That left games. I was pretty good at them, because I could run fast, but athletics was like work, it was everyone for himself, so that was no good for joining, either. Maybe I should try harder at cricket and get into a school team? Not much point. I liked watching people play, but I was hopeless at catching. Football was better, and Maltese had once told me I had 'a good little left foot'. Rugger too, because I never minded tackling. If I put my head behind someone's legs, not in front, I could knock over boys much bigger than myself and not feel a thing. After the match against Bilton Grange, when we'd lost 64–3 and I'd scored the only try, Mr Porch had stood up in the bus and said I'd been brave. That was a start, wasn't it?

I slipped out of bed, picked my dressing gown off its peg, and crept along the corridor to the washroom. It was late now, and Beak must have gone to bed: when I passed the top of the main stairs, there was one feeble light burning in the hall below. The whole school was fast asleep, apart from me. The Gibbon's door was open a crack, but there was only grey air bubbling inside. The dormitory doors were all ajar too, and when I stopped outside Green to listen, I heard scrappy little snores and bedsprings creaking. I reached the washroom, and turned on the strip-light above the basins, which juddered for a few seconds, then settled into a humming white stripe. I wanted a drink, before going straight back to bed. But as I filled my glass I glanced into the mirror, and kept on looking. Admiring ourselves was wrong; Beak said so. It was vanity. And if masters caught us taking too long with our hair after showers, or turning our heads sideways, they said we were like girls and should be ashamed. But tonight I didn't have to worry, and kept staring. Fair hair which wanted to be curly like Uncle Rob's. Nose too big and too squashy. Ears which stuck out like taxi doors, or that's what dad said. A mole on the right hand side of my mouth, which was where I got spots. It wasn't a bad face, but it showed everything too easily – that's what I didn't like. It blushed like a tomato, or went pale, or got bags under the eyes, or crumpled if I worried.

When I'd first arrived at Maidwell, nobody minded who I was. Now they minded all the time. They kept pulling me out of the Wilderness when I disappeared into the trees with my binoculars. Or off the window ledge in Tower when I was working on a new plane. They had plans for me, and said one day I'd be grateful. I had another sip from my glass, poured away the dregs, dried it, and put it back on the shelf. Then I had a last look at myself and stuck out my lips, like mum when she was making sure her lipstick hadn't smudged. Should I start brushing my hair into a fringe? No. Dad didn't like fringes, he thought they were common. Hair should be brushed straight back, with a proper parting. But I couldn't think about it any more tonight. Not about hair, not about other people, not about anything. I turned away from the basins and went back to the light switch. When I clicked it off, and the humming stopped in the strip overhead, the silence suddenly seemed thicker than before. So did the darkness. I had to keep my hands in front of me all the way back to my dorm, because after so much brightness I couldn't see a thing.

CHAPTER FOURTEEN

Beauty

It was hard to believe that business about one dog year being the same as seven human ones. When dad went into the kitchen first thing every morning, to have breakfast before setting off for work, there was such a loony whining and scrabbling on the floorboards it woke up the whole house. I reckoned it meant dogs thought every hour was like a year – at least a year. I told Kit this, and he said, 'Lucky they don't have to go to school, then.' I kept forgetting he hated it as much as me – but he always did keep himself to himself. Perhaps he thought I made a fuss about things, or he felt booted-around because he was the youngest. I don't know. We never talked seriously like that.

But we couldn't pretend nothing was changing. Last year, when I was still ten, I'd stopped going into mum's room every morning for a cuddle in the mornings. Now I just went sometimes, and lay a little way off. Mum seemed quite happy staring at the flies that floated up from the stables, and buzzed round the lampshade in the middle of the ceiling. The longer I watched them, the more I thought they were like tiny horses on a merry-go-round. Their circles were smooth glides up and down, as though they could keep going for ever. 'You don't have to do this, if you don't want to,' mum said quietly. 'What do you mean?' I asked. 'Come into bed.' 'Oh, don't worry,' I said. 'I like it.' I was trying to make her feel better, but she could read my mind.

After breakfast, we collected our tack from the lumber room between the kitchen and the scullery. Kit and mum had their breeches on, but I'd decided they were too much of a palaver. 'The horses will know,' Kit said mysteriously. 'Know what?' I asked. 'If you're wearing jeans, it shows you don't care what you're doing. You've got to look smart if Tommy's going to obey you.' I pushed past him into the yard, making sure my saddle bashed him on the arm. 'It's not the pony club here,' I told him, 'it's just riding.' Mum told us to shut up or the day would be over. Her face was made of shadows when she pulled her hard hat down over her forehead.

If they thought we were going hunting the horses were a pain, barging round their stalls, snorting, banging their doors. On ordinary days, they tried to pretend we didn't exist. Tommy was the worst. Even when I'd slung the saddle across his back, he still kept his head in his manger, mumbling into the corners in case he'd missed some oats. Then he cannoned sideways and tried to knock me over. 'Make sure he doesn't blow out his stomach,' mum called from Serenade's stable, so I dug him in the ribs with my knee and waited for the groan to roll through him before hoiking the girth up a notch. After that, it was time for the bridle. This meant yanking his head out of the manger, wiggling my thumb into the corner of his mouth where he couldn't bite me, slithering the snaffle up his tongue, and finally hoisting the top of the bridle over his ears with my other hand. It was an art, mum said, and I was proud of being able to do it quickly.

We tramped round the yard for a minute, fiddling with our stirrups and deciding which way to go. Over the Heath, then down past the Routledge twins, along the stream, and home the back way? Or the same thing in reverse? It wasn't much of a choice: there were new houses being built everywhere, and more and more farmers who didn't like us going on their land. Across the Heath was best: we reached the open fields sooner, where we could gallop. So off we went, the dogs lolloping alongside with their tongues hanging out even though they weren't tired yet. If anyone passed us we always said hello, and raised our hats; mum said this was important, otherwise people would think we were stuck-up. I thought they'd probably do that anyway. Tommy was only about fourteen hands high, but sitting on top of him made me feel not quite in the world any more, and not quite myself. First I was dandelion fluff, blowing past the miller on his white steps, and the gnome fisherman where Mr Manning lived. Then we were crossing the Heath three abreast, and I was leading the Charge of the

Light Brigade. As we came to Tim's house, I changed into a spy, peeping between the curtains to see if he was inside wearing his Boy Scout uniform.

We came home past the field where the horses lived when they weren't in their stables – the field where I'd stood with dad under the may tree, and the storm had blasted off the blossom. On the way out, I'd had to boot Tommy along, hauling at the reins to stop him lunging at the hedge for a snack. Now there was no need. It was mad, the way he thought someone might have filled up his manger while we'd been away. Was that all he lived for – food? Kit and I were in no hurry, because coming back was the worst part of the morning. It meant mucking out – unsaddling the ponies, stuffing their haybags, slipping on their halters and tying them to a peg in the stable wall, then fetching the wheelbarrow and fork. We lifted out the dung first, sometimes on a cushion of wet straw, sometimes balancing dark green bobbles on the prongs. Then we attacked the bedding underneath, levering up wedges and trundling them off past the greenhouse to the compost heap. It wasn't disgusting, not even when the pee-pong made our eyes water. It was just a chore, and fagging. Mum looked white-faced by the end, and had to lean against the wall by the buddleia bush, getting her breath back. 'Why don't we have a cuppa, then do the tack after that?' she said, as if it was us who couldn't cope. We said yes, because we knew it was her who needed a rest. Tack was easier, anyway. All it meant was soaking grass off the bits, wiping the saddles and bridles with the see-through soap, then arranging everything in the lumber room so it would be ready for tomorrow. It only took twenty minutes, and after that we could do whatever we liked. Kit was right, though. It had been a mistake to ride in my jeans. Even though I couldn't see a mark, they smelled of sweat, and now that would stay with me all day.

It was almost lunchtime, which meant sitting on the Aga if it was winter – the left-hand lid, which didn't burn but still had enough heat to soak up through my bum into my brain. 'Are you hungry after all that exercise?' mum asked, making us feel we'd done something special. 'What shall we have?' She wanted us to say 'Not much', but we never did. We were under orders from dad to make her eat properly, and not only in the evening. So while Kit went off to play with the trains, or sit on Mrs Lambert's back as she polished the hall floor, I slid off the heat and asked what we had in the fridge. Meat for mincing. It meant rattling the cast-iron contraption from the drawer by the sink, bolting it onto the side of the kitchen table, stuffing chunks into the funnel at the top, cranking the handle, and peering at the worms which wriggled out through the grille on the side. Then I sat beside mum while we did runner beans, snipping off the ends with our two knives, dragging the stringy edges. Or broad beans, which I liked more: staring at the heap of bloated pods, saying we had ample and then wondering if there were enough, squeezing each one until it made a soft pop, fiddling our fingers inside and running them along the damp velvet.

If there wasn't any veg in the house, we scooped up the basket from its place by the gumboots, and tramped down behind the greenhouse. We had a chicken run there now – a little one, with a wooden hut inside, which Mr Manning had built as an experiment because he thought we shouldn't have to buy eggs, since we had so much garden. Mum and dad still weren't sure – I'd heard them talking about it from my place on the stairs, saying the chickens were on strike, and if they didn't start laying soon, dad would wring their necks and we'd eat them. I unhooked the basket from mum's arm, saw there was a shrivelled carrot and a useless little bean lying on the newspaper in the bottom, and chucked them over the wire fence. All twelve chickens scampered towards us over the bare earth, and when two of them got to the carrot at the same time, it came alive and turned into a snake as they pecked it. 'Stupid birds,' mum said, in the same dried-out voice dad used for people who got in his way when he was driving. We stalked on towards the asparagus bed, where we discovered we'd forgotten to bring a knife.

Mr Manning had been watching from the greenhouse, and now he came to our rescue, rootling in his lumpy trouser pockets, snapping open a blade, and running his torn fingers along the edge. He didn't do the cutting for us. He watched with his hands on his hips and his stomach sagging forward, waiting for me to make a mistake, or lose my balance and trample on the mound of the asparagus bed. When I didn't, and handed back his knife with the blade pointing towards me, like dad said we must, to show we meant no harm, he grunted and turned over his tongue with a wet slap. Mum and I thanked him as though we hadn't noticed, and waited until we were back in the stable yard before we dug each other in the ribs. I loved her best when we were doing ordinary stuff together. Like the moment we sat down again in the warm kitchen, watching the light turn blue-green as it slid towards us across the coalhole lid. The world felt dim, and slow, and floaty. Serenade was outside the window, her head drooped across the stable door, a string of saliva dangling from her mouth. The dogs lay in their wicker basket; they were asleep too, but Beauty was dreaming, giving kicks with her back feet, which made the wicker creak. The veg-carrier stood on the table with the purple heads of the asparagus jutting out, and a tiny scarlet spider swinging from one of them. Across the hall, Kit was listening to 'Needles and Pins' on the wireless. Beyond that, cars hissed along the hedge. Further still, the millstones churned out their everlasting dry rumble.

After lunch, mum smoked her first ciggie of the day – an Olivier – and although I asked to light it, she never let me. 'It's a revolting habit,' she said, snatching the matchbox from my hand and waving me away. 'I don't want you getting ideas.' 'He already smokes,' Kit said sullenly. 'I've seen him.' 'You do?' mum asked, raising her eyebrows. 'Yes he does,' Kit went on. 'He smokes pine needles wrapped up in loo paper. In his hut at Maidwell.' Mum flapped her hand again. She understood what Kit was up to. He was trying to keep her talking, because as soon as she finished her ciggie it would be time for our rest, and he didn't want that. Neither did I. But we never got out of it, and anyway, something strange always happened in the next couple of minutes. By the time mum had stubbed out, and we'd taken our sweet from the Quality Street tin in her desk, then dragged ourselves upstairs, I always felt sleepy.

As soon as I pulled back my coverlet and lay down, I was wide awake again, calling to mum in her bedroom next door, asking if I could go to the playroom. She didn't answer, which meant she'd already dropped off. So I stayed put. 'You could always read,' Kit said from his bed the other side of the room. He was using his blasé voice, and holding up the *Dandy* like dad when he read the *Standard*, so I couldn't see his face. I grunted, and reached for the pop-star book dad had given me – ages ago now, but I still liked it. It wasn't really a book, just a collection of lists: birthdays, top ten hits, the colour of eyes, and 'current dates'. I was pretty sure I knew what 'current dates' meant but not completely, because lots of people, including Cliff Richard, had put 'mum' as their answer, and nobody's mum could be their girlfriend, could they?

I turned to a page about Gene Pitney; I liked him because of 'Twenty-four hours from Tulsa'. But my mind wouldn't stop in one place, and flipped back to the other day, when I'd sat in the kitchen with mum, telling her I didn't think books were important. She hadn't liked me saying that. 'You'd think books were important all right, if you'd read anything decent. Your comics are junk. I'm sorry, darling, but they are.' It made me think of the hours she sat beside me in the Black Swan at Market Harborough, watching me catch up on my *Victors* during exeat weekends. She only allowed it because she knew I was unhappy. That made me feel pathetic.

I stared at the ceiling so I could think more clearly. OK, so comics were babyish. But what should I read instead? If I looked a long way back, I could see mum giving me Beatrix Potter, and Pooh, and *Peter Pan* and *The Wind in the Willows*. After that, when I was a bit older, there'd been *Zong the Hill Pony* and *Mary Plain*, and *Tim Minds the Shop*. And now, nothing, really. Mum and dad never recommended anything, and neither did people at school. In fact Beak had actually banned the two writers whose names everyone knew: Enid Blyton and Ian Fleming. I didn't mind about not reading Blyton, because she was for girls. But Fleming was different. Mum had a story by him in the whirligig, called *Casino Royale*, and on the cover there was a picture of 'The Author' puffing at a cigarette in a holder, with smoke curling up beside his face. He looked great, so why had Beak banned him? When I'd asked mum, she said it was because James Bond was sexy. I knew books could be like that, because I'd heard people talking about *Lady Chatterley's Lover* on the news, and asked mum about it. 'You'll read it one day,' she'd told me, 'but not yet. You're too young for *Lady Chatterley* – and for lots of other things as well. *The White Rabbit*, for instance.' I nodded again. *The White Rabbit* was also in the whirligig. The cover on that one was an aeroplane flying at night, and it said the story was about a spy who'd been caught by the Germans and tortured. It sounded horrible, but I thought maybe I should try *Casino Royale*. I'd have to wait until mum was out shopping, if it was as bad as all that.

It was three o'clock, and we could stop resting now, but Kit was asleep, with the *Dandy* crashed onto the floor by his bed, and I needed a few more minutes to think. When granny had been mum's age, she'd obviously been a big reader, along with George Victor. There were rows and rows of small fat books in the house in Beaconsfield. But what about the Motions? Dad said he only had time to look at books on holiday, then made his joke about always having to take *The Lonely Skier* by Hammond Innes, which he'd started when we were little but never finished. Grandpa never read anything except *Horse and Hound*. But great-grandpa Andrew must have had a whole library in those huge houses of his. We had one of his books in the whirligig – the *Works of Tennyson*. It was a present he'd given to Jessie.

I got off my bed as noisily as possible, so I was bound to wake up Kit. He lay still. Mum's room was quiet, too, when I creaked past her door, and I didn't look in, because I didn't like seeing her asleep: when her mouth was open, it made me think she was dead. I tiptoed downstairs and climbed back onto the Aga, my head sinking onto my knees. Home wasn't the same any more: suddenly I had to have opinions about everything. And I wasn't the only one who thought things were changing. Dad was always tut-tutting at people when we drove to places nowadays, saying they made him feel part of a dying race. And sometimes mum got so worked up about the road outside, and the new houses, I thought she was going to burst into tears. I'd even heard her talking on the phone to Mrs Franklin, saying she thought we should all move to Somerset, which wasn't overrun like here. I could see why, though. It was just after that horrible fuss we'd had – the worst on record.

We'd set off for our morning ride after breakfast as usual: me, mum and Kit, with Beauty and Wiggy trotting along behind. Mum had chosen the Routledge way, across the Heath towards Tim's house, then uphill past the council estate, where we were on the lookout because someone new had moved in, and they had a bull terrier. We'd seen him once – a big sweaty-looking man wearing a vest and no shirt. Mum said she thought he must be drunk, even though it was half-past ten in the morning. The dog was even more frightening. A bow-legged, grubby white thing with no forehead and a big drooling mouth, heaving around on the end of its lead. I'd never seen a bull terrier before, but I thought it looked like a shark with legs, and said so to mum. She told me they were demons. 'In the old days they were bred for fighting, you know,' she said, dropping her voice as though the dog might overhear. 'They shouldn't be kept as pets at all, really, they're more like hounds. Wild.' I glanced at Kit because I wasn't sure whether mum was exaggerating, but he shrugged. 'I expect they'd eat a sheep,' mum went on, 'if they found one.' 'What about a baby?' Kit asked. 'They'd easily kill a baby.' 'Or a man?' I asked, looking at Beauty, who was tucked in beside Serenade where she couldn't be kicked. How soft she looked, with her white coat and the black patches round her eyes and shoulders, and how like a person with her nervous smiling face. 'Probably not a man,' mum said in a kind voice, which made me think I'd asked a silly question, until Kit came to my rescue. 'I expect they could kill a man if they found him asleep somewhere,' he said. 'They'd latch onto his neck until they'd bitten right through.'

But perhaps we were worrying about nothing. After all, if the man had been in control of his dog that first time we'd seen him, why not again? It was a good question, but there wasn't time for an answer. As we came up to the council estate, the bull terrier flew at us. I heard his nails first, scratching along the cement path beside his house, and whipped my head round so fast my eyeballs banged against the side of my skull. He was bursting through the open gate. Just a blur, with his lead dragging behind him – a strip of tartan, then a jingling chain. He charged straight into Beauty's shoulder like a rugger player, rolled her over, and had his teeth round her neck before I'd even had time to shout. But we'd all seen him. Wiggy had bent nose-to-tail, sneaking back up the lane towards home. Kit was waving his stick and bellowing, 'No! No!' And mum was throwing me her reins, jumping onto the ground while Tommy tossed his head up and down as though he'd swallowed a hot chestnut. Beauty was lying flat on her back with her legs in the air, showing her rows of pink and black titties, and making a high-pitched whine that sounded like a baby. The bull terrier's head levered slowly backwards and forwards against her throat, and he was trembling. A revolting all-over quiver, as though he was about to explode. His tail had arched so far forward, the tip was almost touching the middle of his back, which meant his arsehole stared straight at me like an eye socket with no eye.

I was shouting 'No! No!' too, like Kit, and so was mum now she'd got to the dogs. She lifted her riding crop and whacked the terrier as hard as she could, not caring where she hit him. On the snout, round the ears, across his back, over his piggy eyes, even across his bare bum. I was still churning round on Tommy, but felt I was gazing upwards, seeing her silhouetted against the pebble-dash and the sky. Every time she raised her arm, I thought how thin she looked – there wasn't a chance she'd hit the terrier hard enough to make him let go. In fact she was making him grip tighter: there was blood oozing between his teeth now, and running down one side of Beauty's throat. It was brave, but it was hopeless. Mum looked like she did when we played cricket by Teaser's Hill and she had to throw the ball in from the boundary. Her arm always went floppy, because she didn't know how to do it, nobody had taught her.

Here was someone to help, though. The man we'd seen with the dog that first time. He was wearing the same jeans and the same vest, or one exactly like it, with thin straps over the shoulders. Why had he taken so long? Because he'd been busy. He'd got a kettle in his right hand, one of those new electric ones, which had a little spurt of steam above the spout. And what was that in his other hand? A hammer. Not the kind dad used, with a biffer on one side and a claw on the other. A hammer like a mini-sledge, which I could tell had already been used for hard work, because it had glittering dents and gouges in it. Now I was close, I saw the hairs on top of his shoulders, and a wrinkle of stomach where the cotton got stuck. Was he hot? No, he was fat, that's all, but he could still move fast. He was already beside mum, telling her to stop hitting with her crop and putting the kettle down in the road, where it looked small and silly. Then he knelt with his back to me, so I could see the top of his bum and a spray of much darker hairs. He tilted his head sideways, until he could work out exactly where his dog's teeth had got to in Beauty's neck.

The horses calmed down, and as we gathered in a circle I passed mum back her reins. I didn't want to see her face in case she started to cry, so I looked at Serenade instead. She was taking such big deep breaths, she'd opened her nostrils much wider than usual, and I could follow right up inside them, where the skin was pink and dripping. It reminded me of a telly programme I'd seen about elephants – the way they collected together, when one of the herd fell ill. 'Incredible, how much they understand,' dad had said. 'They're just like us, really.' 'A good deal better than some of us,' mum had said.

The man was holding one of Beauty's paws now, telling mum everything was under control. Then he let go of the paw, picked up his hammer, and stuck the handle inside his own dog's mouth. There was a gurgle, like a sink unblocking, which must have been a growl. The man didn't mind. He started wiggling the hammer. Cranking it so hard, he lifted his dog half off the ground. The teeth even kept hold when the man turned the hammer round, picked up a flint from the side of the road, and walloped it between the dog's lips. The noise was soft and hard at the same time, and a splinter of white flew out. A tooth. There it was in the road, like spit. Kit laughed, not a real laugh but a funny shout, and I could see why. The bull terrier was insane. Something in his stupid flat head was telling him to hang on, even though his own blood had started to soak down the other side of Beauty's neck, which meant she was wearing a red bow tie.

Beauty's eyes were shut. She wasn't dead, was she? She couldn't be: her stomach was moving, steady and slow. Her bare cloudy skin, with the black blotches she liked us to tickle. The man better hurry up, all the same. The hammer and the stone hadn't worked. 'Please help us,' mum said, which was shocking: she never talked like that to people we didn't know. I made myself look into her face but she wouldn't meet my eye, and didn't notice when Kit leaned forward and touched her on the knee. The man didn't pay any attention, either. He was too busy putting down the hammer and the flint, touching the side of his kettle, nodding to himself, and gripping the handle as he scrambled onto his feet again. 'Last resort,' he said, rolling his r's to show he was speaking the bull terrier's own language. Then he stepped up beside the dog, held the kettle directly over his head, and started to pour.

It was hard to say how long we'd been there – maybe hours. But the water was still hot enough to steam as it unwound through the air and burst over the back of the dog's head as if it were hitting a flat stone. Mum said later it was probably the shock that made him let go. I thought it was more likely the heat, and I wouldn't have minded if the dog had been burned right the way down to his brain. There was a high-pitched, long-drawn-out scream, like Cunningham at school when he broke his leg in a rugger match. Then the bull terrier started jabbering, shaking out a heap of little whimpery whines. After that, he set off up the lane towards the Routledge farm with his head almost ploughing through the gravel, and his tail stuffed between his legs so I couldn't see his arsehole or his bollocks any more, just his back legs pumping like joints of meat.

'Thought that might do the trick,' said the man, spinning round and grinning. His face was red and sweaty, and there was blood on the front of his vest in a V-shaped spray. One of his own side-teeth was missing – that didn't seem surprising. But why did he sound so cheerful? Surely he loved his dog? And another thing: why had he been so helpful in the first place? He probably thought we were snobs, clattering past his house every day, looking down our noses at everything. Mum wasn't thinking any of these things, though. 'Is my dog all right?' she said, aiming her voice at the man but staring at Beauty, who was lying on her back, not moving. 'Don't know,' said the man. 'Look, I'm sorry about . . .' But mum interrupted – something she never did. 'Your dog almost killed my dog and I need to get her home. Are you listening to me? I need to get her home as soon as possible'. The man knelt down in the road, then said he had a van round the back and would drive Beauty home if mum told him where we lived. Mum kept nodding her head in quick jerks, like a bird attacking another's bird's egg.

A minute later, the man was settling Beauty onto a tartan rug in the back of his Ford. Then he drove off in second gear without mum even asking, which meant we could stay alongside if we trotted on the road. As we came into the yard, Mr Manning appeared from the greenhouse, and started talking about the chickens laying eggs at last. Mum asked him to put the ponies in the stables – ordered him, really – before heading for the back door with me and Kit trooping behind, and the man carrying Beauty like the crown jewels. When we got into the kitchen, mum went to her usual place by the sink, and the man laid Beauty carefully in her basket. He stroked her head, moving his hand hard enough to widen her eyes a little and show the red inside the lids. She gave one of her half-smiles, and I thought mum wouldn't like that. Beauty was her dog, no one else's. But the man only wanted to make her better, which was why he'd taken the dishcloth from the draining board and begun dabbling at her neck, sometimes standing up to wet the cloth under the tap, then crouching down again and wiping some more.

I was propped against the Aga. This was the second time I'd looked at the man from on high, without him seeing me. He'd put on a shirt before getting into the van, so the hairs on his shoulders were invisible. They must have been wriggling under the cotton as it stretched tight across his back. His other hair – the hair on his head – was plastered in thin stripes, as if his brain was struggling to hold all the things he was thinking. 'Can I help?' said Kit, but there was no answer. I asked the same question, and got the same nothing. It didn't matter, because the man was putting the dish-cloth back on the draining board, even though it was stained with blood. Mum mouthed 'That'll do now', then held open the door into the yard. Her whole body twisted sideways as the man squeezed past. When he turned round on the step and said he was sorry again, she let him finish then said 'Thank you', but so quick-ly I didn't think he heard. Before he could say anything else, she shut the door in his face.

I told myself she was still upset, that's why she was being so odd, but I understood better when dad got home that evening. Beauty was better by then: there was nothing to see on her neck, except where the fur had dried into a faint rusty colour, and she'd eaten her dinner. But mum acted as though everything was still a crisis. When she heard dad's car scrunching into the drive-through, she didn't step outside to give him a hug. She stayed against the sink in the kitchen, so he could see something was wrong as soon as he came into the light. Dad looked round smiling as she started telling him what had happened, then his face changed and he put his briefcase and bowler on the kitchen table. I tried to join in but mum waved her hand, shooshing me, and carried on to the end herself. She missed out some of the worse things, like the noise the bull terrier made when he ran off down the lane with the water burning his head, and her voice kept popping into a squeak then back again. It turned out she wanted dad to do something. She asked him to go and see the man, and tell him he should have his bull terrier put down. And she thought it would be a good idea if dad wore his army uniform. Then the man would listen to him and do what he was told.

Dad ran his squidged finger across the top of his bowler, making a line in the black. His face looked loose, and the skin of his cheeks thickened into definite folds. He changed colour, too; he'd been pinky-grey when he got in. Now he was dim purple. 'My uniform?' he repeated slowly. 'Yes, your uniform. So he can see you're a

Colonel. Honestly, Richard, it's only a matter of time before that beast attacks something else, and next time it'll be even worse. He'll kill somebody. You'll be doing everyone a favour.' Mum levered herself away from the sink and twiddled one of her ciggies from the packet by the Belling. She normally only smoked when she was sitting down with her drink. 'Where are the fucking matches?' she said suddenly. Kit and I looked at each other across the room with our eyes wide: we'd never heard her say that word before, and wanted to get out. Dad cleared his throat, delving in his suit pocket and handing over his lighter. 'Steady on, darling,' he said. 'The boys. Anyway, I don't think I can do that.' 'What do you mean?' mum said. 'See the man,' dad told her. There was something tired in his voice, and I knew what it was. Embarrassment. I looked back at Kit again. He was waiting for me this time, and tipped his head towards the door. 'Sorry mum. Sorry dad,' I blurted. 'We'll go and have our bath now.' We were out of the room before dad said, 'Well done.'

Kit went ahead to run the taps, and I waited in my special place on the stairs, where I could still hear them talking in the kitchen. Mum kept saying everyone would be pleased if the bull terrier was put down. Dad made a long speech, telling her it wasn't his business to see the man himself, but yes the dog obviously was dangerous, and he was quite happy to ring the police and report it, that was the best thing to do, and he'd get on with it right now, but no he wasn't going up there in his uniform. Then there was a silence, and I thought of Beauty in her basket. She hated it when people got cross. It made her nervous, and she'd be smiling at them. So far as I knew, dad hadn't even looked at her neck closely yet. He could tell she was OK. Next thing, mum said he was gutless, which I knew she didn't believe, and he said 'Oh for Christ's sake, Gilly', which was the angriest I'd ever heard him. I knew they weren't just talking about the dog. Mum was unhappy because she didn't like living in Little Brewers any more. She didn't like the cars buzzing along the hedge. She didn't like dad working so hard and being away so much. She didn't like being skinny and tired.

Mum's ciggie smelled foul. The kitchen door was shut tight, but her smoke had wiffled straight upstairs, carried by the heat of the Aga, and now it was rubbing inside my nose like a dry stick. The smell would be in the bathroom, too. Ciggies and hot-water-fug: that was always disgusting. But I couldn't shout down to her now, or ask her to put it out. She'd know I'd been listening, and then there'd be a whole different reason for everyone to be unhappy. I stood up as quietly as possible, and went to get undressed. On my way past the bathroom, I heard the taps stop, and Kit starting to hum. He was soaking already – probably up my end, not the tap-end where he usually went. Little puffs of cloudy air smuggled under the door like Red Indian messages. As soon as they set off along the corridor, they melted.

CHAPTER FIFTEEN

The Cliffs of America

Holidays meant two different things. One was not being at school. The other was going away. No one from Maidwell went very far, except Wallace whose dad was rich and knew people in the Bahamas, and Jardine whose family worked in Hong Kong. Most of us just disappeared down our burrows in the winter and spring, and drove to the West Country or Norfolk for a fortnight in the summer. Dad never liked it to start with; he swooped along in the Daimler, telling mum not to complain as she swayed beside him in the passenger seat. When the roads turned into lanes, he beeped at locals if they didn't keep close to the hedge. At supper he munched up his meals very small, as if he was testing every mouthful for glass. After a couple of days, and mum saying 'There isn't a train to catch' whenever she saw him jiggling his foot, he started to change. He forgot to put on his Bay Rum in the morning so his hair went curly. He bought a toy sailing boat because the rigging was too tangled on the one Kit and I had kept from last year. He held hands with mum if we went for a walk in the evening. 'You see?' mum said to me one night after we'd said our prayers. 'He does like holidays really. It's just that he finds it difficult to relax.' Her face was invisible in the dark, but she was using her determined voice.

Our usual place was the Moorings, in Overy Staithe on the north Norfolk coast; dad always laughed when he said the name, but mum wouldn't explain why. She told me Nelson had come here when he was a little boy, and dreamed of becoming a hero. I knew about Nelson from my Ladybird book, and worked out where he must have stood on the harbour wall, then lay face down in the exact spot. When crabs scuttled over the mud below me I dangled my bacon rind in front of them, so they wouldn't be able to resist. Were they related to the ones Nelson caught? Kit said it was a stupid question, of course they were – but we'd have to leave them now, because it was time for bird-watching on Blakeney Point, which was my favourite thing of all. There were so many different kinds of tern, the *Observer's Book of Birds* hadn't got pictures of them all, and I had to borrow mum's *Field Guide*, which was much more grown up. It even had a complicated cover: a green woodpecker on the paper jacket, and a hoopoe in silver on the blue cloth inside.

I thought we didn't go further afield because Maidwell was so expensive, dad didn't have any money to spare. But when I asked mum about this, she surprised me. 'It's not about money,' she said, emptying her tea dregs into the plastic bucket under the kitchen sink. 'Dad takes me here and there. We went to Corsica. And Amalfi. Remember?' I didn't. 'And then there's the war,' she went on, as if talking to herself. 'Dad had such a foul time after D-Day, he's not all that keen on abroad.' I watched the water ricocheting off her mug under the tap, and remembered the falling-down bodies in my comics, and the jagged shapes with BOOM and KERPOW inside them. I'd always known about dad and the war, but I'd never quite been able to imagine him fighting. No wonder he talked about Krauts not Germans, and sometimes said 'Heil Hitler' when we overtook a VW Beetle. 'Do you think he ever killed anyone?' I said suddenly. 'Who, darling?' mum said, drying her mug. 'Dad,' I said, persevering. 'Oh, I don't know. Probably quite a few people. But Hitler was a very bad man, remember, an awful man.' 'I know that,' I said, and was about to tell her I'd learned about him in History when she cut across me at a right angle. 'France would be very nice,' she said. 'And Italy, that would be even nicer.' She paused, then went on more quickly. 'But we can't think about them. Even without the war and the money, there'd still be grandpa.'

I understood what she meant, but only vaguely. Grandpa went to Scotland every summer, and sometimes at Sunday lunch he asked us to stay with him there. 'It would be so lovely for the boys,' he said, sounding like dad when he was disguising an order. Mum always said 'Yes, it would', but I could tell from the way her eyes went glassy that she didn't really think so. I cornered her about it once, and asked what the problem was. 'You're not ready for Scotland yet,' she said. 'You need to know how to fish properly first, and probably shoot as well.' 'But you told grandpa it would be fun!' I reminded her. 'Believe me, darling,' she said, 'it won't be fun if you can't keep up. Grandpa's not the kind of person who waits for people. And you're still only ten.' 'Don't mope,' she said. 'I'm doing this for your own good. I tell you what, though. We'll give Norfolk and Devon a miss this year, and go to Ireland instead. Then we can see how you get on. If you like it, we'll tell grandpa you're ready.' I stared her straight in the eye and wished I didn't blink so much. It made me look windy, and I didn't want her to think I was anything like that. On the other hand, going to Scotland did sound as tough as joining the army.

We took the ferry to Rosslare, but it was dark and I couldn't see anything. Next morning, the country didn't seem so different from England, except there were more white houses, and the roads got bumpier and bumpier until at last we reached Roundstone in County Galway. Mum took the directions to Louisburgh out of her handbag. 'You should see your faces,' dad said, trying to cheer us up. 'They're as green as alarm clocks.' I peered through the Daimler's little triangle-window: we were halfway up a drive between wet laurel bushes, with a house at the end that looked like a tidied-up version of Little Brewers. There was the same creeper everywhere. 'Oh no,' Kit groaned. 'Why have we come somewhere that looks like home?'

It turned out that Ireland was much odder than we thought. People walked in the rain without bothering to take umbrellas, there were hedges made of fuchsia, and once a year everyone from the village climbed the mountain behind our hotel without wearing any shoes. There was a jetty, too, and dad said he'd buy me a pint of Guinness if I could swim round the end. I did, but when the drink arrived in the bar that evening, he had to help me finish; it dropped into my stomach like a load of cement. 'I've got my bearings now,' he told me, ordering another, and I grinned without knowing what he was talking about. 'He's saying he's sorted out the fishing,' mum explained, putting her hand across the top of her glass and winking – which was another thing she found difficult to do, like throwing a ball. 'Oh, Gilly,' dad said. 'You look as though you're having a stroke when you do that.' She took her hand off her glass and squeezed his arm. 'You'll take Andrew with you, won't you?' she said.

Next morning, I went down to the jetty again with Kit before breakfast. 'Look,' I said, pointing to the milky horizon and suddenly wanting to tease him. 'You can see the cliffs of America from here.' 'Really? Where?' said Kit, shielding his eyes. 'There,' I said. '*There.*' 'Oh yes,' Kit said quietly – then, after a pause, 'What are those people doing? Are they waving?' He was talking so seriously I couldn't resist shading my own eyes for a moment – and that's when he exploded, shoving me towards the water. By the time I got my balance again, he was halfway back to the hotel. He was going shopping with mum in Roundstone, to buy a white fisherman's jersey like the kind Val Doonigan wore sometimes, with patterns in the knitting. It was his treat because I was spending the day with dad, and I couldn't decide whether I felt jealous or not. But when dad and I finally set off with our rods, and sandwiches from the woman in the kitchen, I was too nervous to think about it any more. Were we going to walk all the way to the mountain-top? Apparently. That's what mum had meant, when she said I'd have to keep up. The path looked very long and was littered with sharp stones, and when I thought of the people with bare feet my teeth hurt.

After a while we turned off by a stream, and high-stepped through the heather until we came to a pond. So far so good, I thought. But I made a mistake when I said the pond looked pretty. 'Not a pond, old boy, a *lough,*' said dad, making a phlegmy noise for the *gh*. I stared at the water again: a giant puddle, brown, still as a mirror, with bristly weeds along the far edge, and a purple mountain rising behind. We put our sandwiches on a rock, then dad opened his box of flies. This turned out to be even better than the sweet tin in mum's desk. I'd never seen such pretty reds and blues. He told me some of their names, which were like spells, and tied a yellow one on the end of my line. 'We'll start with yours,' he said, 'and when you've got the hang of it, I'll fix up my own.' It was the first time he'd talked to me like this, being a teacher only nicer, and it made me want to look at him more closely. His hands, for instance. At home they were always nervous, flicking ash off a cigarette, twiddling his signet ring, trembling when he cut the heads off roses, clenching and unclenching on the arm of his red chair in the drawing room. Now they didn't shake, and were long and thin and nifty – even the funny one, which he'd squashed in the deckchair. They felt strong, too, when he came to stand behind me, gripped me round both wrists, and showed me how to flick the rod up to my shoulder, then wait for a moment while the line whistled out behind, then how to fling it forward again, so the line curled past us like a giant signature and lay down on the water. 'The quieter it goes, the better,' he whispered. 'And the further the better, too. They're clever things, fish. Much cleverer than us. And trout have got radar for ears, so we have to be quiet, too.' I immediately lost my balance, and flipped over a weedy stone with my gumboot. It made a splash like a nuclear bomb, but dad didn't say anything. He squeezed me tighter, and we made another cast.

Dad let me try by myself and turned away to fix his own rod. It had felt so easy when he was controlling my hands. I'd thought I must be a natural, and had in my blood all the things I needed to know, just waiting to appear. But as it turned out I had a lot of other things in my blood as well – things that were a real nuisance, and made me catch the grass, and tangle my line, and bung up the reel, and hook my coat. Dad tried not to notice at first, but couldn't pretend for long. 'Don't worry,' he said. 'It's always like this to start with.' He put down his rod to watch, telling me to flick further back, or not so far, or exactly like that, dead right. I made a few good casts, then caught the heather behind me again. This time he shook his head. He wanted to get started himself. So after a few more tries, and a near miss when I found the fly hurtling towards my eyeball like a hornet, and thought I'd be blind for ever, I tidied up my reel as best I could, then sat on the rock beside the sandwiches. Dad was the expert. If I paid close attention, I'd learn eventually.

He looked completely alone – that was the most surprising thing. The heathery wall of the mountain behind him kept blurring in cloud. Gusts of wind thumped the surface of the lough into mucky little waves. Sunlight smashed the clouds, then vanished. But none of this made any difference. The moment dad stepped away from the shore he forgot everything except what he was doing. His brain slithered out of his head and ran down his arms, along his rod, into the line, then sliced backwards and forwards through the air round his head, before disappearing underwater. That's why his face suddenly looked softer, why dark creases had appeared in his cheeks, why the bone of his jaw had come loose. He wasn't in himself any more.

It was like seeing a dead person who was still alive, so I tried to concentrate on other things. Such as how cold it was getting, and how good the sandwiches looked: surely dad couldn't have forgotten about them too? He'd warned me about this. 'The great thing about fishing,' he'd said on our way up the stony path, 'is not minding if you don't catch anything.' 'You mean nothing at all?' I said. 'That's right. If I counted the hours I've spent flogging rivers here and there, and never had a nibble, people would think I'd wasted half my life. But it's not about catching things. It's about fishing itself. That's what counts.' I glanced across to the mountain, then back at the lough again, and didn't believe him. There he was frowning like a demon, crouching forward as he tried to land his fly alongside the reeds on the far bank. He definitely wanted to catch something, and so did I. I wanted to feel a trout wriggling in my hands, then knock it on the head with the special stick in dad's bag, which was called a priest, then carry it back to show mum and Kit, then give it to the woman in the kitchen so she could cook it for supper. But I had to get used to the idea that this wasn't going to happen today, and might not happen tomorrow either. It made me feel colder, and I checked my watch. Kit would be back in our room by now, unpacking his new jersey.

Suddenly dad gave a little whoop, and his rod bent like in one of the engravings along the back landing at home. I leaped to my feet and tiptoed towards him. 'Where is he?' I wanted to say, but that would have been daft. The fish was right there, where the line stretched underwater. A brown wobble, like a penny sinking into a wishing-well. 'He's not going to fall off, is he?' I asked, hoping that sounded sensible. 'Better not,' said dad. He was reeling in faster now, and I could see a stubby nose jutting above the surface. 'He looks OK,' dad said. 'But just to be sure, why don't you go to the bank, and grab him when I get him into the shallow bit?' I could see that was a good idea, and set off towards a little inlet: dad could dangle the fish into that, then I would pounce.

'You can get him now,' dad said, and because that sounded easy too I leaned down and snatched. But the trout was bigger than I'd thought – the water had disguised him. The slime on his body was thick, too, like an invisible layer of clothing, and impossible to grip. No wonder Peter Routledge had said tickling them was diffi-cult: you might as well try to catch soap. My fingers closed round the middle, then squirted immediately off to the tail, where there was even less to grip, though it looked dryer. It didn't matter; the hook was still stuck tight. All dad had to do was keep reeling in, swinging his rod towards me, and in a moment the fish would be through the shallows and onto the bank, where I could whack it with the priest.

I tried to hurry up, dipping my hands into the water and shooshing forward. That was a mistake. My hands hit the line and knocked the hook clear. There was the fly – droopy yellow, lying on a finger of weed. And there was the fish, almost beached on the stones. We were going to lose him, that was obvious. We were going to lose him, and it was my fault. Dad hadn't seen exactly what had happened, he was too far away, but I didn't have any excuse. The gills were already moving faster, getting ready to dive. The two seconds I'd been hunched over, staring, were probably like two years in fish-time. That's why the trout was feeling so much better, and about to make a dash for it. It's why I had to dash too, otherwise we'd talk about it for the rest of the holidays. Mum would decide I wasn't ready for Scotland, and dad would never take me with him again.

I dropped on the fish as if I was smothering a rugger ball, then clambered upright and scooped him onto the bank with a mighty flick. 'What happened?' dad asked, hobbling towards me over the slippy stones. 'Sorry about that,' I said in my grown-up voice. 'Lost my footing. I got the fish though – there he is.' We bent down and inspected him: a glittery little stick, with grass-bits on him like stripes of green blood. 'Shall we knock him on the head?' I wondered. 'I don't think so,' said dad softly. 'He's going of his own accord.' Then he put his hand on my arm. 'Not much of a fish, is he? Just a little fellow.' He picked him up easily, with no sliding, and popped him in his bag. 'Your first,' he said. 'Not mine, dad,' I told him. 'Yours.' He pretended he hadn't heard, and set off along the stream towards the stony path, our two rods bouncing on his shoulder.

Sometimes we called Scotland Scotland, sometimes it was Glen Feshie, which was the name of the lodge grandpa went to, near Fort William. He'd rented it years ago, when he gave up working in the brewery and started farming instead. Dad always made the house sound impressive, but mum wasn't so sure. There were five thousand acres, dad said. Mum said land didn't cost much up there, and anyway it was only bog and rocks. Everything was much grander than Little Brewers, dad went on. And much colder, mum said, with a kitchen so far away from the dining room the meals were always freezing. There's a maid, dad said. She's not a real maid, mum butted in, she's moaning Edith, then rolled her eyes and made a tsk-tsk noise under her breath, which turned into 'Edith, Edith'. I wasn't sure what to make of this – except that dad obviously took it all very seriously.

The summer after Ireland, we caught the sleeper north from London. I'd never been in a bunk before, and it was strange to think of dad climbing the same little steps next door, leaving mum and Beauty on the bottom bed. Kit and I had our own compartment, which made me feel I was living about five years ago, before we had to be sensible all the time. When we found a pot in the cupboard under the corner sink, and saw it had 'Not to Be Used for Solid Matter' written on the side, we rushed next door in our pyjamas and showed mum. She laughed too, and even dad chuckled from his darkness near the ceiling. But when we woke up next morning, climbed into the hired car and bounced off to find the Lodge, she said we mustn't tell grandpa about the pot. He wouldn't think it was funny. Her voice sounded tired, and the vein beat in its dent beside her eye. 'Still,' she said. 'We must make the best of it.' Dad nodded, tightening his hands as we turned off the main road, and I looked around, trying to see what the best might be. The river, for instance, the Feshie: that was beautiful, running along-side the drive and shivering like I supposed a salmon would do. The hills behind were pretty, too: heavier than Ireland, but covered with the same jungle of bracken and heather, which I knew I could get through if I absolutely had to. But the house . . . My mind wouldn't work properly, when it suddenly reared in front of us. It was the spooky hotel in a murder film, with smoke flopping out of the chimneys and ivy round the windows. Even though it was morning, the lights were all blazing, as though something horrible had to be scared away. 'Don't turn round,' Kit whispered to me in the back seat, when we jolted past some outbuildings and braked by the front door. 'What?' I hissed. 'You missed it,' he said. 'A deer. Hanging up in one of those sheds. It didn't have a head.'

'Look who's here!' said grandpa, standing on the front step with his arms out, his silver hair shining. I couldn't tell whether he meant us, or the people squeezing through the porch behind him. Mum had warned us there'd be others. 'It's a kind of house party,' she said. 'It goes on all summer, and it's how grandpa keeps him-self happy.' 'And how he spends all the money,' I whispered, which I thought was safe because I'd heard mum say something like it herself, when she was talking to dad and didn't know I could hear. She smiled, and kept going. 'I don't know who'll be there, exactly. Mrs Johnson, for one,' Mrs Johnson was grandpa's housekeeper; she had a daughter but no husband, and even mum wouldn't tell me about that. Now here she was, bustling forward and wiping her hands on her apron. She kissed me on the cheek, but I didn't mind. What I did mind was behind her. First Joanie, grandpa's girlfriend, with her stomping boots and jam-mouth. And then Beak. Beak! I gawped, thinking this must be a trick. Maybe grandpa had built a model of him with roller-skate wheels that moved like a real person. 'Your mouth's open, darling,' said mum quietly, putting her hand on my shoulder, then turned up the volume. 'Oliver!' she said. 'How lovely! The boys *will* be pleased.' She giggled, but not in a happy way, and pushed me forward. I took a deep breath and shook his hand. Yes, it was the same Beak. The red wax nose melting into the mouse moustache. The black eyes sliding from side to side. And this soft hand still hanging onto my own. The hand which held the cane, while the other hand gripped the back of my neck. 'Hello Andrew, hello Christopher,' he said breezily, squaring his shoulders. He wanted to show us things were different up here: that's why he didn't call us Motion I and Motion II. But of course he was still Beak wherever he was, and I hated him. When his hand drooped, I backed away, then stood beside mum until grandpa let us into the house. I thought if I looked at her now, I'd burst into tears.

'It's ghastly,' mum said, as soon as she got us into our bedroom. That helped, but it didn't change anything. Mum was right about the cold, too. It was freezing in Scotland, with slippy pale blue eiderdowns the colour of glaciers, and pictures of stags on the walls, which had dozens of tiny black flies trapped under the glass. When I went to the window, the mountains had stepped closer, so now they were pressing round the house, leaning their shoulders together and frowning. In the night they'd probably fold over the drive altogether, like the hill shutting over Merlin, and we'd never get home again. 'I tell you what,' mum went on, rubbing her hands together. 'We'll get Mrs Johnson to make you a fire in your own room. And tomorrow we'll go into Fort William and buy some Monopoly, so we can play that while the men do their stuff. Does that sound fun?' It did. Especially the fire. But the best thing of all was knowing mum hadn't said any of this just to make us feel better. She'd said it because she wanted to go home too.

When Edith came sniffing into the dining room to give us our cold soup for lunch, grandpa boomed, 'Well, boys, it's marvellous to see you here', as if he was saying grace. He didn't pay us much attention after that, and neither did Beak or Joanie or any of the other tall tweedy people who came and went. They appeared at breakfast and shouted over our heads, then climbed into the back of the Land Rover to go stalking or fishing or shooting, then came back in time for a bath and supper. To start with, I thought Beak was being kind – avoiding me, so I didn't have to think about school. I soon changed my mind. He didn't think I was worth bothering with. Mum laughed and said I hadn't 'penetrated' – but if Beak wanted to ignore me, I'd ignore him too. And once mum had got the fires sorted out, and the Monopoly, we'd surprise all the grown-ups by catching a salmon. That's the kind of thing a boy would have done in the *Victor*.

As soon as I'd hatched the idea I told mum, and we went on the second day, simple as that, and took Beauty with us. 'She'll be very good,' mum told the ghillie, when he handed her a rod by the out-house where Kit had seen the deer with no head. 'Can I have one too?' I asked, scanning the floor for bloodstains, then staring at the ghillie's caterpillar eyebrows. 'You, sonny?' he said. 'You're a bit wee for the salmon, but you can have a swing with your mother's rod if she'll let you.' I'd have been disappointed, if his voice hadn't been like hypnosis. Mackay at school had a Scottish accent, but it was nothing compared to this. This was like listening to a completely different language, which I understood even though I couldn't speak it. I told him I'd already been fishing in Ireland. 'Oh, you have, have you?' he murmured. 'Catch anything?' 'Yes,' said mum before I had time to answer. 'Some brownies.' That was two lies in one, and I looked at the ground again, hoping Kit wouldn't say anything. He didn't. He just whistled and put his hands in his pockets. 'Very nice too,' said the ghillie. Then he fiddled a pair of half-moon glasses from his top pocket, and perched them on his nose. They looked as out of place as a moustache on the Mona Lisa, but he needed them to check the fly was tied on properly. Then we were off.

The rod was too long and too heavy, so I soon gave up. When mum took over, she wasn't much good either. Her line kept collapsing in spaghetti-tangles, and every time this happened she gave a shriek, which the ghillie said didn't matter because salmon couldn't hear as well as trout. After five minutes she got into a rhythm – which was fine, except it meant she started to look alone, like dad had done in Ireland. I took the hint, and went to sit under the pine trees with Kit and Beauty, out of the way. The silver light bouncing off the river, and the way she had to stretch to get the line back properly: it all made me think she was about to hurt herself.

'Sorry, darlings,' she said in a half-shout because she couldn't turn round. 'I'm hopeless.' 'No,' said the ghillie softly, as if he was a darling too. 'You're doing fine.' He leaned forward to jiggle the line where it came off the reel, making the fly move a fraction in the water. At exactly that moment, his hands were magic as well as his voice. Just by making the tiny tweak, he'd got the fly into a salmon's mouth. He must have, because suddenly the line was going wild. First in slow motion, while Kit and I scrambled to our feet, and then in speeded-up time, ripping off the reel as though it wanted to stretch all the way to Fort William. Everything else was going crazy too. The rod bucked in mum's hands, and the ghillie wrapped his arms round her, like dad when he'd been teaching me. Then he squatted down like a games coach at school, telling her to keep the rod hoisted and her line tight. To let the fish run, and eventually to start reeling in – because look, here was the net, and we were going to catch this fellow, it was a good one, a big one, and we'd show the men when they got back, oh yes we would.

My heart had bounced between my teeth and swelled up, so I could hardly breathe. Kit was goggle-eyed beside me, his mouth sagging. 'Come on, mum,' we said, which was also like games at school. 'Come on, mum.' She liked that. She kept giving her gurgling laugh, leaning backwards sometimes and gasping 'Blimey' or 'He weighs a ton.' Her face was red, redder than I'd ever seen it, with cloudy blotches on her cheeks. She wasn't exaggerating. It really was a heavy fish. And only five or six yards out, now. A bar in the water, like silver. Beauty saw it at the same time and growled. 'She's going to jump in,' I thought. 'She's going to ruin everything.' So I leaped forward just as she dipped into her collie-crouch and flung my arms round her neck, pinning her down. 'Good job, Master Andrew,' said the ghillie, which made me feel like Gordon

Banks, and he went back to mum. 'Keep him coming,' he told her, 'Keep him coming.' He was almost whispering, and dipped his net into the water without making a ripple. I tried to bury my face in the hair on Beauty's neck, where the bull terrier had bitten her, but she wriggled her head round and licked my face. There was biscuit-smell on her breath. When I turned back to mum again, I'd missed the crucial moment. The ghillie was already springing to his feet, holding the net in mid-air with both hands and showing the whole world what mum had done. 'Well done, madam,' he said, with a funny crack in his voice.

'Thank you, thank you,' mum said in a rush, the rod straight in her hand again, and the line blowing across her face so she had to brush it away. She gave such a huge smile I could see all her teeth, even the one with the lead filling. It made me feel the heat inside her, and her blood tearing round. Then the ghillie laid his net on the bank, fiddled the fly from the salmon's mouth, whisked the priest out of his bag, clonked the fish on the head, and lifted it by the tail so we could see it completely. 'A fresh one,' he said. 'A fresh one and a fine one.' I thought archaeologists must feel like this, when they pulled treasure up from the earth. The salmon was like a buried warrior, suddenly yanked into the light. We gazed in silence at the dented silver on his head and jaw. Then Beauty sneezed, and mum said she'd have to sit down. I stayed looking while the ghillie laid the fish on the grass. I told myself I'd never forget, then went over to mum under the pine trees and hugged her so hard she told me to be careful, she felt creaky after all that hard work.

I asked whether we could eat the salmon that same evening, but dad said no, Edith couldn't manage, and anyway didn't we want to freeze him and take him home? That way, we'd have a bit of Scotland to keep with us. He was proud of mum, and talking faster than usual, but he didn't want to make a fuss. After all, grandpa lived here for months on end, every year, and a salmon wasn't headline news. That was fair enough, I thought – especially when dad said he'd come with me to inspect the fish in the scullery, and told me I'd saved the day by diving on Beauty. Later, grandpa interrupted everybody at supper and leaned forward to ask whether I'd like to go stalking with dad in the morning. 'If he doesn't mind,' I said, looking at mum, who was pushing a triangle of baked egg across her plate. 'Of course he doesn't mind!' said grandpa loudly, and stared all the way round the table, holding his fork upright in his hand. Beak was nodding and so was dad. Mum was still prodding her bit of egg.

Dad and I had breakfast early, before mum was awake. She'd put my thick cords out the night before, and my special socks like tweed, and enough jerseys to make me feel like a sausage roll. When I stuck my head round her bedroom door, meaning to say goodbye quickly, she made me come in, turned the light on, and sat up in her nightie to inspect. 'Come on, Gilly,' said dad, patting her shoulder heavily, as if trying to push her under the covers again. 'It's not a fashion parade.' 'Have you got your thing?' she asked, ignoring him. I nodded. My thing was my bear, a small panda-toy I'd got in last year's Christmas stocking, which I'd told her was my lucky charm and came with me everywhere. The fur had worn off one of the legs, and now it was just shiny metal with a sharp edge. When I kissed her goodbye, I was already holding it tight in my coat pocket.

The ghillie was waiting by the outhouse – the same man as yesterday, with the caterpillar eyebrows. When dad said 'You remember Robertson?' I smiled, and shook his hand like an old friend as he said, 'Master Andrew.' 'Robertson will be coming with us,' dad explained. 'And McKenzie' – he pointed across the yard – 'will be there if we need him, won't you, McKenzie?' There was a grunt from an open doorway, and when I looked harder, I saw a gypsy-faced man inside, saddling a pony. I was going to shake his hand too, but 'No time to waste' said Robertson, and clumped out of the yard with the rifle slung across his back. As I set off to follow, dad whispered, 'We know who's giving the orders round here, don't we?' The funny thing was, he didn't seem to mind.

We crossed a flat tractor-bridge over the Feshie, and headed for the high tops. Robertson had given me a stick with a curly handle, which helped clear the way ahead. Even so, it was hard going.

Within half an hour the bracken had turned into heather, which sometimes sprayed as high as my chest, scratching my face and hands, and sending tiny grey moths, or were they dead petals, straight up my nose. Much more of this and I'd get worn out – but the heather soon shrank down into clumps again, and there was short grass which was easy. Were we stalking already, or were we still waiting to begin? We'd begun. Look. We were heading into the wind, so the deer wouldn't know we were coming. Sweat smells, bath smells, breakfast smells, breath smells: everything blew back from us towards the lodge. I turned round, half-expecting to see it all stretched out behind like a banner. Instead I saw two blobs on the drive, which were mum and Kit watching us disappear.

By mid-morning we'd climbed out of our own valley into the next, where the lodge was invisible, and a big mild grey wind was barging around pointlessly, banging off the mountain walls, flattening the tops of the bracken. The sky was low, like a slate roof, and there was no talking but high-stepping and deep breathing. Even dad was puffing, looking round sometimes, making sure I could keep up. I grinned back at him. I'd been ready for this, hadn't I? Besides, it was fun. And I had my bear clenched in my hand in case it turned out not to be. Actually the leg with no fur was useful, because I could dig it into my palm until it hurt, and that made me get a move on. My stick was a help too, now I could see Robertson wanted me to use it like a kind of pole. That's how he was with his own: springing into the air then sinking down, springing and sinking, as if the heather were really water, and he could almost walk on its surface but not quite. 'Well done, Master Andrew,' he said, when he saw me copying, but he didn't look at me for long. He was busy wondering about the stags. Where were they? Close. In fact, much closer than we thought. Robertson had suddenly crouched down and lifted his spy-glass like a pirate. Then he shook his head. False alarm.

At lunchtime we sat in the shelter of a boulder and ate our sandwiches. Venison, which tasted of drains. I chewed carefully, thinking about how I was eating what I was hunting, and remembered Mr Porch telling us about the Picts in History. Had any of them sat here, I wondered, wearing their animal skins and their woad? Or were we the first, the very first people ever to come here? Probably the first. And we were eating almost raw meat, like cavemen. I ran my fingers over the stone, feeling its bumps like mum always said I should when I touched a sculpture. The bright green moss was soft as felt. 'What are you thinking?' dad asked, and I dropped my hand quickly. 'Wondering where all the stags are.' Dad thought this was a good question, and asked Robertson. When Robertson shrugged, I snapped a heather twig and gouged at the rock, chipping off a flake of mica. Now people would know someone had been here before.

When dad gave me a nip from his flask, I thanked him in a perfectly normal voice. I wanted Robertson to think I'd drunk whisky dozens of times, even though it was my first sip, and glowed down my throat like melting iron. Then we were off again, faces into the wind, picking up our feet as though we were hauling through glue. And just when I'd decided we weren't going to see a stag, and I'd have to pretend to Kit that I'd drunk a lot of whisky, to make up for it, I cannoned into dad's back. He'd stopped. Robertson had stopped too. Stopped, and sunk against another big granite lump, so he could lean his spy-glass on the knobbly top and peer ahead. Across the valley, beyond the brown track threading downhill, was a herd of about a dozen. Hinds, mainly, but with a young stag in charge. And a few yards off to his left, another stag. Not so good, this second one. Not so many points on his antlers. And stewing round in circles looking unhappy. Robertson made a flat sweep with his hand, which showed we should lie down.

After that, everything happened very slowly, step by step. First Robertson waved dad alongside him, holding out the rifle. Then dad took the cartridges as well – little brass capsules, like miniature whisky bottles, only thinner. Then he loaded them. Then he snuggled into the heather, getting the right weight over his elbows. Then he cocked his head sideways, peering through the sights. The herd was upwind from us and didn't know we existed. I pulled my panda from my pocket, and pressed my lips to the threadbare head, asking God to let dad do what he wanted. With my other hand, I pressed down the heather for a better view. The second stag wasn't going round in circles any longer. He was fidgeting, huffing his nostrils open, and moaning. These were the last movements he'd ever make. I blinked, and tried to clear my head. In a minute he would stand still, and that would be it. Less than a minute. He was slowing down already, his brain working through the last thoughts he'd ever think. Now he was still. Side on.

Dad fired. It was much louder than I'd expected, like two heavy stones clacking together, and smoke tootled from the end of the gun barrel. Nothing happened on the slope opposite. Had dad missed? The herd was still grazing, and the mothy stag was still watching them. Then the rifle's echo cartwheeled off the hill behind us, and everything exploded. The herd turned into a spray of enormous brown waterdrops, bouncing down the valley with the healthy stag behind them. Their bodies were too big for their delicate leg-bones, and looked as if they might smash onto the rocks at any moment. But they didn't care. They had to get away, no matter what. Only the other stag was left, and I'd be able to look into his eyes soon enough. Except he was sitting down when he ought to be lying. Dad hadn't killed him, that was the problem. He hadn't shot him though the heart. It explained why Robertson was telling dad to hurry up and fire again, to finish him off. And why dad was rocking from elbow to elbow, fiddling open the breech and slotting in a new cartridge. I'd cut my finger on the leg of my panda, squeezing it too tight. 'Come on, dad,' I said under my breath. 'Come on.'

Dad fired again and the antlers jerked backwards, taking the stag's body with them. It smacked the ground so hard, the legs jiggled in the air. 'Shot, sir,' said Robertson, letting his words hang for a moment, then scrabbled to his feet and called over his shoulder. 'Come on, Master Andrew, I'll show you something.' He set off down the slope before I was ready, but he can't have been going at top speed because I soon caught up and so did dad, which meant we all reached the stag at the same time. 'Shot, sir,' Robertson said again, out of breath, but dad said 'No, no' quietly, and shook his head. I stood there gazing. The antlers had hit the ground first, and gouged out little divots; they were cold things, and made death seem ages ago and nothing to do with us. The body was different. That still had life swarming out of it. The raw red tip of the willy poking from its furry sheath. Eyes wet. Whiskery lips pulled back from the teeth – an old man's big yellow teeth, sprinkled with grass-flecks. 'Now, Master Andrew,' said Robertson, dropping to his knees. 'How cold are you?' 'Pretty cold,' I said, realising it for the first time. Robertson was pleased. 'We'll soon have you warmed up,' he said, and splayed his left hand on the ribcage of the stag, flicking his jacket open with his right and pulling a stubby knife from his belt. My eyes wandered across the body: the scurfy skin, and the ginger hairs, widely spaced, like on a pig. The mucky red hole high in the back leg by the hip, and the smaller, tidier hole through the shoulder. That was the way to the heart. It looked too small.

'Here,' Robertson was saying, and my attention switched back to him. 'This'll be warm.' With that, he jabbed his knife into the stag, and pulled it the whole length of the stomach, until he was almost at the sore-looking tip of the willy. The stomach fell open straight-away, so all the slithery hoops and rings and bags and sacks and coils flopped onto the heather. I could see what Robertson was up to now. They were hot, all these blotchy things – they had steam rising off them. Enough to make me blush, anyway. 'Not squeamish, are you?' said dad, looking into my face with a half-smile. 'No, dad,' I said. Robertson whipped off his jacket and pushed up the sleeve of his shirt so it was above the elbow, and he could stretch inside the stag without getting blood on his clothes. He looked like someone exploring a hole in a wall, squirming for-ward until his head was resting on the body, grunting a little, tak-ing care not to puncture anything, then scooping the innards towards him, and at the same time leaning sideways to get clear of their giant mess. Under its thin coat of blood, his arm looked very white, without any hairs.

I bent to look more closely at the shapes I recognised – the beefy heart, and the liver, and the kidneys in their puddingy fat. Robert-son hadn't finished yet. He was working inside the stag with his knife again, nicking off flaps and hinges, tidying until the whole cave was clean. 'Kneel,' he said, and I thought of what King Arthur said to his knights when they'd fought bravely, so did as I was told. 'Now give me your hands.' I did that too. His own hands were warm and soft, and I knew if I squeezed them they would squirt out of my grip like a trout. I let Robertson pull them over the slippy edge of the opening and into the dark red inside. He was looking in my eyes and nodding. 'OK?' he asked, making the 'k' sound as though it was flying. 'Yes, OK,' I said. It was like a furnace, only the heat was perfect, and the wetness made me want to wipe my hands together, as if I were washing. So I let go of Robertson, wringing my hands, and felt the hot blood sliding over my fingers, under the ends of my nails, into my cuts and scratches.

'You try, dad,' I said, twisting round and looking up at him. I couldn't see his face – what was left of daylight had rolled into a ball behind him, and blinded me. But I could tell he was shaking his head. Was he trying to say something? I'd never know what it was, because McKenzie, the gypsy-ghillie I'd forgotten about, was coming up the track towards us, leading the pony by a leather strap. Up to now, I'd been thinking the day was just one thing leading to the next by accident. Actually it had all been planned. Dad and I were always going to walk in a particular direction. We were always going to wait as long as we'd waited. We were always going to find this sickly stag. And the stag was always going to be killed. The only thing that had gone wrong – nearly – was dad's first shot. But that had been all right in the end. And now McKenzie had arrived on cue, heaving the body across the pony's back, lashing it down with hairy ropes. It was like watching dad tie the luggage on the roof of the car when we were going on holiday: throw and pull and tie, throw and pull and tie.

As I turned away, and stood waiting for the signal to start off downhill, I slid one hand into my pocket. I wanted to hang onto something until we were back at the lodge, and everything was normal again. Not my rubbishy panda. One of the cartridges. The second one dad fired, which had killed the stag, and was now so warm in my grip the dried blood on my fingers was beginning to melt and run again.

CHAPTER SIXTEEN

Going Beetroot

I was loitering on the upstairs landing, clearing my throat, squeaking the loose floorboard, pretending to look for clean clothes in the airing cupboard – and at last mum heard me. 'OK, darling, you can come in now.' All I'd been trying to do was get into her bedroom, so I could see her get ready for the dance. Was it another thing I was too old for, like cuddling in the morning? I twisted the handle and stepped forward. Carpet soft as pigeon-feathers, lamplight speckled with talc and scent-spray. I stood still until everything settled down, then took another step. Mum was just as I'd imagined, wearing her black-and-red magician's dressing gown, and dangling her hands so she could dry her nail varnish. 'Come and say hello,' she said with a little pout, as though she wanted to forgive me something. 'I've been trying to for hours,' I told her. 'I just needed some p and q to do my face,' she said, 'you know.' 'Not really,' I said, deciding to stay grumpy for a bit longer, and backing away from the dressing table to sit on her side of the bed. 'I've got a surprise,' she said. I thought it must be something to do with the dance. A new dress, perhaps. 'Beak's leaving Maidwell,' she said. 'Mr Porch is taking over.'

When she stood up and went to the cupboard, her dressing gown sagged open, so I could see the lacy hem of her slip brushing the tops of her stockings. The white shimmered as if she'd suddenly been caught in a spotlight. 'What are you looking at?' Mum folded the dressing gown shut again, tossing the belt-ends across one another in the beginning of a butterfly. 'Nothing,' I told her, but couldn't help blushing. 'I'm thinking about what you said.' I was, too. I had enough questions to last me a week. Had Beak been told to go, or made his own mind up? Had there been a panel, with Mr Porch standing in front like the boy in *And When Did You Last See*

Your Father? Would there still be the Swish? I could feel the skin of my bum tightening, like it did every time I thought about beating, and watched mum stretch into her cupboard on tiptoe, reaching towards the party dresses she kept at the back in see-through plastic bags. 'I'll go and wait in the drawing room,' I said. Mum sank against the empty clothes as though she'd lost her balance. 'Stay, darling. I'll need you to do me up.'

When the new term was about to start, and we were eating the condemned supper on our knees in front of the fire, dad said, 'It's sad about Beak going, but at least he's seen you through most of your time.' Kit and I glanced at one another without speaking, and I said, 'Sure, dad.' I thought if I talked fast like that, he'd see what I really thought of Beak. Dad took the hint, and tried to sound jolly. 'The old boy's been headmaster for more than thirty years,' he said. 'It's right for someone younger to take over. And Beak would never have wanted to make a fuss. That's why you didn't have a party or anything last term. He'd have hated bursting into tears in front of you all.' I stuck my fork into my banger, and four juice-jets squirted out. Beak burst into tears? I wanted to say, 'If he liked us so much, why was he always beating us?' – but dad would think that was rude, so I kept my mouth shut. Anyway, I was concentrating more on Mr Porch: he was the one I had to watch out for now. He was married – that was probably a good thing, even though Mrs Porch had such white skin, and such black hair, she might have been a witch. On the other hand, Mr Porch had always been creepy. He smoked Players with no tips, and coughed so hard his lungs jumped. Also, his knees went pale purple when he took tackling practice.

After the first week of term, I told Jagger Hut that I'd got it wrong. Amazingly, school was better with Mr Porch – even Booster Thwaites thought so, and he'd been Beak's second-in-command. I overheard him in a corridor telling Rhubarb that things were 'much more relaxed in Common Room'. They were in class too: people didn't seem frightened all the time. After another week, I changed my mind. Mr Porch had started whacking people in their dorms before lights out, flicking up his slipper in exactly the same way Beak had done – only Mr Porch never fumbled, and he always swung harder, with the stiff part of the heel bang on target. Then he began Swishing people after supper, and that was harder than Beak as well. But harder wasn't the only bad thing. There was his crocodile smile afterwards, with his lips stretching and the tobacco-teeth glinting. 'I will never betray you,' people sometimes said in my comics. Well, Mr Porch had betrayed us: that's what we said in Jagger Hut, then swore we'd refuse to be prefects.

Eventually everyone at Maidwell was made a prefect – not that it meant much. The masters did all the bossing, and the only person who minded was Stephens, who wanted to be Head Boy, and copied Mr Porch's way of wearing his watch loose so he could jiggle it round his wrist. 'But how will anyone know we're senior?' Stephens asked me one day. 'Surely prefects should be able to *do* things?' 'Like what?' I answered. 'I don't know. Hurry up the stigs in the showers,' he said. When I passed this on to Miller II, he said Stephens would be asking if he could Swish people next. I knew what he meant, but really we thought Stephens was a joke, so it wasn't a problem. Everyone in their right mind knew rules weren't the main worry any more. The main worry was exams, and especially the exam at the end of my last term, when I was twelve, which would decide where I went next. Its name made it sound easy – Common Entrance – but masters said it was the most difficult exam I'd ever take, and if I failed I'd go to a school no one had heard of, and probably end up running a garage or a pub.

Most people went to Eton, which my new friend Bacon always said backwards: Note. I knew about Eton. Grandpa had been there, it was huge, and the boys wore stiff collars. It wasn't for me, though. I was going to Radley College, because that's where Uncle Rob had been to school. He'd liked it, and it was smaller than Eton, which mum and dad thought would suit me better. I was pleased about the small, but everything else bothered me. Was it cheaper than Eton – in which case were mum and dad running out of money? Were the boys there not so clever – and did that explain why it wasn't famous? And was Uncle Rob a good reason for going? He was fun, with his huge hands and his curly hair and his laugh like a door banging. But what about this boy he'd been at the school with – the one who now

taught there, and would be my house master? His name was Mr
Way. What if he turned out to be a second Beak?

I went to see Rhubarb, my English teacher, because he was the
one who talked to me as if I was a grown-up. 'It's a better school
for you than Eton,' he said firmly. We were sitting in his study at
the top of one of the towers, where there was a window seat surrounded by books. Books about God, mainly, including one I
wanted to read when I was older, which was the life story of St
Luke. I liked the sound of him because he was a doctor; a real person who did a real job. 'Better how?' I wondered. 'Radley's in the
country,' Rhubarb said. 'It's a quiet sort of place – you can do your
birding.' 'What if I said I didn't want to go?' I went on. 'You mean
you'd rather be at Eton?' 'No,' I said. 'I mean, supposing I didn't
want to go to that sort of school at all?' Rhubarb frowned; he had
a small hard lump on his forehead, and when his skin furrowed it
turned white. 'Like the boys in the village, for instance?' he said.
'And not board?' 'Yes. Not board any more.' 'Well . . .' Rhubarb sat
back in his chair and put his hands on his knees, making a little
ppppprrr noise like a horse blowing. 'You'll have to talk to your
parents,' he said, then added after a pause, 'But like I say, *why*
would you want to do that? Boys like you are very lucky, you
know.' 'I know, sir,' I told him and stared out of the window.
Someone was wearing in a new cricket bat. I could hear a busy
tok-tok-tok-tok echoing up from the nets.

When I got downstairs I bumped into Bacon, and told him
Rhubarb had said Radley was special, not second best to Eton.
Bacon gave one of his squealy laughs. 'He's paid to do that,' he said.
'No, honestly,' I told him. 'We can't all go to the same school.' That
wasn't quite what I meant, but Bacon wasn't listening. 'At Radley,'
he was saying, 'new boys are hung up on hooks.' 'Hung up how?'
'By their shirt collars.' 'How long for?' 'The whole of their first day,'
Bacon said. 'Sometimes longer.' Then he gave another of his special
laughs and his face went pink – the Gibbon had told him a little
curly tail would burst out of his grey flannels one day soon. She
meant everyone knew when he was fibbing, and that made me feel
better. But I still wished he hadn't said it. All through the next few

months, and even when I finally went into Tower with the other leavers and took the exam, I kept imagining a room like the showers, with white tiles on the walls, and boys strangling on the pegs.

Bacon lived in Norfolk, which I knew because of Overy Staithe and the bird marshes. Another boy at school, Birkbeck, was his neighbour there, and now they were both doing Common Entrance for Eton together. I'd wanted to be Birkbeck's friend ever since Haggie's class, but never dared because he was better than me at everything. He looked nice too, with a long face that was sunburned whatever the weather, and amazingly thick straight brown hair which fell into his eyes so he was always flicking his head like a moorhen, trying to see. I'd decided he couldn't like me, so I just grinned at him when we passed in the corridor, and mugged up on cricket, which was another thing he did brilliantly. In the end, we started talking about it, and found we were friends after all.

Birkbeck always moved slowly, like a farmer coming back from a day in the fields, and this meant he was a good person to take birding. My models didn't take his fancy, though – his hands were too big – and neither did the stories I sometimes wrote for Rhubarb. I didn't mind, because I wanted to learn everything he had to tell me. Like how to do fractions, and bowl googlies, and make pine-needle cigarettes taste better by rolling up bits of cardboard and sticking them inside the end I didn't light.

Then Birkbeck asked me to stay with him in the last summer holidays before our exams, and suddenly we were best friends. Even mum and dad were excited – and I saw why when mum drove me up to his house. There was a chunk of castle beside his village green, like a gigantic mushroom that was starting to go bad, and a private drive behind it, winding along a beech hedge. 'I told you it would be grand,' mum whispered, as she bent towards the windscreen to get a better view. She hadn't in fact, but she was right. The house was almost as big as school. 'You're going to have fun,' mum went on softly, breaking harder than she meant, so the gravel gave a little cough like a rich man clearing his throat.

I spent two days with Birkbeck in Norfolk – watching the Test on telly with his dad, tinkling with his mum among the teacups, then biking off round the farm by ourselves. After that, we went to Scotland for a week, and Birkbeck speeded up because he enjoyed it so much. He had some girl cousins staying, and on the second morning we nipped into their bedrooms when they were out, filled their nighties with jelly fish, then stitched up the head-holes. I couldn't believe the fingers at the end of my arms belonged to me: I'd never done anything like it before. That same evening, I looked down the silver lough behind the house, as if I was seeing all the way home. The inside of Little Brewers was shadowy, and when I imagined mum putting away the cooking things in a cupboard under the sink, I saw how tired and thin she looked. 'You're not homesick, are you?' That was Birkbeck's mother: she'd crept up behind me. I shook my head. There wasn't a word for what I felt. Sorry was too strong, and left out too much, but it was close to sorry.

Birkbeck knew exactly what he was going to do after school. First Eton, then university, then back home to run his dad's farm. Like Bacon. What was I going to do after Radley, he asked, supposing I passed my exams? I told him I hadn't decided. In dad's family, only grandpa had gone to university, and he hadn't been able to stay for long. For dad there'd been the war; it would have been impossible for great-grandpa Andrew; and nobody had thought about Aunt Liz. That's why dad said it wouldn't matter if I didn't go myself. But I had to do *something*. There was the brewery, except dad never encouraged that. I sometimes thought about being a vicar, because I liked the idea of working quietly in the country. But I only believed in God when I wanted something. What about the Forestry Commission, then? Mum said that was a possibility – except when I thought about the forests I'd seen in Scotland, and remembered they were all evergreen, I went off the idea. I preferred other kinds of tree, and seeing the leaves change colour. What about something to do with birds? The Royal Society for the Protection of Birds: that had a smart name. It meant I'd be doing what I liked, and not have to worry when I failed Maths and French and Latin and every other subject apart from English.

Actually I thought I'd probably pass History – and Geography, which was easy because mostly it was about the countryside. But

English was the only one that felt safe. Eyot and I had nearly had another punch-up soon after my last term started, when he accused me of being Rhubarb's pet. 'What do you mean?' I asked him, wishing he wouldn't put his face so close. 'He touches you on the arm when he's marking your essays,' he said. 'In front of the whole class.' Then he flounced off as if that proved everything, and I shouted after him: 'It's not true!' But it was true. Rhubarb did sometimes touch me when I was standing beside his desk. I didn't mind. It showed he liked me, which must have been why he put me in charge of the choir as well, even though I wasn't the best singer in the school, and couldn't hold the alto part in hymns. 'Why do I have to learn alto, sir?' I asked him at our first practice. 'Because your voice is starting to break,' he told me. I had to admit there was a frog in my throat these days, but I thought it was only the ciggies in Jagger Hut.

Sometimes in the break from revision, Rhubarb asked me to walk round the lake with him, so we could talk. 'If you like English so much, you ought to try other things,' he told me. 'Theatre. Music. Things that are like English.' I picked a brown stone from the path thinking someone had dropped a toffee, then chucked it into the water. Theatre? Music? 'Give them a go,' said Rhubarb. 'Let me know how you get on.' I was happy to do that, but I didn't know where to start. I'd never been to the theatre with mum and dad – only pantomimes with grandpa – and Maidwell didn't bother much with acting. Haggie wrote something for her class every Christmas, and years ago, when I was eight and she'd been my teacher, it was a play about a garden. Every boy had to be a different kind of flower, and she'd asked me to be the best flower of all, the lily. It didn't work, though; I couldn't remember my lines, so Haggie asked Innis I to be the lily instead. I took over as the Weedy Flower, which was a much smaller part, and I always went bright red when I said my one line: 'I'm not very robust, you know.' The audience laughed because they thought I was lying. 'Or maybe being ironic,' said mum, which I didn't understand.

I'd hated plays after that, until my talk with Rhubarb. Then I made a plan with the other boys in my dorm, and told the Gibbon we wanted to do something for the last week of term. Not really a play. More like *Sunday Night at the London Palladium*, with each of us doing a turn. She thought this was a good idea, which surprised us, then word spread – and eventually half the school turned up, including Rhubarb and Mr Porch. We had the bay window in Tower dorm as our stage, and just our pyjamas and dressing gowns as costumes, but nobody minded. When I stood up at the beginning and explained what would happen, everyone clapped anyway. I sang 'Drink to me only with thine eyes', which I'd found in Lety's music book, but the best thing was by Vane II, whose mum and dad lived in the Lake District – it was a song about a Cumberland Farmer. Vane was chubby and blotchy and nobody knew he could sing: he wasn't in the choir. But after he'd plastered down his hair with water, and done up the top button of his pyjamas, he didn't look like himself any more. When he opened his mouth he sounded completely different too. People clapped so much, the Gibbon said we'd have to do it again next term 'But I won't be here, miss,' I said. 'Nor will you, Motion I,' she said. 'Nor will you.' Then she dug her thumbs into her stiff belt and had a go at smiling.

I'd never heard anything like Vane's song before. 'It's folk,' he told me after one of our rehearsals; his talking voice was like a chop being slapped on a table. 'What's folk?' I asked. 'It means the song's old,' he said, 'and has to do with the country. There are lots like that. You should find out about them.' I thought so too, but music was confusing. At home we had mum's musicals like *Gigi* and *South Pacific* and *My Fair Lady*, and some crackly 78s which belonged to dad. Most of these were songs by the Inkspots, and if ever I said that word – Inkspot – dad winked at mum and made the clicking noise with his tongue, so I kept it for special occasions. We didn't listen to that sort of thing at school. Musical Appreciation, which was half an hour before lunch on Wednesdays, was Classical: Rhubarb brought the record player from the masters' Common Room and told us we had to listen for the fairy in *The Dance of the Sugar Plum Fairy*, or better still for the cannons in the 1812 Overture. After our talk by the lake, I started to listen more carefully to whatever Rhubarb played, and wondered what he was thinking when he put on quieter pieces and stared up through the cedar branches outside the window. His lips moved, sometimes, as though he was counting. 'No, he's praying,' said Lety, and I wanted to believe him. Sometimes music made me shivery too – the problem was, everyone else yawned so much in Appreciation, or practiced making farting noises by blowing on their hands, it was difficult to hear properly. But Lety, he knew about music. He played chopsticks every day on the piano under the stairs, while we were waiting for the lunch gong. He had lessons with Jenny the music teacher, too, because his dad was French and thought music should be a proper part of school.

Jenny gave her lessons every Saturday: she taught experts like Lety in the morning, then played for the rest of us when it was time for Dancing, which was last lesson before lunch. Nobody could pronounce Jenny's real name, which was like a hedgehog, full of j's and k's and z's, and she had a hunchback and witchy black hair that was meant to be piled on her head like Yo-Yo's, but kept collapsing. Everyone liked her, though, because she wasn't a real teacher, and after we'd divided into pairs to practise the waltz, the quickstep, the Charleston and the reel, she sent her fingers scuttling up and down the keys so fast they started to blur. 'Come on,' said Birkbeck, who was always bossy when I was being the girl. 'Pay attention.' He laid one of his brown hands on my shoulder, curled the other round my waist, and off we went round the hall, trying to miss each other's toes. 'One-two-three, one-two-three,' Mr Porch shouted from his place by the mirror. 'It's a dancing lesson, not a dodgems.' We straightened our faces and tried to concentrate. Birkbeck swallowed a lot, because by now lunch-smells were floating through the swing doors which led to Annie's kitchen.

Dancing was fine, except for one thing. Even though swanky people like Palmer-Carew went to holiday parties where they waltzed or quickstepped, most of us had never heard the sort of stuff Jenny played. We listened to pop music. So, whenever Mr Porch was in a good mood, he said we could end Dancing by doing the twist – which meant Jenny's fingers went mad, as if she was changing into Little Richard. But really Mr Porch thought pop music was like James Bond, and ought to be banned. Dad said it was a racket, too, but even he let me spend my pocket money on records, and didn't mind if they were about love any more, as long as I kept the volume down. After he'd gone to work, mum told me to turn it up again, but pop music was like that. It crept round everything people put in its way. When I was lying awake in my dorm at night, I could hear Yo-Yo listening to Radio Caroline in the ironing room. And even boring-looking newspapers like *The Times* had pictures of pop stars in them these days – usually Mick Jagger being arrested, or Pete Townshend smashing his guitar. I cut them out and stuck them in my scrapbook, starting at the opposite end from my pressed flowers and bird feathers.

Rhubarb hadn't meant Mick Jagger when we were walking round the lake and chatting about music. But now I knew him better, I could tell him about the scrapbook. It turned out he preferred the Swinging Blue Jeans and the Moody Blues to the Rolling Stones, and I thought that was gaga, which was the word mum used when granny said something really insane. All the same, just hearing him talk about pop songs was amazing – and when it came to the Beatles, I almost wished he'd stop: if he liked them so much, how could I keep them for myself? He knew the names of everyone in the group before I did, and one day, when we were watching some juniors play a rugger match against Shipham, the school in the next village, he said his girlfriend had all their records. 'I didn't know you had a girlfriend,' I said, so taken-aback I forgot to call him sir. Rhubarb pushed his glasses up his nose, and rubbed his forehead like he sometimes did when he was getting a migraine. Then I asked, 'Is it Miss Yohanssen?', and immediately wished I hadn't.

Rhubarb wasn't angry – he just wasn't going to answer my question. 'Tell me about this scrapbook,' he said, as if it followed. 'Why don't you cut out other things as well? 'What sort of things, sir?' I said quickly, to let him see I was sorry. 'Things that are happening in the news – then you'll know what's going on in the world.' I wanted to ask why I should be bothered with the world, if I didn't know the people in it, but Rhubarb went on before I could open my mouth. 'You're old enough for that now,' he said. 'You should take an interest.' His voice was serious – sad, nearly. 'It doesn't matter if you don't know who everybody is,' he said. 'You know about

Mr Wilson, and Mr Brown, and Sir Alec Douglas-Home, don't you?' 'Yes, sir,' I said, relieved to be telling the truth. 'Well, then . . .' he said. 'And you know who President Kennedy was, don't you?' 'Yes, sir,' I said, even more eagerly. I could remember hearing when he'd been shot: I was in Camel, and we ran up and down the corridor in our pyjamas before bedtime, taking it in turns to fall over and clutch our heads. 'Well, then,' Rhubarb said again. 'You can start from there, and you can ask me questions when you have any.'

I was about to say yes, I'd like that, when Rhubarb suddenly started shouting at the Maidwell team again. He thought we ought to be able to score from here, if only Fort got a good shove on. 'Use your *legs*, boy,' he bellowed, hitching his scarf tighter, as if he was hurting his throat. I thought this meant he was finished with me – then he started a whole new conversation. 'So what about *your* girlfriends, Andrew? Since you mention Miss Yohanssen, I mean. You must have some – a nice-looking boy like you.' It was strange. I'd guessed that talking about Mr Wilson and President Kennedy was Rhubarb's way of punishing me for mentioning Yo-Yo. Actually *this* was his revenge. Talking about girls. I could tell because Rhubarb was lifting his lips like Beauty when she couldn't decide whether to smile or bite.

'I don't have any girlfriends, sir,' I said, pointing at the scrum; Maidwell still had the ball, but it was stuck because the back row had keeled over. 'Oh come,' said Rhubarb. 'I don't believe you' – and I hung my head. Why did grown-ups think girlfriends were their business? It was ridiculous. Anyway, Rhubarb would laugh whatever I told him, especially if I said I didn't know any girls. There were Birkbeck's cousins, but after the jellyfish in their nighties they hadn't talked to me again. And that only left the girls Kit knew, who were all his age so didn't count. 'Cat got your tongue?' said Rhubarb. I looked sideways at him again, expecting to see more of his snarly smile, but amazingly it had disappeared. 'I'll go into school now, sir, if you don't mind,' I said. When he muttered 'Quite right', I stepped back immediately, before he changed his mind.

I didn't want to stop thinking about girls altogether, just not while standing next to Rhubarb. He might ask me whether I knew the facts of life, if I hung around any longer – and that really would be embarrassing. Beak had given me the Special two years ago, when I was ten. He'd taken me into his study, and after I'd perched on his yellow sofa he picked a book off his shelves and squeezed in beside me. 'Do you know what this is?' he asked, opening the book at a black page which had a white tadpole struggling across the middle. 'Yes, Beak,' I told him, because I didn't want to say anything he'd laugh about afterwards with grandpa. 'Well, that's good,' he sighed. 'It's the great thing about growing up in the country. You learn this sort of thing without even trying.'

If Beak had still been headmaster, he would have given me the Extra Special as well. But now Mr Porch did that, and I'd had mine a few weeks ago. He hadn't said much about men and women. He was more bothered about school, and warned me that if and when I went to Radley . . . I interrupted, and told him I knew what he was going to say. 'Oh?' he put his oily head on one side like a duck. 'About them hanging new boys on pegs,' I went on. Mr Porch frowned, and wanted to know who'd told me that, because they'd have to be punished. I said I couldn't remember, and he tut-tutted and started again. 'No,' he said. 'I wanted to warn you about older boys who might take an interest in you.' I nodded, like I'd nodded when Beak had shown me the picture of the tadpole, without having a clue what he was talking about. Mr Porch watched, and when my head was still again he said, 'Do you know what I mean?' using his slow and husky voice. I swallowed and said, 'No, sir.' As he explained, I thought it sounded a bit like me and Rhubarb – an elder person telling a younger one everything they knew. I couldn't see what the problem was. I'd have to ask someone.

I'd come through the rose garden without noticing, and was crossing the yard outside the changing rooms. Birkbeck: I could ask him. Or Miller II, who was right here in front of me, leaning against the wall and standing on one leg because he was shaking a stone from his gumboot. 'Where are you off to?' Miller II dropped his boot with a wobbly thump, and slid his foot inside. 'Going to look at my traps,' he said. 'Can I come with you?' I wondered, thinking I didn't have to decide whether to ask him my question until we were in the Wilderness. But he caught me off guard. 'I'd rather not,' he said bluntly, and pushed past. It made me feel hollow for a moment, but I kept going towards the changing room because I didn't want him to know I minded. 'It doesn't matter,' I was telling myself, then I looked up and saw one of the windows by the door had been left open. I was going to hit it. I understood that quite clearly. I was going to wallop it with my forehead, and because it was a metal window, propped open with its stiff arm-thing, it was bound to hurt. Here it was, coming closer, coming closer, magnifying fast now because everything else in my head was dodging aside – Rhubarb's nervous teeth, Fort jumping, mum at her dressing table, the jellyfish, boys hanging on pegs, the tadpole, Miller II. The only thing left was the window, which I could tell had been repainted several times because there was a chip on the corner – how strange – it must have been green to start with – green was the colour furthest down.

I woke up next morning in the sick room opposite the Gibbon's bedroom, with a bandage like Captain Pugwash. 'You knocked yourself out,' she said, when she eventually poked her head round the door. 'We had to ring your mum. She's worried you'll have a scar.' 'Will I?' I whispered, hoping the answer would be yes. Then people would ask me about it, and I'd make up something more exciting than hitting the window. The idea made my head ache. 'It's too early to know,' the Gibbon said. 'But I have got *some* news for you.' 'What?' I said, thinking it was typical of her to make me ask. 'You've passed Common Entrance,' she said. 'The Headmaster's had a letter.' My headache suddenly got much worse. Was this a joke? And what about Bacon and Birkbeck – had they heard? 'Your friends have passed too,' said the Gibbon, reading my mind. 'Not that you'll be seeing them, of course, going to Radley.' 'There's nothing wrong with Radley,' I said, thinking the Gibbon wouldn't blame me for being rude if I was ill. 'Did I say there was?' she asked, turning on her accent full blast and checking her upside-down watch. 'No, miss,' I said, shutting my eyes and wishing she'd leave. When she did, the rubber soles of her shoes made a twisty squeak on the lino, as if she was stubbing out invisible cigarettes.

The Gibbon didn't want anyone in her sick room when term ended. So on the second-last day of term she took off my bandage, stuck a plaster over my cut, and sent me back downstairs. That evening we had a sing-song round the piano in the hall, with Rhubarb playing. This was a treat, but because I still felt shaky, I sat on the stairs to listen, under the picture of *Christ's Entry into Jerusalem*. I was thinking about goodbyes. If I didn't tell someone how much I hated Maidwell, wouldn't my feelings stay the same for ever, trapped inside me? Then again, maybe goodbyes were always like this, piled up like parcels that never got posted. More and more of them as time went by. That would explain why old people were sad. Why even mum and dad were sad sometimes. They were stuffed with heaps of old goodbyes.

My head started to ache again, and it was time for bed. But as I got to my feet, and climbed to the bend where I could look down at everyone round the piano, Rhubarb started playing a song I hadn't heard before. 'This is one of my favourites,' he said to no one in particular, and smoothed open the pages of his music book. 'It's a folk song, called "The Ashground".' A folk song, which Vane II said was the sort I liked. I leaned my elbows on the heavy banister and got ready to concentrate. But I didn't have to try. The second Rhubarb started, my head split clean open. He was singing. Up to now, I'd only heard his voice surrounded by others in choir practice. Now here it was alone, sounding softer than I'd expected. The words hung in the air as if they were fireflies in a wood, buzzing and gleaming, then scooting into a deep green silence when others took their place.

> Down yonder green valley where streamlets meander,
> When twilight is fading, I pensively roam,
> Or at the bright noontide in solitude wander
> Amid the dark shades of the lonely ash grove.
> 'Twas then while the blackbird was joyfully singing,
> I first met my dear one, the joy of my heart;
> Around us for gladness the bluebells were ringing,
> Ah! Then little thought I how soon we would part.

Rhubarb kept his fingers on the keys for a moment, and I saw the black stone of his signet ring flash in the overhead light. Nobody moved. There were Birkbeck and Bacon, leaning their shoulders together, and Eyot biting his nails, and Kit half-hidden behind his friend Otter, and Miller II standing alone by the door, and Lety who was frowning because he wished he could play as well as this. I'd see them in the morning, then I'd never see them again. I'd never see Rhubarb again. His fingers rose heavily off the keys, as if they were made of marble, and he started the second verse:

> Still glows the bright sunshine o'er valley and mountain,
> Still warbles the blackbird his note from the tree,
> Still trembles the moonbeam on streamlet and fountain;
> But what are the beauties of nature to me?
> With sorrow, deep sorrow my bosom is laden,
> All day I go mourning in search of my love.
> Ye echoes, O tell me, where is the sweet maiden?
> She sleeps 'neath the green turf down by the ash grove.

This time, when Rhubarb reached the end of the verse, he took his hands off the keys immediately, and rested them on his knees. He wasn't going to play any more: it was time we all went to our dorms. Had he noticed me looking down? I wanted that more than anything. But no, he was too busy closing the piano lid, telling boys to mind their fingers, and not to get overexcited because otherwise they'd never sleep. I turned away past the long-haired prince and the grumpy men in *And When Did You Last See Your Father*, opened the door of my dormitory, and sat in the window-bay until the others arrived. It was dark here when I pulled the curtains shut, and I could hear the moorhens on the lake. The moorhens, and the lake water slopping through the reeds, and the reeds shaking until they started to hiss, and the breeze gliding across my window before it vanished into the Wilderness.

CHAPTER SEVENTEEN

Woooooooogh!

Dad always kept the cellar door locked. He said it was to stop us falling down the stairs, but we managed the ones in the house, so what was the problem? 'He doesn't want us messing around with his wine,' said Kit, and even though this made us sound like thieves I wasn't about to complain. The cellar was spooky. When I opened the coal-flap outside the kitchen window, it looked like the bed of a dried-up river, and that made me think something dangerous must have happened right beneath us, without anyone knowing. There were heaps of soggy cardboard. A sand-pile with a broken shovel stuck in the side. Long white stalks in the hyacinth bowl, all stretched out sideways.

Today we were late and in a hurry. When dad said he wanted me to fill the coal scuttle, because he still had the Aga to do, I got on with it straight away. Besides, I wasn't thinking about ghosts. I was thinking about the new house. After years of searching, mum and dad had found what they wanted, and apparently it couldn't be better. Thirty miles north, mum said, in 'real country' near the Essex–Suffolk border. An old rectory. When she first told me, I said that sounded great, which she didn't think was good enough. 'It is,' she said, with a bubble in her voice like a girl. 'It really *is* great. The village where great-grandpa Andrew used to live. Stisted. Dad went there when he was a little boy, so now we'll be going home.' I couldn't understand why she said this, since Little Brewers was my home, and Beaconsfield had been hers, but I kept my mouth shut. Everyone knew how much she hated the Heath these days, what with the busy road and the new houses.

As I dug into the coal, I made myself concentrate on mum. She was directly above me in the kitchen, telling Kit to get a move on but keeping him back by chatting. 'You're going to love Stisted,' she said, her voice suffocating in the floorboards. 'Yeah,' said Kit; he was wearing shoes with leather soles, and his footsteps cracked like gunshots. 'Stisted,' he repeated slowly, as if hearing the word for the first time. 'How do you spell it?' 'With an "I",' mum said. 'So why's it pronounced like "sty"?' 'I don't know,' mum said. 'Like *pig* sty,' Kit went on – and now it was mum's turn to stamp. I smiled to myself. Kit wasn't so keen to move, because he had friends in Hatfield Heath and didn't mind about the road. That was why mum couldn't tell him to stop being grumpy – she didn't want to upset him. I'd promised to keep him cheerful too, which was fine except it meant pretending I wasn't sad myself, staring round the cellar and thinking there were still places I'd never explored properly.

I banged the coal scuttle against the wall, to give Kit and mum a jump. They stopped talking – then mum called 'We can heeear yoooou', which ended with Kit jumping up and down so hard, the floorboards gave a definite crack. 'Watch out!' I shouted, 'You're going to bust through'. Kit went 'Woooooogh!', which was the noise we made when we were pretending to be scary. I lifted my face and made the same noise back – 'Wooooooaagh!' – then set off to find the stairs. As I reached the bottom step, I turned round. A finger of light had poked into the far corner of the cellar, where the roots of the house disappeared into the earth. Maybe it didn't matter if the whole thing collapsed. It wasn't ours any more.

Mum said more about Stisted on the way over, facing forward in the Daimler but laying her arm across the top of dad's seat so she could twiddle his hair. Normally she never did this in front of us. 'Just one thing, though,' she said. 'You're going to have to use your imaginations. The whole place is a mess, because dad's buying it straight off the Church Commissioners.' 'The who?' Kit and I said together. Mum rattled on. 'The people who sell things for the church,' she said. 'The house is too big for them now, and they're building a new one for the vicar which is right in the village, so much better for him and everyone. But he's still in this house, our house, at the moment. We'll be meeting him when we get there.' 'Why do we have to use our imaginations?' Kit wanted to know. 'Because the house needs a lot doing to it,' mum said. 'You'll see.

It'll be fun.' She pulled down the sun-shield in front of her, and glanced at Kit in the little mirror. 'How much further is it?' he said, as though he hadn't been listening. 'Only a few more minutes,' said mum, then banged the sunshield shut again and muttered, '*Honestly.*' 'I know,' said dad, but louder. 'Honestly.'

At last we could see the village from the main road – or guess it, through the trees on the other side of the valley. 'Not many houses,' said Kit, but mum didn't want to talk now, and neither did I. I was trying to see the Hall. That must be it. A pale yellowy-grey block, left of the church. Normally we called that colour 'lavatory brick', but not today – and anyway, the church was pretty. It had flints, and a wooden spire, and a weathervane which turned right on cue, flashing a gold message. Then I looked back at the Hall again, and dad told me about it. Andrew and Jessie had liked it best of all their houses. She'd stayed after great-grandpa died, and only moved when the army took over during the war. Now it was an old people's home, and the council ran it. Dad said the house was in good shape, but the grounds were completely overgrown. I said maybe I could explore them after we'd moved, like he'd done when he was my age? There was a harumph behind the wheel, and dad's seat shook. When he was a boy he'd come here at Christmas, and everything had been frightening: wobbling up a stepladder to light the candles on the tree, sleeping miles away from everyone else down a black corridor, trooping off to church on Christmas morning past the rhododendrons and the water garden, with great-granny Jessie leading the way in her crackly dress.

The road sank into the valley and bumped over a humpbacked bridge. 'The Blackwater,' mum said, which made it sound like the river in hell; actually it was a skinny thing, and the reed-beds either side were knocked flat. Then came a cheat cricket pitch, where the wicket was bitumen, not grass. Then a mill – 'Like at Little Brewers!' Kit said, though it wasn't like Little Brewers at all, there was no rumbling, and the front was peeling. The trees were bedraggled, too, now we were climbing again, and when we passed the entrance to the Hall I saw its spindly front gate had sunk into a bank of nettles. The house itself was hidden by bare branches. 'All looks a bit miz,' dad said, in the steady voice he used if he thought we were worried about something. I stared at the back of his head, where mum had twiddled a tuft of hair into a curl.

As we followed the edge of the grounds, shadows darkened over the windscreen until we came to a lodge. After that the lane divided – the village off to the right where I could see a school, a pub sign in a chestnut tree, and a brown pebble-dashed house with 'something Institution' written across the front. We turned the other way, into open country. One field, two, then another straggly tree-hedge – thinner than the one round the Hall, with a low iron fence rusting in the undergrowth. 'Here we are!' said mum, and Kit and I sat up straight. The house looked a complete tip. It was meant to be white, but the front was dangled-over with green beard-shapes. Drainpipes snaked everywhere, chocolate-coloured, and one at the side stuck out like a dead arm. The roof was mostly hidden behind a parapet, but so many slates were missing at one end I could see right into the attic. Dad cleared his throat. 'Like mum told you,' he said, 'it needs a lot of work.' 'That'll be fun,' mum said again, touching his arm as we slowed into the drive-way. 'Basically, it's a very pretty house. You can see that, can't you?' Kit looked at me and rolled his eyes.

We bumped through a pothole and stopped by the front door, which was propped open by a stone with a curly fossil. I thought mum and dad might want to hang round the car for a moment, with dad tugging up his trousers and clearing his throat one more time. But they plunged straight inside, mum clutching her handbag and lifting her feet as if she might be about to step in something nasty. 'Come on, boys,' she said, without looking round to see if we were following, or wanting to know what we thought about the smell of damp and cat pee. We did as we were told, then veered off left towards a man's voice calling, 'I'm in here.' It was a drawing room, sort of. Red rugs on the floor. A table covered with papers. Big French windows – beautiful wide windows – and a grass field outside with a bomb-crater dip in the middle. Then further round to the left, a disintegrating brown sofa with a tabby cat yawning on a cushion. And a screen hiding the far end of the

room. The voice was behind the screen, and when I followed mum
and dad to the edge, there he was. A man on a low bed, holding one
hand towards us and stretching the other towards a horrible fusty-
busty fire, with primrose flames licking its windows. 'Are you . . .?'
mum was saying, still hugging her bag. 'Yes,' said the man, letting
his right hand drop, and plucking at his dog-collar. 'I'm the rector,
or whatever you want to call me.' He made no effort to get up, so
we went on standing in our huddle, mum and dad facing forward,
me and Kit waiting for them to decide what happened next. Was
this like the bear outside their bedroom window, which was frightening but turned out to be a joke? No. This was real. This was
where we were going to live.

Wait a minute. If mum and dad liked it so much, why was I
being stuffy? All this broken stuff could be fixed, all this cat-stink
blown away. Kit and I could help. We'd rip out the fusty-busty for
a start. Then we'd tear up the filthy carpets and have a bonfire –
dad loved bonfires. I dug Kit in the ribs, and we peeled off to
explore the rest of the house, leaving mum and dad nattering to
the vicar. First the kitchen with its gas stove like a skeleton and a
window blocked by a wall of cardboard boxes. Then a little sitting
room across the hall, with a bed jammed against the fireplace. A
too-big, too-heavy fireplace, which had lumpy coats of arms either
side, like the heads of gigantic bolts. Did the vicar sleep here at
night? It smelled like it, and the sheets were grey. We nipped round
to the door under the stairs, which roared out cellar-breath when I
tugged it open; much darker and wetter than Little Brewers. Then
upstairs, hopping over a broken step, and into the room where I'd
probably sleep. The bare boards had apples laid on them in neat
rows – fine, except they were mouldy, and the air smelled dark
brown, like their skins. And there was a lawnmower by the basin,
sitting in an oil puddle. Why on earth had the poor old vicar
lugged it up here?

We poked our noses into the other bedrooms, then traipsed out
through the back door. There was no garden. At least, there was a
path round the side of the house, with cat hair wriggled into the
clover heads, but it was only a narrow track. Where the grass

should have been, there was a forest. It was made entirely of thistles, with stalks as thick as my wrist and the heads gone to seed: a
muddle of dead yellow and fluff, stretching right down to that fall-
en-over greenhouse. No thistles in the wood to my right, though –
the trees were too close together. But wait a minute. Was it a wood,
or another bit of the garden? Most of the trees were rubbish – elder
and sycamore shoots. They'd need clearing out as well; it would
take all next holidays, probably. Kit and I looked at one another
and rubbed our hands. Then we went back to find mum and dad,
who were still behind the screen. 'Well?' said mum. 'We love it,' I
told her, and as she raised her eyebrows to show she didn't believe
me, I told her again. 'Really we do. We love it.' That's when the vicar
stopped talking at last. I'd forgotten to think he might love it too,
and want to stay put.

The day the removal men came, Kit and I went to stay with
granny; we only had a week of holidays left, but mum said it
couldn't be helped. Something to do with the lorries being busy. I
didn't mind: I was getting nervous about school, and this would
take my mind off it. Besides, I wouldn't have to see strangers busy-
bodying round our bedrooms, or carting stuff through the open
air. Just thinking about my bed standing under the sky made me
feel cold. 'It's odd,' I said to Kit, the last night before mum came
to collect us again. We were sitting at our bedroom window in
Beaconsfield, after granny had turned out the lights; she did that
an hour earlier than mum, and we weren't sleepy. 'What's odd?' he
said. 'I don't mind about leaving home,' I told him. 'What, never?'
he asked. 'I mean I don't mind leaving Little Brewers and moving
to Stisted.' Kit turned away and looked across the garden to lights
on the main road. He didn't feel the same, but he'd never say so; he
thought it would make him sound wet. After a while he muttered
'Me too', just as I'd predicted.

He stiffened and changed the subject. 'By the way, what's that?'
He pointed at the horizon, where the main road ran towards Ger-
rards Cross, and for a moment I thought he might be inventing
something, so we didn't have to talk about home or school any
more. But he really had seen something. A big yellow smudge out-

side that hotel – what was it called? The Bell. Probably some kind of tarpaulin flapping about – but it didn't make sense, there was hardly any wind tonight. We watched in silence for a minute, and when nothing changed I decided it was a false alarm and picked up where I'd left off. 'I like Little Brewers,' I said, 'but mum's right. The village has changed. Or maybe I'm thinking more about school.' I stopped, waiting for Kit to pay attention. 'Why do you just call it "school"?' he said eventually, in the dried-out voice which was meant to make me feel an idiot. 'It's got a name, you know.' 'I don't like saying "Radley",' I said, as though I was being perfectly sensible. 'Why not?' Kit said. 'Because it sounds lah-di-dah,' I said. Kit laughed. 'It *is* lah-di-dah, you fool. It's a lah-di-dah place.' Then he straightened, and sounded more thoughtful again. 'You want to go, don't you?' I stared at his face, still turned towards the horizon, then down at my hands. I hadn't talked much about changing school – not to Kit or anyone. It seemed strange, now he was asking me directly, but actually it was simple. I couldn't imagine Radley, so there wasn't much point thinking about it. Every time I close my eyes and said the name, all I saw was a long corridor, and boys hanging from hooks like pheasants in a butcher's window.

Kit tapped me on the wrist. 'Hey! Look!' he whispered, and pointed. The yellow thing by the hotel had grown. It wasn't tarpaulin, and it wasn't cars either. It was fire – and there was a fire engine with its lights flashing, the blue kind that made everything ripple. I could see the white windows of the hotel, the pillars round the front door, and the bell on the sign all trembling as if they'd been hit by an earthquake. The hotel was burning. 'What shall we do?' I said, flinging open the window. 'Should we tell granny?' 'Granny!' Kit slapped the leg of his pyjamas. 'Brilliant idea. Yes, go and tell her, so she can rush up there with her hose.' I kept my eyes on the horizon. Tiny men were rushing round their toy engine, like at Beaconscot. I could imagine the badges on their helmets, and their hoses stretched across the car park, and the ladders cranking upright, and the spray of water like a slow-motion sneeze. 'Do you think anyone's been hurt?' Kit asked. 'I'm sure not,' I told him quickly – then realised I hadn't thought. I'd been too busy watching the flames change colour, and telling myself how strange it was to see all this when mum and dad were spending their first night in the new house. There hadn't been time to imagine people trapped in their rooms, or shouting from windows. 'I suppose that's OK,' said Kit. 'If no one's been hurt.' I could tell from his quiet voice that he was thinking about Little Brewers. But I couldn't face it any more, so I turned to him briskly and said 'Yep – only the building', then pulled the window shut. We leaned our heads on the glass for a minute, in case the fire burst out in a new place. When I blinked, I could see the flames still leaping under my eyelids. After they died down, I told Kit I was going to sleep.

Next day, there was a story about the hotel in the local paper: granny showed us. The fire had started in the kitchen, a whole wing had burned to the ground, but no one had been hurt apart from one of the waiters, who hadn't woken up in time. In the picture, roofbeams were lying across his bed. This meant we had something amazing to tell mum when she came to collect us. She seemed perfectly happy to listen, probably because she didn't want to say much about Stisted in case granny decided she wanted to come with us. Eventually, when we were in the car, we started talking properly. The move had gone fine, mum said, nothing much had got broken, the builders and the painters had pretty much finished by the time they got there, the dogs liked it, and Flick had jumped out of the bedroom window because dad had shut her in like you were supposed to do with cats, to stop them running off. 'What about the garden?' I said. Mum laughed. 'Oh, that,' she said. 'A man came to cut down the thistles, but the wood's still waiting for you. It's yours.'

She'd said this before, but I thought there was bound to be someone like Mr Manning who would cut down the rubbish. When we finally dipped over the Blackwater again and climbed through the village, I could see she meant it. The whole background to the house was jungly: branches woven together, old man's beard like a burst pillow, white fungus on the top branches of the apple trees. It really would take weeks to sort out. The main thing was the house, though. I hadn't seen it since the day with the vicar, which was weeks ago now, and I expected things to look smarter. Nothing like this, though. An army must have swarmed over it, patching up the roof, painting the walls white, fixing the pipes, shining the windows. It still looked old – two hundred years old, apparently: there was a brick in the scullery with a date on it. But it felt new as well – like a dead man brought back to life. Or a dead woman. A fragile, lacy old lady like great-granny Jessie, who smiled without opening her mouth, and didn't say much. I'd never looked at a building before and thought I recognised it, the way I sometimes looked at people and knew they were my type. I felt it now, the moment mum turned through the gate. I couldn't think what to say, and when I looked at her I could see she wanted to cry. 'Blimey,' said Kit from the back seat, then again, very slowly: 'Blimey O'Reilly'.

It was just as good inside. The fusty-busty and the pee-stink had already gone, the walls were painted, there was carpet along the hall, and my room at the top of the stairs – the first bedroom I'd had to myself – still smelled of apples but it was delicious, like being in a loft. 'Is something missing?' mum said, standing in the doorway and watching me pace round touching my table, my lamp, my bird books on the window sill. I shook my head. No, nothing was missing. It was just that everything I'd known for years suddenly looked different – even the scratch in the shape of an old man's face on the headboard of my bed. I needed to make them all mine again. When she went along the corridor to see about Kit, I stood in front of the window and took a deep breath. This was my view now. I was above the front door, so I could watch people coming and going. Beyond that, I had a corner of the horses' field, with a big chestnut tree shading the grass. One of the branches looped down below the others, and Serenade had already decided to make it her scratching place. There was a tuft of chestnut hairs stuck to the end, shining and ruffling as the wind blew through them.

I wanted to get started straight away. To hack a path into the wood, make a bonfire, and see mum coming towards me with a cup of tea, telling me I'd done well. But there were too many other things to sort out first. Little things like the doorknobs, which kept coming off because the builders were idiots, dad said. And bigger things like what to do for the ponies. They had new stables outside the scullery – pale wood that came in a flat pack which dad thought was cheap, though it didn't matter because everything worked fine. What about exercising? How would we know where to go? It turned out mum had already been told about a couple of circles. 'Not towards Braintree,' she said, with that bubble in her voice again. 'Braintree's hideous. More towards Coggeshall – that's pretty. There's lots of country out that way, where you hardly see a car, just villages. Priors Green. Greenstead Green. Pattiswick. And I told you about the deer, didn't I? There are deer everywhere. Muntjac. They escaped from Colchester zoo during the war, and now they've taken over.' She might almost have been talking in her sleep, but I liked the sound of what she said – and the trees at home could wait.

On the first empty day, Kit and I went ahead of mum and started saddling-up. After I'd passed Common Entrance, mum had decided I was too big for Tommy, so she sold him and bought a roly-poly skewbald called Lollipop. She hadn't told me until it was all done, but that was OK. Tommy had always been a bit mad, and Lollipop was fat and cosy; it meant mum knew I didn't take riding as seriously as Kit, and that made me feel safe. So did the sight of Lollipop in her stable, standing four-square as a sofa while I slipped the bridle over her ears. Next door, Kit was rustling round Musket. 'I'm surprised,' he said suddenly, almost shouting so I could hear through the partition wall. 'About what?' I wanted to know. 'That you're not making more of a fuss about doing the wood and everything. It's the kind of thing you like.' I thought about this. Was he trying to be nice, or tell me I'd made a mistake because he wanted to go riding with mum alone and see everything before I did? 'I like riding,' I said carefully. Kit changed direction. 'What about school?' he said. 'You've got less than a week of hols left.' 'Yeah,' I told him sulkily, so he could hear he was being annoying. 'It'll be fine. It's my half-term soon – before yours, actually.' I caught my breath, and set about tightening Lollipop's girth. It was silly to argue; we were nervous, that was all.

We set off three abreast in the lane with mum in the middle, heading away from the village and towards Mr Hill's farm. Mr Hill had known dad when they were boys, and didn't mind if we rode over his land, though in fact it suited us to stay on the lane for a bit – that way, we could see how the place fitted together. The thatched cottages with their twisty brick chimneys. The hawthorn hedges. Enormous ploughed fields, much bigger than anywhere near the Heath, with clay-streaks running through them. The funny thing was, everywhere felt lumpy because of the woods, and the apple orchards, and the muddles of oak and ivy on the horizon, which were probably pond-holes – but really it was pretty flat in this direction, away from the Blackwater. It made me feel the usual laws of up-and-down weren't working properly, and Stisted was a secret place. Not scrunched-up like most secrets, but big as the sky, which spread wider with every minute, so by the time the village was out of sight I'd launched into space.

The lane curled past a lay-by where a pale brown stocking dangled in the hedge. 'Canoodling couples,' Kit said, putting on dad's voice. I thought he probably didn't know what canoodling meant, but laughed all the same. When we reached the next gateway, I stopped. I'd been expecting plough, which would have meant we had to go round the headland in single file, but the field was still stubble. We walked on, wondering who was going to break into a canter first. Lollipop obviously thought it should be her; the muscles in her neck were flicking, but I didn't want to start yet. The open field was too beautiful, what with the wood on the skyline like a Roman legion, and the sound of hooves rasping through the straw. Really, it might be all right, learning to be a different person. I rubbed my hand over my face and mum noticed. 'What are you thinking?' she said, poking me in the back with her stick. It was a cane, like a Swish, but yellower, and with big knuckles at the joints. 'Nothing,' I told her, bulging my eyes to show I didn't want to talk about it now.

She got the point. 'Oh boys!' she said brightly, 'I forgot to tell you . . .' Kit and I glanced at each other. This sounded like the start of one of mum's jokes: she was tucking in her chin and smiling downwards. 'The woman in the village shop's got a poster up, which the police gave her, saying a prisoner has escaped from one of the local gaols. They think he's hiding in the woods.' 'What, this wood?' said Kit, going red in the face. 'Well, no, not this wood necessarily,' said mum. She was talking in a kinder voice now, as if she realised she might have scared us when all she meant to do was tell a story. 'A wood hereabouts. He used to be in the army, and they think he knows how to make a tent and look after himself.' Kit was gazing dead ahead, his mouth open. The second I noticed, I realised I wasn't so different myself, with my eyes screwed up to see whether I could spot anything. A hand, perhaps, tweaking back a branch.

'Has he got a gun?' I asked, and for a couple of strides mum said nothing. The horses' hooves were suddenly louder through the stubble. It was the noise dad made when he stroked his hand over his chin, only pricklier. 'Of course he hasn't got a gun,' said mum. 'Why would he have a gun?' She'd meant the prisoner to come and go quickly, but here we were making a fuss. 'He might have stolen it,' I said stubbornly. 'That's right,' Kit murmured, then added half another word I couldn't hear, because mum cut him off. 'I'm sorry I even mentioned it,' she said. 'I thought you'd be interested, that's all.' 'We *are*,' I told her. 'I just want to know if we're going to see him.' I swallowed, then went on. 'You know what? I think we should be very quiet, and not talk inside the wood. Then if this man hears the horses he'll think we're muntjac or whatever deer you said, and we'll be able to spy on him. If he sees us we can gallop away.'

I swallowed again, while everything I'd said turned into pictures. Light falling through the top branches of the wood onto empty tracks and pathways. Silent green tree trunks. Heaps of dead bracken. And suddenly a clearing with a pot slung over a fire, and foxy eyes glaring above a beard. If it went well, we'd get a reward from the police. If it went badly, and the man really did have a gun, he'd take us hostage and I wouldn't have to go to school. When I looked up again, mum was chewing the inside of her cheek. 'We don't mind,' I told her, digging Lollipop in the ribs until she started to trot. My voice was bobbly, which was a pity because it made me sound frightened when I wasn't. It was just Lollipop, jiggling me up and down.

As I went ahead, the huge sky sank down until it was pressing round me like water. There were only a few yards to go before the trees started – oaks, spaced like pillars in a cathedral. When the time came, and I was inside the wood, I'd disappear in a twinkling. I twisted round in the saddle and smiled, to show Kit everything was fine, and he lifted one arm like Peter O'Toole charging on his camel in *Lawrence of Arabia*. 'Wooooooogh!' he shouted, and then again, 'Wooooooogh!' Mum didn't think it was funny. Her hat was pulled forward again, and her face was covered in shadow, but she was scowling. She looked smaller too – hardly bigger than Kit, with Serenade's reins as light as ribbons in her hand. I hoisted my arm to Kit, then steered Lollipop into a gap between a couple of the thickest trees. The change happened so fast, all I could see were shadows, slicing at me like bits of smoky glass.

CHAPTER EIGHTEEN

No Talking

There were four others: Colchester, who walked with his head jerking backwards and forwards like a speeded-up tortoise; Brooks, who was Canadian and needed to shave; Philips, who had spots; and Gimson, who wanted everyone to know he was going to be a GP because that's what his father did. We were the new boys, and we had to share a dorm for our first term. After that we'd get a cubicle each.

We were in the dorm now, and a prefect had turned the lights off. It was our first night, but the amazing thing was, nobody was crying – though it might have been drowned by the racket from outside. Someone called Williams was in the corridor, showing off about his new red pyjamas, which nobody believed he'd been given by his girlfriend. When the prefect came back and told him to cool it, a different noise started. A boy across the quad below my window, playing 'Itchycoo Park'. The first time it came to the chorus, I thought I might get snuffly: mum and I had heard the song when we were in the kitchen together, slicing up beans. But saying goodbye this time hadn't been like Maidwell. For one thing, mum and dad had chatted all the way as if we were going on holiday. Then she treated my housemaster Mr Way like a friend of the family – which he might well have been, with his tweed coat and grey trousers, and his striped army tie. After that, when she walked round the hall I'd be sharing with the other juniors, she was still perky – trying out a gas tap in the cooking-bit, drumming her nails on the ping-pong table. I thought she might be keeping her mind off things, or making everyone think she was the kind of mum who had a job. Eventually I decided she enjoyed the way boys looked at her. All the other mums weighed a ton, and wore suits made of thistles. She was smiling and nervous. Some people might even have thought she was my sister.

It was still difficult saying goodbye. I could tell mum and dad wanted to treat me as if I was more grown up, but none of us knew quite how to do that. In the end dad shuffled from foot to foot, then patted me on the shoulder, and when mum gave me a hug she made sure it didn't go on too long. We were outside the school's enormous red-brick tower, and I thought older boys might be watching, and tease me later – maybe even hang me on a hook. So I did what mum wanted, and squeezed her quickly, shook dad's hand, and left it at that. On my way back inside I saw Colchester and Philips chatting to their parents. Colchester's dad was easily as old as grandpa, and Philips's car was a hearse. That was a relief. If anyone was going to get teased, it was Philips.

Not badly teased, though – or not hung from a peg. Nobody had said anything about that, even as a joke. There wasn't any Swish, either. Mr Way said so, after mum and dad left, when I was sitting round his gas fire with the other new boys. He had a friendly pink face, and a soft voice which couldn't do r's and made me pay special attention – even though he fiddled with stuff on his desk all the time, which was distracting. The pencil pot, the sharpener, the bottle of Nippon ant killer, the letter rack, the page of notes, the paperclips: they all had a perfect place, only he couldn't remember where it was. In any event, I liked him – even the pictures on his walls were good: *A Sleep of Prisoners*; *The Boy with a Cart*. It turned out they were posters for plays he'd directed. And that reminded me. Uncle Rob had said Mr Way used to write poetry years ago, and won the big prize at Oxford. He probably didn't know I'd been told that, so when it came to my turn for a question, I asked him about punishments instead. He stroked his chin, and said beating was 'only a last wesort'. I thought he must be talking about boys who smoked, which dad had already warned me about.

Mr Way said the first thing to do was learn the geography. Each of us had a nanny to help, and mine was Macfarlane, who was a term older than me, had brown crinkly hair, and was famous for being a fast runner. He was ratty when I went to find him, but after I'd told him I was a fast runner too, he cheered up. He said he didn't mind being a nanny; he just didn't want to be slow – then shot off to start the tour immediately. This was fine by me. I'd already noticed that even though I'd only been at Radley for a few hours, time was moving faster. At Maidwell everything had been sluggish and bogged down. Here it was quick as a river coming up to a waterfall. I thought it must be because I was nearly a teenager now. Dad had often said things would speed up as I got older.

Macfarlane showed me my House, first, except it turned out Houses were called Socials, which I thought mum would say sounded non-U. The main bit was Croome's Tower, which had a floor made of mosaic, only nobody had bothered to make a picture in the middle so it was just dirty white. Then came the dorms, which were rows of green cublicles with sliding doors. Then the studies, which we couldn't see inside now because older boys didn't like stigs interrupting. Then the baths, which had a special rule. Macfarlane told me that after I'd been at the school for one term, I'd be allowed one minute in the water, then two minutes after two terms, and so on. 'What about new boys?' I asked him. 'Before they've done a whole term, I mean?' 'First term counts as one term,' said Macfarlane, who didn't speak as quickly as he moved, which explained why people shouted 'Ugggh! Klaus!' at him in the corridors, and screwed up their faces as if they were struggling to understand something. Macfarlane said, 'Don't worry about them. My first name's Nicholas, you see. That's why they call me Klaus.' I wanted to say something pally, but he wouldn't stand still for long enough.

After the baths, we cut across the quad to Social Library – a poky little box with a record player and a billiards table and a couple of rows of paperbacks. As Macfarlane snatched the door open, then threw it shut again, almost chopping my head off, he said, 'It's arranged so Ohm can see what we're doing from his window.' I frowned at him. 'Ohm,' he said again. 'It means Mr Way – because of how he says "armoury".' 'What?' I said blankly. 'Armoury,' said Macfarlane again. 'It's the CCF. That's the Corps. Oh, never mind. The thing is, all the masters have nicknames – you'll get a test in a fortnight, to show you know them – and Ohm stands in his study window a lot, looking at the Library to make sure nothing's going on.' 'Don't you like him, then?' I said. 'We all like Ohm,' Macfarlane said, hurrying back to the quad. 'Wait till he takes you for English, though. He spends half an hour explaining why it says "the" not "a" in someone's poem.'

I'd only be in Mr Way's form if I did English for A-level, which wasn't for another two and a bit years, and I couldn't think that far ahead. Besides, I needed to know more about this test. 'There's a thing called Greybook,' said Macfarlane, 'Though it isn't grey – it's a different colour every term. It's like a calendar of what's happening in the school, and in the front it gives the names of all the masters. You have to learn their initials and their nicknames – I'll write them down for you. Creeping Jesus, that's the Sub-Warden.' 'The what?' 'It means deputy head. The head's called the Warden – he doesn't have a nickname though. The others all do. Goldie. Hoddy. Tooly. Drooper. Smoothy. Wheezer. The Prole. Yoiks. Nipple. Full Strength. Paddy . . .' For the first time since mum and dad had left, panic blew through me: there were hundreds of names. Hundreds of faces. How could I possibly learn them in a fortnight? And that wasn't counting the nicknames for *things*. Macfarlane charged off again through a labyrinth of corridors and side-ways. Little School. Covered Passage. The Mansion. Bigside. The Labs. Clock Tower. The Rears. 'What's the Rears?' I asked, which was stupid because I could easily guess: we'd used the same word at Maidwell. But I had to be sure. 'Have a look,' said Macfarlane, nodding towards the end of a curling brick wall. I peered round, and just as I thought, there was about a mile of white porcelain. On the wall above, in huge capital letters, someone had written WILKINS LIES IN YOUR HAND. Was it the school nickname for willy? Macfarlane said no, Wilkins was the boy-Master of the school beagle pack, and nobody liked him. I nodded, and looked round the wall a second time, because I didn't want to tell Macfarlane the beagles had been started at Radley by Uncle Rob, using grandpa's money. This time I noticed some of the proper loos, especially the ones up the furthest end, had cigarette smoke dribbling over the top of the doors.

Then there was only one more thing to see. Chapel, which was the far end of Covered Passage. It would have been a great place to run, being so long and straight, but Macfarlane said there was always a master lurking somewhere, and it was best to take things steady. He was acting more like a friend now, because he knew the tour was nearly over, and told me that after I'd collected my gown from the school shop tomorrow I'd feel I was flying. I frowned. My gown? 'We all wear gowns,' Macfarlane said. 'Masters wear long ones, boys wear short ones, and scholars have bits of fur on the arms, made of mole or something. You're not a scholar are you?' 'God no,' I said, using the Maidwell voice for something really ridiculous, and Macfarlane grinned. 'I'm not either,' he said, and then, to prove he didn't care, started to run after all. Even if I'd been trying, I wouldn't have been able to beat him to the chapel door.

I expected the chapel to be a small dark place, but it turned out to be huge. 'Freemasons use it when we're not here,' said Macfarlane, with a catch in his voice. I nodded as if I understood what he was talking about, and clicked after him across the black and white tiles. There was a peculiar sweet smell. Candles, probably, mixed with boy-fug, left over from last term. 'That's incense,' whispered Macfarlane. 'Creeping Jesus likes his smells. You know about the Oxford Movement don't you, and how Radley was founded and everything?' I shook my head. 'You'll be finding out soon enough,' he went on. 'You'll probably get a question about it in your test.' I felt another spurt of panic. Radley wasn't like a school at all. It was a kind of village, with its own language, and its own special way of living. Was that a good idea? There wasn't time to decide: when we got close to the gold sculpture-thing behind the altar, which Macfarlane said was called the reredos, and were peering at its glittery carvings of Jesus preaching, a bell rang and we had to rush for supper. Like the other stigs, I got lumbered with stacking plates at the end of the table, which meant I couldn't do any more thinking then either.

I started again after lights out, when the cubicles were quiet, except for the prefect clonking up and down, saying 'No talking' even though nobody was. Brooks had already fallen asleep; his breath was whistling through his nose like an old man's. Philips hadn't, though; he was winding his hand round the metal bars of his bedhead as if he was learning the dance of the seven veils. Was his dad's car really a hearse? Why? Because his dad was an undertaker? I closed my eyes, and saw the Daimler leaving again, with the exhaust-cloud smudging mum's head through the back window. What would happen if I couldn't learn everything in a fortnight? Macfarlane said that after I'd done the real names and the nicknames and the initials, I'd have to get the school rules off by heart as well. Don't walk on the grass unless you're a prefect. Keep the middle button of your jacket done up. Never let your hair touch the tops of your ears. Most of them weren't even written down in the Greybook, which meant I'd have to know them by instinct. I flipped onto my stomach and closed my eyes. Mum and dad would be home by now, but I couldn't walk round Stisted in my head, like I'd done with Little Brewers. I didn't know it well enough yet. If I turned from the hall into the kitchen, there was no Wally clock on the shelf, no Aga, no dogs' bowls. There was just the smell of new paint and sawdust and the builder's roll-ups. When I drifted outside into the garden it was worse: mud where the thistles used to be, like a mashed-up football pitch, and the tangly wood off to the right. It would all be OK in a while. For now, though, home wasn't quite like home, and school wasn't quite like school either.

The bell on top of the Mansion clanked at seven next morning, and an hour and a half later I started my first lesson – in the Slums. This was a black hole next to the Marionette Theatre, but nobody seemed surprised: we were the Lower Remove, after all, the bottom class in the school. I thought that meant our form teacher would be useless. In fact everyone said Mr Morgan was a good bloke, even if he did have a head like a jamjar, and never smiled with the whole of his mouth. My other teachers were decent too, especially Mr Hudson, who took History. He told us we'd be doing the poetry of the First World War, as well as the battles, and I wanted to know: would we have to learn it by heart, like at Maidwell? The poems turned out to be so sad, and so exciting, and the pictures of bombs and dead men and rats and flares were so amazing, it was hardly like work at all. Best of all, it reminded me of the War Memorial at Hatfield Heath, and the portrait of grandpa in his uniform, and that made it feel like part of something I already knew. When I told Huddy, he pushed his specs up his nose, and his eyes grew twice their normal size. 'Maybe other poems will make you feel the same way?' I said maybe they would, but it didn't seem likely.

Apart from the war poets, work was almost impossible. Mr Storey smiled a lot, but I was no good at French. Mr Catchpole the Maths teacher didn't lose his temper with me like he did with other boys, but there was something I didn't get the first time he told us about the binary method, and I never caught up again. Mr Hodson was supposed to teach Chemistry, but the main things that interested him were showing us how to make explosions, and how to snap test tubes by shoving the spout of a tap down the top, then tweaking the bottom. When I told mum about this, she laughed and said 'Oh, *stinks*', which showed what she thought of Chemistry. And Physics, as it turned out – but Dr Cauldwell didn't think there was any point me doing Physics. Or Biology. He said I hadn't got the right kind of brain.

Divinity was taken by the chaplain, Jibber Jenkins. Dad said he looked like a dentist, when he saw him at Matins on my first exeat weekend, but that was only because everything about Jibber was so tidy: his hair, his face, his trousers, his shoes. I liked him, partly because he didn't feel like a real teacher – he was a vicar – and partly because I enjoyed chapel. Once a day the whole school, all six hundred and something of us, squeezed in and thought about more or less the same thing. God, obviously, but God who didn't have much to do with the Bible, and a lot to do with things we wanted but couldn't have. Like winning matches, or doing well in tests. Even though no one talked about it, I knew I wasn't the only one who felt a bit soppy when the services ended, and we saw the sunset fading through the tall windows, and waited for Rats Langridge to pound his knuckles along the keyboard of the organ.

That was why I decided to talk to Jibber, and not Mr Way, when

I needed some help. It wasn't exactly a crisis. I just felt, by the end of my first term, that my plans to do better at work were getting nowhere. Especially with Mr Fisher, who took us for Latin and was the only Radley master who reminded me of the Maidwell ones: a buzzard-faced, pipe-smoking old man with a 'you idiot' voice which scared me so much it made my brain freeze. Jibber's room was at the top of the Mansion. When I pushed open the green baize door which led to his corridor, and heard it thud softly shut behind me, I knew I'd made a mistake. It wasn't that Jibber refused to take me seriously. He said my teachers were quite happy with me, and I was doing well at athletics too. I just felt I'd given him a problem he couldn't solve. 'Do you know what you want to do in later life?' Jibber said, when I was ready to go back through the green door and downstairs into my own world again. I thought of telling him about the Forestry Commission, or the Royal Society for the Protection of Birds, but instead I blurted out I was thinking about the church. It seemed the best way to thank him for letting me waste his time.

Actually Jibber had given me some good advice, even though it took me a few days to realise. He'd told me to make the most of what I already knew, rather than worry about new things. So that's what I did. I remembered I was supposed to be good at games, and started to try harder at rugby, and got into a junior team. And when it turned out I was hopeless at hockey, because I didn't want the ball to smack me in the face, and even worse at cricket, I took up fencing. Gimson said fencing was queer, even though Mr Way taught it. I knew what he meant. All that business with my left hand, and having to hold it up behind me like a broken flower – it was as bad as ballet. But never mind: not many boys did fencing, so I got into the school team, which meant driving to nearby schools for matches now and again, on Saturday afternoons. This was fine when it was a boys' school. If it was girls, they wore suits of armour under their white jackets, and if ever I managed to hit one of them with the tip of my blade, the metal made a weird hushed-up clang. It was either embarrassing or disgusting, I couldn't decide.

Jibber made me remember something else as well. Even though

school was school, there were still country things I could do in my free time. College Pond for one thing, where nobody went much apart from smokers, and which might be good for birds. And there were the games pitches, which Macfarlane said were the biggest patch of mown grass in the country – and even though he was probably fibbing, they were certainly huge. Better still, they had Bagley Wood at the far end, and this was bigger and darker than any wood I'd been into before. I decided to start a new scrapbook for feathers, and keep a bird diary, and get back into the mood of walking round the lake at Maidwell. It was difficult, because my brain seemed to have changed shape, and slipped further away from my eyes and ears. Even so, after I'd walked for twenty minutes over the grass carpet, past the jumbling boys and the masters shouting on the touchlines, then disappeared into the trees to make a list of woodpeckers and blue-tits and thrushes and one day even a redstart, I still felt I wasn't at school any more. At Maidwell, people had always hated boys being alone – they thought we were up to no good. But here they didn't mind. When I told Dr Cauldwell I was interested in birds, for instance, he nodded his mad professor head and made a plan to show me about trapping. We ended up slinging an old tennis net between some apple trees by his science labs, while he ran about waving his arms in the air, and soon the net had two or three bird-leafs struggling in the holes. One of them was a wren, and Dr Cauldwell let me hold it while he put a tiny ring round its leg. The wren's little body felt so shaky in my fist I thought it might be about to die.

I was especially pleased about the netting, because it showed Dr Cauldwell had forgiven me for something embarrassing that happened soon after I got to Radley. It was when Macfarlane was still my nanny. He'd warned me stigs had to do fagging; apparently I was fag to Peterson, who was head of the Social. Macfarlane said there wasn't anything to worry about – the old days, when you were like a servant, and got beaten all the time, were long gone. How could I be sure? Peterson looked about as grown up as dad, except his hair was slicked back and yellow, not slicked back and going grey, and he purred around the place with his nose in the air like Lord Snooty. The thing he liked best was racquets – and that was snooty too, because only about six people in the world knew how to play. Anyway, it turned out Peterson was OK. Mainly he wanted me to clean his shoes in the morning, and his teacup in the evening: otherwise he left me alone. Apart from the day he gave me a few shillings and told me to go to the shop in the village and buy him a magazine. He wrote down the name, and explained I had to pass it to the man behind the counter. It worked fine, until I was walking back up the hill to school and looked at what I'd bought. The magazine was full of pictures of naked women. I'd heard about mags like this, but I hadn't seen one. Were all women that shape? And were breasts always orange when they were young? I came to a dead stop, so I could look at them more closely. That's when a half-timbered Morris Estate drifted alongside, and Dr Cauldwell offered me a lift. As I slid into the passenger seat I could tell he knew what kind of mag I was holding, even though I'd rolled it into a sausage by now, and was gripping it with both hands. How could I explain it was for Peterson, and nothing to do with me? Dr Cauldwell would never have believed it – and even if he had, he'd have reckoned I was sneaking.

Later, I realised Dr Cauldwell didn't mention the mag because he didn't mind. That would have been impossible at Maidwell, because everyone there had pretended girls didn't exist. But I'd only been at Radley five minutes before I twigged that Maidwell wasn't normal, and nor was Little Brewers come to that. I still didn't know any girls, but most boys had met dozens of them in the holidays, and been to dances, and they'd obviously talked about them all the time at their first schools – as well as about pricks and cocks and tools and todgers and tonkas and wanking and wet dreams and tits and pussies and fannies and a whole load of other things that suddenly poured into my head, along with masters' nicknames, and the rules about where I could and couldn't walk on the gravel near Clock Tower. For the first week or so I kept quiet, learning these new words. Then I joined in, and that was that.

Except there was a catch. Although everyone pretended to have a girlfriend, and spent ages hanging round the letter rack waiting to hear from them, no one really knew what they were talking about. When Brown was on dorm duty one evening and overheard some chat about snogging, he laughed and said snogging was all right so far as it went, but compared to fucking it was a waste of time. I hadn't heard many people say fuck since I'd asked mum about it years before, and she'd dropped her spoon in the white sauce, but I thought the other boys wouldn't bat an eyelid. Actually, they were so impressed, it took about two days for us to start talking about girls again – especially because Brown had very tight curly hair, which was already falling out. How on earth had *he* managed to persuade anyone to go all the way? There was no way of knowing, but it proved something. The rest of us were nowhere. Or rather, the rest of us were somewhere else – though not everyone wanted to admit it. Partly because there was no choice, a lot of us were thinking about boys when we were talking about girls.

About halfway through my first term, I twigged this must be what Mr Porch had meant when he'd given me the Extra Special. But by then it was too late. Mr Porch had made other boys sound disgusting, but most of them weren't – especially not the older ones, who invited stigs into their studies. Burrows, who was creepier than the others because he wore a Nazi Iron Cross under his shirt, thought the people who'd designed the school in the first place must have expected boys to be queer. They'd built the chapel so we could gaze at each other across the aisle, rather than having to face the altar. They'd been mingy with baths, so we had to hang around for ages wearing nothing but our towels. They'd forgotten to build our cubicle walls up to the ceiling, which meant we could slither across the top after lights out.

Nobody talked much about this sort of thing – we knew it was asking for trouble. So we gossiped about making bombs, instead. This started by accident, when Johns and Plummer and Mott discovered some Chemistry junk in a loft. They'd got bored one rainy Sunday, noticed a trapdoor, found a ladder with its legs tied together by the kitchen, untied them, propped it up – and the next thing they knew, they were like Carter staring into the tomb of

Tutankhamun. Heaps of test tubes covered in cobwebs. Glass pipes like snakes being tootled out of baskets. Huge ghostly jars which whiffed of sour milk. When the boys got their breath back, they started to load everything down, but of course Mr Way happened to make one of his tours just then, and the whole lot got confiscated.

Johns was good at Chemistry; his dad was a surgeon, and he wanted to be one too. Maybe he felt inspired by all those retorts and pipettes. Or Hoddy, the bonkers Chemistry master. Anyway, Johns stole some magnesium tape and other stuff from the science labs, and started making bombs. Not like the pictures we sometimes saw in the paper, with wires taped to sticks of dynamite. But real old-fashioned ball-shaped bombs, painted black, with a fuse sticking out from the top, and BOMB written on the side in tidy white letters. He let off the first one in a bush behind chapel, when Jibber was shining past. Because it set the bush alight, we wondered how long Jibber spent thinking he might be Moses. The next one went off in the disused sewage works on the outskirts of the village, because Johns knew explosions worked better in tight spaces. The bomb blew a hole in the floor, and it turned out the sewage farm wasn't completely disused after all. There was a giant lake of old shit under the bricks, and a lot of it spurted into the air to make a slow brown fountain. Johns thought this was great, except not many people were there to see. So then Plummer went mad and let off another bomb – a smaller one – in the dining hall when Mr Doulton was halfway up the aisle to say grace one Sunday evening. Mr Doulton was keen on the Corps, and walked as if he was a Roman legionary who had to get from Londinium to Hadrian's Wall before sunset, or else he'd be thrown to the lions. When he heard the boom, and saw the magnesium smoke billowing round Plummer's table, he veered off the central aisle with his lips pressed so tightly together it looked as if he was swallowing his teeth, grabbed Plummer by the collar, and marched him out of the hall without slowing down by even one mile an hour.

That was the end of the bombs; it meant life wasn't so exciting, but most people felt relieved. Radley wasn't really a bomb-making kind of school. A lot of boys smoked cigarettes, a few kept drink in their studies, and at least one was growing cannabis – but his asthma was so bad he could hardly breathe, let alone inhale. That was it, as far as major crime went. People were more interested in being crackers than anything else – like Pease, who kept white mice in his tuck box, or Thorpe, who hid a live chicken in his study for twelve weeks, then ate it for a special treat on the last evening of term. Boys who didn't want to be crackers concentrated on arguing about the school rules, not breaking them. Things like how long we wore our hair, whether we could wear slip-on shoes and bell-bottoms, how psychedelic our ties were allowed to be. We thought they were important because they stopped us connecting with people outside school. At Maidwell, outside had been a secret – Beak and Mr Porch made sure of that. Here, teachers wanted us to think about what was happening in the world. How could we do that, if the rules made us so different? Shouldn't we try to be more like other people, not less?

Jibber thought the answer was to be a Christian, and plenty of masters agreed with him. That sounded fair enough – but we were still teenagers, we hadn't even done our O-levels yet. Nobody would listen to us if we went sailing into the world and tried to make it better. The only thing we could do instead was complain about things at school, and work from the inside out. That didn't sound like much, but if anyone tried to make it mean something, it turned out to be impossible. When Symes said he was going to see the Warden and complain about having to have haircuts once a month, we weren't in the slightest bit surprised when he came back fuming. All the Warden had said was: our parents hadn't sent us to Radley to turn us into pop stars. That was unfair in so many ways, it was difficult to know where to start. When I'd worked through some of the obvious reasons, I realised it was even unfair on pop stars.

At first, I'd only heard of groups that got into the charts, or on *Top of the Pops*. Then I biked into Oxford one Saturday afternoon and bought Bob Dylan's *Greatest Hits* – not because I knew much about Dylan, and not because I thought he'd had many greatest hits – not like Elvis or the Rolling Stones, anyway. I'd just heard a few songs that didn't sound like anyone else, and I thought he looked great. In my last year at Maidwell I'd started to fuss about my hair, combing it backwards and forwards, and wishing my ears didn't stick out like dad said they did. But all that kind of thing mattered much more now. Even if I didn't have Dylan's heap of dark curly hair, even if I was too tall to have an 'I need looking after' kind of expression, even if I didn't walk in that dipped-down, scurrying-out-of-the-rain way, at least I was skinny. That was something.

After I'd heard Vane singing 'The Cumberland Farmer' at Maidwell, then listened to Rhubarb playing 'The Ashgrove', I'd decided folk music was what I liked best. And Dylan was folk music with the volume turned up. It wasn't only his words I loved – though nobody else's felt so much like a thump on the heart. It was the way his voice actually sounded a part of whatever he was saying. Sometimes it was a lying-down kind of voice, sometimes it swerved around like a car on an icy patch, sometimes it felt warm and pressed up against my ear, sometimes it was shouting and telling me what to do. I more or less wore out the *Greatest Hits*, then every other Dylan record I could get my hands on, playing them in the Social Hall and looking up to see Mr Way watching from across the quad, like Macfarlane had said he would.

This might have caused problems – not just because a few idiots thought Dylan couldn't sing in tune, but also because there were dozens of us who used the Hall, only one record player, and not much free time to listen to music. By now, though, people who might have wanted to shove me out of the way had to take me seriously. I had a new friend, and he was the tallest boy around (apart from Shorter), even though he was six months younger than me. Nobody wanted to shove him anywhere. He wasn't exactly in love with Dylan, but he was pretty keen, and he defended me – so long as I defended him, when he wanted to play Jimi Hendrix, or John Mayall or Peter Green or any of the other people I'd never heard before, but liked immediately.

But that was the thing about Sandy Nairne. He was cleverer at work than anyone else, and he knew more about life as well. I realised this the first time he stepped into Social Hall, at the beginning of my second term. I volunteered to be his nanny, because I sort-of recognised him. He was handsome, in a big Scottish way, and I could tell just by looking that he understood things I wanted to understand. There was something hilarious about him too. His green tweed jacket, and his shirt with a nifty strap-thing that buttoned under the tie-knot – his mother had obviously just bought them, but they were already too small. All his buttons were struggling to stay done up, and there was miles of sock between the bottom of his trouser legs and his shoes. He probably grew about an inch the first time we talked, and that made me feel he was ready to burst out of everything.

Sandy's dad had been a boy at Radley before the war, so he already knew a lot about the school. That helped to explain why he looked relaxed, striding along with his bouncy walk and dangly arms. His family sounded completely unlike my own. For one thing, they lived in Surrey; every time my dad said 'Surrey' he made a *tsk* noise, because he'd once met someone from Esher who wore a Gannex coat like Mr Wilson. For another, Sandy's dad had actually met Mr Wilson, because his job was high up in the Ministry of Defence. 'But that's only half what he does,' Sandy said, without realising how extraordinary all this sounded – then went on to explain that his dad also painted watercolours, and some were so good he had exhibitions. And there was more: Sandy had three sisters, a girlfriend, and he knew the Moody Blues sometimes went to his local pub. The Moody Blues! His local pub! The best I'd done was stick a picture of the lead singer in the back end of my flower album. I tried to hide this from Sandy, but when he found out he didn't mind. Everything about my home was as new to him as his was to me. It meant that while I noticed other boys kept saying their parents were boring, or actually horrible, I started to like mine even more. They weren't the people I'd been lumbered with. They were interesting.

At the end of my first year Sandy and I moved into a study together, which mum thought was a joke. Studies were the size of a kitchen cupboard, so how could we two possibly squeeze in, along with our millionth-hand desks and the G-plan chair granny Bakewell had given me? 'I mean, you're a stick insect,' she said, 'but Sandy's the size of Tarzan.' We didn't mind being squashed, I told her. It was how school was – and besides, if Sandy and I wanted our plan to work, we knew tight spaces could help, like they'd done for the bomb at the sewage farm. 'What plan, exactly?' mum wanted to know. That was more difficult to explain. Our plan to be different from other people. Our plan for *style*. Our plan for *thinking*. We weren't interested in the girl on the motorbike, which was the poster everyone else had in their study. It was Jimmy Hendrix we liked. And a big silvery squiggle which turned out to say 'The Soft Machine Turns You On' if you looked at it closely. And a metal wastepaper basket decorated with the Union Jack, which showed we didn't care about any of the old-fashioned things. And the *New Statesman*. And talking about the Sorbonne, so everyone could see we knew what was happening with the students in France.

Sandy and I bought our new study-clobber in Carnaby Street in London during the holidays, when I went to stay with his family. It felt better this way round, because I still wasn't convinced he was interested in country things – and anyway, they didn't sell pictures of Hendrix in Braintree. As it turned out, Sandy's family was even better than I thought. When we sat down to lunch on my second day, I saw the jug of wallflowers on the table had been changed since breakfast. Under my breath I said I liked wallflowers, and Sandy's dad heard me and said well done for noticing, which made me want to move in and stay the rest of my life. And that was before I even thought properly about Sandy's older sister Fiona, who was beautiful like a garden statue, but couldn't be bothered with us because she was reading Dag Hammarskjold.

When I got back to school, I felt everyone had stayed the same, or maybe even slipped backwards a bit, while Sandy and I had got ten years older; I'd been right about time moving faster these days. It was ridiculous that we still had O-levels to take in a few weeks' time, let alone haircuts and rules about walking on the grass to bother with. Not just ridiculous. Embarrassing. When I said that to people, I wanted them to think it was because I knew all about London and girls and pubs. Actually there was something else, which I didn't mention to Sandy. It was all very well for him to bounce through life swinging his arms. He didn't have anything to feel frightened about: he was clever, and good at rowing as well as painting, and he was the same on the inside as he was on the outside. I might be fake, though. Liking Dylan wasn't going to help me pass my exams, and discovering all this other new stuff – none of it felt joined up yet. One minute I knew what I was talking about, the next Sandy had mentioned somebody I'd never heard of before. James McNeill Whistler, for instance. We had a postcard by him on the study wall, of a dark blue bridge over the Thames – if it was so famous, why didn't I know about it already? 'Be patient' – that's what Sandy always said. But how long did I have to be patient? The clock was moving faster and faster, and I had to get my skates on.

Especially after Brookes. He was in the year below me and Sandy, so I probably wouldn't have noticed him if he hadn't been funny, with a gaggle always following him around in stitches. Then suddenly he was in the sanatorium, then I heard he'd gone home, then I saw his friend Bidwell crying in chapel, then I remembered Brookes had always been pale, with a face like a hungry pony, then Mr Way had an assembly and told us Brookes had died. We stood in a ring, all sixty of us squidged into Social Hall, while Mr Way rocked backwards and forwards so the rubber soles of his shoes squeaked like someone struggling to breathe. No one else moved for a long time. I'd never known anyone who'd died – only great-granny Jessie – and held my breath while a ghost shimmied past me, brushing against my arm. Would this ghost keep charging on, and vanish over the horizon like a cloud? Or would it circle round and come back looking to capture somebody else? I went to see Mr Way to talk about it all, and he showed me what Brookes's dad had sent as a memento: a fat book with the middle cut out, where Brookes had hidden his radio during term-time. Mr Way held it in his hand as if he was guessing its weight, and even though I couldn't see his face properly, I knew he was trying not to cry. That made me feel less frightened, but it didn't stop the clock.

Then death turned out to be catching, which is what I'd suspected. Another boy fell ill during the holidays and was buried the same day the rest of us turned up for school. At our first chapel service of the new term we discovered Mr Catchpole my Maths teacher was dead too. This was as bad as Brookes, because even though Mr Catchpole could be tricky and lost his temper a lot, he was one of those grown-ups with a younger version of himself inside, waving through the bars of his face. He had migraines. He sometimes missed patches of stubble when he was shaving. He got carried away on the touchline and looked as if he was having an epileptic fit. We liked all that, and it meant we didn't blame him when people started saying his death had something to do with a boy. What kind of something? No one said, exactly. We only knew that after we'd all gone home on the last day of last term, Mr Catchpole had shut himself in his room in the Mansion, and swallowed a bottle of pills. Nobody found him until the holidays were nearly over, which meant his body had been up there for weeks, staring at the ceiling while the flies buzzed against his window.

After the Warden had told us about Mr Catchpole officially, we made guesses about the boy, then went quiet. Nobody wanted to be the first to start talking about something else. I got round it by sliding off for a walk, even though it was dark now, and we weren't supposed to go on the pitches after sunset. It was a warm night, and the breeze pressed my clothes against my skin, and my skin against my bones. It made me feel closer to Mr Catchpole, and to Brookes, and to everyone else who'd lost their hold on the world before they were ready. When the grass shivered behind me, I glanced over my shoulder. Nobody was there. Just the long yellow rows of study windows, and the cubicles above them. The whole school looked as though it had floated down from the dark sky like a spaceship, and I was the one passenger who'd stepped out to see what this new country was like. I turned left, towards the beech-tree clump. It was colder now, and really I'd have liked to go back and see Sandy. But my eyes had started to water, and I didn't want him to think I'd been crying. I patted my pockets, to see if by some miracle I'd brought my cigarettes with me. I hadn't, and it was just as well. There was someone watching from the beech clump, and judging by the silhouette, it was a master. I changed tack and picked up speed, and when I got into talking range I called 'Hello there', as though everything was perfectly normal. I didn't stop, in case he wanted to have words with me.

CHAPTER NINETEEN

Yellow

Mum had always written twice a week when we were away from home: once on Mondays and once on Fridays. In the old days at Maidwell, Kit and I shared her letters. Now I went to a different school, she made copies using the special paper I'd seen in the second drawer of her desk. I got the top copy, and Kit had the bottom one. I didn't know there was a difference until she made a mistake, and posted them the wrong way round. My usual version of home was warm and dark blue and like talking. Kit's was pale grey and spidery and far off. I felt sorry for him, but not enough to swap places.

Then mum missed a week, and a letter came from dad, so I knew something was wrong before I opened it, because normally he only wrote for birthdays. Mum was ill, he told me, making his words look like lines of soldiers standing to attention. She had glandular fever. But they'd found someone to help clean the house: Mrs Bunton, who lived in the thatched cottage by the ford. And someone to give a hand in the garden too: Mr Woodley. A few days later, mum was back in touch, explaining what it all meant. She had to spend most of the day in bed, even though it was driving her mad – there was so much to do in the new house. Her skin had turned yellow, that was the worst thing. I wouldn't want to kiss her when I came home. While she was saying this, her writing wobbled. I decided we should talk, and went to the school phone-box, which was a cabin by the junior dining hall. The queue went on for ever, and when I eventually got through, there was no answer. Mum must have been asleep.

'It can't be helped.' That's what dad always said when he didn't like something but couldn't change it. I said it too, when I got home and found mum had been fibbing about how much better she felt. She was thin as a stick, threw up if she ate more than a boiled egg, and fell asleep all the time with her mouth open because she was too tired to care what people thought. Her skin really was yellow, too. It made me think the fever had wriggled into her bones, and was turning them bad too. 'What should we do?' Kit said, leaning on the post-and-rails outside the front door. I shrugged. Serenade could lump it and spend the summer eating. We'd have to exercise the ponies, though, to stop them turning into butterballs. It wouldn't be much fun without mum, and dad was only around in the evenings and at weekends – but maybe we could do some exploring. What about the wood behind the house? This was the perfect chance to sort it out, especially now we had Mr Woodley to help. 'Poor mum,' I said, then added 'It's a bloody nuisance' to remind Kit I was at senior school. He jerked his head round and looked me in the eye. 'It is,' he said. 'A *bloody* nuisance.'

Mum told us about Mr Woodley before we met him. 'He complains all the time,' she said, lying back in her big green chair beside the new fireplace in the drawing room. Her voice sounded hollow. 'You know – if the sun's out it's too hot, if there's no sun he's freezing to death. And he's always got a drip on the end of his nose. And he's deaf. Except he can hear well enough when Mrs Bunton says elevenses.' She paused, and took a sip from her teacup, which was full of Complan. Then she sat up straight, and tried to sound more excited. 'He told me that when he was young he ploughed that field beyond the hedge with a team of horses. Isn't that amazing? A team of horses.' She sank back against her cushions, and her teacup rattled into the saucer. I couldn't think of anything to say, and stared across the rails into the sunlight. Serenade was grazing under the oak tree by the bomb-crater dip. She already looked so fat, she'd probably pop if anyone ever climbed on her again.

Next morning, Mr Woodley knocked on the back door after breakfast. I could see what mum meant: he must have had a very tough life. He sagged like a scarecrow, and only just had the energy to pick up his big black wellies when he blundered a step backwards and tugged off his cap. The top half of his head was white as an egg. The rest was so hard and shiny, he must have spent years staring straight into the wind. Whatever he'd been looking for – he hadn't found it. His watery blue eyes were still shifting left-right-left all the time, while the drip at the end of his nose did fish-eye swivels. 'Good morning, sir,' he said, flattening a non-existent tuft of hair before fitting his cap back onto his head. For a second I thought he must be talking to someone behind me, then I realised I was the sir. 'Hello Mr Woodley, I'm Andrew,' I said, as quickly as possible, and shook his hand. It was like holding a piece of polished wood, and the knuckles were too knotty to let the fingers work properly. Then Kit stuck out his hand as well. 'Is it true you ploughed that field over the hedge using horses?' he asked. Mr Woodley scratched the side of his skeleton-head. 'That field,' he said. 'That field and all the fields.' The words turned over in his mouth as heavily as wedges of clay.

We followed Mr Woodley across the yard to the hayshed behind the stables. He'd decided to keep his lunch things here, which made it a good place to make our plan for the wood. Before we got to that, we asked him more about himself. He told us he'd been born in one of the cottages by the front gate to the Hall, and when he was a boy he'd seen great-granny Jessie wearing her long black dress. I expected him to say something sarcastic about that, like Mr Manning would have done. But he didn't, not even when I asked him about his home and he told us there'd been eight or nine children, he didn't seem sure, and they'd all shared a bedroom. 'What about the bath?' Kit asked, really interested, but Mr Woodley didn't hear. After school he'd worked on Macmillan's farm like mum said, and now he lived on the new council estate, Sarcel, which was beyond the village street. He had a wife who didn't come out much because she had swollen legs, and a boy John who worked in the grounds of the Hall. 'Don't know why you want to hear all this,' he murmured, as we reached the end of his story. Everything he'd said made me feel I was listening to Vane's song about the Cumberland farmer again, or 'The Ashgrove'.

The wood wasn't really a wood but a couple of acres where the trees had got out of control. We wanted to keep the ones along the lane, which hid the house from the outside world, as well as the old

apples and cherries which Mr Woodley said were 'meant'. The rest
was rubbish and had to go. Branches had knocked down the wall
which ran round this bit of the garden, and hidden all the old
paths, and now there were killer brambles as well, so the whole
place was tangled as a rainforest. Mr Woodley couldn't think
where to start – and anyway, he didn't want to decide today,
because he needed to do some digging down by the old greenhouse. Although Kit and I were disappointed, we reckoned it
wouldn't be right to start without him. So we took the ponies for a
ride instead.

Next morning Kit burned Mr Woodley's gumboots. He must
have found them in the hayshed after breakfast, while I was
upstairs talking to mum in her room; I could smell the rubber
when I came down with her tray. Kit hadn't done anything like this
for a while, not since carving a chunk off the bedhead during his
rest – but as it turned out, mum might have been behind it. She
knew Mr Woodley's boots were too big, and by the time I got to see
him, she'd already asked Mrs Bunton to give him the money for a
new pair. 'Did he complain?' I wanted to know, when I went back
to the bedroom again. 'Of course he did,' mum said. 'And quite
right too. Kit can't go round the place burning people's wellies, can
he?' Then she burst into laughter, and for a moment I thought she
might be better.

Mr Woodley and Kit and I got most of the wood done in a couple of weeks. Usually we started in the morning with brambles,
because if one of us used the scythe and the other two pulled the
dead stuff away with rakes, we could clear a decent patch of
ground pretty quickly. But sooner or later we found a tree that
wasn't meant, and then we stopped brambling and started chopping. Most of the un-meant trees were elders, which dad said were
a kind of weed, so we could feel him beaming at us even though he
was miles away in London. Besides, elders were fun because they
were easy. The wrinkly bark looked tough but split easily, and by
the time I'd fallen into a rhythm with the axe I was already well
into the trunk, where the wood oozed colourless blood onto my
blade. I knew I'd reached the middle when I got to a tube-thing full

of fluffy pith: that meant the tree would start to topple any moment, especially if Kit stood the other side and caught hold of a branch and pulled. 'Hang on,' I called to him, meaning *Don't let go* and *Wait a minute* at the same time. I needed his help, but I wanted the tree to fall suddenly, in a huge whooshing rush, with the cut-through trunk springing up sideways as stiff and peculiar as the legs of the stag dad had shot in Scotland. If Kit pulled too steadily this didn't happen. There was only a rustling collapse, like an elephant sitting down. The trees that fell slowly seemed to go on breathing for longer, with a more lively green in their leaves. The ones that went down like ninepins died on the spot; their leaves turned from sparkling to dull in a second.

Mr Woodley kept a bonfire going the whole time, and helped us when we dragged the brambles clear. His polished hands were so tough they didn't mind the prickles, not even when whole thorns snapped off their stems and stuck in his skin. He kept swaying gently towards the heap we'd made, bundling up an armful, then swaying away again and dropping his load onto the fire. Kit and I rested as we watched, comparing blisters on the palms of our hands, tugging twigs from our hair, rubbing the bleary smoke into our eyes when we meant to wipe it away. We were in a trance: every day the same routine of chopping and raking and burning, while dad came and went to his work, mum dozed in the quiet indoors, and the rest of the world rumbled by in the lanes out of sight. I wanted the work finished and the wood tidy again, like it must have been ages ago, with sunlight falling onto the old paths and their dragon's-teeth edges. But I wished it would last for ever as well. If we kept going, I'd slip back into the way things had been at Little Brewers, where I'd never had to think.

Then I had an idea. It didn't matter if we finished the wood. There was another wilderness to explore, a much bigger one, down the road in the grounds of the Hall. When I asked mum if I could go and have a look, she said of course; if anyone stopped me and wondered what I was doing, I should simply say who I was. I liked the sound of that, and sat on the edge of her bed while she told me some more about the house. Great-grandpa Andrew and great-granny Jessie had moved there in the 1920s, and before that it had been owned for a long time by a family called Onley-Saville-Onley. 'What, you mean, like Freddie Onley-Saville-Onley?' I asked, not believing her. 'Yes,' she said, 'though actually Arthur not Freddie. If you look in the church you'll see a plaque. And by the way, what's the pub called?' 'Oh,' I said goofily. 'The Onley Arms.' Mum rolled her eyes in her yellow head, and said when Andrew and Jessie first arrived in Stisted they did some good things, like buy a painting for the church. 'What painting?' I asked, without expecting to know – though I did, surprisingly: it was a copy of *The Adoration of the Magi* by Rubens. 'And there were some strange things too,' mum said in a quieter voice. 'Andrew decided all the houses in the village should have numbers, to help the postman, but he didn't dole them out in 1, 2, 3 order. He used the birthdays of his family and people he liked. So the numbers jump around all over the place.' 'How was he allowed to do that?' I asked. 'I don't know,' said mum airily. 'He just did.' Even though she was so tired these days, she still didn't like it when people thought she might be fibbing.

I left Kit raking the edges of the bonfire-rings, and biked off to see what I could find. Sarcel, where Mr Woodley lived, was out of sight beyond the village and wouldn't have existed in Jessie's day. The main street wouldn't have been so tidy, either – or tidy in a different way. Now there was fawn gravel on the road, flowery front gardens, and new pebble-dashed houses squeezed in between the old ones with their half-timbered fronts and twisted chimneys. Some of the houses were asleep – they were owned by people like dad, who were only around at the weekend. A few were awake, though, with old ladies hovering on their front paths waiting for someone to stop, and cats dozing on the little lawns. The Onley Arms was busy, too, with chestnut leaves resting heavily against the top windows. It really was the only pub – the other one, the Red Lion, had been turned into a house and had its name over the door in twiddly metal writing: Rufus Leo. I pedalled past, down the slope towards the church at the bottom of the hill, and told myself to breathe deeply. This was home now. People would recognise my name, if I needed to tell them.

The road swerved left at the village shop, then jinked and ran downhill to Mrs Bunton's cottage by the ford. It was even prettier here, and felt older. Flint cottages, not brick, and piano music. I wasn't making it up, was I? Mum had said there was a music teacher here; she might be taking lessons herself, when she felt better. I started pedalling again, spurting through a fringe of gravel and onto the cement track which led to the lychgate. Apparently there was a painter who lived the other side of the wall on my right. He had a weird name too, Pleydell-Bouverie, and mum said all his paintings were of cocks. Kit said 'Urgh' when he'd heard that, but mum said she didn't mean that kind of cock, she meant chickens. I thought she might have been lying again, because she thought he was too young, so I stood on my pedals and peered over the wall. All I could see were big windows with a few postcards wedged into the corners, their writing faded by the sun.

I dumped my bike and left the back wheel spinning, hurrying in through the gate. Then I slowed down. Something strange had happened. I couldn't have dropped more than fifty feet since the Onley Arms, but I felt about a hundred yards underwater – as though I was wading through thick green, but miraculously still breathing and making headway. The church reared up ahead: the dark-wood spire I'd first seen from the main road, and the rest covered in flints like the cottages. It was difficult to believe I'd been here already, on the last couple of Sundays for Matins. The church hadn't meant much then. It was for mum and dad, and a handful of other people from the village – the old men and women who shuffled up the path in their soft suits when the bell clanked. Now the whole building was sunk into itself, baked and dozy like the graves, with a wave of cow parsley frothing round the bottom of the walls. Here by the lychgate was the grave of the chimney-builder: it must be him, because there were miniature copies of his handiwork either side of the headstone. Further along the path lay the big box-grave, surrounded by iron railings, of someone who'd lived in our house when he was rector: Charles Morgan Forster. His name was on one of the bricks in the gumboot room, and mum said he might be related to the famous novelist. To her surprise, I knew who she was talking about.

Beyond the west end of the church, by the back gate into the Hall, was the grave of Andrew and Jessie: a heavy cross, with their names and dates round the base. He'd been seventy-six and she was ninety-four, though I had to bend down and press away the grass to find that out. I ran my finger-ends over the letters, and remembered great-granny in the sun-house, asking me to turn her round so she could watch me playing croquet with Kit. Then I saw her asleep in her huge four-poster, with the lace cap perched on her sparrow-head, when mum took us to say goodbye. Would I live as long as her? If I did, it meant I'd have another eighty-two years. I straightened and gazed over the graveyard wall, where the ground shelved towards the Blackwater. There was a red combine harvester on the far side of the valley, cutting a field of beans. The dust spewed out behind in a hard little jet, then spread and settled like a picnic cloth.

I didn't need to go into the church today – it was the Hall I wanted. But the back gate looked as though it would collapse if I touched it, so I squeezed behind Andrew's cross, where an empty jamjar stood waiting in case anyone brought flowers, and scrambled over the wall. It wasn't difficult; it just meant shoving aside some laurel branches, before dropping down the other side onto a bed of crinkly leaves. If there was a gate, there must be a path – the one dad had walked down when the family made their Christmas processions. Here it was. It had turned into a valley, with rhododendrons on either side, ramping three or four times my height and fuzzed over with dead honeysuckle. I rubbed the back of my head and pressed on. The ground underfoot was gravel, packed down by years of rain and woven together by moss. Off to the left was a water garden; when I peered through the bushes, I could see mercury-coloured blobs. Had there been fountains? Waterfalls? There must have been, though all I could find now was a channel choked with muck. When I kicked some twigs clear, I caught a deep *glop-glop*, and a gloomy trickle crept forward, then dropped into another, smaller pond below.

Soon afterwards, I reached a turning off to the right. Lime trees.

An avenue. And a walkway between them, where Jessie must have strolled with her parasol, with the hem of her black dress brushing along the ground. Then, a few yards further on, the old summer house with a wooden roof like a witch's hat, and bramble-arms swarming over the window ledges. The sprays were spindly inside, and the leaves smaller, paler green, dipping at my face. It was creepy and smelled of pee, so I decided to leave it for another day, like the pond. It turned out the rhodies stopped a few yards further on, and the path was easier. That high brick wall beside me had probably been the kitchen garden. And those big trees spiralling up from the undergrowth – they looked meant. With their puzzled bark and wiry twigs, they might even be Chinese or Japanese. Why hadn't the council looked after all this? This cedar tree, for instance, with one of its high branches torn off and rusting down-wards like a broken hinge. I could imagine dad tutting and shaking his head. Andrew and Jessie had sat here in this shade, with the same waxy brown seed-barrels littering the ground, while the maid traipsed towards them with afternoon tea on a tray. Did I envy them? Dad might; that was probably one of the reasons he felt sad. I didn't. Everything had turned into a story, and was noth-ing to do with me any more.

I turned off towards the stable block at the back of the house, where the laurel bushes had pressed close to the bricks and left fan-shapes in the damp. Two ghostly grey heads scowled inside one of the windows and disappeared. I was a trespasser. A boy from the village, like the others who'd pushed through before me and scratched their names on the wall. THE HOUSE OF LOVE, it said, in pale blue letters under a foggy window. I looked inside. A bare mattress. Polystyrene cups. Not too bad, just a secret place under the shadows – so I looked again. It was worse than I'd thought. A thick damp half-light. A candle stub. A red sheet with a bluebottle wiping its hands over a neat little stain. I covered my mouth with one hand and spun away – but it was all right. In a second or two the laurels ended, which meant I'd reached the main entrance, where sunlight made everything simple again. The front door: I recognised it from a photograph in dad's album.

The hounds used to meet here, and this circle of grass at the head of the drive was where grandpa had leaned down from his horse to take a glass of sherry.

Another face appeared, bobbing in the window by the door, but this time younger. A man. If I ran now I'd be guilty – so I stood still, and when half the heavy door dragged open I stuck out my hand and gave my name, like mum had said I should. The man had slicked-back mouse-hair and pasty skin. 'Oh yes,' he said, eyeing the grass stains on my hands and knees. 'They said you might be coming over. What is it you want to see?' 'Nothing really,' I told him, but he wasn't listening. 'I can show you the entrance hall,' he said, then turned sharply as if he was squashing me under his heel. I heard mum in my head again, telling me I mustn't mind, I wasn't asking for much, but as I stepped over the threshold her voice suddenly stopped. It was like falling asleep and dropping straight into a dream. The wide sweep of the staircase, the glow of mahogany doors, the fiddly brass handles, the chequered tiles: they all drew slowly together and started to make sense. This must have been where the Christmas tree stood. Where Jessie lifted dad to light the candles.

'And here's Vi,' said the man at my side. 'She remembers your great-grandfather.' I came back to myself, and looked down – and thought I might still be dreaming, she looked so tiny. A walnut-face, and root-fingers locked on their walking stick. 'Vi,' I said, as though we'd known each other for years. Was that too friendly? If it was, Vi didn't mind. She beamed and said, 'I mistook you for Andrew.' The man interrupted before I could think what to say next. 'Vi was married to one of old Mr Motion's gardeners,' he said carefully. 'She lived in the lodge at the end of the drive, didn't you, Vi?' Vi nodded. 'Funny to think I worked here all my life and now I live here,' she said, still beaming. 'Well, I won't keep you. You do look just like him, though. The spitting image.' 'That's nice,' I said, which sounded even more stupid, but Vi just nodded once or twice, as though she'd solved a problem that had been bothering her for ages. Then she shuffled off towards the drawing room, the rubber tip of her stick making little squeaks on the tiles. As the

door closed, I thanked the pale man and walked off into the sunlight before anyone else appeared.

Pedalling back up the main street, I decided to keep the Hall a
secret – not the look of it, or the overgrown garden, or the House
of Love, or Vi who thought she'd seen a ghost. These were all stories, and harmless. What I didn't want to talk about was the past as
a whole – the family past. I thought it would make dad say he felt
part of a dying race. Whenever he'd done that before, I'd thought
he was making a joke. Now I wasn't so sure. Maybe he wanted to
keep close to the past because he couldn't face the present? I didn't
feel like that – not at home, and not at school either. Bouncing
round Social Hall, mugging up on the Greybook, making friends
with Sandy: I was trying to make things different from what had
come before. And the more Sandy told me about his life, the more
I liked the sound of it. So free! If he wanted to go somewhere, he
climbed on a train and nobody minded. So talky! His family dis-
cussed things all the time, and changed their minds, and didn't feel
they'd hurt someone if they disagreed. Although Sandy never said
it straight out, I knew he felt things at Stisted were old-fashioned.
The way people said they loved animals but spent most of their
time trying to kill them. The way they never talked about anything
properly, just dashed around complaining. The Rolling Stones?
Ought to join the army. French students? Prison. Strangers moving into the village? Oiks. Mr Wilson? Common little man. The
Coggeshall ringroad? Hideous, and typical of Mr Hill to make so
much money in compensation: he was already rich as Croesus.

I wanted to talk about all this to mum – she was the obvious
person. But how could I say anything, without criticising home? I
had to admit, some things were starting to bug me. Dad made out
the Mos had been posh for centuries, with their big houses and
everything, but it wasn't true. A hundred years ago, great-grandpa
Andrew had been sticking on stamps, like mum said. It was his
brain that made him interesting, not his money or his swank. Why
didn't people see that, and say brains mattered, like they did in
Sandy's family? I knew I could ask mum, and she'd understand.
From the way she talked about George Victor the doctor, and her

supper with Peter Ustinov, and granny's friend Joan Kunzer, who knew about John Betjeman and the fish knives, and *The Nutcracker*, she'd probably have agreed with me. But only when we were alone together. If she said anything out loud, that would be disloyal, which was impossible.

I decided to put off talking to mum until later, when she was well again. But I had to tell *someone* at home. Apart from Mrs Bunton and Mr Woodley, there was only Kit. It was more difficult to connect with him these days, because he was still living in the old, slow Maidwell time, and my new, faster time meant that I'd sped away from him. On the other hand, he was still my bro, so it was worth a try. I found him beyond the stables, digging one of his holes with Wiggy. It was a year since we'd finished clearing the brambles, and the grass under the apple trees had joined up, so it was difficult to tell whether this part of the garden was old or new. 'Hi,' I said, suddenly feeling awkward. Kit said nothing and stayed kneeling, resting one hand on Wiggy's back while she scrabbled at the soft earth. Was there a rabbit's nest here? It was impossible to tell; Wiggy often dug for the hell of it, even when the earth was packed so tight between her nails she could hardly stand. 'Well?' Kit said, glancing round. 'Are you making an announcement?' 'Should I be?' 'I don't know,' said Kit. 'You look all puffed up. What's the matter? It's not dad going on about hair and trousers again, is it?' 'No,' I said quickly, realising this was my cue. I must either shut up now, or tell him as much as I could. I took a deep breath and rushed through everything I'd been thinking about: country things, town things, Sandy, the Labour party, trains, the Rolling Stones. Kit stayed kneeling while I rattled on, sometimes looking into the hole, and sometimes whispering to Wiggy, telling her to keep going. I thought he might not be listening, but when I finished he said calmly. 'If home's so awful, how are you going to make it better?' 'Home's not awful,' I said, shocked to think I'd given him that idea. 'That's not what I'm saying. But I'm going to change a few things.' 'Such as what?' 'Such as hunting,' I said. 'I'm not going to do that any more. Or shooting.' 'We hardly ever do any shooting,' Kit said, still calm. 'Dad's always complaining he never gets enough invitations.' 'No, well, hunting mainly,' I said, wishing I'd never even started this conversation. I should have waited and talked to Sandy.

'Dad will be annoyed,' Kit said, resting on his heels at last and wobbling the loose skin on the back of Wiggy's neck. 'You can stop now, old girl,' he said. 'There's nothing there. No rabbits.' When Wiggy heard 'rabbits' she started scrabbling furiously again, spraying up little handfuls of earth. Kit got some in the eye and clambered to his feet. 'He'll just have to get annoyed,' I said, 'because that's not the only thing.' 'What do you mean?' Kit asked, fishing a grey hanky from his pocket, folding the corner into a triangle, then poking at the corner of his eye. I couldn't tell whether he still thought I was stupid or not; his voice was too level. 'What do you mean, "what do you mean?"?' I said. He tucked his hanky back into his pocket and folded his arms. 'I mean, *why* do you want to give up hunting and everything? Because you feel sorry for the animals?' 'That's part of it,' I said. 'But not the main thing.' 'What, then?' 'Because of what it represents,' I said, wishing it didn't sound as though I'd swallowed a mouthful of mud. 'What it *represents*?' Kit echoed. I took another deep breath. 'I want to live differently,' I said. Kit stared me full in the face. 'Different from mum and dad?' he said, speaking more slowly. 'It's not them,' I said. 'It's things round them. Not so much bellowing. More *thinking*.' Kit slowly lifted one hand to his ear. 'I don't hear any bellowing,' he said. I kicked the ground, showering up another spurt of dry mud. 'Forget it,' I said. 'I knew you wouldn't understand'.

I thought our talk was over for the time being, but when mum came down for tea, and sat in her green chair with her rug pulled round her, Kit started again. 'Andrew's giving up riding,' he said suddenly. Mum was midway through a mouthful. 'Oh really, darling?' she said, with crumbs in her voice. 'When did you decide that?' 'Hunting,' I said. 'Maybe riding. I haven't decided.' 'He wants something else,' Kit went on. 'And he's going to vote Labour. When he's allowed to vote, that is.' I glared at Kit but couldn't see his face: he was sitting with his back to the French windows. 'Is this something to do with school?' said mum, putting down her cup. 'I don't know,' I told her, which was a lie. 'Maybe it is to do with school, yes.' 'And what sort of something else do you want?' Even though she was talking seriously, I kept expecting Kit to interrupt, or laugh, and glanced at him again. He was rubbing his knuckle into Wiggy's ear because he knew in a minute it would make her give one of her helpless little grunts. 'That's the thing,' I said, as quietly as I could. 'I don't know. Maybe it's got something to do with moving house, and seeing the Hall. As well as school, I mean.' Mum stretched out her hand, and rested it on my knee. 'It's OK,' she said. 'We'll talk about it again . . .' She looked across at Kit, meaning we'd wait until we were alone, but he noticed. 'Oh, don't mind me,' he said, pretending to be more upset than he was. He half stood up, than sank down again. He was side-on to the window now, and I could see his jaw was set. 'Though come to think of it, this isn't a very good time for you to talk to mum, is it bro? You'll be going out rabbitting in a minute. Or is that something else you're giving up?' 'I am giving it up, actually,' I said, pushing my chin forward. Then I got to my feet and went upstairs to my room. I'd been playing the *White Album* earlier in the day, and now I put on the first of its LPs again, turning up the sound to max so it would sound as if the aeroplane at the beginning of 'Back in the USSR' was landing on my desk.

Dad got home late that night and there wasn't time for us to talk, even if I'd tried. The next few days were no good, either. Kit and I had a week before term started, and nobody wanted a row when we had school to think about. All the same, I noticed dad kept finding more time than usual to ask me things, even when he knew the answers already. What games would I be playing next term? Had I got all the clothes I needed for my trunk? Maybe he was being kind because he knew we hated the end of the holidays. Or maybe mum had said something? I thought so. Especially on our last Sunday afternoon, when dad asked me to look at the roof with him, because he thought some of the slates might be loose. I made a face at mum, but all she said was, 'Be an angel. You know how dad hates heights'.

We climbed the stairs in single file, dad in the lead but half turned round and saying we must watch out for the attic ladder, it would take off somebody's head one of these days. Dad had obviously decided to be patient, especially because we were doing something he hated. After we'd hooked open the little door in the ceiling, and the ladder had shot down like a gigantic spear, just as we'd predicted, he actually laughed. 'We must get that fixed,' he said. I took the hint and went first, climbing almost vertical, and squeezing through the trapdoor into the half-light of the attic. There was nothing valuable up here, but still, it felt like a treasure cave. Black box-silhouettes. Dustsheets. The zizzy smell of pine. And what was that cot doing? Was it really the one I'd slept in when I was a baby? I ran my hand over the white wicker sides, and my fingers looked as thin as mum's. 'Everything OK?' dad called, hesitating on the ladder below me. 'It's cold,' I told him. 'Cold?' he repeated. 'Well, there's a kind of breeze,' I went on. There was, too: a sullen flap, like a gust trapped years ago, and nearly dead but not quite. 'I don't believe you,' said dad brightly. He was only talking to keep his mind off climbing.

I found the latch for the window onto the roof, and was warm as soon as I had it open. There was no view yet, only the chimney stack, streaked with piebald sparrow-mess. All I had to do was get round the side, then turn to give dad a hand. But I didn't want to move. I wasn't scared. I just felt a weird kind of laziness, half in and half out of the attic, as if I'd got stuck being born. 'Are you all right, old boy?' That was dad again, but right behind me now; he must have made it to the top of the ladder, and was talking to my legs and bum in the gloom. 'Sorry, dad,' I shouted, and levered myself forward. A couple of heaves and I was upright, leaning against the chimney. 'What's it like?' Dad was poking his head through the little window behind me. I waved one arm, to show it was safe, but stayed leaning against the bricks. The roof turned out to have a narrow walkway between the slates and the parapet. If I kept a hand on the parapet top, and put one foot in front of the other like a tightrope walker, I'd be fine. And the slates themselves were great – pitched and folded so they made a whole little valley-world.

Dad had his shoulders through the attic window now, and

although he was smiling I could tell it was fake. His face was pale green. 'Don't worry,' I said, and wavered off down the walkway, leaning inwards in case I started to wobble. A couple of yards and I was clear of the chimney stack, where I could look over the side of the house. There was mum's car outside the front door, with a white splodge on her roof. And there was Serenade, dozing by her scratching post at the edge of the chestnut. She had no idea I was watching – but in the branches above her a pigeon fixed me with his grey button eye, wondering whether I was dangerous. I ignored him and kept going until I reached the corner. From here I could see the whole of the big field, and the rabbit-place in the far corner, and beyond it the dark muddle of the Ashground. Further still, beyond the horizon, was the Hall with its lost paths and cloudy windows. None of that was interesting now. All I wanted was the bird-feeling of swooping down through the warm air, and rising again with a single wing-clap. Then plunging and lifting again, while the grass-waves rolled beneath me, each one different and each one the same.

'Shall we get started?' When I turned round, dad was out of the window entirely, leaning against the chimney stack so he didn't have to see the drop. He had both hands clamped to his sides, and was frowning hard at the slates. 'Is everything all right, old boy?' he said, and for a second I thought he meant: was I safe on the roof? Then I realised he'd brought me up here so that we could have the chat he'd been practising for days. I couldn't believe it. This wasn't the place to talk – not when he wanted to throw up. 'Yes, I'm fine,' I said sunnily. 'It's great. I can see right to . . . "I didn't mean that,' dad interrupted, flicking me a quick glance, then fixing on the slates again. His face had turned from green to white, and his thumbs were tucked inside his fists like a soldier. But I still couldn't talk to him. Not now, maybe not ever. 'Honestly, I'm fine,' I told him, in a quiet voice to show I understood what he was asking. He nodded, then cleared his throat. 'Sure?' 'Sure, dad.' 'That's good,' he said, then paused, and we both stared at the roof as if we'd forgotten why we were there.

After a minute I had to change the subject because he wasn't going to; he was braver than me about that. 'You can see where the slates have come loose,' I said. Dad looked up again, smiling and relieved. 'Well, yes,' he said. 'You can, can't you? I tell you what. I'll point, then you can nip up and give them a shove. Does that sound OK?' 'Yes, dad,' I said, and thought he must have talked like this during the war, when he was giving orders, only without so many pleases and thankyous. It made me spring into action, but when I put my foot on the roof and started to climb, my shoes wouldn't grip. 'Bare feet, I think,' dad went on, without moving a muscle. So I took off my shoes and socks, and he was right. My skin stuck to the slates like Spiderman, and after I'd fixed the first few I got the knack completely. I scampered up the slopes, then down into the hollows, tweaking out twigs and moss-blobs, not thinking about the breeze, or the cuts in my finger-ends, or the drop from the parapet. There was no danger of falling. None at all. Nothing existed, except the shimmer of sun, the scrape of the slates fitting back into place, and dad's voice calling, 'Up a bit. That's right. Now across. Now down a bit. There you are. Yes, that's right. Well done. Well done.'

CHAPTER TWENTY

Wasting Skin

The foreground was bog, painted splodgy green and brown except where water was starting to fill the creek. Then it was silver. It reminded me of Blakeney on the Norfolk coast. Dad was always in a good mood when we spent holidays there, and the marshes had so many birds it was like being on safari. But the clouds in the painting were what I liked best. Big slabs of orange and purple across the bottom of the sky, greeny-blue in the middle, where the V of geese were flying, and white at the top. That was the clever bit. One of these white clouds looked like a swan: the beak and neck and shoulders were perfectly clear if you half-closed your eyes.

I tried to explain this to Sandy, when I told him dad had given me the painting for doing better in my O-levels than anyone thought I would. Actually five out of six didn't seem that hot to me, especially since I'd got the lowest grade possible in everything except English. But mum and dad didn't agree. They thought a pass was a pass, and now I could drop all the impossible subjects, like Chemistry and Maths, and concentrate on things I liked better. English, obviously – but I wasn't much good at any other subjects. History and Geography, I decided in the end. History because Sandy was doing it, and he could give me a hand. Geography because it was to do with Nature. 'Your dad gave you a *painting*?' Sandy said. 'A painting by *Peter Scott*? Why?' 'Because I asked for one,' I said, wishing I hadn't told him. 'And it's not a real painting, it's a reproduction.' Sandy folded his arms, frowning and smiling at the same time. When I finished telling him about the cloud-swan he was making the same sniffy face. Sandy had been talking about art ever since he climbed out of his cot; I'd only just started, so I was bound to make some mistakes. Not that this was a mistake. I liked the picture. It was hanging above my bed at home, and dad had written a message on the back, saying well done.

I was never angry with Sandy for long. He was my best friend, and there were too many things I needed him to tell me. Anyway, we were senior now, and didn't have time to waste. We had to show everyone else we were different. We'd asked Mr Way to let us move our study to the top of Croome's Tower, away from the others, and turned it into a kind of grotto. The Hendrix and the Soft Machine posters were a help, but we had a lot of new stuff as well, including the Blind Faith LP with the naked girl on the cover, holding a model aeroplane. It looked a bit pervy, but that was the point. If Mr Way objected, he'd cheer up when he saw my drawing of Thomas Hardy, stuck beside the George Frederick Watts self-portrait. Mr Musset had let me use the Art School for this, even though I'd stopped doing Art when O-levels finished. I'd watched *Far From the Madding Crowd* because of Julie Christie, then happened to see Hardy's face in a photograph and liked it.

We weren't the only ones who saw things were changing. Mr Milligan had retired. He'd been Warden for ages and I'd hardly met him, except to take him my report card from time to time, when all I could think about was his knuckles: they were so hairy he must have looked like a monkey under his shirt. The new Warden was Mr Silk, who was young and had a pretty wife and two little girls, which made the school more like a family. The masters approved too. Mr Silk was a games genius, but he was brainy as well. He'd been a friend of Siegfried Sassoon, and even people who hated poetry knew Sassoon was a hero. Not that anyone would have guessed Mr Silk was clever: he had a huge square face, a stride like Goliath, and sang so loudly in chapel he almost blew out the windows. But he had a great smile, and must have spent hours staring at school photographs, because he already knew my name, and shouted it juicily whenever I passed him in the corridor. It sounded as though he was urging me over an invisible finishing line: 'Good morning, *Andrew*.'

Even Mr Way liked him, and that was surprising because Mr Silk was noisy and energetic, and Mr Way was quiet. I'd realised this my first night at the school, which was three years ago now, when Mr

Way had sat me down in his study with the other new boys and told us we must see him if ever we felt homesick. He'd said the word with such a sorry click at the end I'd thought he must be feeling it himself. I had been to see him once or twice. Not to talk about homesickness, because I didn't feel that too badly any more. But about how to deal with my Latin tests, which I could never pass because Mr Fisher was so frightening. And about what to tell mum when she wrote and said Beauty had died. And how to help dad when granny Sunbeam fell into the sea at Dunwich, and drowned. Every time, Mr Way did the same thing. He stayed at his desk, hunched forward in his tweed jacket and army tie, and said nothing for a bit. Just fiddled the paperclips and pencils on his desk into straight lines, and sometimes checked the lid of the Nippon ant killer, while I sat in the chair beside him and waited. He was thinking, and didn't have an answer ready for everything, which I liked. When he'd worked out what he wanted to say, he kept it simple. I should do my best with Mr Fisher and not worry too much. It was OK to miss pets as much as people, even if it was embarrassing. And as for granny Sunbeam – he didn't quite know what to say about that, apart from how sorry we must all be. I nodded, but the truth was, Kit and I had never seen much of granny, and most times she ignored us. It was dad I felt sad about, because he bottled up his feelings, and never talked about them. I sat back in my chair and let the burble of the gas jets mix with the softness of Mr Way's voice. It made me feel sleepy and wide awake at the same time, so his words slid into my head without leaving a ripple.

Now Mr Way was a sort-of friend, and I was in his English set for the first time, I mustn't let him down. Other people weren't so sure. Nixon said it was pathetic, spending hours looking at a single word in a poem, and going through *Troilus and Cressida* line by line. Not to mention *The Knight's Tale*, which didn't even have any farting in it, and poems by John Clare who was a peasant. And oh, had I heard? Mr Way had arranged for his classroom to be painted a peculiar kind of salmon pink, which would help us concentrate. Pink? No wonder he ran the fencing club.

Even though Maidwell had turned poems into a kind of punishment, I thought they must be OK if Mr Way liked them. Besides, they were different from home – more or less opposite to dad's side of home – and that was important. But the strange thing was, when Mr Way came into our first class, he looked snappier than usual, more like a soldier. He was walking quickly, with papers shivering in his right hand and his left fist swinging as though he was marching. For a moment I thought he must be angry. Then I realised he couldn't wait to tell us what he knew. This was nothing to do with the books on our syllabus. It was a poem he thought we'd like. He slapped his papers onto his desk, and looked me in the eye. A poem by Thomas Hardy. I knew if I smiled back, the others would see, and think I was a teacher's pet. So I just opened my anthology at the page number he gave out, and listened as he read:

> I look into my glass,
> And view my wasting skin,
> And say 'Would God it came to pass
> My heart had shrunk as thin!'
>
> For then, I, undistrest
> By hearts grown cold to me,
> Could lonely wait my endless rest
> With equanimity.
>
> But Time, to make me grieve,
> Part steals, lets part abide;
> And shakes this fragile frame at eve
> With throbbings of noontide.

There was a prickly silence when he finished; nobody wanted to answer the first question. It wasn't shyness that stopped us. We were puzzled. Why had Mr Way chosen such a strange poem to start with? We were sixteen: what did we know about old age? Then I looked at the words again, saying them over slowly, and they stopped being just words. I could hear a man singing to himself, in a shadowy room by a log fire. The meaning was still there, but something else, too – something like sadness for the man. Sadness for everything, in fact. For his life nearly over, for mine starting, for people I'd never met. I pushed the book away from me carefully, as if I might find the poem sticking out of my chest like a weapon. It reminded me of the film *Khartoum*, when General Gordon stood at the top of the steps, and someone in the mob chucked a spear at him, and he staggered, and seemed not to feel it, then sank down.

Nothing like this had happened to me before – but the poem reminded me of 'The Cumberland Farmer' and 'The Ashgrove', and everyday things I loved, such as peering into a bird's nest and seeing the eggs when I hadn't expected any. Come to think of it, the sound of the words made the whole of Stisted gush through my mind like floodwater. All I had to do was say them, close my eyes, and I saw the horses' field glittering with frost, and the bomb-crater dip with a window of ice in the bottom, and the Ashground in the distance, and the old man of the poem standing in mum's bedroom, gazing at himself in the mirror on her dressing table. The old man whose face I'd already drawn, and pinned on my wall in the Tower study. 'Now who would like to tell me something?' said Mr Way at last, rubbing his palms together. I put up my hand without knowing what I was going to say.

'It's about an old man who wants to be a young man,' I said; it seemed best to stick to basics, and not mention songs or firesides. 'That's a start,' said Mr Way with a half-smile. 'Anything else?' This was difficult. What did 'else' mean when you were talking about a poem – was it the sadness I'd felt? 'The words are very simple,' I said. 'Apart from "equanimity", of course.' Then I paused and had an idea. 'It tells us what he's feeling, but not straight out. We're sort of inside him.' Mr Way smiled again, full on this time. It made me want to smile back, but I knew that would make me look greasy. Besides, Nixon had his hand up. 'Yes?' said Mr Way, raising his pale eyebrows. 'This throbbing, sir,' said Nixon. 'What sort of throbbing are we talking about here, exactly?'

That evening I took Hardy off my study wall and wrote his name underneath my drawing, copying his own handwriting as best I could. It was frustrating. I couldn't describe clearly to Sandy

what I felt about the poem, any more than I'd been able to tell Mr
Way. But Mr Way kept me behind afterwards, and explained there
were other Hardy poems in the anthology: one about the oxen at
the Nativity, and one about the Titanic. I read them as soon as I
could, and hovered in the classroom after the next English lesson.
Were there other poems Mr Way thought I might like? He told me
to come and see him when he was doing report cards, and
although I turned up feeling a bit of a fool, Mr Way pretended not
to notice, and lent me some books from his shelves by the gas fire.
One was a pale-green brick with black and red lettering on the
spine: I'd been staring at it across the room for years, wondering
what it was: *The Dyer's Hand and Other Essays*, by W. H. Auden,
Faber & Faber. Almost none of these words meant anything. The
other book was much thinner, and the lettering dim because it had
been in the sun. A whole book of poems called *The Less Deceived*.
Mr Way said the man who wrote it had been to St John's College in
Oxford, which was where Mr Way had been too – only they'd
never met because of the war. Mr Way had almost known someone
who'd actually published a book? It was unbelievable – especially
since the poet was called Philip Larkin, which seemed funny to me,
not like a poet's name at all. After I'd taken the book back to my
study and started reading, I enjoyed the poems as much as
Hardy's; they gave me the same mysterious feeling of discovering
things I didn't realise I already knew. And there was something
else. Mr Way had cut out a new poem by Philip Larkin, and glued
it inside the front cover. Amazing. Everyone else cut out pictures of
girls or cricketers or cars, and stuck them on their folders. Mr Way
cut out poems. I'd better not tell Nixon that.

Mr Way lent me several books over the next few weeks, but neither of us made a fuss about it. I read them quietly, then gave them
back, and we talked about them for a while in his study. Seamus
Heaney. Ted Hughes. Sylvia Plath. William Wordsworth. Edward
Thomas. John Keats. T. S. Eliot. I didn't have to sound expert, or
write essays: the only thing Mr Way wanted to know was which
poets I liked and which I didn't. The problem was, I liked nearly all
of them – especially Edward Thomas and Wordsworth – and every

one made me want to write something myself. Partly to be like them, and partly so I could get inside their skin and understand them better. Without knowing quite what I was doing, or even what I wanted to do, I started jotting down lines after prep when the light was going, and I felt the evening-mixture of sad and safe, which was my favourite mood in poems. 'What are you up to?' Sandy wanted to know, and when I didn't answer he scooted his chair across the study floor to have a look. 'Poems?' he asked, in a flat voice. I nodded. 'What are they about?' It was a good question. They weren't about anything. They were just words, thrown like stones at whatever happened to be passing through my mind. They made my thoughts stop and turn round to look at me. Memories of the field at home, or the overgrown gardens in the Hall, or people I'd read about in the paper, or dad in the war. 'Oh, nothing,' I said, putting my hand over one I'd written recently, and felt especially proud of. It was about leprosy. 'What sort of "nothing" is that?' said Sandy, stabbing a finger down between my own, and landing where it said 'you'. 'Who's "you"?' he went on. 'It's not really a "you",' I said. 'It's me' – though that sounded idiotic. 'As long as it's not *me*,' Sandy said, and went back to his essay.

I wanted writing to feel normal, but there was too much I didn't understand. Surely people had to be older, and probably dead, before they could call themselves poets? And they probably had to have read a lot of books. On the other hand, now I'd started, I couldn't stop. It was more like turning the tap on a steam pipe than anything to do with thinking. One twirl, and a jet rushed out. But that's when the next problem came along. After the steam had cleared, I could see that whatever I'd written sounded like the person I'd just been reading. Philip Larkin, if it was a poem about not having a girlfriend. Seamus Heaney, if it was a poem about the stable yard at home. Auden, if it was a poem written like a telegram. T. S. Eliot, if it was a poem made up of bits and pieces. 'You should show those to Ohm,' Sandy said, when he noticed I'd started keeping them in a special folder. So I did. And Mr Way made me sit in the chair by his desk again, and talked about what I'd written as seriously as if it was by Hardy.

He told me to read more, too, so I wrote to mum and asked: could she send £20 because I needed to go into Oxford and buy some books? When the money came, I pedalled off through Sunningdale, then over Folly Bridge where the lorries always tried to flatten bicyclists, then stood in front of the Modern Poetry section in Blackwell's. I was lost. The shelves stretched for ever, and were stuffed with names I'd never seen before. Faber were usually good, so I bought a couple of them: Norman Nicolson and Vernon Watkins. Then Wilfred Owen and Robert Graves because they'd been in the war. And Rimbaud because he was queer – Burrows had told me about him. Then E. E. Cummings because Mr Way said he was sometimes good and sometimes sugary and I needed to see if I could tell which was which. After I'd got the books back to school, and stroked the jackets, and written my name inside and the date, I took them with me to Social Hall, to make sure everyone could see what I was up to.

That's when the real difficulties started. I couldn't make head or tail of Vernon Watkins. His language was waffly, and didn't connect with anything I knew, so there weren't any head-pictures. E. E. Cummings wasn't much good either: the poems crawled over the page, and had some words joined-up, and didn't use capitals – but when I'd unscrambled them and put them back together again, they nearly all seemed soppy, not just some like Mr Way had said. Rimbaud was good: he didn't make sense in the usual way, but he fizzed round my brain like one of mum's energy tablets when she dropped them into a glass of water. Owen was even better – though he seemed the queer one, more than Rimbaud, even. Did Mr Way know that? Perhaps I'd got the names in a muddle.

Then something came out of the blue. My knees hurt. I'd first noticed a few months ago, before O-levels. When I told Sandy, he said it was growing pains, which he knew all about. But they wouldn't go away, and Miss Laing the Social Matron reckoned I'd got a knock playing games. A knock on both knees, and no bruises? It didn't make sense, but I decided not to go on about it, because knees were a bit daft. A silly word for silly things. If I took a few days off games I'd probably get better. Mum thought so anyway, when I wrote and told her. She said it sounded like arthritis, which she had in her hands: why didn't I wear a copper bangle, and see if that helped? I told her the school would think it was jewellery, and tell me to take it off.

If anyone had something worse than a runny nose or an upset tummy, Miss Laing sent them to the infirmary, which was a sore-looking red-brick dump near the Science labs. It seemed as bad on the inside, thanks to Sister Boddy, who ran the place and was like a grown-up version of Miss Gibbon at Maidwell – except her uniform was dark blue, not wishy-washy green. I asked Ransome about her, because he was often ill, and knew her better than most people. He said she was fine; we only thought she wasn't because of the Cough and Drop. He had a point. The Cough and Drop happened once a year, when a doctor made the whole school turn up in alphabetical order, ordered us to take down our trousers, then cradled our bollocks in the palm of his hand while telling us to clear our throats. Sister Boddy stood at his side the whole time. Sandy worked out that she must have seen roughly ten thousand cocks in her life.

When I told Sister Boddy about my knees, she paid more attention than I expected. I was taken off games, and sent to the Radcliffe Hospital in Oxford to have X-rays. No games was good, because it meant I had more time to lie around in my study thinking about poems. But suppose I was pretending to be ill, so I could get out of things I didn't like? I thought carefully, trying to worm my way under my skin and into my bones. Some days my knees hardly hurt at all – when the weather was dry, for instance. On other days, I really wasn't making it up. There was a weird deep-down ache in my joints, as if they needed oiling. And that's what it looked like on the X-rays, too. They showed the lining of my knee-bones was rotting away, and Sister Boddy said there was a special name for it: contro malacia patella. 'Will it clear up by itself?' mum asked, when I rang to put her in the picture. I told her nobody knew the answer, which she said was nonsense: we needed an expert opinion. This sounded bad, but at least it made me feel important. And suddenly a good deal worse. So much worse, it was difficult to walk any more, and I had to have a stick, which meant everyone could see there was something wrong with me. Sandy thought that must be awful, but I didn't mind. I was an invalid and writing poems. When I looked back only a few months, and saw myself on the roof trying not to upset dad, it was like watching a stranger.

The expert was Dr Osmond Clarke, and his consulting rooms were in Harley Street in London. Mum came with me to see him, and her woolly ankle-boots looked embarrassing as we padded up the red carpet onto his floor. It turned out to be OK, though. Osmond Clarke wasn't smart and London-y. He was a fisherman and small – there was a picture of him on the mantelpiece, holding up a salmon so huge he could only just get its tail clear of the heather. And he had an early Christmas card from Giles, whose cartoons from the *Daily Express* we had in the downstairs loo: apparently Giles had hurt his thumb, and Osmond Clarke fixed it for him. I could see what mum was thinking. What was good enough for Giles would be good enough for me. After Osmond Clarke had asked me to take off my trousers, and made me lie on a narrow bed, and prodded and poked at my knees like mum said he would, I agreed with her. Osmond Clarke might look like a garden gnome, with his dinky beard and his twinkly specs and his stubby legs, but he was definitely an expert. He told me to get dressed again, then sat the far side of his enormous desk, put his neat little hands into a steeple under his chin, and said there were three choices. I could have one leg in plaster for a bit and see if it made any difference. I could have cortisone injections in both knees – which 'would hurt, but can do marvels'. Or I could have my kneecaps taken out. Mum lifted her bag off the floor by her comfy boots, and held it tight on her lap. Her face had lost almost all its yellow now, but in full sunlight the colour was still there, lying under the skin like bad water low down in a pond. 'If you say so,' she said eventually, speaking to Osmond Clarke but staring straight at me. 'In that order I think, starting with the plaster.'

I went back to school, the doctor arrived, and my left leg disappeared into its stiff white sausage. There wasn't the faintest chance

I was a fraud now. Boys I hardly knew came up and told me it was hard luck. People stood aside in doorways when they saw me rowing towards them on my crutches. Even Mr Fisher said he was sorry – which made me think Mr Way had told him I'd started writing poems. This was all fine: it helped to be the centre of attention. But it was tiring, dragging one leg around, and my plaster tickled so badly it was driving me insane. When I scratched inside with my ruler, dead skin trickled out by my ankle, and smelled disgusting.

When I got home for Christmas, it didn't feel like a holiday. I couldn't walk anywhere. I couldn't sit in the front of the car, because there wasn't room for my plaster. I got fagged out before everyone else, and that made me grumpy. Kit took every chance to escape, and since that meant he was often alone with mum, I felt jealous as well as bored. On the other hand, they were doing things I was glad to be missing. Hunting most Tuesdays and every Saturday, while I lay on the sofa in the drawing room and read my poetry books. When dad came back from work in the evenings, I didn't have to explain what I was doing. As far as he was concerned, books and invalids went together like horses and carriages.

Early in the new year, mum and I went back to Osmond Clarke and he cut off the plaster. My leg looked scraggy as a chicken's neck, but he said that was normal, and took some more X-rays, which he sent to the hospital in Black Notley, a few miles up the road from Stisted. Soon mum and I were talking to a new doctor, in a Portakabin as it turned out, with a broken window and a plywood floor that bounced when I hobbled across it on my crutches. We decided he knew what he was doing, because he stared at the pictures for a long time before speaking. The plaster hadn't worked, and now it was time for the cortisone injections. He'd start giving them to me right away if that was all right? There was no time to lose, and he had a bed behind this screen . . .

Osmond Clarke hadn't been kidding. The injections hurt, even though my head felt about half a mile away from the rest of me when I watched the needle fiddle under my kneecap, then down into the joint. They made life more complicated, too. There was nothing to show I had anything wrong, apart from my stick, which meant people didn't feel so sorry for me. When mum's friend Mrs Hill dropped in, for instance, bringing some late Christmas presents, she just hollered up to my bedroom from the hall – 'So glad you're on the mend' – then stamped after her terrier, which had barged into the kitchen looking for a fight with Wiggy. I sat at my desk and closed my writing book, and tried to imagine the cortisone dribbling through my joints, coating the end of my bones or whatever was supposed to happen. It wasn't doing any good: there was still the same ache, only now it felt sharper. 'Is the needle *really* that big?' Kit wanted to know, when he came to tell me Mrs Hill had gone, and the coast was clear. 'Like a *knitting* needle?' 'Yes,' I told him, 'like a knitting needle', and made sure I got the inside track, next to the banisters, when we went downstairs again.

Mum and I went back to see Osmond Clarke, and waited for him to shake his head. The first time in his rooms, we'd sat on these same slippery red chairs with the curly arms, and everything had been an adventure. We hardly ever came to London, and as soon as we were done here we'd go to Selfridges. But now I was stuck in a kind of tunnel and wanted to reach the end, no matter what. Osmond Clarke wanted that too, and said 'I'll book you into the London Clinic', pointing with the gold nib of his fountain pen towards what looked like a mansion block at the end of his street. 'I'll do your left leg first, and then we can look at the other one in a few months' time.' I felt my kneecap jerk like a goldfish in a plastic bag, and waited for him to say something else. Suddenly he was standing with his hands behind his back, as though he didn't want me to see them any more. Mum took the hint, and led the way to the door. I felt Ozzy was being pathetic: I didn't mind seeing his hands, even if they were about to pick about inside my skin. I wasn't thinking about him at all, really, just wondering what would happen about school. I should have been going back in a week's time, to start my second term with Mr Way and show him the poems I'd written during the holidays. Not many, but enough to prove it wasn't just a craze. I could already see my empty desk in the Croome's Tower study, and then, in a second flash, a plain white hospital room. Everything was pulled out of shape. Even the walls were smeared and dragged and turning into something else, like the swan that was actually a cloud in the Peter Scott painting above my bed. Then there was Mum's voice, billowing through scraps of sleep-mist, and the room started to settle. I had a cage over my leg. Dad would like that, when he came to see me in a little while. He'd think I was being brave.

CHAPTER TWENTY-ONE

The Ashground

Mum called it the London Clink, not the Clinic, and I was a prisoner there for a fortnight. Even though she stayed with friends in town, so she could sit with me every afternoon, she got a new bedroom ready for me at home as well – the little drawing room on the ground floor to the right of the front door, so I wouldn't have to climb stairs. Or maybe she rang Mrs Bunton, and asked her to do it. I wasn't sure, because my brain wouldn't work properly. For the first few days I couldn't see my leg – just the cage – and because it felt close up and far away at the same time, I thought maybe Osmond Clarke had chopped it off by mistake. Then I started to know it was there, and couldn't sleep. By the time I got home, I felt stupid as a plank.

Mrs Bunton said: how could I bear it, having so much time to myself? But there hardly seemed to be any. Mum's friends kept dropping in. The postman brought letters from Sandy, which I took a long time answering, as if we were really chatting. Mr Nash came twice a week – a nervous, dangly man who wore a pale mac whatever the weather, and smelled of mothballs and did physiotherapy. That meant draping a mini-sandbag over my ankle and telling me to hoist my leg: I could, after a fortnight. I always felt worse after his visits, and wondered whether he wasn't 'overdoing it' like mum said, but I looked forward to seeing him. Mr Nash was different from everyone else who came to the house. He voted Labour, and he thought private schools should be abolished, and he'd heard of Wordsworth, and when I played him Bob Dylan's 'All Along the Watchtower', then the Jimi Hendrix version, he said he liked Dylan better which I thought was the right answer, even though it was a close-run thing.

After a month, my leg stopped hurting as much. I loved being able to read for a bit, then doze for a bit, then listen to music for a bit – all without anyone interfering. I loved the ceiling crack like a map of the Thames, and the smell of cold ash from the fireplace in the morning, and the muddle of brown flex under the lamp, where the cat snoozed. Best of all, I heard the life of the house going on round me – feeling part of it but separate. Mrs Bunton stomping after the hoover on the top landing. Mum in the kitchen, clattering away the plates from last night, then turning off the radio and calling Wiggy because she was ready for her ride. Serenade jingling in the stable. Mum knocking on my window with the handle of her crop to say goodbye, then hollow hoof-noises scooping down the tarmac into the lane. And when she came back, the rest of the whole long day doing house things. Deciding what we wanted to eat. Making shopping lists. Wondering how Mr Woodley was doing. Watching mum wheel the telly into my room so we could see the news together. Hour by hour, I sank down to somewhere I'd never been before. The layers of ordinary time, of being-ill time, of not-school time, were all piled above me like the picture of rock formations in my Geography book.

I wasn't out of sight. People were holding off until I felt better – Mr Way especially. He wrote me a few letters saying get well soon and then, when I was ready, he sent me lists of books to read, and ideas for essays to write. He said he didn't want me to fall behind, but that wasn't the whole story. He remembered about poems as well: I'd probably like Thom Gunn, and *The Hawk in the Rain*, and *Comus*, and I could try Shelley. I asked mum to look in Hannay's bookshop next time she went to Braintree, but she came back saying they didn't have a Poetry Section, just a *Complete Shakespeare*, and if I wanted anything I'd have to order it. I made a face, but it just went to show how special poetry was. Anyway, the thing I liked best about being ill wasn't reading, it was talking to mum. The daytimes in between her chores, when she sat in the red chair under the window, with the chestnut taking deep breaths behind her, and we turned things over like people playing with stones in a stream. Or the evenings when we were waiting for dad's car, and the clock slowed down, and the light in my room changed to dim green thanks to the tree. Serenade stood by her branch snorting now and again, and the rabbits bounced round their corner of the field because they'd got bold, now there was nobody taking potshots at them.

I didn't want to admit it, but there was always a wrinkle when dad came home. It was partly because he was tired, and hadn't shaken all the work-wasps out of his head. And partly to do with the way mum and I glued together while he was in London. We weren't ganged up against him; we'd got so used to each other, dad couldn't always understand our jokes or know what we were talking about, and it made him impatient. Drinking his whisky fast, in straight-back gulps. Jiggling his foot more than usual. Asking me what I'd been doing all day, as if I was slacking, not mending. Maybe I was slacking. The more days I spent in bed, the soggier my head felt – and was I inventing it, or could I feel my 'good' knee getting worse, even though I was hardly using it? That meant I'd probably be back in hospital soon, then in bed again for weeks afterwards. What was the point of trying to get better now? I asked Mr Nash, but he shook his greasy black hair over his eyes like a pony. It wasn't his business. When I threw the same question at mum, she made two faces at the same time. One was a frown which showed she was sorry, and didn't want anything to hurt any more; the other was a smile, because it meant we'd have extra time together.

Osmond Clarke couldn't fit me in for a while, so by the end of the spring, when I could walk again with my stick and it would have been holidays anyway, life got back to normal. I still couldn't do any of the stuff I'd been about to give up – such as taking my gun round the field, or following the last few days of hunting. And since dad now left me out of conversations about this kind of thing, I started to feel I'd won all the arguments, without even having to start them. Occasionally I made sure by clutching my knee when I was poling round a corner, and wondering aloud how I'd ever grip a saddle. But I soon realised I didn't need to do that. Dad wasn't bothered because I'd stopped hunting; he wanted to know what was I going to do instead? Write poetry all day?

No one had ever tried to persuade me to go into the brewery, but I liked driving past pubs and looking at the signs, thinking if it said 'Ind Coope' the people inside might know dad's name, because Ind Coope were his employers, now they'd bought up Taylor Walker. And it was fun hearing him tell the story about the brewery in Brackley, where there was a beer-tank the size of a swimming pool: someone had fallen in once and drowned, but nobody noticed until all the beer had been drunk. Apart from that, dad never tried to make his work sound especially interesting. Most of the other people in his building were sharks. There was hardly a chance to get out of his office and talk to publicans, which is what he'd liked best in the old days. 'I'll show you, if you like,' he said, halfway through the holidays when I was more or less well again. 'You can come to London with me one evening, and we'll visit some pubs together, like I used to do.' I looked at mum, the other side of the fireplace. 'Would you enjoy that?' she asked in her surprised voice, which was smaller than usual. 'Sure,' I said, suddenly interested. 'I've got my stick, and we'll be in the car won't we? It'll be fine.' It was the first time dad had asked me to do something like this, and I felt about twenty-five years old.

I took the train to London and met dad in his office in St John Street, up the road from Smithfield. When the taxi drove round the edge of the market before dropping me off, and I saw the meat-porters standing in the shade, still wearing their bloodstained white overalls, I was ashamed. Dad must see this every day, and I knew nothing about it. In fact his whole week was a mystery: he never said much about London, except that the streets were filthy and the people had no manners. Now here it all was: a complete world. The car park outside his office, which was a bomb site left over from the war, and had a Globe-Trotter luggage office on the far side: that explained why dad had given me a Globe-Trotter suitcase for school. And Vera, dad's secretary, who sent him a card at Christmas that made mum click her tongue, like when she was trying to get Serenade over a ditch, but who turned out to be about as sexy as Miss Laing. And dad's huge wooden desk, which had belonged to great-grandpa Andrew, along with the paintings on the wall. They weren't real paintings but coloured sand; it had been dribbled into shapes incredibly carefully, to make a picture of dray horses pulling a cartload of barrels. And dad himself with his black hair shining, taking me down the stairs with his hand on my shoulder and introducing me to everyone. After that, we slid away in the Daimler through back streets which he turned out to know as well as the lanes round Stisted. When we stopped at the first pub, a man leaped out from behind the bar to shake his hand like a friend.

It reminded me of that day when mum and Kit and I had watched dad doing his army training on Salisbury Plain. Dad never showed off about things, but he turned out to be a big man away from home, in the other places he belonged. He wasn't always trying to keep things the same, either, which is what I'd started to think. He'd left the army now, for instance. He'd loved it but he'd given it up, just like I wanted him to think I'd loved hunting and shooting, but had given them up. It's what happened in the grown-up world. Soon he'd see I knew how to cope, even if I did have a walking stick and wrote poetry. In the next pub we went to, for instance, a fight broke out between two drunks by the slot-machine, and it didn't freak me out in the least. If it hadn't been for my stick, I'd probably have helped the barman bundle them out-side into the street. Or that's what I told dad, anyway, when it was nearly eleven and we started driving home along the A11. *Whack, whack, whack*, went the slipstream from the Daimler as it ham-mered against the lamp posts. I was determined to stay awake all the way home, even though I'd also been determined to show dad I could drink a decent amount of beer, and could hardly keep my eyes open.

'You have to understand,' mum said, when she came to wake me next morning, after dad had left for work again; I was having a lie-in because she thought my leg might need a rest. 'Your father was brought up very strictly. You know what grandpa's like. And as for granny Sunbeam . . .' She hung her head and I stared at her, won-dering. After my day with dad on the roof, and now the evening in London, I knew there was even more to him than I'd thought. I might play him some of my records, and see if he liked the Keith Moon drum solo on my Who LP. Mum couldn't be jealous could she? Now I'd had my night out with dad, she wanted me to have one with her. She'd bought tickets for *The Nutcracker*: hadn't she always said she'd liked it, and because I was old enough at last, and reading all these poems . . .? 'It isn't really the sort of thing dad enjoys,' she said, and patted me on the hand. I told her we ought to be able to do different things together, and she looked at me with her eyes narrowed, as though that was the most grown-up thing I'd ever said.

I watched *The Nutcracker* with my shoulders sloped and my neck straight, so I could feel empty and concentrated at the same time. I'd tried it when I was being confirmed, in case the spirit of God wanted to rush in, and even though it hadn't worked then, it seemed right for now. When I looked across the huge dizzy space of the Festival Hall, it was like having a dream of falling. The wooden cliff-walls. The conductor waving his arms about and nobody thinking it was funny. And the dancers – real people, with sweat on their faces, grunting when they took off and landed. I wanted to squeeze mum's arm, but that was the sort of thing boys did to girls. So we sat there not moving until it was over, and the applause burst like a star exploding. Then we went to Hatchard's, where we got the *Collected Poems* of Siegfried Sassoon, and also his *Memoirs of a Foxhunting Man*, because mum said that even if I wasn't going to follow hounds or do that sort of thing again, I shouldn't forget it: it was part of my inheritance.

'My childhood was a queer and not altogether happy one. Circumstances conspired to make me shy and solitary.' I knew from the moment I started the *Memoirs* that it was going to be the best book I'd read: the mixture of country things and family things, the little boy snug in his life but outside it at the same time, and the war on the horizon, which was going to change everything and make it impossible for Sassoon to know where he fitted in. It was a story with grass-seed on some pages, and smears of plough on others, and made me think of mum every time I opened it, because she'd written 'Andrew, with love from his mother' on the blank page at the front. That showed how good she thought it was. She never usually said 'mother'. When I stared at her writing – the blue ink with the needle-eye hole in the upright of the 'h' – I realised only two or three people had given me a book before. And then, because I liked it so much, she gave me a record as well – Beethoven's *Pathétique*, played by Julius Katchen. I listened to it in the evenings, before dad got home, while mum was cooking sup-per in the kitchen with Kit, and turned it up loud enough for her to hear. 'I love this bit,' she called along the hall, whenever the music slowed down. So did I. It had something to do with the breeze flipping over the chestnut leaves outside my window, show-ing they were already brown underneath.

By the end of the holidays, mum and I were stuck together more tightly than ever – but she seemed just as keen for me to get out and meet people. That's how I found Jane: because there was a party nearby, and I didn't want to go because I knew my legs would hurt, but mum said I had to. When I came back and told her Jane was pretty, and lived on the marshes near Maldon, and I wanted to see her again, she said 'Oh good' surprisingly quickly. So Jane and I did meet a few times, and after a while we decided we were boyfriend and girlfriend even though we hadn't kissed properly. The one time we tried, when we were walking on the marshes, Kit jumped out of a bramble bush and put us off. I was annoyed because I wanted to kiss her – she was beautiful, like a Roman coin – but at the same time it was a relief. I didn't want to think much about girls. When I told Sandy, he wrote back and said I'd certain-ly want to think about them when I'd found the right one.

He was probably right, but I couldn't do anything about it. Mum and I had been back to Osmond Clarke, and he'd looked at my second knee. It had got worse, and he'd better do the operation soon. That meant the London Clink again, and missing most of the winter term, and more letters from Mr Way with ideas for reading and essays, then back to school properly in the spring. Mum and I walked down the red carpet and out into Harley Street much more slowly than last time. There was no adventure about being ill any more; I knew exactly what to expect. Painful weeks with the cage over my leg. Mr Nash and his mini-sandbag. Visits from Mrs Hill. The fug of the little drawing room, and the coals dying in the grate when mum and dad eventually turned off the bedside light and tramped upstairs past my head. I slid my hand through mum's arm, and we headed towards the Marylebone Road, looking for a taxi to Liverpool Street. The first knee had got me out of a lot of things, but the second night hurt more and I was being a nuisance. I told mum I was sorry, but she was the one who started crying while we stood on the pavement. 'I didn't cook you properly when I was carrying you,' she said, trying to make it a joke. It didn't sound like a joke to me, it sounded like nonsense, and I told her so when a taxi stopped at last, and I helped her into the back.

I was wrong; nothing was the same second time round. I didn't spend so much time in the Clink, or with Mr Nash, because my body had learned how to get better quickly. Mr Way sent me new books to read, including the poems of Alexander Pope, which looked too long but turned out to be wonderful, especially after I'd cut out Aubrey Beardsley's illustrations to 'The Rape of the Lock' and stuck them on my cupboard door. 'Is that what I think it is?' Mrs Hill wanted to know, going beetroot as she bent to look at one of the sylphs. The real difference was mum, though. Just as I was starting to hoist the mini-sandbag, and thinking I'd be ready for school halfway through the Spring term, she got glandular fever again. I hauled myself upstairs to her bedroom after the doctor had gone, and found dad standing at the end of the bed. He had his thumbs tucked inside his fingers, which showed how upset he was. 'It's quite wrong,' he said, in a big voice which hunted off through the room looking for something to blame. 'People can't get glandular fever twice. The doctor said so himself.' Then he shook his head at mum, and pulled his lips into a straight line. Now I was looking at her properly, her face did look yellow against the white pillow. 'We'll have to get some help,' dad was saying. 'You can't do anything, darling, and neither can you, Andrew. But we've got to keep the place ticking over.' 'There's Mrs Bunton,' I said, without thinking properly. 'Mrs Bunton!' dad exploded, and to cover my mistake I swung forward and kissed mum on the forehead. Her skin smelled of talc, but there was something underneath which was sour and hot and curled up like a cat. It must have been the fever.

It meant I couldn't be an invalid any more – so while mum lay in bed upstairs, and the yellow flushed through her like dye in a river, I cranked away at my leg-exercises, and caught up with Mr Way's essays. Last winter, home had been like a secret, which mum and I had kept to ourselves. Now it was like a mouse's nest with the roof torn off. We had Deborah to help shop and cook – she was the daughter of a friend, and everyone liked her, but she was always *there*. And neighbours kept hallooing in and out of the front door. Or Mrs Bunton bounced round the house in a panic, thumping the hoover into the furniture. Or Jane rang up, and sometimes came round to sit with me, then mum, then me again. I watched the spring sunlight stretching across the fireplace in my bedroom and felt guilty. My knees weren't my fault, but I should have been at school. I was jealous when Sandy's letters arrived. I wondered what else Mr Way would have told me to read, if I'd been snapping at his heels. When dad decided that because there was so little spring term left, I might as well put off going back to school until the summer, I looked at the carpet between my knees and realised guilty wasn't quite right. It was more like plain miserable. 'Oh, what's the point, dad?' I said. 'I've been away so long I'll never catch up.' Dad leaned forward. 'But old Way thinks your work's fine,' he said. 'He's not worried at all.' I kept staring downwards, not meeting dad's eye, and eventually he went next door and got a drink. It was just like mum said. We didn't like scenes.

Mum stayed the same dingy yellow for weeks, as though she'd been inefficiently smoked. Then for no special reason, and with no warning, she was suddenly better: up and about, wearing her light blue jersey with the roll neck, and her cement-coloured trousers with the zip on the side, which was how she'd looked last winter only now she was out of date. I was out of date too, in my navy jumper with the spotty green handkerchief round my neck. I told her that perhaps we'd been unconscious for years, like Sleeping

Beauty, and she looked at me with her eyes half-shut, so I couldn't tell whether she thought that was funny. But it made me think. The poems I'd been writing in the last few weeks: they weren't breathing real air. I went to the bathroom, and looked at myself carefully in the mirror, as though I might find I'd sprouted a beard, or grown hair down to my shoulders like Tennyson. What I saw was chubby and pasty, with perfectly normal hair except it was brushed too carefully. I thought if dad didn't know me, and passed me in the lane, he'd say I looked like one of those people who needed a good kick up the arse.

'It's girlie,' Kit said, 'the stuff you and mum do together.' I could see him through the kitchen window, digging another hole with Wiggy by the greenhouse, while mum sat me down at the table and said it was high time I knew how to cook a few basics. 'For later,' she said vaguely, and set about showing me how to take the skin off coley, or jam beef cubes through the mincer, or wash cabbages and keep an eye out for slugs in the plughole afterwards. We never cooked anything fancy, apart from chicken-liver pâté, which was my favourite starter, and sometimes mum turned away with her hand over her mouth because the thought of eating anything made her feel sick. Then there was shopping – in Coggeshall, on Thursdays, because that was the day mum had her hair done, and I could get everything we needed, while she disappeared into Leslie's Salon. Mum said Leslie was queer as a coot, and told me not to come into the Salon because 'he'll eat you alive'. But somehow I always ended up seeing him after all. I'd usually had a chat with Stephen by this time – Stephen who ran the antique shop over the road – so Leslie didn't seem anything out of the ordinary with his bright red shirt and carrot-coloured hair. Anyway, he was funny, and the day I told him I was keen on Wilfred Owen he rushed across to Stephen's shop and came back with a second-hand copy of Sassoon's *Rhymed Ruminations*. When we got home mum said it showed what a nice person he was, but dad rolled his eyes. He was always in a bad mood on Thursdays, because although mum liked having her hair done, she left the salon looking as though there'd been a disaster. It was the dryer, which she sat underneath like an astronaut waiting for blast-off. After a day, when she was messier and prettier again, dad cheered up.

I needed to talk more about what I was reading and writing. At school there'd have been Sandy and Mr Way. But at home? Mum worked out what I was feeling, and brought it up when we were sitting in the drawing room, waiting for the evening news. She was lying back in her green chair, resting her head on a cushion she'd covered with one of her flower-tapestries. 'Do you remember bringing your stories into the bedroom at Little Brewers?' she asked. I did, but I'd forgotten. Now I could even see the writing book in my mind's eye – the dark blue cover and the red spine. 'Absolutely,' I said, and went on thinking. Perhaps writing was in my blood after all? 'I'm not an expert or anything,' mum went on, 'but you can always talk to me, you know. You did before, except they were stories of course.' I smiled. Sometimes, when she was off guard like this, she sounded so tired it made me think there was something wrong with her deep down. Something far worse than glandular fever. Her face was hollow as a corpse. Then I looked again, and she was OK – her mouth closed and her eyes wide. 'So shall we do that?' she said, sitting up straight because the news was starting. 'You can tell me what you're reading, and show me what you're writing, and we can have a plan – I can't think why we haven't done it before.' This time I laughed properly. 'I've been ill, mum,' I said. 'We both have.' She nodded without answering, because Richard Baker was already speaking.

We decided to have a routine. At the end of the week, I copied out everything I'd written in the last few days, gave it to her, and we talked about it on Monday after dad had gone to work. There were two or three poems usually, but because they were still word-explosions, and I didn't understand them myself, it was difficult to answer mum's questions. The parts she liked best were scenes she recognised: the pond behind the veg patch, or the view across the field in the evening, or the poem I wrote about Beauty, who'd been dead for a few years now, but still wriggled through our talk as if she was alive. Sometimes mum said she wished I'd write in the old-fashioned way, meaning sonnets, but I told her modern poets didn't do them any more, then wondered if that was true: hadn't I seen a sonnet by Seamus Heaney? After a while we changed tack, and talked about what I'd been reading. Not whole books, but pages I chose, such as the letter from Rupert Brooke to Ben Keeling where he said he wanted to look 'at people and things as themselves – neither as useful nor moral nor ugly nor anything else, but just as being'. I was impressed by that, and so was mum; she'd given me Brooke's letters, for my last birthday. 'You know we've got his poetry in the whirligig?' she said. 'Whose?' 'Rupert Brooke's,' she said – and when I went to the corner of the drawing room there it was: a fat blue leather book, which it turned out had once belonged to her father George Victor. I felt a fool, even if it had been hidden among the Iris Murdochs and the C. P. Snows. 'So there is a book of poems in the house!' I said, calling across the room more loudly than I meant. 'Five actually,' said mum, fiddling one of her Oliviers from the packet on the arm of her chair, and sticking it in her mouth with a little stab. 'I counted them the other day. I think that's above the national average. There's an anthology called *Other Men's Flowers*, and great-grandpa's Tennyson, and the Brooke of course, and John Betjeman, and Francis Thompson. I won him as a school prize. You should try – you might enjoy it.' Then she set off into 'The Hound of Heaven', and our sort-of-lesson was over for the day:

> I fled Him, down the nights and down the days;
> I fled Him, down the arches of the years;
> I fled Him, down the labyrinthine ways
> Of my own mind; and in the mist of tears
> I hid from Him, and under running laughter.

We had our chats indoors, so it was more like school. But now summer was starting, I did most of my reading and writing outdoors. In the garden first, lying on one of the folding sun-beds dad kept in the garage, which had spiders living in their legs. As the metal heated up, the spiders escaped and crawled over my hands: pale sandy brown and light as a tickle. I brushed them off and went back to the poems of Andrew Marvell, which I'd bought second-hand in Stephen's shop. While I was reading his poems about gardens, I gazed down the lawn towards mum's herbaceous border and saw the words zoom off the white page like flies, vanishing into the laurel bush. It made me wonder how much I was understanding, if words kept turning into things. Or *how* I was understanding, at least. Mr Way would have to explain. We'd talk about that when school started again, along with all the other questions about poems that mum couldn't answer, which I had on a list in my bedroom.

Vanishing across the field towards the Ashground was even better than reading in the garden. The name made my head swim, it was so like the song Rhubarb had sung when I left Maidwell: 'The Ashgrove'. *Down yonder green valley where streamlets meander, when twilight is fading, I pensively roam.* It wasn't twilight, and I wasn't especially pensive, or not like the man in the song anyway, because I wasn't missing *my dear one, the joy of my heart.* On the other hand, bluebells really had been growing in the wood a few weeks ago, and there still was a blackbird singing. I stopped at the entrance, which was a huge shaggy doorway that must have been made by a tractor, and stared at the brown path ahead. If I walked all the way, and came out by the sugar beet clump, I'd be close to the Hall, wondering whether to keep going past the House of Love and the old water garden, then home through the village. But that was all the past, and I'd come here for me. The Ashground was my place – where I could read and write and doze and be invisible.

I'd got Jenny with me, the Norfolk terrier we'd bought as a puppy after Beauty died. She was still tiny, like a furry wind-up bug, and although everyone knew she belonged to mum, she liked me best because I was the one who spent most time lying down. It meant Jenny could hop onto my stomach and be a book-rest. Mum said that made her lazy, but Jenny liked walks, and to prove it she stood by the back door and whined whenever she saw me carrying my writing book. Crossing the field she stayed close, bobbing through the grass tufts like a cork in a stream, but now we were at the Ashground, where the ground was smooth because it was covered in last year's dead leaves, she scooted off sideways to mind her own business. There she was now, pretending she'd seen a rabbit, while I set off down the brown path and the trees closed round me at last.

Ash, mainly – that's why it was called the Ashground – and though the name sounded old, most of the trees were young: pale grey trunks wavering like plant stems underwater, and thin leaves overhead. Maybe there'd always been an ash wood here, and the owner cut them down every so often, then replanted. Where the path sloped towards the centre, I came to a deep hollow that felt as ancient as Stonehenge. An uprooted tree guarded one side, dribbling dry earth and ivy. Had a charcoal burner worked here once? My hand tightened round my writing book, as I imagined him looking like a cross between Robinson Crusoe and one of Robin Hood's Merry Men. Either of those would do. This feeling of age got even stronger when I stepped forward a few paces and the path spilled into a glade. These were the tallest trees in the wood, which meant they'd probably been here for ages: their top branches met in a cathedral arch, and light squeezed through like chips of stained glass.

I veered right, where the trees shrank again, and the ground dipped into a little valley. The rumpling here was tyre tracks left by the tractors last time they smashed through, lopping off branches and hauling out stumps. By now most of the damage was softened – bright moss had swarmed everywhere, smothering the wobbly flints and clay-lumps. This is where the bluebells grew best, bursting through in a torrent every April, then dying back and leaving their juicy leaves shining like weed. They squeaked when I stepped onto them, as though they had voices. Stranger still was the faint turquoise glow that stayed after the flowers had gone. And the ash trunks beating with a faint pulse. And the leaves taking hold of one another, then darkening above me.

I wanted to reach the opposite side of the valley, where I was furthest from the path and could see anyone coming before they saw me. Not that anyone ever did come this way – apart from the tramp of course. Sapling branches slashed at my legs as I crossed the dry bed of the stream in the valley bottom, climbed a few paces, and stretched out on a bed of dry moss. I rolled sideways and pulled a pencil from my pocket, then opened my writing book. I was waiting for the same feeling I had in the garden, when I saw poems float off my page and escape down the lawn. Now I needed words to come from the branches, and the seedcases which spiralled down onto my book. I prodded a curl of leaf debris with the end of my pencil, then breathed out heavily and watched it lift off my page and disappear. It was no good. I'd have to walk a little further, then come back and try again. Everything would still be here. I closed my book silently, to show myself how patient I could be, and stood up. Where had Jenny got to? There she was, bounding down towards the dry stream because she knew it was always like this.

I stamped over the bluebell-floor, then back through the skinny trees and onto the main path. It meant pressing into the wood before doubling back, but the tramp's car was always worth seeing. A Ford Cortina someone had burned and abandoned years ago, before the trees grew so close together. Everything that could have been taken from the wreck was long gone – the tyres, the electrics, the dials – but not the windows and not the seats. Dad said it was an eyesore and he was right. The charred metal was disgusting, with its rusty spurs and spikes, and its sour stink of pee. Worse still was thinking what might have been wrong with the man who left it here, his lights lurching among the tree trunks and his wheels churning in the leaf mould. Had he been on the run from someone? Was he a criminal hiding the evidence? My skin tightened as I picked the brambles apart, and peered inside the car.

The tramp had been here, maybe even yesterday. The sweet wrappers were still shiny, and the empty Kia-Ora bottle smelled faintly of whisky. Who was he? Mum said the old fellow with the floppy trench coat we sometimes saw on the top road, but that was too easy. He was more likely someone we never saw. Someone who opened this battered door after dark, when everyone else was asleep, sat on this orange seat behind this bony steering wheel, munched his chocolate and drank his drink, then gazed ahead through the the windscreen. Someone who did by night what I did by day. Looked at the moonlit pillars of the ash trees, and the leaf-clouds rustling above them. Looked, and waited for the Ashground to strain at its moorings in the earth, then felt them break as the air in front of him lifted and opened, before he began his slow plunge forward into tomorrow's daylight.

CHAPTER TWENTY-TWO

Shut-Eye

It's the day after the accident, and dad hasn't come home yet. Kit and I talk to him, though – he rings after lunch, while Kit and I are helping granny and Ruby in the kitchen. Kit goes to listen in the sitting room, while I take the extension upstairs, perched on mum's side of the bed. The news is the same: mum hasn't come round after the operation, but dad keeps talking in case she can hear. Us, the dogs, Serenade, friends, the weather, Mr Woodley – anything he can think of. Last night he slept in a chair they brought from the nurses' coffee room. 'Did you get any shut-eye?' I ask him. 'Not much,' he says, using the I'm-not-complaining voice which makes me think of him in the war, hiding under hedges on his way through France. Does he think mum's getting better? Long gaps open between his answers, and sometimes between the words as well, when I listen to the air trampolining along the line between us. Mum might die any minute. She might even be dead by the time he goes back to her room.

Kit and I put down our phones at the same time, so my receiver gives a weird double tingle. I like thinking we're bound together at home, helping dad. All the same, I stay on the bed alone for a moment longer, and listen to Kit padding through the hall below, into the kitchen. There's the burble of him giving granny and Ruby the latest, and the scratch-scratch of the dogs' feet across the lino. The dogs know something bad has happened, and are creeping about the house as though we're going to thump them. Hangdog, that's the word. Then Kit runs the tap, and the pipe behind the sink gives its wobbly groan. 'Those bloody plumbers,' I hear mum saying. 'They never got it right.' Her voice reminds me I mustn't look round the bedroom. Not at her dressing table. Not at the photographs under the glass lid. Not at the hanging-cupboards with her clothes waiting for her to come back. Not at her book on the bedside table: *Summoned by Bells*, by John Betjeman. She can't understand why I don't want to read it. It's poetry, isn't it? 'Not my kind of thing, mum.' So stupid. Now I'll take it into the hospital and go through it aloud with her. That'll make up for being a moron.

I stretch forward, meaning to take hold of the book carefully so I don't lose mum's place, then the pipe noise shuts off in the kitchen and I lose track. I should be downstairs with Kit; he'll wonder where I've got to. But the silence in the bedroom is too heavy. The silence and mum's lemon smell. Without thinking why, I slither off the bed onto my knees, fold my arms on the counterpane, and lay my head on my hands. 'If you're there, God, make mum get better.' The words crawl out of my mouth and lie among the green cotton-tufts like worms. Disgusting. I never pray. But I am praying, even though I don't know what I'm going to say next, and can only think about the counterpane, how if I pull it back there'll be the eiderdown underneath with its paisley swirls, and below that the yellow top-blanket, and below that the sheets mum slept in. The dent of her head might still be on the pillow. 'If you make her well again, I promise to do something with my life.' Ridiculous! My eyes snap open, so the counterpane ridges surge at me in waves, then I scramble to my feet. What does 'something' mean? Or 'do', come to that? It's bollocks. I run my hand quickly backwards and forward over the bed, as if I'm brushing away a spillage of sugar.

Dad rings again after six, like he promised. When he's done, Kit and I sit in front of the telly and watch the headlines. The news is still Christmassy – shopping bonanzas and a pile-up on the M1 and a missing child. Now I'm thinking about Reginald Bosanquet, the newsreader. Is he sloshed? Mum says he looks like a boozer, with his squashed red face. What do I look like, listening? Drunk too, I expect – my mouth's hanging open. And what about granny? She's taken over mum's green chair, stretching out her legs on the long stool. The way her eyes swim across the ceiling, goggle at the telly for a moment, and slide off sideways: it's difficult to know if she even realises what's happened.

Ruby's under the other lamp in dad's chair, so she can see to do her knitting. *Clock click clock*: it's a bed-jacket she's started, pale blue, and the weave is very loose, like soft chain mail. Every now and again she presses it flat across her lap with one hand, and counts under her breath. What if mum never wears it? I glance sideways at Kit, next to me on the sofa. He's staring at his hands – the only one who isn't pretending. Telly isn't interesting. News isn't interesting. Knitting isn't interesting. Being awake isn't interesting. 'Come on,' I whisper. 'Upstairs.' He nods without looking at me.

Some time before morning, the wind swings round to the west. I feel it as soon as I wake up; the air's wetter, and when I push open my red curtains, the last snow has melted. Yesterday there were dabs and squiggles on the branch-ends of the chestnut. Now they're soggy-looking and the grass below is clear. I could go for a walk later, but I won't: there might be an emergency, and I have to be here in case. It's the worst thing, this waiting. In limbo, mum would say. If she were dead already we'd be making plans, looking forward and backwards. Now we're just stuck. Stuck, while time crawls on towards the end of the year. Two more days, then good-bye 1969.

Dad calls after breakfast, and says he won't ring again until six this evening. Kit and I decide we'll go for a walk after all, as soon as we've seen to the ponies. They're like the dogs. They know something's wrong, and stand quietly against the side wall while we scrape their wet bedding off the stable floor. In the end, Wiggy can't resist making a dash for a bobble of dung, but Kit growls at her and she drops it immediately, with a hacking noise in the back of her throat to show she never meant to take it in the first place. Then we set off down the garden, past mum's border and under the ash tree, alongside the greenhouse and the veg garden, through the fence into the bottom half of the field. 'Listen to the moorhens,' I say, when two of them clatter across the pond on the far side of the garden wall. 'Look at that,' when we find a new rabbit trail. Kit doesn't answer, chewing his thumbnail as he walks. He knows I'm only trying to cheer him up, but when Jenny gets on the scent of one of the rabbits and starts her cork-in-a-millstream rush through the grass, he laughs. 'Stupid girl,' he says and puts on a burst of speed. By the time I catch up, he's looking back at the house with his hands in his pockets, like a man inspecting somewhere he might want to buy.

'What do you think's going to happen?' he says. Now we've stopped walking, I realise the day's colder than I thought. Stringy feathers of snow lie in the bottom of the bomb-crater dip, and the trees are squeaking in the Ashground behind us – it's two of the old tall ones, with their top branches mashed together, so they rub when the wind blows. 'What do you mean?' I ask. 'I'm sure they're doing everything they can. The doctors . . .' Kit knows all this, we've said it dozens of times before. 'I don't mean that,' he says. 'I mean what's going to happen *here*? Even if mum gets better, we can't go back to how it was.' He pauses, and I turn round so we're looking at the house together. A plover swerves up from the field by the garden railing – I'm surprised we haven't disturbed it already, but they sit very tight, plovers. Plovers. Lapwings. Peewits. Three names for the same bird. And when the females are nesting, they pretend to be wounded, and flop down a long way away from their young, to lead predators away. I think of telling Kit this, but he's still looking at the house. So tidy! Like a child's drawing. Boxy white, with the laurel bush in a dark cloud to the left, and smoke climbing straight up from the sitting-room chimney. 'Mum *will* get better,' I say. Kit nods once, before setting off back. We keep close to the hedge, then slip through the yard door in case granny hears us and wants to talk.

Kit wonders whether I'd like to spend some time in my room alone, and when I say no he pulls a face. 'I thought you might want to write something,' he tells me. He means to be kind, but it makes me feel stupid – as though I might be thinking of myself, not about mum. 'I'm going to keep everything that's happened,' I say, remembering what I told myself yesterday. 'What, you mean the last couple of days?' Kit asks. 'No, I'm going to keep *everything*. The whole of the past, locked up inside my head. Just as it was.' 'You can't do that,' Kit says, sucking in his bottom lip to show he's concentrating. 'Whatever happens next will interfere with it. And anyway, you'll want to understand it. That'll change it all.' 'I know,' I tell him. 'I don't mean I won't think about it – I expect I'll think about it for ever. I just mean I'll keep it safe inside me as well. Separate.' Kit nods, slowly. 'And write it down eventually?' 'Perhaps,' I say. 'But not now. Now I want to be with you.'

That's how we get through the rest of the day. The little sitting room, the one I used as a bedroom when my knees were bad: it's our playroom now, and too small for granny and Ruby to sit with us. We listen to records with the volume low – *Music from Big Pink*. When Kit says we should sort out the toy cupboard, I give him a hand. He crouches inside, so his head and shoulders disappear, and passes out my old army toys and bits from the train track at Little Brewers. The rocket launcher we could never get to fire, not even when dad and Uncle Rob helped. The troop carrier with most of the green paint missing, because this was the one I used to scoot off the bottom step of the hall stairs. The grey plastic railway bridge with the Michelin Tyre advert, and Wiggy's chew-marks up one side. 'More than I thought,' Kit says, when we've set them in rows on the carpet. It's taken half an hour to fish them out, and now it'll take another half an hour to put them back. That's the main thing.

At six, when we're expecting the phone to ring, there's a long crunch of wheels outside the front door. Kit and I are in the sitting room. We've been watching *The Magic Roundabout* – it's miles too young for us, but mum thought Dougal the furry dog looked like Jenny and that made us like it. Now here's the news: no more snow, though it'll stay cold. As the car stops, Kit and I look at each other with our eyes narrowed. It'll be Mrs Hill, checking to see if we're OK. We don't want that. We turn off the telly, click on the Christmas tree lights, and reach the hall in single file. The front door has swung completely open, and no one's there. Only the white frame, then the black air, then the ghosts of the railing and the chestnut tree. Did we invent the sound of the car? We stop still, and I can hear the phone creak in its cradle by mum's desk, getting ready for dad's voice.

But here is dad. He must have parked the Daimler in the garage round the corner, come to the front door and opened it, then gone back to collect something he'd forgotten. The something is in his hand – a plastic Marks and Sparks bag. And it's full, with a stiff tongue flopping between the handles. Mum's stock. That's what she was wearing. It was round her neck when she stood in my bedroom, when she drove me to the bus stop, when she leaned forward in the Hillman and waved goodbye. Then I look at dad. He's framed in the doorway like a portrait, but we've forgotten to turn on the hall light, so everything about him is grey. Hair, overcoat, suit trousers, shoes. Even the plastic bag is grainy, the colour of old snow. He hasn't seen us yet, that's why he's still wiping his feet on the mat, bent forward so his face is hidden. And it's his face I want to see, because everything he knows will be written there. When he glances up at last, in the second before he sees us watching, I think I've made a mistake. It isn't dad after all. It's someone who looks very like him, a man whose skin has come loose from his skull and is about to drop clean away.

Now he's turning over his right shoe, wiping along the outside edge of the sole: his black brogue shoe, with the shine he's kept in spite of everything. In the exact moment I open my mouth to speak, he looks up and flinches, as though we've chucked him a ball to catch in the dark. 'Hello, you two,' he says. 'I wondered who you were, standing there.' What do we do next? Three days ago, in the car park at the Swan with mum, I had a moment's fangle, not knowing whether to kiss her goodbye. It's different with dad. I can't remember kissing him since I was little, in the back bedroom at Little Brewers, when he tickled me with his Desperate Dan bristles. I move slowly forward, in step with Kit, but I needn't have worried. Dad's seen all this coming and made a plan, that's why he's doing everything slowly. He puts down the plastic bag, which sags open further, and shows mum's waistcoat along with the stock. Then he stretches his two arms round our shoulders. Then he pulls us against his chest so we can rest there for a moment. Then he leans his chin on our heads in turn. The cigarettes and trains are in his overcoat, and a new bitter smell I don't recognise.

After we've pulled apart, dad hangs his overcoat on its peg by the downstairs loo and goes through to granny and Ruby in the kitchen; they're getting a stew ready for supper. Five minutes later, he comes into the sitting room holding a glass of whisky, and we're ready for him. We've got a beer each, and we've lit the fire and drawn the curtains, and now we're sitting on the sofa with the Christmas-tree lights behind us. When the door swings open and bangs against the chair behind, where no one ever sits, it's only Wiggy coming to collapse in front of the fire. Dad says: 'When are you going to learn to close it, you great lump?' He always does that.

Dad stands with his back to the flames and pokes Wiggy with his toe – hard enough to leave a ruffled V in her coat. She's something that went wrong in his life: mum bought her as a gun dog, and she turned out to be too fat. Dad complains about it sometimes, but it's not serious. All the same, it makes me remember his other difficult things. His squashed finger and his bitten-off tongue. Grandpa. The war. Changes at the brewery. Granny Sunbeam dying in the sea, and dad having to identify the body when it washed up a week later – almost unrecognisable, mum said. Now mum. Most people would decide they were unlucky, but dad's never done that. He tightens his jaw and keeps going. I stare into my beer and wait for him to start.

I already know everything he's going to say. How the accident happened, what it's like in the hospital, how we must be patient. But dad's decided to go through it again from the beginning. It helps, listening to his voice hesitating then pressing on, watching him swirl the whisky in his glass and sometimes turn round to hoof a lump of coal safely onto the back of the fire. Mum's still unconscious, he says, but sometimes he thinks she can hear him talking, because her eyes move from side to side. He can see them, rolling under her eyelids. And the doctors are doing everything they can. The nurses are marvellous – one of them has a sister who lives in the village, and it turns out mum took this woman some flowers from the garden once, when she was ill. 'When can we see her?' says Kit suddenly. Dad frowns, then looks towards me as though he wants me to explain. I can't help him, because it's my question as well. I've been too caught up with thinking about him.

The crumples in his trousers have completely demolished the creases. He must have slept with his knees bent, in that chair beside mum's bed.

Dad goes to the curtains, tweaks them apart, and pushes his head through to see into the field outside. He's a science fiction man, being sucked from one dimension to another. Except his left hand is clenching and unclenching in the way it always does, and the thumbnail is scratching the material – what did mum say it was called? Not satin, but smooth like that. And shiny, so the dragons in the pattern shimmer against their green background. Brushed silk, that's right. Then dad turns round and comes back to the fire; he's been crying. 'I'm not sure about seeing her,' he says. 'The thing is, mum's been very knocked about.' 'We know about her hair,' says Kit. 'Ruby told us.' Dad swallows and peers into his drink again. 'It's not just that,' he says. 'It's the bruising. A lot of the bruises are coming out now, so she looks worse than she did to start with.' 'We don't mind,' says Kit. 'No, we don't,' I add quickly; 'She's still mum'. Then dad makes me feel I've been slapped on the back of my head. 'Not really,' he says. 'She's not mum at the moment. Not any more.'

Eventually dad tells us we can see her in a couple of days. That's better than we thought, so Kit and I lean back into the sofa and take a mouthful of beer. But when dad goes on again, I realise he can't have understood what this means – how we need all the time between now and then to think and get ready. 'We've got to keep ticking over,' he says in his soldier's voice. 'Mum would want us to do that.' Dad stops again, and swallows hard. 'I want you to see your friends like normal,' he says eventually. 'And I want us all to go to the Butlers' party tomorrow night.' Kit and I lean sideways as though we're tobogganing round a corner. I'd forgotten about this – we both had. The Butlers live ten minutes up the lane, and they asked us weeks ago. They always do, at Christmas time – us and a dozen other friends, and usually it's fun. Now it's impossible. We'll have to wish people a happy new year. They'll have to wish us one. 'I know it'll be difficult,' dad's saying. 'But we can't hide away and stop living, mum would hate that.' 'The Butlers would understand

...' I say. 'It's not about the Butlers,' dad tells me sharply. 'It's about us. It's for us.' I can't answer that, and neither can Kit. 'Great, then,' dad says, with a smile to show we agree. 'Dinner jackets I'm afraid, but I expect they're clean, aren't they? Anyway, you're a dab hand with the iron Andrew. You can sort something out.' 'Sure dad,' I say, and watch him finish his whisky in a gulp. Then it's time for supper.

The hospital rings during the night but I don't hear the phone. The doctor thinks mum's taken a turn for the worse, and dad ought to know. Should he drive in straight away? No, they'll ring again if it looks really bad; he needs his sleep. An hour later they do ring again, to say she's better. 'Funny way to give you a good night's sleep,' I tell him at breakfast. 'Funny way to end the year,' he says, then gets ready to leave the house again. When I go upstairs to help him pack more things for mum, I see he's already made the bed, smoothing and folding the corner like an expert, and plonked mum's little white zip-up suitcase on top. It makes me think of him as a soldier again, at camp on Salisbury Plain. He used to share his hut with a man who had only one eye, and when this man took out his false eye at night he sometimes dropped it, so it rolled across the floorboards like a marble. 'What happened then?' Kit and I used to ask, though we knew the answer. 'He went grubbing around for it,' dad said, 'and when he'd found it, he popped it in his mouth, gave it a good suck, then stuck it back in his eye. Of course.'

Dad's forgotten to pull up the coverlet, so the case sinks into the eiderdown as it fills with mum's things. The yellow and the green nightie from the top drawer in her cupboard. The lumpy shawl she wore the last time she had glandular fever – Ruby knitted that. Her blue-backed hairbrushes and the handy mirror from her dressing table. And a photograph too – one of us all together on the beach at Mersea. It was so cold that day, Kit wouldn't swim unless he was allowed to wear his shirt, and Mr Round's hat. There he is, sitting under the concrete breakwater, looking like a mut in a cartoon. Dad turns him face-down on the nighties, and closes the lid. A minute later, we're waving him off from the front step. The exhaust-plume wanders after the car, lifting its hands, but disintegrates before it reaches the gate.

When dad gets home again at six, there's nothing new to report – though we collect in the sitting room as though he's going to make a big announcement. Mum has been asleep all day. He's kept talking to her, but she never reacts. I want to say that doesn't sound like sleep to me, but as I try out the words in my head, they sound angry – and I'm too tired to feel angry now. I've been shrinking like a balloon all day. Is it selfish? That's what I wonder, after we've trailed upstairs to change for the Butlers' party. I'm in my bedroom, gazing between the open curtains into the chestnut branches. I should have spent the day belting round the house helping Ruby. Or thinking about mum as fiercely as I could, to keep her alive. All I've wanted to do is sleep, like on a boring journey, getting the miles done, so when I wake up I'll be in a new place with the travelling behind me.

We drive to the Butlers in silence, me in the front beside dad, Kit leaning forward in the middle of the back seat. This is the first time I've left home since the accident, and as the headlights prowl along the hedges, then suddenly telescope along an empty track, I see everything has taken a step back from me. I remember the names of the trees, and where the puddles come, and how long it takes to get from this flint cottage to this broken gate, but nothing's mine any more. It's the same when we reach the Butlers, only worse. Mr Round, with his boxer's face and natty velvet smoking jacket: I've known him all my life, but feel I've never met him before. Or Mrs Round, with her jittery laugh and mud under her painted nails. The questions are what I expect, though. How are we managing? Is granny driving us mad? As we go through to eat, Mrs Hill puts her chubby hand on dad's arm. She wants to hear something nobody else knows, but dad is staring into the fire. There's nothing he hasn't said already.

It's pheasant, which I usually like. Tonight it makes me feel sick: the sweaty yellow fat between the skin and the meat, and the fiddly bones in the legs. Never give them to the dogs, mum says: they'll get stuck in their throats. Nobody minds, though. They probably think I'm being brave, coming at all, and I want to tell them it's got nothing to do with bravery. When supper ends, things gets more complicated. Mr and Mrs Butler clear the dining table and spread out the green baize cloth for roulette; the grown-ups will play until it's time for Andy Stewart and Big Ben, while the children go upstairs for Murder in the Dark. 'Do whichever you like,' Mrs Butler whispers in my ear, and I remember I like her; she gave me Bullfinch's *Mythology* when I was having my knees done. I glance across the table at dad, who's still talking to Mrs Hill. He's being polite, smiling and nodding, but I can tell he's hating it because the muscle in his jaw is making its rabbity chew-shape. When he looks across at me and winks, I wink back: that's the sort of thing a friend would do. Then I give him a smile as well, and tell Mrs Butler I'll stay put and watch the roulette.

But first I need a pee. Someone's using the downstairs loo, so I trot upstairs – and when I reach the top landing the lights suddenly switch off. Murder's about to start. I know how it works. Everyone draws lots to choose the murderer, but that person doesn't say it's them, and when the lights go out, they tiptoe around looking for a victim. Sometimes they kill with a tap on the shoulder, sometimes by pretending to strangle. It depends on how much they like their victim – boy-murderers who fancy girl-victims often kill them very gently, so they can brush up against them, and maybe even kiss them as they die. When it's done, the murderer has thirty seconds to get away, then the lights go back on and everyone has to work out who-done-it.

I remember where the bathroom is, and set off along the landing with my arms straight in front, in case I bump into something. I'm thinking about the corridor to Tower dorm at Maidwell, when Eyot jumped at me without warning and I clobbered him on the nose in pure funk. Then it had been completely quiet, except for my shoes squeaking along the lino. Now there are squashed giggles from the bedrooms on either side, and a sweet scent-patch when I pass the airing cupboard. Everyone's so pleased to be away from the grown-ups, they sound half-drunk. Pleased to be away from us, too, I should think. They're sorry for us, but we're a bore. Which reminds me: where's Kit? How can he stand being up here with these babies? I get the answer when I reach the bathroom and flick on the light. 'Turn it off, you idiot,' a girl's voice shouts down the landing. But I don't, I just pull the door shut behind me. Kit's sitting on the edge of the bath with his chin in his hands. 'Hello,' he says steadily, smiling as if he always knew it would be me. 'Do you think we can go home yet, or will dad want to stay until midnight?' I'm about to say 'Midnight' when the girl's voice shouts down the landing again. 'I told you to turn that bloody light out. It's coming under the door and you'll give everything away.' As she finishes, another voice gives a watery gargle, and a body clonks onto the carpet. By the time Kit and I come out of the bathroom, the lights are blazing again.

It is after midnight when we leave, but we've managed to avoid most of the new year stuff. When everyone else crowded round the telly to watch Moira Anderson sing 'Auld Lang Syne', Kit and I lay low in the kitchen. Now we're home, and dad asks whether we want to have another drink before bed. Ruby's left a note to say the hospital rang, everything's the same, but she and granny have let the fire go out and the black grate looks cold. Dad wants company – he's already twiddling a ciggie out of his packet, offering me one. I thank him and say no, taking off my tie to show I really am dropping. But when dad starts to poke the ciggie back into the packet, and looks downwards with his face crumpled, Kit nudges me and I change my mind. We won't say anything new, but that's not the point. I click on the standard lamp above mum's chair and turn off the overhead, so everything's softer. Jenny waddles through from the kitchen and hops into mum's place under the warm light. Tomorrow we'll go to the hospital. That's what dad promised.

But Sister rings as we're finishing breakfast, to say mum's worse again, and dad leaves alone. He doesn't come home for the rest of the week, when it's only two days before Kit and I have to go back to school. After supper, we take him upstairs because he wants to see how we're getting on with our packing: do we need to buy anything for the new term? No, we're fine, we tell him. 'Jolly good,' dad says, turning to go down to the sitting room again. I stand in his way and fold my arms. 'Tomorrow,' he says, without looking me in the eye. 'We'll go and see her tomorrow.' 'Thank you,' Kit and I say together, but quietly, in case he changes his mind.

We set off after lunch. The hospital is in the middle of Chelmsford, and as dad swings round the last couple of roundabouts and pulls through the big iron gates, I tell myself to concentrate, so I don't miss anything. It's difficult, though. The lime trees by the X-ray hut, for instance: now it's started to rain, I can't tell what's wet and what's old leaf-goo, shining on the roof. And the names of other hospital departments on those big blue signs: I don't know what most of the words mean. And the fat woman wearing a flowery house-dress, clutching a bunch of tulips and trying not to show her knees. The man taking her arm must be her son. Does it mean her husband's dying?

'Whoof,' says dad, sighing as he turns off the engine. He usually sits still for a moment after he's done that, wriggling his shoulders and listening to the engine cool. Now he can't wait to get going, and opens the door so hard it knocks the side of the van next to us. Kit and I grin at each other. It helps, having dad like this. 'Filthy rain,' I say, when we catch him up at the front door. 'Filthy,' he says. 'Shall I lead the way?' I smile at Kit again as we fall in behind – he's wearing his green jersey, his favourite, but it's too small and his wrists show. I hadn't noticed that before. Mum will. We've forgotten to have a haircut too. We'll have to do that tomorrow morning, otherwise there'll be a rumpus when we get back to school. 'All right?' says dad, marching forward without looking round. 'Yes thanks,' we say together, and I make myself focus again. We're in a high hallway now, with a notice board covered in fluttery papers. It's like school. So is the metal staircase. One of the old parts of school, where masters hate teaching and boys smoke in the evenings.

When we turn left, everything's busy again. There's a long ward off to the left, with floppy plastic doors that don't fit properly, so when I peer in I might as well be looking through a mask. A few drowned visitors are slouched at bedsides, while others are floating slowly to their feet, leaning forward, plumping up a pillow. Cards! Everyone has Get Well cards, and we haven't. I should have made one – mum would have loved that. What have I been doing these last few days? Nothing. My hands flop down to my sides. Is this mum's room here, this splintery wooden door? It can't be. It says 'Sister' on a pale green sign, and dad's knocking. She won't be like Sister Boddy will she, or the Gibbon? Not at all. She's like Ruby, only more bustling, with short silver hair and gold specs. That's all I have time to see, because I'm listening to what she's telling dad. This woman I don't know has the secrets I want. She's been talking to mum, and washing her, and turning her, and putting her cheek against her face, as though she's loved her all her life.

'And these must be the boys,' Sister says, as though she's only just noticed us. Kit and I tell her our names, but of course she knows them already. 'A nice-looking pair,' she says, which would normally make us smile, but not now. It reminds me how mum used to say people had to be tough to work in hospital. Sister might look like Ruby but she's made of steel – and I'm still thinking about this when Kit catches us off guard. 'Where's mum's room?' he asks roughly, as though he thinks Sister might suddenly say we can't go in. Sister's not used to people talking like this, and pouts her lips so I expect she'll say, 'All in good time young man, all in good time.' But she remembers what's happened to us, and relaxes again. 'Your father knows the way.' she says. 'He'll take you.' 'Thank you.' I say, because I want her to know it's best like this, just the three of us, and as dad sets off again she turns into her office. 'Mrs Lucas,' I think, when the door shuts behind her. That's who she's like, not Ruby. Mrs Lucas at the Barn. I shake my head, because if I remember for a moment longer I'll be back in the dark little study again, being accused of something I never did. And from there I'd have to run up the flinty path to find mum by the car, knowing she'd make everything OK.

Dad nods towards a door on the right, which has a glass panel above the handle – thick glass, with black threads running across and down. It's so the nurses can check on mum, without having to go right in. Do I want to look through as well? I can't decide – but I don't have to. The door suddenly whisks inwards, and there's a nurse slap in front of me. Red-haired. Skinny. Almost white face – quite pretty actually. 'Oh! Hello!' she says. Irish, but soft, Dublin or somewhere, not the north. 'There I was hiding from you! You must be Andrew!' She stands on tiptoe and peeks over my shoulder. 'And you'll be Kit! Hello Kit!' There's elastic in her voice, as though she's given the right answer to a question in a competition, and is about to get a prize. 'I was helping your mum with her little problems,' she rattles on. 'It's quite a business, what with the tank and everything. We've done it now, though, we're right as rain. Oh, and hello there, Colonel Motion, I nearly forgot you. How are you today?' I turn round to dad, expecting him to look annoyed, but when he says 'Hello, Bridget,' I get it. He talks to Bridget every day, and every night sometimes. She knows more about mum than anyone. She's probably seen him cry.

I'm moving forward now, thinking this is the moment when I'll know everything. But as I come to a standstill at the bed-end, there's too much muddle, and I can't see straight. Charts. Zigzag lines. The oxygen tank, like an astronaut's gear. Cards on the bedside table. Waxy apples and yellow roses. Who bought them? Dad? He didn't say. Surely not flowers *and* apples – he doesn't do that sort of thing. It all means I don't see mum for a moment. Then I do, and I've got everything wrong. She's not lying flat, she's propped on a big bank of pillows – one has the name of the hospital embroidered in red thread. Her hair isn't all shaved off, either – it's only cut very short, especially on the left side, where there's a silly little sticking plaster. The bristles are much darker than her hair when it was long. And so is the bruise dark. A strawberry splodge like a birthmark, where the blood has oozed through the skin round her left eye, and along the cheekbone under her mask. The mask that's attached to a tube leading to the oxygen tank, which turns every breath into a hiss. I can't get past it to see mum's really mum. I can't tell how much of her is alive and how much is machinery.

'Hello, darling,' says dad; he has to speak up, so mum can hear above the hissing. 'I've brought the boys to see you.' What's meant to happen next is a miracle. Mum has been waiting for us like the princess in a fairy story, and now we're here she'll suddenly wake up and smile and be well again. As I stare at her eyes above the mask, they bulge under the closed lids, roll softly from side to side, then settle again. That's all there is, just like dad said. But it's OK – there's something else I can try. Mum's arms are stretched on top of the blanket, and I press one hand into the crook of her elbow as I bend forward to kiss her forehead. My hand and my head get their messages at the same time, so strong I have to shut my eyes to keep my balance. My hand feels the heat in her arm, and its skin-niness, as though I'm touching bare bone. And my head fills with her smell: someone's been rubbing talc on her – that's the first layer. The real smells are underneath. Sweat, and ammonia, and more sweat. That's where mum's sunk down to. 'Hello,' I whisper. 'It's me. Can you hear me?' This time her eyes don't move, and after I've stayed hunched for a moment longer, breathing as deep as I can, I step back and make room for Kit.

Dad's been putting clean nighties in the bedside cupboard, though mum's still wearing her hospital gown. He's red in the face when he stands beside me again, and I can see tears trapped in the creases under his eyes. 'What do you think?' he says. He's never spo-ken to me like this before; he's always known the answers himself. I slowly shake my head, but I don't answer him because just for a sec-ond I can see the future. Mum's going to die. Maybe not soon, she's too much of a fighter for that. Maybe not here. But eventually. She's never going to recognise us or speak to us – not for years. And even when she wakes up again, she's never coming home.

When Kit leaves mum's side, his knuckle flips the oxygen tank and gives a tinny clink that deepens as it dies into the metal. 'You can definitely hear us,' he says. 'Can't you mum? Definitely.' We stare at her face, but there's still no movement, and I think if she came to now, and found us waiting in line like this, she'd make a joke about it. 'You look as though you're going to burst into song' – something like that. Her voice fades, and Bridget stomps back in, so we have to squeeze against the wall and make space. 'Grand to see the boys, isn't it, Gillian?' she says, pressing her finger-ends on mum's wrist. Gillian? No one calls mum Gillian, except granny when she's cross. I look at my watch, sneaking back my sleeve so no one can see, and wonder why I might be bothered about the time.

But we've already been in the hospital half an hour. I suppose that's another new thing – the way the clock lies doggo, then suddenly leaps forward. I'll have to hurry if I want to notice everything and remember it. White walls. White ceiling. Grey metal radiator under the window. Grey pipes round the skirting board. Porridgy curtains and a window. 'Don't get in a fret,' I hear mum say. 'You can't worry about everything at once. Take it slowly. I'm not going anywhere. Now come and talk to me.'

I pull up one of the blue plastic chairs by the oxygen tank and take mum's right hand – just the ends of her fingers, because there's a drip stuck into her skin higher up. They look chilly as a statue, but turn out to be clammy. I keep hold, while dad and Kit stand by the window, talking about the rain. I must concentrate, so she can feel I'm here even if she can't see. Following the veins along the inside of her arm, then travelling over the shoulder of her stiff gown, up the side of her neck and round the edge of her mask, until I get to the mole on her cheek. The stub-end of a wiry black hair has started to sprout from the middle. Mum must have clipped that in the old days, or tweaked it out, and I never knew. She must have hated it, and not wanted anyone to see. I'll do it for her now, when we're alone together. It'll be one of our new secrets. My eyes keep moving, poring over her closed eyes, over the birthmark-bruise, and onto her forehead. 'I'm getting old,' she said the other day, rubbing her frown-lines. Kit said, 'Never mind. You'll get your bus pass soon', and she swatted at him but missed, so her wedding ring clinked against the Aga rail. Like Kit's knuckle on the oxygen tank a minute ago. I can see where the lines would come, if she could frown – pale scratches in her skin. Then I'm looking at her spiky hair again. Were they careful when they reached her other mole, the bigger one on the crown of her head? They must have used a barber's buzzer, hurrying to get her ready for the operation. She hated it when I was brushing her hair at the dressing table and knocked her mole by accident. Maybe they even cut her? I can't tell without lifting her forward, and I mustn't do that, I'd only hurt her.

When I stand up and kiss mum's forehead again, her sickly-sweet talc smell whooshes back, then fades. Where's dad got to? He's not there when I turn round. 'Having a ciggie,' Kit explains, slipping into my chair. I go to the window and look back at him. As he leans forward to mum, his green jersey stretches across his shoulders, and I can see through the little holes in the knitting: he's wearing one of his school shirts already. It makes me wince, thinking of him packing his trunk alone, and I turn away to look through the window. The sun's gone – when did that happen? And how come we're so high? I thought this was only the first floor. I can see right over the car park and the outbuildings, through the lime trees by the front gate, and along the street outside the hospital, where the headlights and the lamp posts look fuzzy in the drizzle. It's already gone 5.30. Shop-owners are locking their doors, and in the department store opposite a woman with no shoes is edging round a huge stack of saucepans, sticking a red SALE sign in the window.

When we leave mum this evening, that'll be our way back – that road to the left of the big store. We'll take it tomorrow as well, and all the other days. The days turning into weeks, and the weeks into months, and the months into years. It'll lead us past more shops first, and pubs, and traffic lights, and zebra crossings, and after that the suburbs, and eventually through the beet fields above the Blackwater. It's midnight-dark there already, but I can see well enough. The lane swerving towards the humpbacked bridge, alongside Mrs Bunton's cottage, and over the dry ford. We'll slow down as we come into the village, and see the church off to the left, with the graveyard waiting, and the ramshackle gate into the old water garden. Beyond that, filling the horizon, the Ashground will be stirring as a breeze works up the valley behind us, but not so strong that I will hear the branches shuffling, certainly not from the house, which is another two minutes beyond the hedge-trees. The light will be shining above the front door because I remembered to turn it on before we left, knowing granny and Ruby wouldn't, and because mum used to do that if we were going to be late, so when she saw it through the branches, even though we weren't quite home yet, she could always say 'Here we are', and pause, then almost repeat herself as if she didn't believe what she was seeing: 'Here we are at last.'